The Science and Politics
of Racial Research

William H. Tucker

The Science and Politics of Racial Research

University of Illinois Press

Urbana and Chicago

© 1994 by the Board of Trustees of the University of Illinois
Manufactured in the United States of America
C   5   4   3   2   1

This book is printed on acid-free paper.

Library of Congress Cataloging-in-Publication Data

Tucker, William H., 1940–
    The science and politics of racial research /
William H. Tucker.
        p.   cm.
    Includes bibliographical references and index.
    ISBN 0-252-02099-5 (alk. paper)
    1. Eugenics—United States—History.   2. Racism—United States—
History.   I. Title.
HQ755.5.U5T83   1994
305.8'00973—dc20   193-47673
                                                                    CIP

TO THE MEMORY OF MY FATHER,

J. Sheldon Tucker

Contents

Preface

Like many books, this one was motivated in part by annoyance—annoyance that in some quarters the innate inferiority of a race is still considered a proper scientific question even though a century and a half of concern with this issue has produced nothing of scientific value and has fostered considerable sociopolitical mischief. In the present climate of overreaction to political correctness, however, there is a danger that vigorous criticism will not be distinguished from the desire for proscription. I wish to declare forcefully that social theorists and researchers have the right to pursue the topic of their choice without threat or harassment. At the same time I wish to exercise my own right to argue in the following pages that this particular line of research has been scientifically unproductive and socially harmful.

Although many people have encouraged my work on this project, I owe a special debt of gratitude to my good friend and colleague Daniel Hart, whose careful reading of an earlier draft helped improve the final manuscript immeasurably. Lawrence Fuchs at Brandeis University also made a number of extremely helpful suggestions, especially regarding the conclusion. While the book has benefited substantially from the comments of these persons, naturally the responsibility for the opinion and the analysis is mine alone. I am also beholden to my friends in the German Department at Rutgers, Christine Cosentino-Dougherty and James Rushing, for their tutelage that enabled me to read some of the eugenics literature from the Third Reich. I owe thanks as well to the staff at the Robeson Library at Rutgers-Camden for locating and obtaining all sorts of obscure materials.

At the University of Illinois Press Richard Martin has been very supportive of this work, and Jane Mohraz's meticulous editing has done much to improve it.

Finally, I am both fortunate and grateful that Monica has tolerated my long fixation with this work, not to mention the piles of clutter that made

my office into an obstacle course. Her unwavering support and patience
has played no small part in its completion.

Just as I began thinking about this project, my father, a truly remarkable person, died. When my progress on the manuscript seemed impossibly
slow, I was sustained by the thought that he would have wanted me to
persevere. It is to his memory that I have dedicated this book.

Introduction:
To Make Nature an Accomplice

I N 1947 Henry E. Garrett, full professor and chair of the Psychology Department at Columbia University, president at various times of the American Psychological Association, the Eastern Psychological Association, and the Psychometric Society, fellow of the American Association for the Advancement of Science, member of the National Research Council, and for ten years editor of the American Psychology Series, authored an article in the scholarly publication *Scientific Monthly* entitled "Negro-White Differences in Mental Ability in the United States." In support of his sharp disagreement with those who desired to explain away race differences as "somehow reprehensible and socially undesirable," Garrett cited a study of the comparative abilities of sixty-eight white and sixty black babies from two to eleven months old. Each baby had been given a series of mental tests constructed for use during the first two years of life from which a "developmental quotient"—essentially an infant IQ score— had been calculated. The average DQ for the white babies was 105, for the blacks, 92; the average DQ for the whites was higher than for the blacks at every age level, with the degree of superiority ranging from two to twenty-five points and averaging thirteen. From these results Garrett concluded that the blacks' consistently lower performance could not possibly be explained by a difference in environmental opportunities. In addition, he noted, the comparison of American whites with blacks, who frequently had some degree of mixed ancestry, did not represent "true racial differences." Garrett consequently expected an even greater disparity between the performance of African blacks and European whites.[1]

Perhaps mindful of the importance of finding these "true racial differences," some years later Hans J. Eysenck, world-renowned social scientist, founder and head of the Psychological Department and Laboratory at the Institute of Psychiatry of the University of London, and author of more than fifty books and hundreds of articles in professional journals, compared the performance of black African babies with white norms on measures of development. The African children showed a consistent precocity until age three, after which they fell behind white children. Like Garrett, Eysenck found it "implausible" that such an "astonishing difference" at the early ages could have been produced by "socio-economic differences or other extrinsic variables." The fact that these differences were opposite from those considered by Garrett did not prevent Eysenck from arriving at the same conclusion concerning blacks' innate inferiority. Eysenck found the superior performance of the black infants consistent with a little-known "general law in biology according to which the more prolonged the infancy, the greater in general are the cognitive or intellectual abilities of the species."[2]

In the United States we have come to take for granted the widespread manipulation that characterizes public media-centered culture. Every time we turn on television or look through a magazine, someone is trying to persuade us to buy a product, vote for a candidate, or adopt a point of view. But we also cherish the notion that there are safe, protected areas, oases of reason, effectively insulated from attempts to sell consumer goods or political ideologies. Here, where the atmosphere is less hysterical, calmer, more serious and reflective, scientific inquiries, disinterested in political agendas and influenced only by objective evidence, can transcend ideology in the pursuit of truth. Indeed, it is exactly on the basis of such disinterest that scientists stake their claim to public trust and respect.

There are, however, critics within the scientific community who maintain that much social research is somewhat less than a model of objective inquiry. George Albee, a professor of psychology at the University of Vermont, offered the following opinion in his address to an American Psychological Association conference as a recipient of the Award for Distinguished Contribution to Community Psychology:

> I have come to believe that I have had the whole "scientific" process reversed. Instead of facts being useful as the objective building blocks of theories, rather it is more accurate to say that people, and especially social scientists, select theories that are consistent with their personal values, attitudes, and prejudices and then go out into the world or into the laboratory, to seek the facts that validate their beliefs about the world and about human nature, neglecting or denying observations that contradict their personal prejudices.[3]

These are strong words, but it is difficult to account in any other way for the identical conclusions of black inferiority Garrett and Eysenck derived from antithetical evidence.

Such consensus in the face of contradictory data is not an isolated occurrence in research on racial differences. When one scientist found at the turn of the century that blacks generally performed better than whites on tests of memory, he explained that their superior mnemonic ability was "naturally expected" since "in both races . . . the memory is in decadence from primitive conditions, but . . . the blacks are much nearer those conditions."[4] A decade later a famous English researcher found that on tests of memory the sons of the rich displayed "complete superiority" over the sons of the working class, a result that led him to the obvious conclusion that a disciplined memory was characteristic of greater intelligence.[5] Yet when a well-known contemporary psychologist found that poor and black children with low IQ scores had excellent memories, he concluded that memory should not properly be considered a component of "intelligence."[6]

Early demonstrations that blacks had a quicker reaction time than whites were also offered as proof that "the negro is, in the truest sense, a race inferior to that of the white" since faster reflexes were claimed to be a characteristic of lower intelligence. "Men, in proportion to their intellectuality," wrote a scientist who had found whites to react slower than both Indians and blacks, "should tend less and less to quickness of response in the automatic sphere."[7] But when research many years later showed faster reaction times for whites, this too became evidence for white intellectual superiority. Speed of reaction was now offered as an indication of "brain activity," and a leading social scientist even claimed (incorrectly) that Muhammad Ali had "a very average" reaction time.[8]

Though blacks have almost always performed lower than whites on paper-and-pencil tests, even the rare occasion on which they have scored higher has somehow also confirmed their inferiority. When two researchers found that blacks did better than whites on simple arithmetic problems, they explained that "the more complicated a brain, the more numerous its 'association fibers,' the less satisfactorily it performs the simple numerical problems which a calculating machine does so quickly and accurately."[9]

Differing evolutionary theories have also been able to produce identical conclusions about black inferiority. Many scientists in the 1920s claimed that blacks were the evolutionary predecessors of whites and that "Negroid stock," having evolved long before whites, was thus not only older but closer to its anthropoid ancestors, both physically and mentally; blacks were intellectually inferior to whites because they had evolved earlier.[10] A few decades later a distinguished anthropologist proposed that blacks had crossed the evolutionary threshold into homo sapiens long after other races and thus had had less time to develop; blacks were intellectually inferior because they had evolved later.[11]

Some studies of group differences have not violated the rules of logic as much as they have strained the bounds of credibility. In 1913 the famous psychologist Henry H. Goddard administered mental tests to a sample of newly arrived immigrants at Ellis Island, which had been carefully selected to omit both the "obviously feeble-minded" and the very few of "obviously high grade intelligence." In the group thus remaining—what Goddard called "the great mass of 'average immigrants,' "—he reported that 83 percent of Jews, 80 percent of Hungarians, 79 percent of Italians, and 87 percent of Russians were "feeble-minded." Probably anticipating the appropriate term for these results, Goddard informed his readers that "many a scientific discovery has seemed at first glance absurd." Nevertheless, he insisted, "it is never wise to discard a scientific result because of apparent absurdity," especially when it had come from a "fair and conscientious" analysis of the data.[12]

It appears Albee has not exaggerated. Although some of these examples might be dismissed as "cheap shots," egregious exceptions noteworthy by their contrast with more sober, restrained investigations that are the norm, many of them are not so much counterexamples to the mainstream as they are organic extensions of it. For over a century there have been scientists obsessed with proving that minorities, poor people, foreigners, and women are innately inferior to upper-class white males of northern European extraction.

Though some of these researchers have been overt racists, civil libertarians and social liberals have also been responsible for many foolish claims. Edward M. East, for example, a Harvard geneticist in the 1920s, "could see no reasonable excuse for oppression and discrimination on a colour-line basis . . . [and had] no sympathy with a regimen of repression on the part of the whites." He was positively outraged over someone "who is denied a seat in a Pullman car, a restaurant, a theatre, or a room in a college dormitory" due to the "gaucheries of a provincial people, on a par with the guffaws of a troop of yokels." Nevertheless, as a scientist, he concluded that blacks were physically as well as mentally inferior and had little of value to contribute to the higher white race. "Gene packets of African origin are not valuable supplements to the gene packets of European origin," wrote East; "it is the white germ plasm that counts."[13]

The scientific conflict over genetic differences between groups is now well into its second century. Unlike other, more traditional scientific controversies, in which the argument diminishes as new discoveries are made or as scientists with opposing views retire or die away,[14] the bitter dispute over race has arisen anew in each generation, to be debated all over again in almost exactly the same terms but with a fervor that seems more theological than scientific. Nor has the argument confined itself to academic journals and scientific conferences; the subject of racial differences has been debated in barrooms and cocktail parties and, for a scientific issue, has received unprecedented coverage in the popular press. Despite the length and intensity of the debate, however, there has been no significant advance in scientific knowledge. Although the techniques of data analysis have become increasingly sophisticated, the arguments on both sides have changed very little. Contemporary scientists often sound indistinguishable from their predecessors of thirty, sixty, or ninety years ago. More than a century of research has produced a lot of heat but virtually no light.

"No Political, No Religious, and No Social Prejudices"

The truth is that though waged with scientific weapons, the goal in this controversy has always been political; indeed, the debate has no strictly scientific purpose or value. The question of genetic differences between races has arisen not out of purely scientific curiosity or the desire to find some important scientific truth or to solve some significant scientific problem but only because of the belief, explicit or unstated, that the answer has political consequences. The claim that one group is genetically less desirable or capable than another has invariably been part of what Marquis de Condorcet called an attempt "to make nature herself an accomplice of political inequality."[15] Rather than an injustice that needs to be rectified, social and political oppression thus becomes the rational—indeed, the unavoidable—reflection of natural differences.

The first suggestion that inequality should be based on nature occurred over two thousand years ago when Aristotle observed that "there are species in which a distinction is already marked, immediately at birth, between those of its members who are intended for being ruled and those who are intended to rule."[16] Applying an idiosyncratic technique for the measurement of individual differences—though one not all that different from the method used twenty-two hundred years later by the famous English scientist Sir Francis Galton—Aristotle distinguished those to be ruled as differing from others in power of reason "as the body differs from the soul, or an animal from a man," and he concluded that "it is thus clear that, just as some are by nature free, so others are by nature slaves, and for these latter the condition of slavery is both just and beneficial."[17]

Although Aristotle's reference to innate, empirically observable distinctions suggested a quasi-scientific justification for slavery—in Thomas Hobbes's words, "as if master and servant were not introduced by consent of men but by difference of wit"[18]—it was not until the nineteenth century that the linkage between science and politics was made explicit. At that time U.S. doctors and anthropologists began to assess intelligence through various anatomical and physiognomic characteristics in scientific attempts at a linear evaluation of racial and ethnic groups, and in England Galton began to study the dichotomization of nature and nurture that eventually led to the psychometric tradition. As these two lines of investigation merged at the turn of the century, a movement arose that attempted to derive moral and behavioral guidelines from what were claimed to be scientific-physicalist laws. Questions of human rights and freedoms—who should vote, who should be educated, who should have children, who should be allowed into the country—were transferred from their appropriate place in the domain of political discourse to the domain of science. In particular, an understanding of racial differences was claimed to be the key to social progress; public education, social harmony, national welfare, indeed the future of the species were all said to depend on it. What began as the study of hereditary characteristics thus quickly burgeoned into a presumptuous field marked by immodest pronouncements on the limits of democracy, the necessity of racial segregation, the futility of education, the biological inevitability of vast socioeconomic disparities, and the necessity for controlling the birthrate of certain groups.

The belief that the operation of science was synonymous with the termination of politics made appeals to scientific authority a powerful strategy for influencing public policy. Critics of the obsession with racial differences could easily be dismissed as emotional and unscientific, preferring sentimentality, idealism, and wishful thinking to the perhaps unpleasant but nonetheless undeniable truths that emerged from impartial data; the researchers had scientific objectivity and rigor on their side. As Karl Pearson, one of the greatest contributors to contemporary statistics, wrote in the introduction to a 1925 article on Jewish immigration to Great Britain, "We have no axes to grind, we have no governing body to propitiate by well advertised discoveries; we are paid by nobody to reach results of a given bias. We have no electors, no subscribers to encounter in the market place. We firmly believe that we have no political, no religious and no social prejudices. . . . We rejoice in numbers and figures for their own sake."[19] Thus unencumbered by bias of any kind or by political or economic pressure, Pearson was led, by the numbers and figures, to conclude that Jewish immigrants were mentally and physically inferior to the native English population, that the newcomers would develop into a "parasitic race," and that there was "no evidence that a lessening of the aliens' poverty, an improvement in their food, or an advance in their cleanliness will substantially alter their average grade of intelligence, and with it their outlook on life." Naturally, Pearson concluded, "there should be no place" in society for such a demonstrably inferior group, an opinion that was soon to be shared by the leaders of another European country.[20]

As a consequence of this viewpoint, for more than a century nature has been played as a trump card in political arguments on the side of repression. Sometimes scientists have only hinted at significant, and ominous, implications. The psychologist Lewis Terman, an early developer of the IQ test, insisted, for example, that a "less naive definition of ... democracy ... will have to square with the demonstrable facts of biological and psychological science."[21] More often, specific proposals have been offered, most of which are intolerable in a free society. When a medical journal reported the latest scientific finding in 1907—that the brain of blacks was "more animal in type and incapable of producing those thoughts which have built up civilization"—the editors found it "dreadful that we did not know these anatomical facts when we placed a vote in the possession of this brain which cannot comprehend its use" and hoped that it was not too late to deprive blacks of the franchise.[22] A popular 1933 scientific textbook opposed efforts to eradicate discrimination against blacks because these efforts ignored "biological and social facts."[23] A group of scientists in the late 1950s and 1960s attempted to overturn the unanimous Supreme Court verdict that struck down school segregation on the grounds that blacks were intellectually inferior to whites. The logic underlying all these proposals viewed political inequality as the natural consequence of biological inferiority; science should demonstrate the latter so society might have appropriate justification to implement the former. As one writer who opposed equality for blacks early in the century frankly admitted, unless blacks were "racially inferior," the "denial of ... equality appears as a colossal injustice, an immeasurable wrong."[24] The role of science was to confirm that no such injustice was taking take place.

Since the mid-1960s, in a social atmosphere much less tolerant of blatant deprivations of civil rights, the science of racial differences has encouraged more subtle political implications. For example, poverty among blacks was explained by some scientists as the economic consequence of natural inequality. Blacks' claims of continuing racial prejudice could thus be dismissed as "social paranoia" since the real problem lay in their genes. As one well-known psychologist noted, "Failure to succeed is less apt to be perceived as personal failure if one identifies with a group which is claimed, justifiably or not, to be discriminated against. Having the status of an unprivileged caste, real or imagined, makes personal failure more tolerable."[25]

Some scientists also insisted that government programs of assistance to the poor, which had originated with Lyndon Johnson's War on Poverty, could be justified only if there were no genetic differences in ability between races. Thus, they argued, their "proof" that such differences did exist made these programs scientifically unsound.

Finally, even when the results of research have not been intended as justification for policies of repression and discrimination, they turn out to be made to order for the proponents of such policies. Whenever scientists have concluded some group to be genetically inferior, some of the investigators have wound up in either organizational or informal alliance with right-wing political groups, often fascists or racists who have been more than pleased to use scientific authority as a source of prestige for their own doctrines. The use of science for this purpose has generally been accomplished with the cooperation of, or at the very least without protest from, the scientists. That is, although it has usually been the ideologues in these coalitions who have fired the shots, the scientists have furnished the ammunition with no reservations over its use.

Though it might be argued that the political exploitation of scientific results is a *misuse* of science, the following chapters demonstrate that the effort to prove the innate intellectual inferiority of some groups has led *only* to oppressive and antisocial proposals; it has had no *other* use. Indeed, there is no "legitimate" application for such a finding. Even if there were convincing proof of genetic differences between races, as opposed to the flawed evidence that has been offered in the past, it would serve no purpose other than to satisfy curiosity about the matter. While the desire for knowledge, whether or not it has practical value, is not to be denigrated, a judicious use of our scientific resources would seem inconsistent with the pursuit of a goal that is probably scientifically chimerical and certainly lends itself to socially pernicious ends.

1

"Helping Along the Process": Social Science and Race in the Nineteenth Century

SCIENCE first turned its attention to the concept of race in 1735, when the great biological taxonomist Carolus Linnaeus grouped human beings into four varieties—red, yellow, white, and black. Though skin color was the primary basis for this categorization, Linnaeus also distinguished the races by personal characteristics specific to each; the whites, for example, were described as keen minded and innovative, the blacks as lazy and careless.[1] The assumption that mental and moral traits were associated with race was to inform many scientific investigations during the next two hundred years.

The Linnaean system was revised and extended in 1781 by the physiologist Johann Friedrich Blumenbach, generally considered the founder of modern anthropology, who added esthetic judgments to personal traits as possible elements of racial classification. Blumenbach was the first to use the term *Caucasian* because he considered the most beautiful race to have originated on the southern slopes of Mount Caucasus in the Georgian area:

> the stock displays, as we have seen, the most beautiful form of the skull, from which, as from a mean and primeval type, the others diverge by most easy gradations on both sides to the two ultimate extremes (that is, on the one side the Mongolian, on the other the Ethiopian). Besides, it is white in color, which we may fairly assume to have been the primitive color of mankind, since as we have shown above, it is very easy for that to degenerate into brown, but very much more difficult for dark to become white.[2]

At the same time that natural scientists were taking these first taxonomic steps, another approach to imposing order, not just on human beings but on all of nature, was reaching the peak of its popularity. The concept of the great chain of being, rooted in the Aristotelian notion that inequality was the foundation of natural order, flourished throughout the eighteenth century and well into the nineteenth. Its basic premise was the existence of a hierarchy that allocated every form of life to its appropriate rank in the great chain, from the lowest position to the highest; biological variety was thus synonymous with natural inequality.[3] This was a pervasive belief throughout the natural philosophy of the time, and it even found frequent literary expression. Alexander Pope's *Essay on Man*, one of the best-selling works of the late eighteenth century, did much to popularize the notion that "Order is heaven's first law, and this confest, / Some are, and must be, greater than the rest."[4]

Although the great chain placed humans at the pinnacle of earthly creatures (the chain, of course, continued beyond humans through various heavenly beings to God, the Creator), it was but a small step to apply the same concept of hierarchical ordering within the ranks of humankind, a step that seemed only natural to Europeans as they came into increasing contact with people of color from newly discovered lands. The hints of relative racial merit contained in the scientific tradition, with its attachment of personal traits and esthetic judgments to skin color, soon merged with the assumptions of the great chain, and the creation of a vertical ordering of the races became an accepted task of science. There was, however, no single index or criterion on which such a scale could be based. The doctors and scientists who carried out these early studies consequently turned to predominantly physiognomic and anatomical gradations, searching for those characteristics that would distinguish higher animals from lower ones and noble races from savages.

Frequently these methods placed blacks somewhere between humans and other animals. In 1799, for example, the eminent English physician and surgeon Charles White concluded on the basis of anatomical and physiological evidence that blacks were a completely separate species, intermediate between whites and apes. The feet of blacks, their fingers and toes, their "gibbous" legs, their hair, their cheekbones and chin, the length of their arms, the size of their skull and sex organs, and even their body odor placed them much closer than Europeans to "brute creation," according to White. Data that did not fit this model were appropriately finessed. Body hair, for example, present in much greater abundance among lower animals and whites than among blacks, should have suggested by White's own logic that the blacks were the "higher" life form, but it was the "noblest" of animals, he observed, "the majestic lion, the king of the forest . . . and . . . that most beautiful . . . animal, the horse," that shared with whites the trait of long flowing hair.[5] Exceptional capabilities exhibited by blacks only constituted further proof of their proximity to infrahuman species. For example, the superior memory some blacks displayed, White maintained, was an ability shared by a number of domestic animals, like the horse and the dog.[6]

As he "ascend[ed] the line of gradation," White came "at last to the white European," that superb first link in the chain, the one "most removed from the brute creation, . . . the most beautiful of the human race," and unquestionably the most "superior . . . in intellectual powers." In a famous paean to the magnificent natural assets of that group to which he belonged, White inquired, rhetorically, where else could be found

> that nobly arched head, containing such a quantity of brain . . . ?
> Where the perpendicular face, the prominent nose, and round projecting chin? Where that variety of features, and fulness of expression; those long, flowing graceful ringlets; that majestic beard, those rosy cheeks and coral lips? Where that erect posture of the body and noble gait? In what other quarter of the globe shall we find the blush that overspreads the soft features of the beautiful women of Europe, that emblem of modesty, of delicate feelings, and of sense? Where that nice expression of the amiable and softer passions in the countenance; and that general elegance of features and complexion? Where, except on the bosom of the European woman, two such plump and snowy white hemispheres, tipt with vermillion?[7]

Setting an example followed by scores of researchers during the next two centuries, White declared his lack of malice toward blacks; his only purpose was "to investigate the truth, and to discover what are the established laws of nature." He fervently proclaimed no desire to see blacks oppressed just because they were a separate species, of greater biological proximity to anthropoids than to Europeans, and hoped that nothing he said would "give the smallest countenance to the pernicious practice of enslaving mankind."[8]

White got his wish. His catalog of similarities between blacks and apes was *not* substantially exploited by the defenders of slavery—but probably not because they found his views unreasonable. Indeed, there had been previous attempts by proslavery writers to classify blacks with "oran-outangs"—the earlier term for what is presently called a chimpanzee—in the great chain, though they had lacked the wealth of scientific detail that characterized White's argument.[9] For that matter, even some opponents of slavery gave indications of similar thinking: though Thomas Jefferson would eventually observe, concerning blacks, that "whatever be their degree of talents, it is no measure of their rights,"[10] he also wrote of matings between black women and the "Oranootan."[11] An elaborate empirical proof of its victims' inferiority had not yet become a tactical necessity for the defense of slavery, however; at the time the "pernicious practice" was an unquestioned fact of economic life. Of course, it was implicitly assumed, even if not customarily articulated, that blacks were by nature subordinate to whites in the chain of being. As one slaveholder rather eloquently remarked at the turn of the century, "Nature, governed by unerring laws, which command the oak to be stronger than the willow, and the cyprus to be taller than the shrub, has at the same time imposed on mankind certain reflections, which can never be overcome. She has made some to be poor and others to be rich; some to be happy and others to be miserable; some to be slaves and others to be free."[12] No data were yet required to verify this self-evident proposition. Slavery was viewed as an expression of the harmony between natural law and social organization.

Science vs. Freedom

Some twenty-five or thirty years later, however, chattel slavery in the United States had become the target of an abolitionist assault determined to expose the contradiction between the subordination of blacks and the universal equality recognized in both the Declaration of Independence and the society's traditional religious teachings. In response to this attack, the defenders of slavery moved to make their underlying premise more explicit, believing that a clear demonstration of black inferiority as an unalterable fact of nature would completely justify their position. As one of them frankly admitted about the empirical claim, "If this be not true, American slavery is a monstrous wickedness."[13] This approach marked the first appearance of a new ideological position, one insisting that science was an appropriate source of moral authority. Logically flawed but politically appealing nonetheless, it became the basis for an ongoing campaign to establish a scientific rationale for first slavery and then various forms of postbellum racial oppression.

"Diseases and Physical Peculiarities"

A number of proslavery doctors, in particular, authored reports scrutinizing the anatomy and physiology of blacks. The results were predictable. John H. van Evrie, for example, produced the lengthy analysis *Negroes and Negro "Slavery,"* elegantly subtitled *The First an Inferior Race; The Latter Its Normal Condition,* in which a detailed examination of every body part led to the subtitle's conclusions. To begin with, he found that dark skin was physically incapable of expressing many of the emotions displayed by whites—"the blush of . . . modesty," the "bloodless white" of grief—an indication to van Evrie that such emotions did not exist for blacks. In fact, he concluded, since poor health produced an "ash-color" in blacks and a "clouded" skin color in whites, equality between the races became possible only when "disease and unnatural conditions prevail."[14] Van Evrie also found that blacks lacked both "the brain . . . [and] the vocal organism" essential to music: "the negro . . . neither perceives nor can he give expression to music," and "therefore such a thing as a negro singer is unknown." The hands of blacks he judged coarse and blunt, preventing any possible achievement in such fields as art or surgery. This poorly developed sense of touch was only confined to the fingers, however; throughout the rest of the body he noted an oversensitive tactile sense, which caused a fifty-year-old black to howl like a schoolboy from a few simple lashes with an ordinary switch. He remarked on the contrast between this oversensitivity of the skin and "the obtuse sensibility of the brain and nervous system," which enabled blacks "to bear hanging very well."[15] Finally, the overall structure of the black figure—the relation of limbs and spine to the "narrow and longitudinal head"—led van Evrie to conclude that the race was incapable of "direct perpendicular" posture. If those foolish reformers desiring to educate blacks were actually to get their way, he explained, the broader forehead produced by such an effort would destroy the delicate harmony between head and body, rendering blacks "utterly incapable of locomotion or of an upright position at all"—education would make it literally impossible for blacks to stand on their feet. In contrast to all these anatomical indications of black inferiority, van Evrie found that the broad forehead and straight lines of the white "stamp him the undisputed master of all living beings." This supremacy, he insisted, was obvious even to animals: a desperate lion or tiger never seized a white, according to the doctor, but frequently preyed on blacks, whom the animals instinctively recognized as inferior beings.[16]

Though van Evrie's polemic was intended to influence lay opinion, particularly in the North, many southern doctors wrote for their peers, both professional and regional. Samuel Cartwright, chairman of a committee appointed by the Medical Association of Louisiana to report on the "diseases and physical peculiarities of the Negro race," presented the committee's findings in a southern medical journal. Though his conclusions were similar to van Evrie's, Cartwright's discussion of black physiology exhibited the greater technical sophistication expected in a professional publication. He described in some detail how not only the black man's skin but also "his bile, . . . his blood, . . . the brain and nerves, the chyle and all the humors" were all "tinctured with a shade of the pervading darkness." Furthermore, according to Cartwright, blacks had a brain smaller than that of whites from which nevertheless descended larger nerves, causing what little intellectual power they had to be diffused into "nervous" energy appealing only to the senses. In contrast to van Evrie, Cartwright found blacks capable of producing music but not the kind that involved "understanding"; it was music with "melody, but no harmony . . . mere sounds, without sense or meaning."[17] Finally, he explained, a deficiency of red blood caused by "defective atmospherization" allowed all the dark humors and bile in blacks to "predominate." This insufficient supply of red blood, when conjoined with the smaller brain and excess nervous matter, constituted the "true cause," in Cartwright's analysis, "of that debasement of mind" in blacks. There was some hope for improvement of this detrimental condition, however: "Under the compulsive power of the white man, [blacks] are made to labor or exercise, which makes the lungs perform the duty of vitalizing the blood more perfectly than is done when they are left free to indulge in idleness. It is the red, vital blood, sent to the brain, that liberates their mind when under the white man's control; and it is the want of a sufficiency of red, vital blood, that chains their mind to ignorance and barbarism, when in freedom." Freedom was the cause of physiological illness in blacks, and slavery was the cure. Slavery, wrote Cartwright, improved blacks "in body, mind and morals."[18]

In keeping with this analysis, Cartwright paid particular attention to "drapetomania," that disease of the mind that caused slaves to run away to freedom. "With the advantages of proper medical advice, strictly followed," this malady could be almost entirely prevented, said the doctor. The prescription for both cure and prevention, he explained, was to treat blacks like children—to show "care, kindness, . . . and humanity" as long as they were appropriately submissive, but should they dare "raise their heads to a level with their master," to "whip . . . the devil out of them" until they returned to "that submissive state which it was intended for them to occupy."[19]

Although Cartwright's report was obviously somewhat less than objective, the federal census of 1840 suggested that he might not have been altogether wrong about the salutary effects of slavery. In the *Boston Medical and Surgical Journal* (later to become the *New England Journal of Medicine*, one of the most prestigious medical publications in the country) Edward Jarvis, a specialist in mental disorders and eventually president of the American Statistical Association, analyzed the census data on the incidence of insanity. Jarvis found no geographic difference for whites, obtaining approximately the same rate of insanity in the North as in the South. For blacks, however, the proportion of "lunatics" in the free states was ten times that of the slave states, so that in the South blacks suffered considerably *less* from insanity than whites did, while in the North their rate of insanity was six times that for whites. New Jersey, the southernmost northern state, had the lowest rate of black lunacy above the Mason-Dixon line but still more than double that of its neighbor Delaware, the northernmost southern state, which had the highest incidence below the line; for blacks Mason and Dixon had apparently drawn a line between freedom and sanity. Despite his personal opposition to slavery, Jarvis could not avoid the obvious interpretation: "Slavery has a wonderful influence upon the development of moral faculties and the intellectual powers; and refusing man many of the hopes and responsibilities which the free, self-thinking and self-acting enjoy and sustain, of course it saves him from some of the liabilities and dangers of active self-direction." By keeping the mental powers of blacks "comparatively dormant," Jarvis wrote, their minds had been saved from "mis-direction or over-action," yet further proof, he concluded, that "in the highest state of . . . mental activity there is the greatest danger of mental derangement; where there is the greatest mental torpor, we find the least insanity."[20]

Only sixty days later a sheepish Jarvis reappeared in the same journal to disclaim completely the statistics on insanity among free blacks. On reflection he had become suspicious about the "extraordinary and unaccountable proportion" of insane northern blacks, especially in the New England states: the farther north the state, the higher was the incidence of black insanity until in Maine one out of every fourteen blacks was a victim of this condition. Upon checking the original reports, Jarvis found that in many northern New England municipalities the number of blacks reported insane was larger than the total number of black residents. For example, in seven Maine towns that listed absolutely no black inhabitants, a total of twenty-six blacks had been reported as insane; similar inaccuracies were discovered throughout the northern states. Jarvis expressed the hope that all of the original documents would be reviewed in Washington and the errors remedied. In the meantime he admitted being "disappointed and mortified" over his prior conclusions, "but having unconsciously sent forth error, we take this our earliest opportunity to correct it."[21]

These hopes for immediate rectification were somewhat naive. Not only did the errors remain uncorrected, but the inaccurate data provided a field day for slavery's ideologues, who offered self-serving interpretations of this lunacy-latitude correlation, which horrified genteel southerners by conjuring up the specter of hordes of savage black maniacs, converted from faithful slaves by the inevitable consequences of abolition. One southern magazine, apparently not content even with the differences in the erroneous data, presented a table, allegedly derived from the census, in which the black population of each northern state had been reduced by about one half. Since the number of lunatics was not changed, the omission of half the free black population had the effect of approximately doubling the rate of black insanity in each northern state; now,

1.0 out of every 6.7 blacks in Maine was a lunatic, whereas in Louisiana the ratio was 1 in 4,031.[22] Furthermore, the article noted, if *only* slaves had been included in the data from the southern states, the ratio would have been even higher; presumably, the large number of insane free blacks in the slave states had lowered this index of mental health from the height that could have been achieved by enslavement of the entire race. The *Southern Literary Messenger* also contributed an interpretation of the data, which, though unsigned, was introduced by the editor as the product of a "vigorous and comprehensive mind." Undeniably sensitive as well, the author expressed great sympathy for the "unparalleled" suffering of blacks in New England, who had succumbed in such large numbers to the evils of freedom; it was, he said, truly "dreadful." In addition to this proven harm to the mental stability of blacks, however, the anonymous writer also worried that freedom made them more vicious and thus more dangerous to whites. If the South were ever foolish enough to consent to abolition, "where," he inquired, "should we find penitentiaries for the thousands of felons? Where lunatic asylums for the tens of thousands of maniacs?" If blacks were "suddenly turned loose," what kind of life would be possible, he wondered, "in a country where maniacs and felons met the traveller at every crossroad?"[23]

Jarvis fought back strenuously against this political exploitation of data he knew to be seriously flawed. Turning to sarcasm, he termed the numerous instances of black insanity that had been reported in towns without any black residents "disorders [which] exist there in a state of abstraction, . . . fortunately for humanity, where they are said to be present, there are no people to suffer from them." The census data, he continued to insist, were "a bearer of falsehood to confuse and mislead," and again he called for a review and correction of the errors—for "the honour of our country, . . . medical science, and . . . truth."[24] Jarvis also led the American Statistical Association to petition Congress for revision of this section of the census.

These efforts were in vain. Indeed, some federal officials who had been informed of the errors continued to cite the data in support of slavery. Secretary of State John C. Calhoun, under whose jurisdiction the census had been conducted, resisted all efforts to acknowledge the errors. At the same time he wrote to a foreign opponent of slavery that abolition would be "neither humane nor wise," because the census had shown that free blacks "invariably sunk into vice and pauperism, accompanied by the bodily and mental inflictions incident thereto—deafness, blindness, insanity and idiocy—to a degree without example," whereas the more fortunate blacks in the slave states flourished "in number, comfort, intelligence and morals."[25] As the clearest evidence for this wretched condition of free blacks, Calhoun cited the statistics on idiocy and insanity in Maine and Massachusetts, the two states where Jarvis had just documented in detail the most outrageous errors.

Seventeen Cubic Inches of Brain

Though the medical case for black inferiority could perhaps be dismissed as proslavery propaganda, during the 1840s and 1850s a group of "genuine" scientists emerged to proclaim blacks a separate and inferior species rather than just members of a less developed culture. Less vulnerable to a charge of bias or political interest, these authorities provided irresistible evidence for those who maintained that racial equality had to be proven a biological fact before it could be entertained as a political policy.

The most prestigious member of this group was the great Swiss naturalist Louis Agassiz, who immigrated to the United States and assumed a professorship at Harvard. After his death Agassiz's private correspondence was published by his widow, Elizabeth Cary Agassiz, herself well known as founder and first president of Radcliffe. In 1978 the Harvard paleontologist Stephen J. Gould compared the original letters with the edited versions that had appeared in print and for the first time made public some of the omissions. Just prior to his own conversion to the theory that blacks constituted a separate species, Agassiz had described his first personal contact with "men of color," domestics at a Philadelphia hotel:

> I experienced pity at the sight of this degraded and degenerate race . . . it is impossible for me to repress the feeling that they are not of the same blood as us. In seeing their black faces with their thick lips and grimacing teeth, the wool on their head, their bent knees, their elongated hands, their large curved nails, and especially the livid color of the palms of their hands, I could not take my eyes off their faces in order to tell them to stay far away. And when they advanced that hideous hand towards my plate in order to serve me, I wished I were able to depart in order to eat a piece of bread elsewhere, rather than to dine with such service. What unhappiness for the white race—to have tied their existence so closely with that of negroes in certain countries! God preserve us from such a contact![26]

Having delivered himself of such a peroration in private, Agassiz went on to offer his public statements as the disinterested pronouncements of the man of science. His first major article on race differences began by emphatically denying any possible connection with political matters in general or slavery in particular. "Let the politicians, let those who feel themselves called upon to regulate human society, see what they can do with the results," he wrote; scientists had the "right to consider the questions growing out of men's physical relations as merely scientific questions." Some thirty pages later, however, this wall of separation between science and politics was showing signs of decay, as Agassiz suddenly offered a more practical motivation: scientists had "the obligation to settle the relative rank among . . . races," because it would be "mock-philanthropy and mock-philosophy to assume that all races have the same abilities . . . and that in consequence . . . they are entitled to the same position in human society."[27] By the penultimate paragraph the facade had completely crumbled: the fact that the "submissive, obsequious, imitative negro" displayed a "peculiar indifference to the advantages afforded by civilized society" compelled Agassiz to conclude that "human affairs with reference to the colored races would be far more judiciously conducted, if, in our intercourse with them, we were guided by a full consciousness of the real difference existing between us and them, and a desire to foster those dispositions that are eminently marked in them, rather than by treating them on terms of equality."[28]

While support from the internationally recognized Agassiz conferred his prestige on the "American school of ethnology," it was the Philadelphia physician Samuel George Morton who contributed the definitive empirical evidence, the data that supposedly clinched the case for black inferiority. From his collection of over eight hundred skulls from throughout the world Morton had calculated the cranial capacities of different races: the various Caucasian subgroups ranked highest on this measure, American Indians much lower, and "Ethiopians," a common designation for blacks at the time, last. Morton's method for determining internal skull capacity was impressive for its cautiousness and painstaking attention to detail. In brief, the skull cavity was filled with white pepper seeds that were then transferred to a tin cylinder from which the volume of the cranium could be read off in cubic inches.[29] Later when Morton found inconsistencies in the data obtained in this fashion, he changed to lead shot one-eighth-inch in diameter to yield more reliable results.[30] His research received almost universal acclaim for its devotion to objective data and its freedom from doctrine and dogma.

Nevertheless, it was undeniable that Morton had begun with his own preconceptions. In *Crania Americana*, his first major publication, he prefaced the data with a lengthy description of racial characteristics: the Caucasians had given the earth "its fairest inhabitants" and were distinguished for the "highest intellectual endowments," whereas American Indians were "averse to cultivation," and blacks were "the lowest grade of humanity." More specific subgroups were given more specific characterizations: the "Esquimaux" were "crafty, sensual, ungrateful, obstinate and unfeeling, and much of their affection for their children may be traced to purely selfish motives"; one Indian tribe was "altogether repulsive, . . . slow and stupid," with a "vacant" expression of face. As usual the choicest epithets were reserved for various black groups, as Morton dwelled obsessively on the minute details of their appearance: one was the "nearest approximation to the lower animals," another was "filthy, . . . gluttonous, . . . licentious," and yet another was "repulsive in the extreme."[31] On looks alone it was clear to Morton that these people were incapable of civilization.

Despite these indications of ethnocentrism, the data could still be considered on their merits; certainly a mathematical measurement could not be accused of a personal or political bias. Of course, underlying the procedure was the assumption of a simple and direct relationship between the size of the brain and intellectual ability. As one historian has pointed out, almost all of the skulls in the three highest Caucasian subgroups had belonged to white men hanged as felons, and it would have been just as logical to conclude that a large head indicated criminal propensity.[32] Nonetheless, the erroneous belief that skull size reflected intelligence had widespread currency in nineteenth-century literature and science. In the "Adventure of the Blue Carbuncle" Sherlock Holmes examined a hat and drew the "obvious" conclusion that its owner must be "highly intellectual." When Watson inquired about the basis for this deduction, "for answer Holmes clapped the hat upon his head. It came right over the forehead and settled upon the bridge of his nose. 'It is a question of cubic capacity,' said he; 'a man with so large a brain must have something in it.' "[33]

The nineteenth-century discussions of this belief seem quite comical today. In Holmesian fashion hat sizes were indeed compiled and offered as evidence of intelligence by those unmindful of Thersites's reminder that Agamemnon was "an honest fellow enough, . . . but he has not so much brain as ear wax."[34] Personal vanities also played an amusing role. Charles Caldwell, a medical professor, announced unblushingly to a large audience that "there are only three great heads in the United States: one is that of Daniel Webster; another that of Henry Clay; and the last . . . modesty prevents me from mentioning."[35] In a published exchange that went on for some months, another adherent to the bigger-is-better doctrine silenced an opponent with the observation that in his experience "those who deny the . . . importance of the brain's volume have small heads."[36]

Even if cranial capacity *were* a valid indication of ability, Morton's data contained serious error that was not discovered until Stephen J. Gould recently reanalyzed the original measurements.[37] First of all, he found that Morton had failed to consider or correct for the effect of stature on cranial size. For example, at one point Morton used a female sample of "Hottentots" and a male sample of Englishmen to support the superiority of the latter. Larger people have larger skulls, but certainly body size is no indicator of intelligence, and Gould pointed out that recognition of this factor alone could have accounted for all important differences in brain size among races. In addition, there were various miscalculations and omissions in the original analysis, every one of which worked in favor of the final conclusion of white superiority. Morton omitted small-brained subsamples (like the Hindus) from the Caucasian mean, while including such subsamples (Inca Peruvians) in the American Indian mean. Some individual large skulls of unfavored races were conveniently omitted from the final calculations, and some means were incorrectly rounded off to the nearest cubic inch, the direction of the error being upward for white subsamples and downward for black ones.

Finally, Gould noted that the difference between whites and blacks decreased dramatically after Morton changed from white pepper or mustard seed to lead shot as the "filler" for determining the brain's volume. Though Morton had made the change to increase the consistency of his measurements, the new values obtained with the more reliable lead filler produced a substantial increase in the average black skull volume but relatively little alteration in the white one. This result suggested to Gould that much of the originally reported difference had been due to the "pack" factor. With seed, if a specimen was known to be from a "smart" race, the skull cavity might be filled more tightly than a skull from a "stupid" race; the unyielding lead shot was less susceptible to this subtle source of bias. Though Gould did not find any indication of intent to deceive on Morton's part, he summarized Morton's research as "a patchwork of fudging and finagling in the clear interest of a priori convictions."[38]

While Morton himself made no public statement of support for slavery, he was hardly chagrined when others found his conclusions admirably suited for that purpose, and in some ways he seemed to encourage it. When told, shortly after publication of his latest book, that John Calhoun would "appreciate the powerful support" it offered for the South, Morton suggested that one of the few copies available at the time be sent to him. In subsequent correspondence between the scientist and the secretary of state, Morton supplied further anthropological evidence to bolster the antiabolitionist case.[39] When he died unexpectedly at only fifty-two, the *New York Tribune* noted that "probably no scientific man in America enjoyed a higher reputation among scholars throughout the world," but the *Charleston Medical Journal* paid a more blunt tribute: "we of the South should consider him as our benefactor, for aiding most materially in giving to the negro his true position as an inferior race."[40]

Agassiz and Morton agreed that the "lower" races were distinct species incapable of abstract reasoning, but for the most part they left it to others to spell out the specific political consequences of these scientific facts, a task that one of their colleagues pursued with a vengeance. Josiah Clark Nott, a southern gentleman, physician, and internationally recognized ethnologist, liked to refer to himself as an expert in "Niggerology," and his articles and addresses in support of slavery frequently appeared in journals representing the opinions and aspirations of the Old South. Despite being a slaveowner, Nott consistently proclaimed himself "at heart an emancipationist" if only it could be proven that blacks would benefit from freedom; however, all the scientific evidence demonstrated to him that blacks were an inferior species who had already attained their "greatest perfection" under slavery.[41] Appearances alone were sufficient for Nott to reach this conclusion. In his leading anthropological text, *Types of Mankind,* one set of illustrations compared the upright skull of a white with the more gradually sloped skulls of a black and a chimpanzee. "A man must be blind," noted the accompanying discussion, "not to be struck by similitudes between some of the lower races of mankind, viewed as connecting links in the animal kingdom; nor can it be rationally affirmed, that the Orang-Outan and Chimpanzee are more widely separated from certain African and Oceanic Negroes than are the latter from the Teutonic . . . types."[42] Nott, however, apparently took precautions just in case there *was* some problem with the reader's vision: Gould has noted that the black's skull was falsely extended to accentuate the desired impression.[43]

In addition to this visually compelling testimony, Morton's data provided Nott with the ultimate confirmation of black inferiority—those "seventeen cubic inches" of brain that separated the "lowest" race from the "highest"—the "Teutonic."[44] In the face of such evidence, concluded Nott, "unless some process [could] be discovered by which a Negro's head may be changed in form, and enlarged in size," there was no possibility for blacks to function in a free society. Only the "strictly-*white* races," he explained, the Anglo-Saxons, who were "destined . . . to conquer and hold every foot of the globe," could exist under stable republics; the "*dark*-skinned races"—not only the blacks, according to Nott, but also most French, Italian, Spanish, and Portuguese—were "only fit for military governments."[45] Since the cause of their plight was anatomical, education could not improve the servile position mandated for blacks by science. In fact, Nott observed, "the negroes who cannot read and write are more moral, more pious, more honest, and more useful members of society" than those who had been made "vicious" through education.[46]

It was therefore not a matter of what Nott called "abstract notions of liberty and slavery"; indisputable scientific facts compelled him—or so he claimed—to support a system of social relations that he would otherwise find objectionable. He once reminded a Mobile, Alabama, audience, however, that emancipation would also destroy "the prosperity, happiness, and political power of the Southern States."[47] It seemed that the dictates of science converged nicely with other motivations that were less sublime.

A Search from Top to Bottom

The American school's insistence that blacks were not just inferior but a completely separate species presented both cultural and scientific problems. Since this claim contradicted the biblical version of creation, it was unacceptable to many southern fundamentalists. Then, too, the customary scientific criterion for distinguishing two species was either their inability to crossbreed or the infertility of their offspring. Because the former test could not withstand abundant hostile evidence from numerous clandestine experiments in southern laboratories, the American ethnologists settled on a new variation of the latter, insisting that mulattoes were "bad breeders," whose reproduction would gradually decline until they completely died off.[48] This contention would not remain tenable for very long either, but the eventual resolution of the taxonomic question in favor of a single species in no way diminished the practical usefulness of Morton's data.

Indeed, the difference in cranial capacity became just one of a number of anthropometric measures, unencumbered by theoretical baggage, that were extensively investigated both before and after emancipation, not so much to prove black inferiority but to identify its bodily manifestations. The presumptive inferiority of blacks became the basis of a search for associated morphological or anatomical signs; any characteristic on which blacks differed from the white standard of perfection was a likely candidate. Extensive overlap on many of these measurements was largely ignored in favor of an obsessive quest for differences, often relatively inconsequential ones, which could then be cited as profoundly significant. If one measure proved unsuitable, it was discarded and replaced with another that would yield the desired results.

The exterior of heads was subjected to as much scrutiny as their interior. In 1852 Peter Browne announced the results of his microscopic observations of human hair. He had found certain "canals" in the hair of whites that did not exist in the hair of blacks, and since, according to Browne, "a greater variety of apparatus" indicated greater perfection, he drew the unavoidable conclusion: "The hair of the white man is more perfect than that of the negro . . . we will not, perhaps, be wandering astray, in ranking the hair of the head of the white man *as a perfect hair.*"[49]

Though first investigated some sixty years earlier,[50] another characteristic of considerable interest during the mid-nineteenth century was the facial angle, defined as the angle that the frontal plane of the face—a line approximately tangent to the upper lip and forehead—made with the horizontal; that is, the farther back the forehead relative to the chin, the smaller the facial angle. To measure this index, a special instrument bearing some resemblance to a protractor was devised, and it produced results that again indicated the greater proximity of blacks to lower animals. Putatively superior beings, those claimed to possess greater beauty as well as intelligence, were marked by larger facial angles. The idealized statues of Greek deities yielded values as high as a hundred degrees, while blacks were typically measured at between sixty and seventy degrees, apes lower, and dogs lower still. Small facial angles were characterized by a nose whose line diverged considerably from the vertical, often referred to as a "snout," and by a projecting jaw termed "prognathous," as opposed to the more upright or "orthognathous" jaw of "higher" specimens. Noting that "those animals with the longest snouts are always considered the most stupid and gluttonous," one of Morton's followers observed that the "animal aspect" of the prognathous blacks could not "fail to strike an unprejudiced observer."[51] In 1865 the great English biologist Thomas H. Huxley, though an outspoken opponent of slavery, contributed his famous observation about "our dusky cousins." "It is simply incredible," wrote Huxley, in anticipation of the imminent abolition of slavery, "that, when all his disabilities are removed, and our prognathous relative has a fair field and no favor, as well as no oppressor, he will be able to compete successfully with his bigger brained and smaller-jawed rival, in a contest which is to be carried on by thoughts and not by bites."[52]

Also a subject of extensive investigation was the cephalic index, a measurement of the general shape of the skull, defined as the ratio of its breadth to its length multiplied by one hundred to eliminate the decimal point. Ratios below seventy-five indicated skulls that were long and narrow, termed "dolichocephalic"; those between seventy-five and eighty, slightly broader or "mesocephalic"; and even rounder heads with ratios above eighty were called "brachycephalic." Just as beauty and intellect were conveniently linked in the facial angle, so dolichocephalics were claimed to be both the most physically attractive and the most intelligent. Objections arose to this classification, however. The French scientist Paul Broca, inventor of the cephalic index, had no argument with other anthropological claims of the time. He agreed that intellectual inferiority was associated with "a prognathous face, ... black ... skin, wooly hair," while "white skin, straight hair and orthognathous face" were the "equipment of the highest groups." But Broca, whose own head was round-shaped, found equating dolichocephaly with intelligence less convincing. In a sudden show of insight he noted that the scientists who posited this link were themselves from countries in which the dolichocephalic type predominated and concluded that there was "a natural tendency of men, even among those most free of prejudice, to attach an idea of superiority to the dominant characteristics of their race."[53]

Even more serious, the skulls of some "lower races" turned out to be unexpectedly dolichocephalic, placing them in the same anthropometric category as that of the highest ranking subgroups of white Europeans. One infrequent solution to this problem was to acknowledge the data and to change the rules of classification; if blacks were dolichocephalic, then some writers had no qualms about labeling long heads the "lowest varieties" of mankind and round heads the "highest."[54] The more common response was to salvage the purported link between narrow heads and large intellects through the ingenious distinction between frontal elongation, the mark of white superiority, and occipital dolichocephaly, a lengthening of the rear of the cranium that produced a deceptively similar outward appearance of the skull, yet with no increase—in fact, with a diminution—in that portion of the brain responsible for intelligence.[55] Indeed, these bulging back portions found in the brains of the inferior races often produced behavior the untrained eye might find similar to that of whites; however, the discerning scientist could tell the difference between, for example, the "blind passions, ferocious instincts, and animal courage" that could be traced to the savage's occipital brain area and the "true courage, frontal courage, which we may call Caucasian courage."[56]

Heads were not the only object of anthropometric examination. In the continuing search for anatomical characteristics that would suggest the similarity between blacks and apes, arm length also came in for scrutiny. The ratio of lower arm to upper arm was investigated but produced little interest when it turned out that on this measurement whites were closer than either blacks or American Indians to apes. The difference from the fingertip to the kneepan proved more satisfactory: due to their longer arm and shorter body, blacks measured about 60 percent of the average distance for whites, placing them appropriately closer to the "anthropoids."[57]

Moving down the body, attention was focused on the sex organs. The French anatomist Etienne Serres found that the distance between navel and penis remained small throughout life for black males while it increased for whites, and he offered this disparity as evidence of black inferiority—what Gould has called "the rising belly button as a mark of progress."[58] Many doctors seemed almost obsessed with the sexual anatomy of blacks; just the titles of their journal articles suggested this preoccupation. In papers like "Genital Peculiarities of the Negro" and "Hymen of the Negro Women" physicians noted the "massive proportions" of the black penis and the "atrophic condition of the external genital organs in which the labia are much flattened and thinned, approaching in type that offered by the female anthropoid ape, . . . lemur and other pithecoid animals."[59] This exaggerated anatomy naturally produced an appetite to match, and scientists remarked on the similarity between the "*furor sexualis* in the negro . . . [and] similar sexual attacks in the bull and elephant." Invoking the South's worst nightmare of sooty desecrators unleashed by abolition, they attributed these outbursts to the "changes in the social . . . status of the negro race" that had occurred "in states cursed by carpet-bag statesmanship."[60] One physician insisted that the attempt to educate blacks was "gross folly" because it would not "reduce the large size of the negro's penis" or "prevent the African's birthright to sexual madness."[61] Meticulous anatomical measurement had again found blacks unable to profit from schooling; they were too small at one end and too big at the other.

Many of these anthropometric studies appeared during the period of intense dissatisfaction with Reconstruction, thus providing a welcome source of scientific justification for the politics of disfranchisement and segregation. The scientific finding that blacks were condemned by their nature to be hewers of wood and drawers of water could certainly not be changed by a mere act of Congress, a point emphasized by some politicians in great detail during the congressional discussions of postwar legislation. In his opposition to Reconstruction, for example, Congressman James Brooks explained to his colleagues in the House that the difference between blacks and whites was "essential, organic, throughout, from the crown of the head to the very sole of the feet. The negro is a different creature, with a different brain and different structural organization." As support for this contention, Brooks presented all the contemporary data on hair, skull size, facial angle, length of the leg, size of the foot, and even shape of the nostrils. Appended to his lengthy address was a chart taken directly from Nott's text, *Types of Mankind,* listing twenty-three varieties of interracial matings, which Brooks had retitled "The Miscegenation in Preparation for Us." The only "sound" policy, he concluded, could occur "where ethnology is discussed scientifically."[62]

From Comparison to Competition

While anthropometrists were scouring the anatomical landscape willy-nilly in search of the signs of black inferiority, Charles Darwin first proposed the theory that was to revolutionize biology. In place of a supernatural power responsible for the creation of all life, Darwin offered a simple mechanical explanation for its "evolution," thus denying the existence of any essential difference between the origin of human life and that of animals. He argued that evolution took place through "natural selection," a long gradual process in which organisms change through chance variations that turn out to produce differential reproductive success. This theoretical breakthrough had little impact on the conclusions of the anthropometrists. From their point of view the anatomical evidence was just as valid whether blacks had been created inferior or had evolved that way over tens of thousands of generations according to a process "decided among the prehistoric Protozoa."[63] The latter outcome seemed no less permanent than the former.

The Preservation of Weaklings

Of greater importance than Darwin's work itself to the scientists of race was "Social Darwinism," a mixture of oversimplified biology and opportunistic politics that arose as the dominant sociological thought of the late nineteenth century. In his pioneering work *The Origin of Species* Darwin had posited that those biological variations conferring some survival advantage on an organism in the "struggle for existence" were more likely to be preserved and transmitted to offspring. Darwin was careful to explain that this concept of "struggle" was intended "in a large and metaphorical sense including dependence of one being on another." Thus, for example, "a plant on the edge of a desert is said to struggle for life against the drought, though more properly it should be said to be dependent on the moisture."[64] In place of these cautious qualifications, however, Herbert Spencer, the major exponent of Social Darwinism, preferred to stress the "survival of the fittest," an inappropriate use of the superlative that converted the subtle dynamic suggested by Darwin's metaphorical "struggle" into Spencer's more sensationalized, literal version: the "struggle for existence," a *bellum omnium contra omnes,* in which purposeful cruelty was transformed into nature's method for biological progress.

Spencer's approach to evolution was intended to provide a normative framework for moral decisions. The replacement of creationism with evolution seemed to Spencer to undermine the authority of the Bible, indirectly raising doubts about the whole basis of ethics and the traditional notion of life's purpose, a lacuna that he sought to fill with a new goal, one derived from science: the continued evolution to "higher" forms of life. In place of traditional moral injunctions, now deprived in Spencer's opinion of their sacred origin, he offered a new foundation for a new morality, a religiosity without religion. "My ultimate purpose," Spencer acknowledged, "has been that of finding for the principles of right and wrong, in conduct at large, a scientific basis."[65]

This scientifically derived system of ethics recognized that "pervading all Nature we may see at work a stern discipline which is a little cruel that it may be very kind." That is, a certain "salutary suffering" was viewed as the inevitable price of evolutionary progress, and attempts to avoid it would only thwart nature's method for preventing "vitiation of the race." The moral corollaries of this view ranged from benign neglect of the weak and helpless to their extermination. Traditional notions of humanitarian assistance to the poor and needy, the losers in the Social Darwinist struggle, would only do biological harm to posterity. Such aid was a "spurious" philanthropy, preventing fatalities from hunger and sickness, which might seem harsh when considered individually but which when "regarded . . . in connexion [sic] with the interests of universal humanity," Spencer found "full of beneficence—the same beneficence which brings to early graves the children of diseased parents, and singles out the intemperate and the debilitated as the victims of an epidemic."[66]

As a consequence, the Social Darwinists opposed all governmental programs for charity, free meals, or other benefits for the undeserving inferior. Similar reasoning also justified opposition to the regulation of minimum wage and working hours, free public education, and all those other "socialistic" institutions, which, by improving the lot of the poor, would shield them from the just consequences of their own inferiority and pave the way for society's degeneration. Even modern advances in public health were seen as unnatural interference with biological progress since they contributed to the artificial preservation of weaklings.

During the late nineteenth century Social Darwinist theory exerted tremendous influence on both academic and popular thought. It was an important contributing factor to the decision to found sociology departments in a number of American universities and motivated many of the people who chose to study that discipline. Spencer's books alone sold over 300,000 volumes in the United States, a phenomenal total for works in technical fields like philosophy and sociology.[67] His ideas were so prevalent that Oliver Wendell Holmes, in a dissenting opinion, felt constrained to remind his colleagues on the Supreme Court that Spencer was *not* part of the United States Constitution.[68]

Though popular on both sides of the Atlantic, Spencer became a veritable hero to the American business classes—and for good reason. His message that misguided philanthropy was a crime against nature and society provided balm for their conscience as well as relief for their taxes. More important, in an era of robber barons and the beginning of imperialist interests, here was a law of science that positively sanctified rapaciousness. Spencer had provided a model of inevitable competition in which, as Bertrand Russell reportedly once noted, victory was promised to those who most resembled capitalists. If acts of compassion or loyalty were merely vain attempts to reverse the biologically ordained fulfillment of evolutionary destiny, then exploitation was not a mark of selfishness and unscrupulous ambition; it was the means to a biologically improved human being and a more harmonious universe. One could attain the highest principles of science by abandoning them everywhere else. Scientific and social progress, not to mention prosperity, could be ensured by the suppression and elimination of the weak by the strong, by the triumph of machine gun over bow and arrow, by unrestrained trade and competition, and by generally "sticking it to the other guy" with impunity. The business tycoons themselves were some of the loudest voices in the chorus of praise for ruthlessness. To justify the absorption of the smaller lines by the larger ones, the railroad magnate James J. Hill proclaimed that "the fortunes of railroad companies are determined by the law of survival of the fittest." Andrew Carnegie's biography described how his discovery of Spencer brought him round from theology and the supernatural to the "truth of evolution." John D. Rockefeller, a man intimately familiar with the practical details of competition, summarized the economic implications of Social Darwinism in a famous metaphor: "The growth of a large business is merely a survival of the fittest.... The American beauty rose can be produced in the splendor and fragrance which bring cheer to its beholder only by sacrificing the early buds which grow around it. This is not an evil tendency in business. It is merely the working-out of a law of nature and a law of God."[69]

"A Great Flood of Light"

Social Darwinism also extended the ubiquitous struggle for survival to units other than individual members of the society. The same kind of competition for resources supposedly took place at an intraindividual level, as different bodily systems vied for the same store of nutrients. For example, an acquisition by the nervous system, the foundation of intelligence, implied a loss for the reproductive system and vice versa. This was claimed to be especially problematic for women since reproduction was supposedly their major function. In the 1875 best-selling book *Sex in Education* E. H. Clarke, a professor at the Harvard Medical School, detailed the case histories of young women whose intellectual efforts resulted in a physique "where the milliner had supplied the organs Nature should have grown." If a woman put as much effort into education as a man did, he explained, then either her brain or her "special apparatus" would suffer. Excess intellectual effort by women would only produce scholarly invalids, "pale, weak, neuralgic, dyspeptic, hysterical, menorraphic [sic], dysmenorrhoeic [sic] girls and women" with arrested breast development, and as an illustration Clarke described the tragic case of a woman who, believing that she was a man's intellectual equal, "strove with noble but ignorant bravery . . . and died in the effort."[70] In Social Darwinist analysis there was inevitably an inverse relationship between intellectual activity and fecundity, which threatened to decrease the proportion of intelligent families in the population and produce biological deterioration of the society. For some unexplainable reason, however, physical work did not similarly attenuate fertility, and all those poor but hard-working women with numerous progeny constituted much of the threat by their tendency to outbreed the more cultured yet supposedly less prolific elements. To hold the biological line, the only hope was for many of the poor to succumb to the struggle at an early age, preventing the proliferation of their kind.

Even more significant, the Social Darwinists extended the concept of the struggle for survival to such larger aggregates as nations and races. Just as competition between individuals was necessary for evolutionary progress because it resulted in the early and unmourned demise of biologically inferior organisms, so the conflict between larger entities was claimed to be a valuable mechanism for ridding the world of inferior races. There was, wrote the British scientist and ardent Social Darwinist Karl Pearson, "one way, and one way only, in which a high state of civilization has been produced, namely the struggle of race with race and the survival of the physically and mentally fitter race." This contest was to be carried out, he explained, "chiefly by way of war with inferior races, and with equal races by the struggle for trade-routes, . . . sources of raw material and of food supply." Though Pearson acknowledged that the struggle between races meant "suffering, intense suffering," he maintained that only by prevailing over the "inferior races" has "mankind . . . arisen to the higher intellectual and deeper emotional life." Indeed, he warned, "when the sword shall be turned into the ploughshare, . . . when the white man and the dark shall share the soil between them, and each till it as he lists . . . when that day comes mankind will no longer progress; there will be nothing to check the fertility of inferior stock."[71]

To the anthropometrists' empirical investigations of black inferiority Social Darwinism now added significant theoretical consequences. For social scientists of the time the study of innate racial differences became the central problem, the key to understanding human societies. Such studies had always been informed by overtones of competition, at least since Agassiz had discovered science's "obligation to settle the relative rank among . . . races." Now that only the fittest races would survive, racial comparisons became a zero-sum game in earnest, one in which an admission of black accomplishment might lose important evolutionary points for whites. Of course, achievements by blacks had often been denigrated. Uninfluenced by Spencerian thought, in 1866 Josiah Nott had dismissed Frederick Douglass, though "unquestionably the most brilliant" of his race, as "nothing more than . . . 'a pestilent fellow' . . . [who] has just brains enough to talk fluently about matters he does not comprehend."[72] By the time of Douglass's death in 1895, Social Darwinism was at its peak, and his obituary in the *New York Times* was more concerned with "confiscating" his abilities for whites than denigrating them. Acknowledging Douglass's distinction, the *Times* suggested that

> it might not be unreasonable, perhaps, to intimate that his white blood may have had something to do with the remarkable energy he displayed and the superior intelligence he manifested. Indeed, it might not be altogether unreasonable to ask whether, with more white blood, he would not have been an even better and greater man than he was, and whether the fact that he had any black blood at all may not have cost the world a genius, and be, in consequence, a cause for lamentation instead of a source of lyrical enthusiasm over African possibilities. It is always more or less foolish to credit or discredit a race with the doings, good or bad, of a particular member of that race, but if it must be done, plain justice should see to it that the right race gets the glory or the humiliation.[73]

Social Darwinism also produced a dramatically revised interpretation of slavery. Previously, the assertion of black inferiority had been the most common justification for their enslavement. As additional evidence that this role was not only appropriate for but also beneficial to its victims, the medical-scientific literature had proven that blacks thrived under subjugation. There were reports of slaves who "frequently" lived from 150 to 175 years, "several instances recorded" of their having surpassed 200 years, and more systematic data that showed consistently lower rates of disease and much greater longevity among slaves than among both free blacks and whites.[74] Now, however, it appeared that slavery had been *too* beneficial for blacks, artificially shielding them from nature's struggle and allowing them to flourish in what one Social Darwinist called a "hothouse existence."[75] The data on blacks' health and longevity now became evidence of the unfair advantage that slavery had granted them, an advantage that emancipation had finally forced them to relinquish. Social Darwinist thinking thus became the basis for a new kind of argument against slavery, one that welcomed its abolition not on traditional moral grounds but so that blacks would be forced out from behind its protective veil and into "open competition" with whites.

From this point of view, of course, the purpose of attaining freedom for blacks was to allow for their elimination. When two races attempted to coexist, there were only two possible outcomes, according to Social

Darwinist science: "amalgamation" or extermination of the weaker. For both sociocultural and allegedly scientific reasons there was little support for the former path. Happily for the Social Darwinists, the "conceded" inferiority of blacks left little doubt about who would prevail in the latter case. The racial struggle was generally agreed to be an unequal contest, "a game of chess," the popular author Edward Eggleston called it, "with a fully developed giant intellect . . . sitting on the one side, and a child on the other, that scarcely knows a pawn from a king." Eggleston concluded that "a great flood of light is let in upon our American Negro question the ultimate solution of which should now be manifest to all."[76] This "ultimate solution" may not have been planned with the same efficient brutality as that "final solution" to be implemented a few decades later, but the two were close relatives in the Social Darwinist family, sharing a common goal of genocide and justified by a similar scientific rationale.

The prospect of black extermination was viewed as a remedy more than a tragedy. There was little to regret in the survival of the fittest; it was an inevitable law of science and the natural process of improvement. "If [blacks] were the highest form of human life," William Benjamin Smith, a Tulane University professor, assured the public, "we might be concerned . . . [but] to the clear, cold eye of science, the plight of these backward peoples appears practically hopeless. They have neither part nor parcel in the future history of man."[77] The scientific literature did, however, contain some different opinions on the appropriate posture of whites toward the imminent disappearance of their racial competitors. G. Frank Lydston, a professor of medicine, believed that "there might be much of benefit to ourselves in retarding the march" of black extinction, though, of course, it would not be desirable to prevent it altogether. Lydston seemed particularly concerned that as blacks became more "degraded" on their way to the inevitable, their criminal behavior would also increase, and he suggested "penile mutilation" as one route to their improvement.[78] Charles S. Bacon, another physician, did not doubt the "*eventual* elimination" (emphasis added) of blacks in the United States, but since the latest census data indicated that the "race is not doomed . . . in the immediate future," he suggested "helping along the process of extinction," though he did worry that three million cheap black workers might be "too valuable an economic factor to be eliminated."[79]

On one point all the Social Darwinists concurred: there were to be no shortcuts for blacks on the evolutionary path. Just as humanitarian assistance to the poor was claimed to produce biological deterioration, all attempts to provide assistance to blacks through political or social reform were opposed as leading to the same catastrophic results on a racial level. The natural process of evolution was the only method for true racial improvement, and it could be neither replaced nor supplemented by "philanthropy." John Roach Straton, a professor at Mercer University, explained in detail the futility of any attempts to provide instant enlightenment for "savages from . . . [a] low plane of evolution":

> The Anglo-Saxon has reached his present high civilization after a long and laborious struggle upward. Through a series of well-defined steps, he has risen from barbarism to his present plane. The system in which he now dwells is the logical outcome of all that has gone before, and consequently, the white man of today is thoroughly suited to his environment. Now, it is reasonable to think that since Anglo-Saxon civilization is the culmination of a series of steps, all the steps must be taken before it can safely be reached. To suddenly introduce another race, therefore, to any step in the series, and then to attempt to hurry it over the steps in the hope of having it reach and occupy the culminating one, must be a hopeless undertaking.[80]

As Tulane's Smith concisely put it, it was impossible "to rise from the floor to the roof without ever traversing the intervening space."[81]

In particular, for the Social Darwinists this meant that attempts to educate blacks were useless. Racial improvement was claimed to be "organic," whereas education was "extraorganic." That is, education did not produce an improvement of "the stock," a change that could be passed on to the next generation, whose children would be as ignorant as ever. Instead, it only allowed blacks to imitate their superiors without achieving that real, biological progress whites had taken centuries to realize. In fact, insisted Eggleston, the campaign to educate blacks would only hasten their numerical decline by enticing them away from manual labor, the one role for which they were fit. "Viewed in this light," he wrote, "the otherwise nonsensical . . . policy may really be regarded as a blessing in disguise."[82]

Any assistance whites provided blacks was, like slavery, an artificial intrusion into the evolutionary process, depriving blacks of the salutary suffering of the racial struggle. Though perhaps intended with the most honorable of motives, such aid was doomed to failure. There was only one way to avoid the "destructive influences" caused by what one social scientist called the "easy conditions of life": blacks had to refuse and be refused "every offer of direct interference in [their] own evolution."[83] According to this view, such benefits of U.S. citizenship as education and exercise of the franchise were to be withheld from blacks for their own good, and even those patronizing gestures once known as the white man's burden were now claimed to lead to the demise of blacks. Whereas policies of racial oppression had previously been rationalized as an implication of science, now they *were* science, part of the organic process of evolutionary improvement. In a classic catch-22, many of the adherents of this position frankly maintained that long before enough generations had passed to make blacks "a capable and reliable race" deserving the same rights as everyone else, they "will have been practically eliminated from the American continent."[84]

The Social Darwinists kept an obsessive eye on health and population trends to monitor their expectations. The first large-scale postwar analyses suggested, *horrible dictu*, that the black population was actually increasing *faster* than the white—apparently, exposure to the struggle was not having the anticipated effect—and E. W. Gilliam, a sociology professor, pronounced it "morally certain" that at their present rate of growth blacks would "overwhelmingly preponderate" in the South by 1980. As a "remedy" for this problem, he encouraged colonization, in other words, the forced deportation of blacks to some territory outside the continental United States.[85] His ominous predictions gave way to more encouraging news in 1896, when the economist Frederick L. Hoffman published *Race Traits and Tendencies of the American Negro*, an exhaustive study based on more than fifty years of demographic, anthropometric, and medical data, including the census reports of 1890. Gilliam's error, Hoffman pointed out, had been his complete reliance on the higher birthrate among blacks and his failure to realize that their deathrate was also becoming ever greater than that for whites. Thus, in spite of their fecundity, noted Hoffman, "in the struggle for race supremacy the black race is not holding its own," and eventual extinction was inevitable.[86] Most scientists agreed that a major factor in this decline was urban conditions. Blacks were steadily abandoning the simple health of country life for the "unsanitated throngs" of the city, where tuberculosis, typhoid fever, and other diseases stood ready as a "two-handed engine of death." Yet the same authorities insisted that neither socioeconomic nor sanitary conditions played a significant role in these statistics. "Even under the same conditions," wrote Hoffman, blacks were "still subject to a higher death rate"; it was a matter of "racial inferiority."[87] Tulane's Professor Smith pointed out the "obvious" reason for this excessive vulnerability: blacks were "histologically ... inferior" to whites, their tissues offering "ready lodgement to the invading bacillus [and] ... far less stubborn and protracted resistance to such inroads when once in progress."[88] In the face of such favorable indications, the cruelties of forced deportation no longer seemed necessary. Whites did not have to *do* anything other than segregate blacks and wait for nature to take its course; it was not expected to take very long.

These scientific proclamations were welcome news to many southern politicians, and some of the chief southern demagogues contributed articles to northern magazines, outlining their racial concerns in the language of evolution and Social Darwinism. In one such publication John Sharp Williams, a senator from Mississippi and once the House minority leader, explained that the South's major problem was "the physical presence of the negro." Even though he noted that blacks were declining in numbers as a result of "God's law of evolution, the survival of the fittest and the extinction of the unfit," Williams desired to find some "way in which the existing processes of natural evolution can be accelerated." He dismissed any signs of improvement among blacks as "only a veneering" imposed by a superior race, not the result of true evolutionary change: "it was habit and not nature."[89] "Pitchfork" Ben Tillman, a senator from South Carolina and perhaps the most extreme racist in Congress, offered a similar analysis in his call for repeal of the Fourteenth and Fifteenth amendments.[90] Such men would not have otherwise risked offending their fundamentalist constituencies by paying heed to "Darwinist" analyses, but the opportunity to exploit contemporary scientific authority for the South's cause was, no doubt, irresistible, especially if it could bolster their case to a northern audience; in such a context certainly the folks at home would understand.

A New Alien Threat

Social Darwinist thought also contributed to the beginning of an alliance between the anti-immigrant parochialism of New England and the racial ideology of the South. As the great waves of so-called less desirable immigrants began to pour over the Northeast in the late nineteenth century, some scientists viewed the newcomers through the Social Darwinist prism and found them not far removed from blacks on the evolutionary ladder.

The Irish were a particular target of complaint at the time. In 1881 Edward A. Freeman, an Oxford professor, toured the United States, praising Teutonic solidarity and proclaiming that "the best remedy for whatever is amiss in America would be if every Irishman would kill a negro and be hanged for it." When this remark proved to be rather unpopular in some quarters, Freeman demurred that he had been only joking, but once secure again in England, he noted that many had approved his recommendation and that most of those who disagreed did so because "if there were no Irish and no negroes, they would not be able to get any domestic servants."[91] Freeman's words might have been in jest, but others remarked more seriously on the inferiority of the two groups. The biologist Joseph LeConte, one of the South's most distinguished scientists, found the "lower races already doomed [to extermination] by the laws of nature," but he offered one possibility that might save them "from the inevitable"—a "judicious crossing" of the "marginal varieties of different races,"[92] that is, those relatively close to each other on the evolutionary spectrum. This clearly implied the mixture of blacks with the Irish, considered the lowest Caucasian variety at the time. As the historian Allan Chase has noted, such a guided evolution would presumably yield a race a little smarter than the blacks and a little stronger than the Irish.[93]

Other leading scientists of the time found many of the new immigrants to be almost as much of an evolutionary menace as blacks were. The biologist Edward Drinker Cope, for example, maintained that neither group was fit for the ballot. In addition, he called for the "return of the African to Africa"[94] and restrictive immigration to exclude "the half-civilised [sic] hordes of Europe."[95] Cope seemed aware that these measures were in conflict with "so-called human rights," but he insisted that such "abstract" concepts had to yield to rights derived from scientific law. "The pure idealist will sustain the former," he wrote, "but the wise man knows that he must bow to the latter."[96] The chief example of the latter for Cope was *the right to pursue a course of progressive evolution without obstruction by unnecessary obstacles.*" The inferior people who constituted such obstacles had to be removed from the path of progress. Of course, Cope recognized that these people would object, but, he frankly maintained, their "preferences . . . must be . . . disregarded."[97]

Another prominent scientist who regarded blacks and immigrants as a similar problem was Nathaniel Southgate Shaler, dean of the Lawrence Scientific School at Harvard. Blacks he termed an "alien folk," unfit for civilization, who had "no . . . place in the body politic," while the new class of immigrants was no more capable: they were "by birthright . . . inferior, . . . in essentially the same state as the Southern negro."[98] He did feel that by bringing blacks to America against their will, whites had incurred a moral debt. Even if blacks were destined for extinction by natural law—"perhaps . . . a beneficent end"—"they cannot be allowed to perish," Shaler wrote, "without the fullest effort in their behalf."[99] No such generosity was owed to the newcomers, who, after all, had come to the New World voluntarily. Indeed, the lesson to be learned from the blacks' presence was not to perpetuate the same kind of problems by allowing the unrestricted immigration of a whole new group of inferior aliens. Shaler was careful to distinguish between the new arrivals, predominantly from "Latin" countries like Italy, Spain, and Portugal, and that worthier peasantry from Germany and the Scandinavian nations, where one found "the Aryan variety of mankind." It was in the Catholic countries that the masses contributed little more to the commonwealth "than the cattle of the fields," according to Shaler; there the stock had been of a lower caste for centuries, and the little talent that did exist had been systematically eliminated by the celibacy the church had imposed on the few capable men and women.[100]

Although it soon became obvious that blacks were not going to disappear from the United States, the immigrants would eventually replace them as the chief obsession of the Social Darwinists, at least for the first quarter of the twentieth century. While blacks might not have been declining in number, they were certainly not displaying the newcomers' exponential increase. Besides, the combination of Jim Crow laws and geographic isolation in the rural South kept the overwhelming majority of blacks separate and unequal, in contrast to the immigrants, whose social and political presence in the major cities would appear more threatening to the older American stock.

The beginning of the century, however, would bring with it not just a new menace but a new and more sophisticated version of Social Darwinism imported from abroad. While American social theorists were primarily concerned with the struggle against the "lower" races, an English scientist was attempting to foster interest in the other end of the human spectrum.

2

For a Twentieth the Cost: Francis Galton and the Origin of Eugenics

I F PHILOSOPHY was the mother of the sciences, then long after the other children had left home, the Social Darwinists were still keeping her company. On the other hand, the almost totally atheoretical anthropometrists were scientific waifs, who had left home at a such an early age that they had no recollection of parentage. The man who reunited this family was the English gentleman-scientist Francis Galton.

One of his biographers calls Galton a "Victorian genius."[1] For the first half of his life Galton was a kind of scientific dilettante—an inventor, African explorer, geographer, and meteorologist, who made significant contributions in each of these fields; an innovator of statistical methods; and the author of a definitive work on fingerprints. But Sir Francis—he was knighted by Edward VII in 1909—did not find his true passion in life until middle age, when he began to focus his considerable abilities on the study of heredity.

Galton had such an obsessive desire to collect data—to classify, organize, measure, and tabulate—that he once acknowledged it as "almost a danger" to himself.[2] In a letter to his sister when he was eighteen, he prefaced his description of a traumatic experience in which he almost drowned by noting that it had occurred "at 17 minutes and 45 seconds to five."[3] Sixty-five years later neither age nor poor health had altered this concern with precise data, as can be seen in Galton's description of a "sudden severe shivering" in a letter to his niece: "The amplitude of the shiver was remarkable and interesting; my hands shook through a range of fully 7 if not 8 inches."[4] His published papers in the prestigious British scientific journal *Nature* included such analyses as an operational definition of audience boredom at a public lecture based on the frequency, amplitude, and duration of fidgeting[5]—a boring speaker produced an

average of one movement per minute per person—and a comparison of
the number of brush strokes made by a portrait artist with the number of
stitches in an ordinary pair of socks.[6] Two months' worth of unpublished
data collected twice a day on his attempt to relate the "flavor, freshness,
body and softness" of his cup of tea to the amount of tea used, the amount
of water, and the temperatures of the pot, water, and mixture at various
moments in the process of preparation was found posthumously in Galton's
personal papers.[7]

Although these instances of simple measurement, many of them no
more than careful counting, were certainly valid, when Galton turned to
more complex traits, the results were much more subjective. He often
insisted on the simpleminded assumption that all behavioral measurements should fit a mound-shaped and nicely symmetric distribution. For
example, in a study of temperament as an hereditary characteristic he
asked the "compilers of family records" to classify each individual as
good-tempered or bad-tempered. When about one-quarter of the almost
two thousand records were subsequently placed in each of these two
categories and fully one-half were not placed in either, Galton declared
this distribution of results itself proof of the procedure's validity. "Whenever
a group is divided into only three classes, of which the second is called
neutral or medium," he explained, the very "nomenclature" demanded
that there be an equal number of cases on either side of this middle
group. Since the compilers of the records had, in fact, produced such a
result, Galton concluded that "their judgments are shown to be correct."[8]

In particular, Galton was enamored of the "law of deviation from an
average," his term for the normal or bell-shaped distribution. When he
learned that the Belgian statistician Lambert Quételet had found the
distribution a successful approximation for various physical measurements,
Galton immediately decided that this "wonderful form of cosmic order"
was, willy-nilly, appropriate for all sorts of behavioral measurements.[9] In
a discussion of the "blind gregarious instincts of cattle," he even applied
it to the independence of oxen. He observed that the great majority of
these animals experienced "mental agony" when separated from their
fellows, a terror of segregation that helped keep the herd together. A
small number—only one out of every fifty—displayed "a self-reliant
nature," and these rare "fore-oxen" were the "born leaders," who grazed
apart or ahead of the rest. At the other end of the spectrum he also noted
those few members of the herd "showing a deficiency from the average
ox-standard of self-reliance, about equal to the excess of that quality
found in ordinary fore-oxen." Since the difference in independence between
the rare fore-ox and the average specimen was, according to Galton,
equal to the difference between the rare excessively timid specimen and
the average, he concluded that "the law of 'deviation from an average' "

was applicable to "independence of character among cattle," just as it was to a trait like human stature.[10]

These examples of pseudomeasurement, stemming from Galton's supreme confidence in the validity of his idiosyncratic methods of quantification, suggested the spirit of the Enlightenment gone astray. The appearance of careful empirical observation, quantitative thinking, universal application of principles, and other elements of the scientific approach gave many of his investigations an image of scientific respectability that belied their dependence on his personal perceptions as a substitute for objective measurement. Galton's contemporary, the Scottish physicist Lord William Kelvin, had noted that knowledge of science begins "when you can measure what you are speaking about, and express it in numbers,"[11] an observation that Galton seemed to reverse: whatever *he* expressed in numbers became, ipso facto, science.

If this worship of *idola quantitatis* was Galton's methodological bias, class prejudice was its social counterpart. Able to trace his "ancestry and collaterals" back through twelve centuries of Norman dukes and French and Anglo-Saxon kings,[12] Galton felt a contempt for the masses of ordinary people that he took no pains to hide. Indeed, his passion for measurement was often placed in the service of his social prejudice. The trait of gregariousness in cattle, for example, was of interest to Galton primarily insofar as it provided a model for the study in humans of

> the slavish aptitudes, from which the leaders of men, and the heroes and prophets are exempt, but which are irrepressible elements in the disposition of average men. I refer to the natural tendency of the vast majority of our race to shrink from the responsibility of standing and acting alone, to their exaltation of the *vox populi*, even when they know it to be the utterance of a mob of nobodies, into the *vox dei*, to their willing servitude to tradition, authority and custom. Also, I refer to the intellectual deficiencies corresponding to these moral flaws, shown by the rareness with which men are endowed with the power of free original thought.[13]

Except for the occasional reference to an animal, Galton's subsequent description of cattle was hard to distinguish from his preceding characterization of the average human. Few oxen, he wrote, had much "originality and independence of character. . . . They are essentially slavish. . . . No ox ever dares to act contrary to the rest of the herd, but he accepts their common determination as an authority binding on his conscience." Finally, Galton noted that these same "blind instincts" of the cattle herd had been "deeply ingrained into our breed," especially in "the black population of Africa," and, surveying contemporary society in general, he remarked that "a really intelligent nation . . . would not be a mob of slaves, clinging together, incapable of self-government, and begging to be led. . . . Our present natural dispositions make it simply impossible for us to attain this ideal standard, and therefore the slavishness of the mass of men, in morals and intellect, must be admitted in all schemes of regenerative policy."[14]

Even when a superior mind supplied intellectual leadership to these slavish masses, in Galton's view they were still incapable of benefiting from it. "Every tutor," he wrote in one book, "knows how difficult it is to drive abstract conceptions, even of the simplest kind, into the brains of most people—how feeble and hesitating is their mental grasp—how easily their brains are mazed—how incapable they are of precision and soundness of knowledge." When he listened to "men and women of mediocre gifts" discuss a scientific lecture, Galton found it "positively painful" to hear the "mere chaos of mist and misapprehension." The average mental ability, he observed, of even the well-educated audience was "ludicrously small."[15]

In addition to his obsession with measurement and his Victorian social bias, a third major influence on Galton's work was his attitude toward conventional religion. Though an agnostic, Galton bore none of the intellectual animosity of contemporaries like Thomas H. Huxley, and he would acknowledge religion's beneficial effect on the lives of others, even while simultaneously observing to Karl Pearson, his friend and protégé, "how impossible it would all be for you and me."[16] This condescending attitude was at least partly due to Galton's perception of the religious nature as one that alternated between "adoration and self-sacrifice," on the one hand, and "sensuality and selfishness," on the other. The religious displayed a "disposition . . . to sin more frequently and to repent more fervently than those whose constitutions are stoical, and therefore of a more symmetrical and orderly character," Galton wrote, clearly thinking of himself in the latter category, and in characteristically statistical terms he explained that "the amplitude of the moral oscillation of religious men is greater than that of others whose *average* moral position is the same."[17] Galton even published an empirical investigation of the "efficacy of prayer," in which he demonstrated, for example, that the likelihood of infant death showed no relation to the degree of piety of the parents. Similar analyses all indicated that prayer yielded little in the way of objective results, although Galton acknowledged its subjective comfort in times of tragedy.[18]

Galton, however, was not so much opposed to conventional religion as he was disappointed in it. It was vague and mystical, it was unprovable, and it certainly provided no clear direction for human improvement, all of which made it unsatisfactory to the man of science. In one of his discussions of heredity Galton even referred to specific biblical passages on the fertility of marriage and the establishment of families, and he complained of his inability to determine whether these statements were "to be understood metaphorically, or in some other way to be clothed with a different meaning to what is imposed by the grammatical rules and plain meaning of language."[19] Clearly Galton was seeking a more practical substitute for religion, something more in consonance with his scientific turn of mind.

The confluence of these factors—scientific, social, and religious—only needed some catalytic element to turn the rich, capable, and energetic Galton from his earlier dilettantish activities toward a single cause to which he could wholeheartedly commit himself. That catalyst was the theory of evolution. When Galton first read *Origin of Species,* it marked a turning point in his life. In the discoveries of Charles Darwin, his first cousin, Galton saw the opportunity to raise "the present miserably low standard of the human race" by guiding the evolutionary process.[20] He now had an outlet for all three of the influences on his thinking, one that would dominate the rest of his life, from 1865 to 1911.

"The Highest Caucasian and the Lowest Savage"

Galton devoted his scientific efforts to the investigation of hereditary influences, especially on differences in intellectual ability. For Galton the study of heredity was a science that could predict the past. There was no trait so trivial or obscure that its origin could not be somehow traced to a previous family member, a technique of analysis that the English scientist often applied to himself. Galton attributed his own "statistical proclivity" to at least a half-dozen "remarkable instances of a love of tabulation within two degrees of kinship of myself." With no intent of parody, Galton ascribed his interest in biology to the "hereditary bent of mind" of his maternal grandfather, Erasmus Darwin, the ancestor he shared in common with cousin Charles.[21]

Actually, before any data had been gathered, Galton was quite certain that, in the "convenient jingle of words" he resurrected from Shakespeare, "nature" reigned supreme over "nurture."[22] Whether it was "character, disposition, energy, intellect or physical power," he insisted that "we each receive at our birth a definite endowment . . . [of] the various . . . qualities that go towards the making of civic worth."[23] The evidence that Galton presented for these claims of heredity's "omnicompetence" was of questionable value, however. For his study *English Men of Science,* for example, he obtained ninety-one written replies to the question "How far do your scientific tastes appear to have been innate?" After categorizing fifty-six of these open-ended answers as "decidedly innate," he concluded from the show of hands that the "origin of taste for science" was hereditary. In fact, Galton became a little testy over disagreement. He complained of the "conceit" of those who were "too proud to acknowledge their indebtedness to natural gifts" and was particularly exercised over the "vanity" of John Stuart Mill, who did not regard himself exceptionally gifted and believed that any child of average capacity was capable of great learning if properly taught. Fortunately for Galton, few of the scientists in his study were affected by such conceit; when the majority agreed with his belief in heredity's power, he found their judgments to be the "cool and careful analysis" of thinkers who were "manly, honest and truthful."[24]

In 1869 Galton produced *Hereditary Genius,* his most well-known work. Though the original publication did not define the "natural ability" that was the book's chief concern, in the preface to the 1892 edition he clarified the term as that ability "a modern European possesses in a much greater average share than men of the lower races." Although such a definition sounded similar to the claims made by American scientists at the time, Galton's approach was actually considerably more sophisticated. Having chosen to concentrate almost exclusively on the difference in ability between *groups,* the Americans had focused their attention on those physiognomic and physical distinctions they hoped would minimize the overlap between blacks and whites; when overlap did occur, they tended to ignore it. Galton's focus, however, was on *individual* differences; he was more interested in the "continuity of natural ability," the "enormous . . . range of mental power . . . between the greatest and least of English intellects" as well as between "the highest Caucasian and the lowest savage."[25] This emphasis on individual differences also meant that the higher "savages" might be better endowed than the lower Europeans. The difference between races was thus statistical in origin, a difference between the averages of overlapping distributions, and could not be assumed to hold for any two individuals.

From this point of view the first task was to develop a system for classifying ability on some sort of standard scale. To accomplish this, at least conceptually, Galton resorted again to the "law of deviation from an average," that is, the normal curve. His reasoning was that since this distribution provided a good approximation of the actually observed data on such physical measurements as height and chest size, "then it will be true as regards every other physical feature—as circumference of head, size of brain, weight of grey matter, number of brain fibres; and thence, by a step on which no physiologist will hesitate, as regards mental capacity."[26] Galton did not bother with the usual scientific procedure of first gathering data to see how they were distributed. Untroubled by the absence of any empirical measurements, he merely decreed ability to be normally distributed on the grounds that other measures were, a scientific fiat concerning intelligence that has been with us ever since.

Galton partitioned the normal curve of ability into classes A through G, extending upward from the average and separated by allegedly equal degrees of merit, and parallel classes a through g, extending downward. Just as he decided that fore-oxen exceeded the average cattle in independence by the same amount that the average exceeded the "peculiarly centripetal" types, Galton declared that "eminently gifted men are raised as much above mediocrity as idiots are depressed below it." Due to the steep taper of the normal distribution, the "mediocre" classes a, b, A, B—the middle of the curve—contained more than two-thirds of the population, and when c and C were added, the six groups accounted for 95 percent. Class D included the "mass of men who obtain the ordinary prizes of life," E was higher yet, and F was the lower bound of the truly superior individuals. Even though there was not yet an operational procedure, a test of some kind, for assessing an individual's appropriate placement on this spectrum of ability, in theory Galton could now compare the relative positions of groups from two different populations. These comparisons could be rather farfetched. For example, he proclaimed that "the class F of dogs, and others of the more intelligent sort of animals, is nearly commensurate with the f of the human race, in respect to memory and powers of reason. Certainly the class G of such animals is far superior to the g of humankind."[27]

The more important comparison, of course, was between races. In contrast to the gut-level reaction of Louis Agassiz, Galton was not repulsed by blacks' appearance. On the contrary, in an amusing letter written from Africa to his brother, he marveled at "the Hottentot Ladies . . . endowed with that shape which European milliners so vainly attempt to imitate, . . . figures that could afford to scoff at crinoline." Charles White's hormones might have been stirred by those "plump and snowy white hemispheres, tipt with vermillion," but for Galton not even the most ingenious European use of steel springs, whalebone, and "caoutchouc" (i.e., rubber) could compare with the "handiwork of a bounteous nature," and the consummate measurer boasted of the dexterous use of his sextant from afar to collect data on these objects of his admiration.[28] Ability was another matter, however, and Galton did not allow his favorable reaction to appearances to prejudice his objective judgments of intellect. There were some blacks, he observed, "considerably above the average of whites," but "their" classes E and F corresponded to "our" classes C and D. That is, the distribution of ability for blacks was displaced two grades below that for whites.

The evidence for this conclusion was almost entirely anecdotal. In his own African travels Galton had seen behavior he called so "childish, stupid, and simpleton-like" that it made him "ashamed" of his own species. Moreover, other travelers often had to "confront" native chiefs, undoubtedly the most capable of the blacks, and yet in his discussions with "competent persons" Galton had seldom heard "of a white traveller meeting with a black chief whom he feels to be the better man."[29] It is true that such self-serving opinions were generally characteristic of Victorian ethnocentrism. As the historian Raymond Fancher has concluded, however, in a comparison of Galton's accounts of African behavior with those of other contemporary explorers, "Galton stands out as a relatively extreme case, ... invariably ... the one more prepared to believe and tell the worst about Africans."[30]

Since Galton lacked a usable operational definition for ability, his proof that all individual differences in ability were caused by heredity was also largely impressionistic. He selected a group of the most noteworthy individuals in a number of fields—judges, commanders, statesmen, scientists, poets, artists, musicians, and others—and he showed for each group that accomplishment in that field ran in families. As additional evidence that opportunity mattered little compared with heredity, Galton cited the United States, where he found culture far more widespread and education of the middle and lower classes far more advanced yet the country still intellectually impoverished. "The higher kind of books, even of the most modern date, read in America, are principally the work of Englishmen,"[31] wrote Galton, either disdainful or unmindful of the wealth of serious American writers of the time—Henry Thoreau, Thorstein Veblen, Walt Whitman, Ralph Waldo Emerson, Nathaniel Hawthorne, Herman Melville, William James, Emily Dickinson. To demonstrate that even the most diminished circumstances were no barrier to the emergence of true eminence, he also presented a true-life version of Oliver Twist, the Dickens protagonist whose upper-class heredity transcended his parish workhouse upbringing. Galton described the childhood of Jean Le Rond d'Alembert, the illegitimate child of a distinguished artillery officer and an ex-nun turned "adventuress," who had involved herself in political intrigue. Abandoned in a public market as an infant and "put out to nurse as a pauper baby to the wife of a poor glazier," d'Alembert nonetheless managed to attain the "first rank of celebrity" in mathematics and philosophy, becoming a member of the French Academy at age twenty-four.[32] Despite such intimate familiarity with the meretricious details of d'Alembert's background, Galton failed to mention that the infant's father took immediate steps to locate his son after the abandonment, had the king's physician personally entrust the child's upbringing to the glazier's wife (who must have known that this was no ordinary foundling), and ensured that the boy received an excellent education at the best private schools and colleges.[33]

Though Galton published many other scientific works after *Hereditary Genius*, he never did settle on a suitable operational definition for "natural ability." He gathered a considerable amount of data based on his belief that powers of sensory discrimination would be highly correlated with intellect. At first these attempts seemed encouraging to Galton, especially when men turned out to display more acute sensitivity than women on such psychophysical tests as the ability to discriminate between weights of "just perceptible difference" or to hear tones of extremely high pitch.[34] When these test scores did not correlate well with "social eminence," however, he lost interest in them as a measure of ability. This lack of a measure of intellect might have been an annoying problem from the scientific point of view, but it proved no obstacle to Galton's social agenda.

"The Science of Improving Stock"

Galton's concern for scientific advance was always overshadowed by a different motivation, one more sociopolitical in nature and informed by his upper-class bias. In a letter to the geneticist William Bateson, he frankly acknowledged his first priority. "To increase the contribution of the more valuable classes of the population and to diminish the converse" was his primary purpose, Galton wrote, and "an exact knowledge of the true principles of heredity would hardly help us in its practical solution."[35] More important for Galton than the scientific details of evolution was the possibility for rational control of its direction. Here, finally, was the opportunity for him to do something constructive about his bête noire— common people. "The average man," observed Galton in his president's address to the Anthropological Institute of Great Britain and Ireland, "is morally and intellectually an uninteresting being . . . of no direct help towards evolution." When he considered a group of such persons, Galton found its repulsiveness even greater than the sum of its parts. It constituted, he said with undisguised contempt, a "mob of mediocrities," who might be regarded "with complacency" by "some thorough-going democrats" but were "to most other persons . . . the reverse of attractive."[36] It might now, however, be possible to remove these objectionable weeds that were overrunning the garden of humanity. After experimenting with the neologism *viriculture* to describe his approach, Galton finally settled on the term that would eventually label a movement. "Eugenics," he suggested, should be adopted as "a brief word to express the science of improving stock, which is by no means confined to questions of judicious mating, but which, especially in the case of man, takes cognizance of all influences that tend in however remote a degree to give to the more suitable races or strains of blood a better chance of prevailing speedily over the less suitable than they otherwise would have had."[37]

This principle quickly became Galton's idée fixe, furnishing the underlying purpose behind much of his scientific work. His initial proposal for a eugenics program appeared four years *before* publication of *Hereditary Genius,* the work presenting the scientific position on which the program was based. In the very first paragraph of that book Galton declared the social significance of its scientific conclusion: the inheritance of natural ability now made it "quite practicable to produce a highly gifted race of men by judicious marriages during several consecutive generations."[38] It was thus necessary to demonstrate the minimal effect of environment as an ideological requirement of eugenical sociology. If environment could exert influence on ability, the "breeding" approach would not be the only method for human improvement.

Although Galton first coined the term *eugenics,* the concept had been described previously. In *The Republic* Socrates explained that only by breeding from the "best as much as possible could one produce the best hunting dogs and most noble cocks. . . . It is also the same with the human species. . . . There is a need for the best men to have intercourse as often as possible with the best women, and the reverse for the most ordinary men with the most ordinary women; and the offspring of the former must be reared but not that of the others, if the flock is going to be of the most eminent quality."[39] No less an egalitarian than Thomas Jefferson also once remarked on the possibility of producing "a race of veritable aristocrats" through selective breeding.[40] It was not until Galton, however, that anyone suggested a serious plan for implementing such a premise.

In his first description of an actual eugenics program, published in a popular magazine, Galton envisioned an annual public ceremony in which the "Senior Trustee of the Endowment Fund would address ten deeply-blushing young men." These worthy specimens, chosen for their "foremost places . . . in . . . qualities of talent, character, and bodily vigour" would be offered the opportunity for marriage to one from a list of ten young ladies similarly chosen for "grace, beauty, health, good temper, accomplished housewifery, and disengaged affections, in addition to noble qualities of heart and brain." In recognition of the "paramount interest" the state would have in the "extraordinarily talented issue" resulting from such unions, the marriage partners would receive five thousand pounds from the public coffers to defray the cost of maintaining and educating children, and "the Sovereign herself" would give away the bride at a ceremony in Westminster Abbey. Galton concluded this first brief account with rhapsodic speculation on the "galaxy of genius" that might be created if only "a twentieth part of the cost and pain were spent in measures for the improvement of the human race that is spent on the improvement of the breed of horses and cattle." He foresaw the introduction of "prophets and high priests of civilization into the world."[41]

Galton eventually elaborated on this rather fanciful scenario, outlining, again in a popular magazine, the elements of a long-term approach to the implementation of eugenic principles. He began by pointing out the present sources of threat to evolutionary progress as an incentive for his program. Chief among these were the "allurements" of the cities, which attracted the better stock to areas that then subjected them to poor sanitary conditions. This meant that the struggle for existence was not producing intellectual improvement but instead was favoring those persons most able to withstand urban diseases, a characteristic Galton dryly commented was "not necessarily foremost in the qualities which make a nation great." As evidence he noted that after the potato famine the Irish face became more prognathous—every educated person knew who that made them resemble—because those who survived the starvation "were more generally of a low and coarse organization."[42]

If natural selection could make the Irish noticeably more prognathous in merely one generation, there was reason for great optimism, if only the process could be guided in a more productive direction. Maybe it would never, in George Bernard Shaw's words, turn a pond of amoebas into the French Academy, but Galton expected "marvelous effects" within 166 years—his calculation for five generations—and he proceeded to outline his eugenic plan, a program to institutionalize his own contempt for the mob of mediocrities. The goal of this program would be to "build up . . . a sentiment of caste" among those who are naturally gifted so they would not squander their hereditary endowment by marrying out of their position. To prevent fraudulent claims, an agency would be formed to collect accurate information on pedigrees, biographies, and accomplishments, all of which could then be used to publish "a 'golden book' of natural nobility," an official seal of approval for superior heredity, "for it would be no slight help for a man to state on undoubted grounds, that not only is he what he appears, but that he has latent gifts as well . . . that his children are very likely indeed to prove better than those of other people . . . that he and his family may be expected to turn out yet more creditably than those ignorant of his and his wife's hereditary gifts would imagine. This would make it more easy for him than for others to obtain a settled home and employment in early manhood."[43]

Assistance for such truly worthy individuals would constitute *real* charity, Galton noted, not that counterproductive type that helped the poor and thus only increased the extent of the very problem it was intended to alleviate. In particular, Galton emphasized that the eugenic creed should be taught to the "most valuable" youth, who would then receive a diploma, "a patent of natural nobility." They would learn that a suitable choice of marriage partner would ensure that their children would be superior to the children of other people, and they would thus find it "base to ally themselves with inferior breeds."[44]

Galton acknowledged his scheme might not be universally popular, especially with those who harbored that "undeniably wrong" democratic feeling that "men are of equal value as social units, equally capable of voting and the rest." He believed, however, that the talents of the elite would be so overwhelmingly obvious that "democracy notwithstanding," their superiority would be recognized without envy, though "very possibly with some feeling of hostility on the part of beaten competitors." But, he maintained, this hostility would only strengthen the sentiment of caste, for the elite would withdraw from areas where they were not appreciated and establish cooperatives in the country, where they would be unlikely even to associate with persons not of their own level. In any case, the result would be inevitable: rapid proliferation of the gifted families and decay of those not so favored. Galton envisioned this as a natural process occurring with little "severity"; the elites, he felt, could be relied on to treat their lesser counterparts "with all kindness." Such gracious treatment would, however, only be due those who accepted the appropriate limitations on their behavior; those who failed to do so would merit a less benign response. If the poorer stock "continued to procreate children, inferior in moral, intellectual and physical qualities," Galton wrote, "the time may come when such persons would be considered as enemies to the state, and to have forfeited all claims to kindness."[45] Although he provided no elaboration on this ominous note, others would follow in his footsteps with more specific suggestions.

While Galton's program implied a society of extreme social rigidity, there might still be some small chance for someone to begin life lacking hereditary recognition but attain it through evidence of actual accomplishment. Even this slim hope was foreclosed, however. There was a world of difference, in Galton's view, between two persons gifted with similarly high qualities: an individual might possess such talents by being an "exceptionally good specimen of a poor race or an average specimen of a high one." The former case still offered no prospect for long-term biological improvement, for "so long as the race remains radically the same," he insisted, "the stringent selection of the best specimens to rear and breed from, can never lead to any permanent result."[46] This statement might seem a direct contradiction of the basic eugenic principle of "breeding from the best," but Galton provided a simple resolution: there was a difference between the truly gifted, who could be counted on to produce similarly talented descendants, and those who had been serendipitously favored by biological variation and whose progeny were thus more likely to revert to their lower ancestral level. Only the former group, not just superior individuals but also members of superior stock, could be relied on for the evolutionary long haul; attempts to make biological progress with the latter was a hopelessly Sisyphean task. Not even the union of *two* gifted persons would be preferable, according to Galton, if they came from inferior backgrounds; "two ordinary members of a gifted stock" would still produce far superior offspring.[47] Only an untainted pedigree could provide hope for future generations.

Just as the American Social Darwinists extended the concepts of struggle and survival from the individual to the racial level, Galton also moved from his earlier Golden Book fantasies and caste sentiments to larger racial and political pronouncements. A "low race" could survive the struggle, he found, only if "the few best specimens" were allowed to become parents, and even then "not many of their descendants can be allowed to live." To avoid such "terrible misery," he offered a more "merciful" solution: the "substitution" of a higher race for a lower one.[48] For example, in Africa, where he claimed blacks had failed "to sustain the burden of any respectable form of civilization," Galton considered various schemes of substitution that would eliminate blacks yet not inconvenience Europeans by subjecting them to the intemperate African climate. Since the Europeans were destined to control Africa anyway, according to Galton, one possibility was for them to assist the "more suitable" subraces on that continent to "spread and displace the others." However, he speculated, even with such assistance "it may prove that the Negroes, one and all, will fail . . . to submit to the needs of a superior civilization than their own" and that they would have to be "replaced by their betters."[49] Consequently, another possibility was to introduce a new competitor—"the Chinaman"—into the African struggle: "The gain would be immense to the whole civilized world if he were to outbreed and finally displace the negro."[50] Such suggestions were neither inhumane nor exploitative from Galton's point of view. Whenever a lower and a higher race came into contact, he noted, "one must yield and . . . there will be no more unhappiness on the whole, if the inferior yields to the superior than conversely, whereas the world will be permanently enriched by the success of the superior." Thus, he concluded, opposition to "the gradual extinction of an inferior race" was "quite unreasonable."[51]

Spreading the Faith

Galton's Darwinist epiphany also allowed him to replace the "old teleology" of conventional religion with a new faith, one based on the "solidarity" he now found with the natural laws of the universe, "among which the hereditary influences are to be included." This new understanding provided Galton "serenity during the trials of life and in the shadow of approaching death,"[52] but he was not content merely to announce the subjective comfort he derived from this belief; his writing began to take on an increasingly evangelical tone. If evolution was the purpose of the universe, then it became for Galton a "religious duty" to follow "Nature's direction." However one chose to understand the concept of deity, evolutionary development was clearly its "Work," and humans were thus called to facilitate the aim of the "divine Worker." To Galton, the ultimate craftsman's method was clear: "the life of the individual is treated as of absolutely no importance. . . . Myriads of inchoate lives are produced in what . . . seems a wasteful and reckless manner, in order that a few selected specimens may survive and be the parents of the next generation. It is as though individual lives were of no more consideration than are the senseless chips which fall from the chisel of the artist who is elaborating some ideal form out of a rude block." If individual life was by divine intent subordinate to evolutionary progress, then a truly religious outlook would be concerned "primarily [with] the future . . . and only secondarily [with] the well being of our own contemporaries." Galton's faith therefore preached celibacy, instead of charity, for the poor—to prevent them from inflicting their "feeble constitutions, and petty and ignoble instincts" on future generations.[53]

This was not religion in some metaphorical sense that Galton encouraged; he meant the word quite literally. "The direction of the emotions and desires towards the furtherance of human evolution, recognized paramount over all objects of selfish desire," he wrote, "justly merits the name of a religion." Only this creed could deal effectively with the "serious evolutionary difficulties" that Galton saw on the English horizon: "poverty, toil, and an unduly large contingent of the weakly, the inefficient, and the born-criminal classes"; the failure of attempts at social reform "owing to the moral and intellectual incompetence of the average citizen"; and "signs of approaching anarchy and of ruin." Galton believed that traditional religions would be powerless in the face of such crises, whereas the eugenic faith could quickly diminish "the inefficient multitude of weaklings" by pursuing that evolutionary path that accorded with both the process and purpose of the cosmos.[54] This same eagerness to diminish the inefficient multitudes had informed many of Galton's scientific claims, and although he maintained that his social agenda was a consequence of scientific truth and religious obligation, it appeared to be more the opposite: both scientific truth and religious obligation were the products of social ideology.

Galton's Impact

Until the last ten years of his life Galton's campaign for eugenics went largely unnoticed in the United States. There were a few exceptions, however. John Humphrey Noyes had founded the Oneida Community in Putney, Vermont, in 1841, originally as a Christian Communist society, whose members swore allegiance first to God and second to Noyes as God's true representative. In place of more traditional family structures, they instituted a system of group marriage, and when Galton began to encourage the stud-farm mentality for improving human "stock," Noyes was very impressed. In an 1870 article entitled "Scientific Propagation" Noyes explained that "some of the vilest forms of existing society" actually had beneficial eugenic effects. For example, since a polygamist had to obtain and support many wives, thus establishing his superiority to his fellows, such a practice would lead to "breeding from the best, which is more than can be said of monogamic marriage." Also, he observed, since slave masters had exercised control over propagation, their use of "animal breeding" principles had, in fact, elevated the black race.[55] Noyes found the childless Galton too meek to face the obvious implications of his own theory, though. "Every race horse, every straight-backed bull, every premium pig tells us what we can do and what we must do for man,"[56] declared Noyes, a man ready to meet his scientific obligations. In the 1870s his community began a Galtonian experiment, in which the men signed a resolution offering themselves "to be used in forming any combinations that may seem to you [Noyes] desirable," while participating women pledged to abandon their own "right or personal feelings in regard to childbearing, . . . rejoice with those who are chosen candidates . . . and cheerfully resign all desires to become mothers, if for any reason, Mr. Noyes deem us unfit material for propagation."[57] The experiment produced fifty-eight children before being abandoned by the Oneida community.

In 1883 in the *Atlantic Monthly* Henry W. Holland also attempted to inform the American public that Galton's eugenics had now brought morality "within the circle of the physical sciences." Like other Social Darwinists of the time, he worried about the threat to the superior "Teutonic race" from both blacks and "the more prolific Celt." So many paupers and criminals from abroad constituted yet another danger, and though Holland understood that "America as the asylum for the oppressed" was obligatory Fourth of July rhetoric, he warned that it was "wicked folly from [the] scientific point of view." Aware of the latest insights from England, Holland noted that "Galton's law" was "squarely across the path" of many of these inferiors, and "the sooner they die quietly out the better."[58]

For the most part, however, eugenics attracted little attention on either side of the Atlantic until 1901, when Galton delivered a lecture to the British Anthropological Institute, sounding all the old themes: heredity's overwhelming influence; the resultant normally distributed scale of human value, with "the mediocre class as far below the highest in civic worth as it stands above the lowest class with its criminals and semi-criminals"; relentless contempt for the poor, who "degrade whatever they touch"; diplomas for the genetic elite and encouragement of their intermarriage; and the appeal to "religious obligations." One new consideration was raised: Galton had always believed that some people were born worth more than others, but now he described actual attempts to calculate "the worth of a child at birth according to the class he is destined to occupy when adult."[59] Though this might have sounded like something out of Jonathan Swift, Galton was quite serious and claimed this actuarial problem to be of great importance, since the child's potential monetary value could then be used by the state to determine the appropriate expenditure for care and maintenance. This address, also published in the United States,[60] was the starting point for a dramatic increase in public interest in eugenics. The next few years brought a flurry of activity in both the United States and England: journals were launched, fellowships were endowed, and laboratories and public information societies were established, many named after Galton. Another country in which eugenics found a welcome reception was Germany, where there was particular interest in Galton's claim that the Jews maintained a "*parasitical existence upon other nations.*"[61]

Undeniably, Galton made some scientific contributions. His focus on the similarities and differences between individuals who were related to each other in various ways became the basis of contemporary behavior genetics, and he was the first to prospect in that rich mine of hereditary information, twins. But his scientific work remained subordinate to his social agenda, and he was consequently not even aware of his most important discovery. He enunciated the modern concept of continuity of germ plasm at least a decade earlier than August Weismann, who is usually given credit (Galton's accomplishment was acknowledged in an 1889 letter to him from Weismann).[62] To the founder of eugenics, however, this physiological mechanism had seemed of little significance in its own right; indeed, one historian has claimed that Galton apparently forgot his own work on the subject.[63] For Galton the only reason to be interested in such a topic was its role as a scientific postulate for his social campaign.

Galton's more significant impact was as founder of the movement that was to have such enormous influence during the quarter-century after his death. Basically, Galton did for Herbert Spencer's ideas what John Maynard Keynes had done for Adam Smith's: he justified the intrusion of public policy into a competitive arena in which it was previously claimed to have no place. Galton shared many of Spencer's beliefs in the competition that led to the survival of the fittest, but where Spencer insisted that government interference in the struggle would only prove an unwarranted burden to the favorites in this race, Galton was concerned that without the right kind of intervention some underdog might displace nature's intended winners from their rightful position. To ensure that the evolutionary struggle had a happy ending, laws had to be passed, social plans made, and policies enacted, and between 1905 and 1930 they certainly were.

In addition, Galton set the tone for the "eugenics era," and many of its excesses were committed in his name. Like him, the movement was to be characterized by the most simpleminded notions about the hereditary nature of personal traits, a contemptuous disdain for the poor, and racist attitudes toward blacks and immigrants from "inferior" races, beliefs all espoused with religious fervor. The most oppressive policies would be justified with a moral arrogance, born of the certainty that they were the ineluctable social consequences of scientific truth. The worst was yet to come.

3

Applying Science to Society: The Eugenics Movement in the Early Twentieth Century

CERTAIN that they had discovered the scientific holy grail, the eugenicists were eager to apply it to all of society's problems and redeem humanity's hope of paradise. As Ellsworth Huntington, a professor at Yale University and president of the American Eugenics Society, explained in a book on the goals of eugenics, the potential to control the evolutionary process was the latest of the "five most momentous human discoveries," the first four being tools, speech, fire, and writing. The fifth promised to be "the greatest of all," according to Huntington, not just transforming the environment, as the others had done, but for the first time allowing us "consciously and purposefully to select the types of human beings that will survive." "Today," he wrote, "we are beginning to thrill with the feeling that we stand on the brink of an evolutionary epoch whose limits no man can possibly foretell."[1] For the eugenicists the knowledge now existed to place the millennium within reach, if only it were put into practice.

Such boundless optimism represented the natural extension of the Enlightenment's faith in the untrammeled use of reason, the conviction that rationalism could liberate the human mind from the bonds of myth, superstition, and revealed religion in favor of the truths derived from science. This belief in reason, approaching deification, meant not only that nature could be studied and understood but also that the resulting knowledge could furnish the basis for the rational conduct of all human affairs. Biology and the newer human sciences—psychology and sociology—would now solve social problems, just as physics and engineering had solved architectural ones, thereby removing many social issues from the unscientific realm of partisan politics. This was, at first, an exciting idea—the possibility that reason could replace religion, emotion, and other nonrational bases for social policy—with an obvious appeal for intellectuals, and courses in eugenics were offered at Harvard, Columbia, Cornell, and other major universities. The seemingly altruistic emphasis on collective social benefit and the improvement of future generations was an additional attraction for progressive thinkers and liberal social reformers, such as Emma Goldman, George Bernard Shaw, Margaret Sanger, and Scott Nearing, who were early supporters of eugenics. At its outset eugenics promised to link scientific and social progress by exercising rational control over the reproductive process and hence the very path of evolution.[2]

The original Enlightenment theorists, however, had also realized that the freedom from arbitrary authority necessary for the exercise of reason was inseparable from individual political rights and freedoms; knowledge and liberty were two facets of the same gem. In contrast, scientific knowledge stimulated rampant self-righteousness and moral arrogance in the eugenics movement, encouraging intervention in areas of behavior where respect for privacy as well as freedom would suggest forbearance and justifying attempts to abridge political rights and liberties. In the interests of "tomorrows that sing" many eugenicists considered it their duty to control the behavior of the less enlightened; governmental and theological tyranny was to be replaced with the tyranny of nature.

After all, in the eugenicists' opinion the very future of the country was at stake. They saw the traditional American stocks being overwhelmed by the "fecundity of mediocrity." This meant that in the Social Darwinist struggle the biologically superior elements were in serious danger of succumbing to the sheer number of "degraded" types. If something were not done to reverse this trend, it would not be the meek that would inherit the earth; it would be all those paupers, degenerates, and members of inferior races, who were outbreeding their betters. Shifting the domain of discourse away from politics provided a means to attain oppressive policies on the grounds that they were a scientific necessity. As such views came to dominate the movement, those progressives who had been attracted to eugenics as a strategy for human improvement became disenchanted and abandoned their interest in the concept.

Eugenicist Principles

Those who called themselves eugenicists constituted a professionally heterogeneous group: within its ranks were biologists, animal breeders, psychologists and other social scientists, institutional administrators, criminologists, social workers, and activists for overtly racist and nativist political organizations. The eugenics movement could never claim a broad popular base; indeed, its upper-class Anglo-Saxon leaders harbored Galtonian attitudes of contempt toward most of their class inferiors. The professionals' "expertise," however, ensured that eugenics had a significant impact on important social issues in the United States during the first thirty years of the century.

These diverse constituents were held together by a common adherence to the legacy of Social Darwinism, that the traditional bases for sociomoral decisions had to be replaced by the teachings of science. Albert E. Wiggam, author of some of the most popular works on eugenics, even insisted that human beings had had no idea of *how* to be "righteous" prior to the recent scientific discoveries. Indeed, he maintained, "had Jesus been among us, he would have been president of the First Eugenics Congress." The principal commandment offered by this scientific morality was "the biological Golden Rule," which differed from the traditional version, Wiggam explained, by including "the unborn" among those "others" whom one should treat as one wished to be treated. This emphasis on the welfare of future generations, of course, reflected the Social Darwinist opposition to assistance for the poor on the grounds that charitable attempts to eliminate economic poverty would foster a biological poverty leading to an increase in the number of paupers. Only the application of eugenics, a plan for the conscious and intelligent control of evolution, wrote Wiggam, could furnish "the final program for the completed Christianization of mankind."[3]

Enlarging the Selective Sieve

The first corollary of this belief was that progress of every kind—military, medical, social—was a mixed blessing, producing technical advance while destroying the function of natural selection as a regulator of human quality. "In our most highly civilized countries," observed the well-known geneticist Charles Benedict Davenport, "the process of elimination of the unfit animal strains is largely reversed."[4] All the efforts "to improve man's lot . . . are hastening the hour of his destruction," insisted Wiggam, every new advancement producing yet further deterioration in the innate qualities of human beings, creating ever more "weaklings, paupers, hoboes and imbeciles."[5]

The biologist S. J. Holmes observed that warfare had once been a eugenically wholesome activity in which the race had been improved by extermination of the unfit. However, "modern civilized warfare," he complained, had become "one of the most potent agencies for elimination of the best blood and the propagation of weaklings."[6] The Harvard geneticist Edward M. East joined Holmes in pining for the good old days of biologically progressive warfare but noted that modern strife was not

without some redeeming eugenic value. True, he noted, the best specimens were more likely to be killed, leaving reproduction to the inferior,
but "the disease-rate of armies is high, and presumably the weaker
succumb." Despite this latter salutary effect, East did not find the situation very encouraging and conjectured that perhaps the only way to
reverse the present "organic retrogression" and "restore the biological
role of warfare" would be "a complete triumph of civilization with gases
and bombs annihilating whole populations."[7] Presumably, given a chance
to start again with the advantage of eugenic knowledge, society might
produce a biologically worthier product this time.

An even greater eugenic threat than the hawk or the dove was the
stork. The eugenicists saw the combination of medical advances in child-
birth and humanitarian principles as truly a two-edged sword, reducing
the infant deathrate but swamping the society with unfit children. East
particularly complained about improvements in prenatal care and child
delivery available to the poor through clinics and public hospitals, finding
them "superficially . . . very commendable. They satisfy our sympathies,
our urge to do for others as we would have others do for us. But
each . . . is unsound biologically. Each nullifies natural elimination of the
unfit. Physically defective women are encouraged to become mothers.
Weak infants are carried through babyhood. Incapable men are persuaded to transmit their lack of ability regularly and often."[8]

Many new developments in medicine were similarly suspect. Herbert
S. Jennings, a geneticist at Johns Hopkins University, explained at the
annual meeting of the National Tuberculosis Association that chemical
therapy—the treatment of certain diseases with manufactured thyroxin
or insulin—could provide a remedy for defects in genes but that such a
remedy would not prevent the same genes from being passed on to
descendants, who would have to submit to the same chemical treatment,
causing the society eventually to accumulate a great stock of these
defective genes. This scenario was not an attractive one to Jennings, who
preferred a "race in which, through lack of skill in synthetic chemistry,
defective genes have been cancelled as they arise; so that each individual
bears within himself, in his stock of genes, an automatic factory for the
necessary chemicals." Jennings proposed the slogan "Every man his own
hormone factory!" as a more constructive approach to future generations.[9]
Other eugenicists even opposed the search for a cure for disease. A
scientist who made such a discovery might win the gratitude of some
individuals, wrote one university professor, but "he . . . would deserve . . . the
execration of his race as its deadliest and most insidious foe" for providing
the "inferior an equal chance with the superior in the propagation of the
species."[10] Wiggam also emphasized the dangers of "coddling" the unfit
with medical panaceas; only "vice and disease," "nature's methods of

racial purgation," could produce those strong survivors who would truly be "biological 'darlings of destiny.' "[11]

Most social reform proposals of the time, measures designed to improve the quality of life for the poor, were also unsound according to the eugenicists. In *Applied Eugenics,* the leading textbook on the subject, the biologists Paul Popenoe and Roswell Johnson analyzed a number of these proposals. They found state-subsidized old age pension, the concept eventually enacted as social security, to be dysgenic since it would reduce the economic obligations of the ordinary working man to his parents and thus allow him to afford more children. "Superior" families would, of course, not encounter this problem since the parents in such families, being naturally gifted with greater earning capacity as well as thrift and foresight, would have provided for their old age, and a "superior man" would therefore be under no economic pressure to limit the size of his own family to support his parents. On the other hand, in "inferior" families the parents would have made no adequate provision for their old age, and to support them, a son would have to reduce the number of his own children. This eugenically favorable result would be reversed by any sort of old age assistance to the poor, though. Popenoe and Johnson's text consequently not only opposed such a program but also recommended that support of poor parents by their children be made compulsory, "a step [which] would not handicap superior families but would hold back the inferior." Proposals for a minimum wage law fared no better: Popenoe and Johnson frankly maintained that "poverty is in many ways eugenic in its effect" since "it is desirable that, in one way or another, it be made impossible" for some men to support a family. Compulsory education was a more complex issue. Since a child in school, instead of at work, was a source of expense rather than of revenue to the parent, compulsory attendance would be eugenic, again discouraging the poor from having more nonproductive mouths to feed. But this beneficial effect would be diminished, warned Popenoe and Johnson, by free textbooks, reduced carfare for schoolchildren, or any other measures designed to decrease the cost of education; these they vigorously opposed.[12]

Other eugenicists applied similar interpretations to policies already enacted. East, for example, opposed prohibition on the grounds that it had been passed "chiefly in order to prevent the feebly inhibited from drinking themselves to death, and to enable them to raise larger families to maturity."[13] Wiggam offered a eugenic analysis of legislation designed to reduce the infant deathrate by requiring employers to grant unpaid leave to women in the late stages of pregnancy who were employed in shops and factories. According to Wiggam, a study of women who had to continue working at such times showed that their husbands were "either weak and puny or else shiftless and lazy." The real problem, he claimed, had nothing to do with the mothers' working conditions; "the children died from weak heredity." The real solution was simple: "the parents should never have been allowed to get married and the children should never have been born."[14]

Almost all environmental improvements that produced better conditions of life for the masses were dismissed by the eugenicists as, at best, "palliative," incapable of producing a change in "blood." Not even "a thousand years of educating or improving" the population would produce any permanent impact, noted Wiggam, because the next generation would always be created "not from the improved body cells, but from the unimproved germ cells."[15] At worst, the attempts at improvement were harmful, enlarging what East called "the meshes of the selective sieve" so that more inferiors might slip through.[16] "Give educational facilities to all," warned Francis Galton's protégé, Karl Pearson, "limit the hours of labor to eight-a-day—providing leisure to watch two football matches a week—give a minimum wage with free medical advice, and yet you will find that the unemployables, the degenerates and the physical and mental weaklings increase rather than decrease."[17]

To the eugenicists there was but one scientifically effective method for human progress: selection of only the "best specimens" for parentage. "Our only hope . . . for the real betterment of the human race," insisted the geneticist Davenport, "is in better matings."[18]

Naming the Undesirables

Although Galton's original approach to the selection of parentage had encouraged propagation of the "better stocks"—"breeding from the best"—the American eugenicists paid no more than lip service to this principle. In practice, they were almost totally preoccupied with the other end of the human spectrum, and control of the "unfit" became the movement's obsession. Of course, Galton had also been concerned with the "mob of mediocrities," but in place of this vague reference to the less desirable, the twentieth-century eugenicists were eager to name names. The most threatening germ plasm, they claimed, came from southern and eastern European immigrants, blacks, and "degenerates" and from that great mass of ordinary working people who were judged too dull to make any worthwhile contribution to the society or the polity.

First on this list of undesirables were the "new" immigrants: southern Italians, Slavs, Poles, Jews, Hungarians, Greeks, Russians, and others. Between the 1860s and the turn of the century the number of immigrants from northwest Europe had remained fairly steady, while the number from southern and eastern Europe grew 200-fold, increasing from less than 2 percent to more than 70 percent of the total.[19] The eugenicists viewed this trend with alarm. The new arrivals were no longer that "aryo-germanic" stock, whose qualities, "bred into its proto-plasm since the stone age," had produced such unparalleled successes in the New World. The "blond, blue-eyed race" was now faced with a tremendous influx of the "black-haired and black-eyed race," and the eugenicists predicted "blood-chaos."[20] They saw the Nordic purity of American blood threatened with contamination from these "vast throngs of ignorant and brutalized peasantry . . . beaten men from beaten races . . . the worst failures in the struggle for existence."[21] In addition, the eugeni-cists worried that, once here, these inferior aliens were proliferating at a frightful rate. The well-known sociologist Edward Alsworth Ross warned the country of "conquest made by child-bearing," because the newer immigrants treated their women as mere "brood-mares," weapons to be spent "brutally" in the silent struggle with the older Americans.[22] (According to the eugenicists, the superior American stock was further burdened in this contest by modern feminism, which, wrote one Harvard professor, removed the "best" women from marriage and motherhood, possibly leading to "the entire extinction of British and American" intelli-gence within the next two or three generations.)[23] In response to the alien threat the eugenicists campaigned vigorously for legislation, and their efforts were rewarded when the Immigration Restriction Act of 1924 slammed shut the golden door at Ellis Island.

The eugenicists judged blacks even more biologically undesirable than immigrants but paid them much less political attention. Of course, they encouraged and supported the southern antimiscegenation laws and the Jim Crow policies that kept blacks separate and unequal, but there was no campaign of antiblack propaganda anything like the systematic and relentless barrage directed against the immigrants. Since it was generally accepted at the time that blacks were less intellectually capable than whites, the eugenicists felt less need to convince the public of this "fact"; well into the 1940s national publications could refer to blacks in rather demeaning ways with little fear of producing controversy. Then, too, blacks were not considered politically volatile at the time; unlike the immigrants, "negroes are never socialists and labor unionists," observed one prominent member of the eugenics movement.[24] Even more important, though there was a slow growth in the black population, it was remaining fairly stable compared with the exponential increase in the number of immigrants. In 1907 more than a million newcomers passed through Ellis Island—over twelve thousand on one day alone—and to the eugenicists it was this steady stream of new inferiors that constituted the immediate danger. Immigrants were a much greater social and economic threat than blacks were, and as they began to populate the cities, the established families deserted the urban melting pots just as, fifty years later, the immigrants' children would flee the inner cities when threatened by the influx of blacks and Hispanics.

For the "degenerates" the eugenicists recommended sterilization, and eventually over forty-five thousand persons in thirty states would be sterilized under state laws enacted largely through the eugenicists' efforts.[25] The statutory language typically eschewed the emotionally toned term *degenerate,* which had already done yeoman service in convincing legislatures of the need for such measures, in favor of the more clinical sounding designation, *socially inadequate person,* defined as one who "fails chronically in comparison with normal persons, to maintain himself or herself as a useful member of the social life of the state." Subsumed under such a description were the so-called feebleminded, the insane, alcoholics, certain criminals (the "delinquent and wayward"), epileptics, the diseased (including those with tuberculosis), those with impaired vision or hearing, cripples, and the dependent—"orphans, ne'er-do-wells, the homeless, tramps and paupers"[26] (a definition that, as the English geneticist J. B. S. Haldane pointed out, would include Milton, Beethoven, and Jesus).[27] Although sterilization was directed at persons because of their individual defects rather than their ethnic group membership, the eugenicists often took pains to ensure the public that the effect of these laws would fall disproportionately on the foreign-born and blacks; good American stock would not be significantly precluded from propagating their kind.

Finally, their scientific assessment convinced the eugenicists that many average Americans were simply inferior—not just those against whom the sterilization laws were directed but millions more, perhaps half the population, who were not so degenerate as to be included among the ranks of the "socially inadequate" but were nonetheless clearly incompetent. The existence of this larger group suggested that the full entitlements of citizenship had been granted too generously, and the eugenicists suggested proposals for restricting the franchise and the right to education. In fact, many of them believed that science had raised serious questions about the very feasibility of democracy, and they urged the consideration of various elitist schemes that would make society more consistent with the latest scientific results.

Eugenics and Genes

In essence, the eugenics movement began as an extension of the principles of animal husbandry to human beings. Some of the most enthusiastic early adherents were the animal breeders themselves, who were delighted to find their own specialized knowledge suddenly offered as the basis for all human progress. Armed with this newly discovered expertise, the breeders regularly warned the public of the dangers threatening "pure" American stock. As W. E. D. Stokes, a well-known horse-breeder-turned-eugenicist, wrote, even a single drop of "cur blood" ruined good breeding stock among humans just as it did for animals; in either case any attempt at "cross breeding" would only produce "worthless mongrels." Yet "pure healthy New England blood" had already been so tainted by "rotten, foreign, diseased blood . . . [from] the imported scum of the earth," according to Stokes, that there were only four thousand men left in the entire country whose ancestral history could ensure any biological improvement. To protect "the rights of the unborn," he proposed the careful compilation of hereditary records, which, in addition to registering any foreign taint, would grade each man from A to F "according to his worth as a sire"—F would signify "a 'blank,' a male only in name."[28]

Although this stud-farm mentality was truly the basis of the eugenics concept, the more sophisticated scientific underpinnings for the movement came from the newly developing areas of genetics and the social sciences. Indeed, it was probably to replace the stud-farm overtones with a more prestigious scientific image that the American Breeders' Association, one of the most important eugenicist organizations, soon changed its name to the American Genetic Association and, at the same time, changed the title of its publication from the *American Breeders' Magazine* to the *Journal of Heredity*.

"Immortal" Unit Characters

At the beginning of the century the study of genetics became an exciting new field when Gregor Mendel's laws of heredity were rediscovered after lying in obscurity for some decades. Many leading geneticists flirted with eugenics, and as the ultimate source of scientific authority on germ plasm and heredity, these scientists were quickly pushed to the fore to act as point men for the movement. In the initial outburst of enthusiasm that greeted the rediscovery of Mendel's work, many researchers in this new field naively assumed that complex human traits would behave like the simple "unit characters" that he had studied. Just as Mendel's classic experiments had shown that single genes acting independently had influenced the color and wrinkling of peas, the early geneticists expected that human traits were similarly attributable to the action of individual genes. The eugenicists viewed this prospect with religious ecstasy. There was an element of "immortality attached to each Mendelian unit character," wrote one scientist, which gave "a new racial meaning to the concept of the soul."[29] If more complex characteristics did indeed follow a Mendelian pattern of transmission, it would be a simple matter to construct eugenic programs that would perpetuate desirable traits and eliminate undesirable ones.

This search for unit characters produced some fascinating results. One researcher identified a gene for "nomadism," the tendency to impulsive, unreasonable, and habitual wandering, and one for "thalassophilia," the more specialized tendency to leave home specifically for seafaring experiences.[30] Another exhibited a family pedigree chart which demonstrated that the Jewish "facial expression" was a simple Mendelian trait resulting from the action of a single gene.[31] A surgeon with the Public Health Service studied Jewish immigrants at Ellis Island and concluded they possessed a unit character for a paranoid attitude of superiority to others (nicely explaining their claim to be "the chosen people").[32] A University of Virginia professor wrote that the "really desirable negro traits," such as "capacity for routine, cheerful temperament, vivid imagination, rhythmic and melodic endowment," were *"unit characters and as such may be transmitted . . . by simple control of matings"*; presumably, a sensibly designed eugenic program would take care to preserve them.[33] One of the state laws included the inherited unit character of chicken stealing as grounds for compulsory sterilization.[34]

More important, of course, to the eugenicist goal of breeding better persons were the traits clearly affecting the quality of human stock. Most of these were conveniently compiled in two essential books for eugenic field-workers, both authored by Charles Benedict Davenport, probably the movement's major scientific voice. A Harvard Ph.D. in biology and member of the prestigious National Academy of Sciences, Davenport was secretary of the Committee on Eugenics of the American Genetic Association and director of the Eugenics Record Office, the clearinghouse for research in the field. In *Heredity in Relation to Eugenics* and *The Trait Book* he discussed each of the many unit characteristics that were inherited "independent of each other" and could thus be "combined in any desirable mosaic."[35] There were single genes for various physical capabilities; for different kinds of mental ability, such as musical, mechanical, artistic, and mathematical; and for specific personality traits, such as matter-of-factness, inadventuresomeness, and unconversationableness. Then there were the single genes with particularly undesirable effects, such as epilepsy, insanity, and "shiftlessness," the Mendelian trait that supposedly led to pauperism, along with the unit characters subsumed under the term *feebleminded*—sexual immorality, criminality, and narcotism. Mental defectiveness, originally thought to be due to a single gene, was later differentiated into a number of independent subtypes, each one again claimed to be a unit character: "number-defectiveness, attention-defectiveness, memory-defectiveness, imagination-defectiveness, emotion-defectiveness, inhibition-defectiveness, moral-defectiveness."[36] These conclusions typically came from an inspection of family records in which a trait was traced from one generation to the next. The use of such data also provided Davenport with a ready excuse when there was difficulty in accounting for a trait within the Mendelian framework: doubts about paternity. This was especially useful in explaining the sudden appearance of ability from seemingly commonplace origins, since "not infrequently," Davenport noted, "a weak woman has had illegitimate children by the wayward scion of a great family."[37]

Disharmonies and Determinism

One important consequence of the existence of so many independent unit characters was the fear that they might combine in some undesirable fashion. The great dancer Isadora Duncan supposedly once remarked to George Bernard Shaw that should they produce a child together, such an offspring would be favored with *her* body and *his* mind; Shaw worried that the child might inherit the opposite pairing. The eugenicists would have found little humor in the exchange. They issued regular warnings of the threat posed by various "disharmonic mixtures."

In particular, the eugenicists were concerned about deleterious genetic combinations resulting from the union of different racial backgrounds. By 1917 the wave of "new" immigrants was near its peak, and in New York State two-thirds of the population was either foreign-born or the children of foreign-born. As a consequence the eugenicists saw "mongrelization" taking place in the United States on a colossal scale. In a widely cited address Davenport explained the kind of genetic problems these intermixtures were producing. If, for example, a member of a tall race like the Scottish, whose internal organs were well adapted to their large frames, mated with a member of a short race like the southern Italians, whose shorter bodies housed similarly well-adjusted viscera, Davenport predicted that some of the hybrids of these two races would be affected by a harmful mismatch: "children with large frame and inadequate viscera— children of whom it is said every inch over 5' 10" is an inch of danger; children of insufficient circulation. . . . children of short stature with too large circulatory apparatus."[38] These bizarre expectations were obviously based on the belief that size of body and internal organs combined in simple Mendelian fashion, but even if such a notion were true, there would seem to be no more reason to fear such a physical disharmony in hybrids than in children produced by a tall and a short member of the same race; body size and viscera would be unit characters in either case. Nonetheless, Davenport went on to cite a list of similar hazards, like the union of a large-jawed, large-toothed race with a small-jawed, small-toothed one that was the cause of the "irregular dentation" exhibited by so many children of "hybridized" Americans.

Not all the incompatibilities of race mixture were merely physical; Davenport also provided a new patina of scientific sophistication for longtime claims about the psyche of the mulatto. Even before the Civil War, a southern journal had typically described mulattoes as "the *worst of criminals* . . . who inherit, in some degree, the superior intellect of the white, while they retain much of the cunning and ferocity of the black."[39] At the turn of the century, "A Southern Woman's View," which appeared in a national magazine, informed the rest of the nation that in the South "every white woman lives next door to a savage brute," a mulatto with "enough white blood in him to replace native humility and cowardice with Caucasian audacity."[40] Davenport's genetic analysis was not unlike these earlier descriptions. He explained that mulattoes combined "an ambition and push . . . with intellectual inadequacy which makes the unhappy hybrid dissatisfied with his lot and a nuisance to others."[41] Presumably the ambition came from the white parent of this misfit, and the inadequacy from the black. Davenport concluded that miscegenation necessarily meant disharmony and that a "hybridized" people were inevitably badly put together, dissatisfied, and ineffective.

Although this kind of analysis was most common in the United States, where the melting pot was filled with the greatest assortment of ingredients, researchers in other countries with ethnic minorities recorded similar instances of disharmonic crossings. The Norwegian scientist Jon Alfred Mjöen, for example, studied "a certain type of humans, which enjoyed very little respect" in his country, "the hybrid between Lap [Laplander] and Norwegian." He found that many of these "half-breeds" were "disharmonious" genetic combinations, whose main feature was an "unbalanced mind," often resulting in "stealing, lying, drinking." As an illustration of this problem, Mjöen presented photographs of two young, bare-breasted prostitutes, one of whom, he explained, had entered the oldest profession because of "unfortunate circumstances," while the other's degradation was due to "disharmonic race mixture."[42]

Although these claims of hybrid disharmony were not based on any verifiable empirical data at the time, some years later Davenport finally obtained anthropometrical measurements and mental test scores from a sample of Jamaican blacks, whites, and hybrid browns. He grudgingly acknowledged that "on the *average*" the browns did not do badly on the tests, but he found more of them "muddled and wuzzleheaded."[43] Davenport's major finding, empirical proof at last of the physical disharmony caused by a black-white mixture, was that the mulattoes had inherited the independent unit characters for long legs from their black parent and short arms from their white one, placing them at a disadvantage in picking objects up from the ground. As the geneticist William Castle, himself once a strong supporter of the eugenics movement, later pointed out, however, the measurements on which this conclusion was based showed that the average arm and leg length for blacks was half a centimeter greater than for whites, with the browns in between. Thus, in the worst case—a brown has the average black leg length and average white arm length—this disharmony would cause the misfit hybrid to stoop one centimeter farther, about three-eighths of an inch, to reach an object on the ground.[44] It would, of course, be difficult to conceive of this additional centimeter as a serious handicap. Even if his analysis were accurate, Davenport failed to consider the opposite case, in which a hybrid might inherit a short leg and long arm and thus have a competitive advantage.

Such simplistic notions of the hereditary mechanism produced a correspondingly rigid belief about its importance. Davenport, for example, viewed all behavior—"sincerity or insincerity, generosity or stinginess, gregariousness or seclusiveness, truthfulness or untruthfulness"—as the result of "germinal determinants"; criminals, poets, artists were all "born and not made." He therefore saw little reason to praise admirable acts or condemn wicked ones; in either case the individual's behavior was only "the necessary product" of an inevitable process that had been "decided at the time the two germ cells united." The only appropriate reaction by society, Davenport maintained, was to encourage production of "the largest number of effective socially good offspring" and "to restrict the product of the bad organism."[45]

Health issues were viewed in the same deterministic way. It was "not poor conditions" that created disease, in Davenport's analysis, but "poor blood, . . . non-resistant protoplasm." When menial occupations produced the highest deathrates from "consumption," he explained that the workers were "largely Irish who . . . lack resistance to tuberculosis." High cancer rates in Maine were similarly attributed to "the presence of one or more races . . . which are non-immune to cancer." Disproportionate disease and death among blacks were explained as the hereditary tendency of "this folk of jungle origin [to] wither away in . . . the white man's . . . large cities."[46] Perhaps the most harmful conclusion of this sort was Davenport's insistence that pellagra was an hereditary disease, particularly affecting certain strains of inferior southern poor—"white trash"—even in the face of overwhelming evidence that it was a vitamin deficiency disease, easily curable through proper nutrition. The historian Allan Chase has described in detail how the "great pellagra cover-up" launched by Davenport and the eugenics movement obscured the legitimate scientific data on the subject and led directly to "millions of completely avoidable premature deaths, chronic degenerative diseases, deformations, and otherwise needlessly wasted lives."[47]

Even those eugenicists with a more sophisticated approach to the hereditary process were often no less deterministic. Edward M. East, for example, was a brilliant researcher and pioneer of the multiple gene theory, which allowed scientists to proceed beyond the unit character pronouncements so stubbornly championed by Davenport and helped resolve the conflict between Mendelian genetics and the biometrical tradition of Galton and Pearson. Nevertheless, he too insisted that heredity provided a fixed amount of talent in "Nature's bank, deposited for the individual at conception." East even found heredity the cause of a child's "fire-scarred face or amputated finger": there were genetic reasons that brought "the first urchin . . . to set fire to a chicken-coop, or the second . . . to build an aeroplane."[48]

For some scientists, genetic determinism provided important insights into the past as well as the present. The MIT geneticist Frederick Adams Woods, one of the founders of the American eugenics movement and often referred to as the "American Galton," found not "a grain of proof" that "environment can alter the *salient mental and moral traits* in any reasonable degree from what they were determined to be through innate influences."[49] Since, he claimed, this must have been as true for kings and rulers as for anyone else, heredity became "the master key of history," and, as a geneticist, Woods proclaimed himself the only objective historian, the only person who understood that history was really a subdiscipline of biology. Every other historian's work he dismissed as one-sided, narrow, dogmatic, half-true, and, of course, "always deficient in scientific method."[50] This magnificent objectivity produced Woods's "gametic interpretation of history," that rulers had always been genetically superior to common people; "royalty" was just the name applied to those families that, because of their superior heredity, had produced the most ambitious, energetic, and intelligent persons, those who had succeeded "in getting and keeping the most of what most men want." In this analysis the highest intellect and the greatest wealth were necessarily conjoined in an aristocratic class, or more properly a genetic caste, and the formation of aristocracy was thus an inevitable biological process, "an impulse lying in the germ-plasm."[51]

Applying Genetic Knowledge

Some of the early geneticists regarded their discoveries as the magic bullet for all social problems. East was particularly jubilant, envisioning a modern-day New Atlantis, the Baconian society based on science (though he noted with a touch of disappointment that as yet "no scientists have been enthroned, as Bacon hoped").[52] He saw in the genetic advances not only the principles for biological improvement but also "the makings of a broad and practical social philosophy applicable to numerous questions connected with public health, penology, education, suffrage and immigration."[53] The immediate problem, in East's opinion, was the "diffusion" of all this new scientific knowledge: professionals, ordinary citizens, and especially elected officials had to be made aware of genetic findings in order to help their clients, cast sensible votes, or make intelligent sociopolitical decisions. If only the word could be spread, he maintained, a "new social structure" was within reach, one based on reason rather than "mysticism."

Science might open the door to paradise, but if many of the geneticists had their way, just as many would be kept out as invited in. Certainly blacks would not be allowed to cross the threshold. According to East, they had no genetic value to contribute. "Gene packets of African origin," the geneticist explained, "are not valuable supplements to the gene packets of European origin; it is the white germ plasm that counts."[54] Happily, this exclusion was not expected to cause any controversy since "the negro is a happy-go-lucky child," who accepted his limitations and was glad to have them. "Only when there is white blood in his veins," wrote East, echoing Davenport on the disharmonic nature of mulattoes, "does he cry out against the *supposed* injustice of his condition" (emphasis added);[55] dissatisfaction was created within the otherwise uncomplaining black only by the presence of internal agitators.

A number of geneticists drew similar conclusions about the germ plasm of the recent non-Nordic immigrants. Of course, the scientists left room for exceptions. "There are undesirable English, Scotch and Germans in this country," noted East, "just as there are desirable Italians, Greeks, and Armenians."[56] On average, however, the former were genetically superior to the latter, and to some extent, he concluded, ethnic prejudice had a "sound biological basis." Davenport acknowledged that "the modern biologist is coming to rely less on the idea of races or groups and to realize that, in nature, we have only individuals."[57] Nevertheless, he found that the "original American stocks" had carried the hereditary traits of ambition, courage, independence, and love of liberty, and he warned that the continued influx of immigrants from southern and eastern Europe, bearing a different genetic makeup, would cause the population to become darker, smaller, more "mercurial," and more likely to commit violent crimes.[58] Woods observed that the "hereditary temperament" of the Slav caused "him to yield much more easily than his Nordic neighbor to the temptation of mob violence." As evidence for the instinctive Nordic "horror of anything other than well organized government," Woods noted that Germany and Austria had avoided the postwar "lawlessness and economic upset" experienced by the Slavic nations. The

United States had no reason to fear "internal upheaval," he concluded, "as long as the Nordic element remains in a reasonably pure condition and in a substantial percentage of the whole population."[59] Not all the geneticists were as sanguine; East, for example, claimed that the United States would have been better off physically, mentally, morally, and economically if immigration had been restricted in the mid-nineteenth century. Its present population would have been no smaller without the newcomers, he maintained, because their presence had caused a severe decline in reproduction of the original "superior types," which had "been forced to the wall by the avalanche of progeny begotten by the horde of aliens."[60]

Some germ plasm was so defective, insisted the geneticists, that society had to prevent its transmission to the next generation. Davenport emphasized the increasing urgency of sterilization as the number of capital offenses, the "crude" though effective method for controlling "defective strains," steadily decreased.[61] He did not view this as a violation of anyone's rights; forced sterilization was merely the exercise of society's obligation to protect itself by "annihilating the hideous serpent of hopelessly vicious protoplasm."[62] The Johns Hopkins geneticist Herbert S. Jennings viewed "a defective gene" as an almost palpable enemy. It was, he wrote, "the embodiment, the material realization of a demon of evil. . . . Such a thing must be stopped wherever it is recognized. The prevention of propagation of even one congenitally defective individual puts a period to at least one line of operation of this devil. To fail to do at least so much would be a crime."[63] If "defective" genes were evil demons, sterilization would become an act of exorcism.

Essential though it might often be, according to the geneticists, even widespread involuntary sterilization could not begin to address completely the problem of genetic defectives; there were just too many to prevent them all from reproducing. East, for example, claimed that there were more than twenty million "morons," genetically incapable of simple literacy, and yet another twenty million "dullards," who did not justify the effort necessary to prod them through grammar school.[64] If "reasonable" sterilization laws were enacted in every state, about one million of these undesirables would be prevented from reproducing their kind, and "the effect would be excellent," he observed, but that would still leave over nineteen million morons, not to mention all those dullards, whose activities would have to be "restricted" in some way if the scientific paradise were to be regained. At the very least their presence suggested to East that "our whole governmental system is out of harmony with genetic common sense."[65] A more scientific approach, he explained, led immediately to the "relinquishment . . . of Jeffersonian democracy." "Men are not created equally free or essentially equivalent," he maintained. "But we have labored to achieve democratic perfection by assuming that suffrage can be exercised wisely by anyone reaching the age of twenty-one years, provided he or she has been properly moulded into the American pattern by a primary school education. . . . [and] this is not a well-ordered scheme."[66] To rectify this unsound practice, East recommended replacement of the "one man, one vote" concept with "plural voting for the higher grades of trained intelligence."[67] In addition, he supported sharply increased educational qualifications for suffrage.[68] Though their presence would still be undesirable, at least incompetents would not taint the political process with a genetically defective ballot.

These repressive measures were not offered as *political* proposals; they were the rational application of newly developed knowledge, the scientific method for creating a better society. Moreover, the scientists who made the recommendations did not consider themselves political actors; they were messengers of truth, merely informing the public of the latest triumphs achieved from the scientific attack on the human experience. They presented themselves as the ultimate in disinterested objectivity, meriting society's trust precisely because their only motivation was the desire for truth. "If a new theory appears which is better substantiated than the one [a scientist] holds," East informed the public, "he will give up the latter at once."[69] Opposition to policies derived from science could thus be dismissed as the forces of ignorance, bias, or mysticism, the protests of people who were incapable of setting aside their emotions and analyzing social problems "rationally."

Second Thoughts

As the eugenics movement became increasingly attractive to reactionary political elements, many of the geneticists began to have reservations. Having climbed onto such an initially enticing bandwagon, they eventually found themselves on a runaway coach. Most, however, chose to do little about it beyond getting themselves back on safe ground. The well-known genetic researcher Thomas Hunt Morgan, for example, resigned from one of the committees of the American Genetic Association and, in a letter to Davenport explaining his action, cited the "reckless statements and unreliability of a good deal" of what appeared in the *Journal of Heredity*, the association's official organ and the scientific outlet for some of the worst racists in the eugenics movement. Nevertheless, he expressed "no desire to make any fuss" and promised to remain a member of the association "for the sake of the *Journal.*"[70] Some geneticists took issue with some specific element of eugenicist doctrine while remaining within the fold in other ways. Jennings, for example, opposed the movement's anti-immigrant statements and even testified at the congressional hearings on immigration restriction,[71] but he continued to support steriliza-tion and denigrate the value of "chemical" treatments for genetic diseases. Even East once made a cursory reference to the "pernicious" propaganda circulated by the "amateurs" in the movement,[72] though he subsequently offered some of his most antidemocratic proposals, apparently oblivious to the similarity between *their* "propaganda" and *his* "scientific" conclusions.

One outstanding exception to the geneticists' reluctance to take a public stand against the eugenics movement was Raymond Pearl, a Johns Hopkins researcher and early supporter of eugenics, who in 1908 had endorsed the new scientific concept, which, he predicted, would elevate the quality of the race by "breeding better men."[73] Though a member of the Galton Society, the movement's eminent inner circle founded by Davenport, Pearl became dismayed with much of the eugenicist doctrine by the early 1920s, and in 1927 he launched the most serious public attack made by a geneticist. In a popular magazine he scored the "stupidity" of assigning such complex and heterogeneous phenomena as poverty, insanity, crime, and prostitution to the action of single genes and accu-rately summarized the political nature of the movement:

> The propaganda phase has always gone along hand in hand with the purely scientific, from the very beginning of the development of eugenics. And in recent years the two phases have largely lost their original disparateness and have become almost inextricably confused, so that the literature of eugenics has largely become a mingled mess of ill-grounded and uncritical sociology, economics, anthropology, and politics, full of emotional appeals to class and race prejudices, solemnly put forth as science, and unfortunately accepted as such by the general public.[74]

It was too little too late though. By this time the eugenics movement had developed sufficient momentum from other quarters that the defection of many geneticists was hardly a fatal blow.

Social Science, Race, and Immigration

When the geneticists became disenchanted with eugenics, they tended simply to ignore the movement and concentrate exclusively on their basic research. With the exception of Davenport, their interest in eugenics had never been more than a brief detour, a distraction from their main interest, and when the distraction lost its allure, it was discarded. Researchers like Thomas Hunt Morgan probably avoided more outspoken criticism of eugenics to steer clear of a draining controversy that might encroach on their laboratory time and reduce their scientific productivity.

For social scientists, especially psychologists, eugenics was no detour, though; it was the main route. In the early part of the century psychology suffered from an embarrassingly low academic status, often enduring criticism and even ridicule from the more established fields.[75] In their desire to attain respect—from the public as well from their academic peers—the psychologists entered into an essentially Faustian bargain, abandoning the distinction between an objective attempt to understand behavior and the creation of ideological support for a social order informed by eugenicist and other elitist principles. In return for their scientific soul, the psychologists would receive recognition, influence, and prestige; they would be taken seriously.

This contact between science and ideology took place primarily on the terrain of measurement. In a society marked by increasing vocational complexity and consequent specialization of talent, psychology promised to rationalize the allocation of human resources by quantifying an individual's psychological traits. Not only would this objectification of human beings allow the placement of each person into an appropriate role with its correspondingly appropriate remuneration, but also such a scientific assignment of social duties and rewards could terminate social and political conflict. The psychologists left no doubt that their science was equal to this task. Robert M. Yerkes, a well-known Harvard psychologist, assured the public that "man is just as measurable as is a bar of steel": though it might take the experienced scientist some time, eventually "imaginativeness, skill, courage, honesty, inventiveness, or any similarly and seemingly intangible . . . ability [could] be measured." Indeed, Yerkes concluded, even "the value of a man [could] be appraised."[76]

Of course, this ambitious projection of psychological assessment was largely ignored in favor of almost total reliance on the development and use of "mental tests." Although psychologists paid lip service to the importance of other traits, the measurement of "intelligence" became their main obsession. One common explanation for this emphasis was the claim that intellectual and moral traits were highly correlated. Edward L. Thorndike, a Columbia University professor of psychology who authored some fifty books and was undeniably the most influential educational psychologist for forty years, regularly produced articles in popular magazines insisting that "the abler persons in the world . . . are the more clean, decent, just, and kind."[77] Or as Wiggam, ever the eugenics movement's most enthusiastic publicity agent, assured the public, "*righteousness* and *intelligence*. . . are carried together . . . in the germ cell."[78] Intelligence was thus the basic index of human value, and the measurement of these other traits, associated as they were with intelligence anyway, became a matter of less significance. In addition, the mental test provided a seemingly objective, quantifiable measure that could be used to rank genetically transmitted ability, thus making it the ideal instrument for that central task of the eugenics movement, the identification of the "better stocks."

Almost immediately upon its introduction in the mid-1910s, the mental test replaced the anthropometrists' techniques and quickly became accepted as a convincing measure of human worth. Ecstatic at the thought of measuring the value of a human being and too awed by the importance of this discovery to display any false modesty or self-restraint, the early mental testers encouraged a total reorganization of society in which each person would be accorded his or her genetically appropriate place as determined by a test score. Naturally, persons with higher test scores, those endowed with greater worth, were entitled to greater rewards as the socioeconomic recognition of their biological superiority. As Henry H. Goddard, one of the major American developers of the intelligence test, insisted, " 'D' men are worth and should receive 'D' wages; C men C wages (which are higher), etc."[79] Ensuring greater ability its economic due was only the beginning of the test's social usefulness. The English psychometrician and ardent eugenicist Charles Spearman maintained that merely

> an accurate measurement of every one's intelligence would seem to herald the feasibility of selecting better endowed persons for admission into citizenship—and even for the right of having offspring. And whilst in this manner a suitable selection secures a continual rise in the intellectual status of the people taken in mass, the same power of measuring intelligence should also make possible a proper treatment of each individual; to each can be given an appropriate education, and therefore a fitting place in the state—just that which he or she demonstrably deserves. Class hatred, nourished upon preferences that are believed to be unmerited, would seem at last within reach of eradication; perfect justice is about to combine with maximum efficiency.[80]

A Platonic paradise was expected to arrive on the wings of a forty-minute paper-and-pencil test.

Within a decade after the development of the mental test, it had become both psychology's principal method and its major substance. In 1924 the Stanford psychologist Lewis M. Terman, probably the most influential proponent of testing, observed with satisfaction that well over half of all researchers in psychology were working with tests, and the percentage of new Ph.D.s following the same path was even higher. Having kept their part of the bargain, psychologists were more than satisfied with the return. "It is the method of tests," noted Terman, that has brought psychology down from the clouds and made it useful to men; that has transformed the "science of trivialities" into the "science of human engineering." The psychologist of the pre-test era was, to the average layman, just a harmless crank, but now that psychology has tested and classified nearly two million soldiers; . . . is used everywhere in our institutions for the feeble-minded . . . ; has become the beacon light of the eugenics movement; is appealed to by congressmen in the reshaping of national policy on immigration; . . . no psychologist of to-day can complain that his science is not taken seriously enough. And is not most of this change . . . due to the mental test?[81]

Psychology had influence and respect, and eugenics had scientific support. Neither side had reason to regret the alliance.

A Result of "Apparent Absurdity"

Even before data from the new mental tests had been gathered, many social scientists had already made up their mind about the intelligence of blacks and immigrants, whose very appearance often constituted suffi-cient evidence of their genetic inferiority. Edward Alsworth Ross, for example, one of the leading sociologists of the time, proclaimed himself too fair-minded to pass judgment on immigrants as they arrived "travel-wan up the gang-plank . . . [or] toil-begrimed from pit's mouth or mill gate." But even when they were "washed, combed, and in their Sunday best," he was struck by the large percentage of "hirsute, lowbrowed, big faced persons of obviously low mentality," who looked totally out of place in civilized clothes, "since clearly they belong in skins in wattled huts at the close of the Great Ice Age." To the sociologist's "practiced" eye, wrote Ross,

the physiognomy of certain groups unmistakably proclaims inferior-ity of type. I have seen gatherings of the foreign-born in which narrow and sloping foreheads were the rule. The shortness and smallness of the crania were very noticeable. There was much facial asymmetry. . . . In every face there was something wrong—lips thick, mouth coarse, upper lips too long, cheek bones too high, chin poorly formed, the bridge of the nose hollowed, the base of the nose tilted, or else the whole face prognathous. There were so many sugar-loaf heads, moon-faces, slit mouths, lantern-jaws, and goose-bill noses that one might imagine a malicious jinn had amused himself by casting human beings in a set of skew-molds discarded by the creator.[82]

Similar methods informed the conclusions of William McDougall, an internationally recognized professor of psychology at Harvard. A series of lectures on anthropology and history delivered by McDougall at Boston's Lowell Institute was eventually published as the book *Is America Safe for Democracy?* with an appendix entitled "Commentary on the Proposition that All Men Are Born with Equal Capacities for Moral and Intellectual Development." This appendix/commentary consisted solely of three pictures. The first was an impressive portrait of Abraham Lincoln, who, the accompanying caption explained, "by virtue of his qualities of character and intellect, rose from a very humble station to a position of the highest responsibility and power . . . and so filled that position as to gain the unbounded admiration of all men and all nations." The aristocratically slender neck, the high forehead, the steady gaze, the solemn and reflective expression, and the resolve etched into this face all told the reader that lack of opportunity was no barrier to a man with these natural endowments. The next two pictures were photographs. One showed a man with tan or light brown skin, who was identified as a Borneo village chief McDougall had met while engaged in anthropological fieldwork. The twinkle in his eyes and faint smile playing across his lips suggested McDougall's favorable opinion of this pleasant-faced man—though certainly not as favorable as his assessment of Lincoln—and the caption confirmed that through "his high intelligence, his humane feeling, his firmness of character, and statesmanlike foresight, he acquired a great moral influence. . . . [which] he used . . . to bring to an end . . . chronic tribal warfare." The last picture showed a dark-skinned black man with large lips, broad nose, expressionless eyes, and perhaps a trace of a scowl, his round head merging almost necklessly into his shoulders. He was identified as a "representative specimen of the inferior type of the Ila-speaking people" from northern Rhodesia. Though McDougall acknowledged having no information whatsoever about this individual's moral or intellectual qualities, he clearly believed the the photograph supplied everything he needed to know. "The most resolutely optimistic humanitarians will hardly claim him as a 'mute inglorious Milton,' or even as a 'village Hampden,' " wrote McDougall about this unknown subject; "nor is it easy to suppose that they could contemplate with equanimity the substitution of the Anglo-American stock by persons of this type."[83]

In this atmosphere of absolute certainty the results of mental tests merely provided additional confirmatory evidence. Indeed, had the data conflicted with already received opinion, the new instruments would probably have been invalidated as measures of intelligence and discarded; some earlier tests of ability had already suffered such a fate when they failed to yield the expected racial ordering.[84] But the happy consonance between IQ scores and existing beliefs now provided the eugenics move-ment with that ultimate source of credibility, scientific data—"measured facts," as one researcher called them.[85]

The tests were soon applied to blacks. Just prior to the first use of these tests the psychologist M. J. Mayo had studied the "mental capacity of the American Negro" by comparing the performance of blacks and whites in school. When whites did better, he attributed their superiority to "race heredity" since it was clear to Mayo (in 1913, no less) that "everything in the power of educator, philanthropist and law giver has been done for the equalization of opportunity." Though he acknowledged that the hereditary difference might be a small one, it was nevertheless significant as an assurance of "social progress and racial supremacy." Such an important issue needed further confirmation, however, and as a careful scientist, Mayo encouraged use of the new mental measurements "to ascertain the relative worth of races."[86] This recommendation was implemented only months later by Josiah Morse, a professor at the University of South Carolina, in an effort to apply "the spirit, methods and instruments of science to . . . important human problems." When white children in one public school system in his state attained higher scores than the blacks, Morse found the implications so obvious that "it need not be pointed out what radical changes would have to take place in our educational theory and practise" based on racial differences.[87] Since the schools were already rigidly segregated, presumably this referred to the type of education blacks should receive. In addition, Morse found that blacks with lighter skin color had greater variation in scores, thus produc-ing more scores at both the upper and lower end of the black distribution. This managed to preserve both the two previous, and seemingly contra-dictory, claims about miscegenation—that the hybrid was a "deterioration" from the "pure" black and that white blood improved the intelligence of blacks.

Investigation of the latter effect, the so-called mulatto hypothesis, became an obsession for some psychologists. The researcher George O. Ferguson, for example, emphasized the importance of distinguishing between various degrees of racial mixture: a true mulatto, offspring of a pure white and a pure black; a "quadroon," the child of a white and a mulatto; an "octaroon," the child of a white and a quadroon; and the child of a mulatto and a black, a combination for which he contemplated but (thankfully) rejected the term "sambo." When Ferguson then adminis-tered intelligence tests to schoolchildren in Virginia, he concluded that "the intellectual performance of the general colored population is approxi-mately 75 percent as efficient as that of whites," but that for pure blacks, blacks three-fourths pure (the sambos), mulattoes, and quadroons the figures were 60, 70, 80 and 90 percent, respectively.[88] (No doubt with this sort of research in mind, the black psychologist Horace Mann Bond, in a description of a number of black children with high IQs, once remarked on the good fortune that these bright children had not yet been classified as mulatto.) More willing than Josiah Morse to specify the implications of his study, Ferguson explained that blacks should be trained for "manual work," the only "sort of education ... which will avoid great waste."[89]

Although blacks were considered intellectually inferior, the intelligence of the recent immigrants was a much more pressing practical concern. Unlike the blacks, most of whom were still living in segregated conditions at the time and hence posed little threat of any kind, the "immigration issue" was widely regarded as the nation's major social problem. Among other questions concerning the immigrants' fitness was their putatively high rate of "mental defectiveness," a condition physicians from the U.S. Public Health Service were initially responsible for detecting. Prior to the development of tests, this diagnosis was determined exclusively through an individual's appearance, and one official from the Public Health Service noted the physical stigmata associated with those easily recognizable types of degeneration, the idiot and the imbecile: a low forehead, large ears, irregular teeth, dull eyes, a "stupid" expression, short limbs, and "thick, sallow, and greasy" skin.[90] The more serious problem, however, was the identification of that higher type of mental defective, the moron, whose appearance was "near normal." Being less easily recognized, warned another Public Health Service official, the moron immigrant was less likely to be deported and, if allowed into the country, would "immediately start a line of defectives whose progeny, like the brook, will go on forever, branching off here in an imbecile and there in an epileptic, costing the country millions of dollars in court fees and incarceration expenses."[91] Fortunately, according to the Public Health Service, even in these more difficult cases, an Ellis Island medical examiner was "an expert in the system of diagnosis by inspection": "An officer, with experience, becoming familiar with the different races, ... can tell at a glance the abnormal from the normal as they pass him on the line." This diagnosis was informed to a large degree by an immigrant's nationality—yet another characteristic the competent inspector determined "at a glance"—so that a "defect" in an immigrant from "a race of high mental attainment" might nevertheless be "a normal condition" for "other people who have not attained the same grade of development." For example, an English or German immigrant who was as "evasive as ... the Hebrews" would strongly suggest mental defectiveness.[92]

Despite the official statements of confidence in this procedure, it clearly left much to be desired and, from the psychologists' point of view, provided an ideal opportunity to demonstrate their professional expertise as well as the usefulness of their latest instrument. In 1911 the psychologist Henry H. Goddard made the first of several visits to Ellis Island. A recognized expert on the study of "feeblemindedness," Goddard had been appointed secretary of the major eugenics association's committee on that topic and had originated the idiot-imbecile-moron nomenclature together with the IQ scores corresponding to each level. Though initially discouraged by the immensity of the diagnostic problem—five thousand immigrants a day were being examined by only a dozen physicians—Goddard set about proving the mettle of his science: "We picked out one young man whom we suspected was defective, and, through the interpreter, proceeded to give him the test. . . . The interpreter said, 'I could not have done that when I came to this country,' and seemed to think the test unfair. We convinced him that the boy was defective."[93]

This encouraging result quickly led to more ambitious demonstrations. One of the "laboratory workers" from the Vineland, New Jersey, Training School for the Feebleminded, where Goddard was research director, selected a number of immigrants she thought appeared "defective," and, when tested, every one of them scored "below normal." A person with experience, Goddard explained, "gets a sense of what a feeble-minded person is so that he can tell one afar off."[94] Moreover, when tests were administered to two larger samples of immigrants judged feebleminded, one by the Vineland workers and one by the regular medical inspectors, Goddard reported that the physicians were correct less than half the time, "while of those selected by the experts seven-eighths were rightly chosen." In yet another full day's observations he found the experts picked out more than five times as many feebleminded than the physicians did, a result which, when combined with the differing rates of accuracy, suggested that the latter were recognizing only 10 percent of the true defectives. Goddard was obviously proud of these results, though he professed no desire to disparage the physicians' efforts: "They do not pretend to be experts on feeblemindedness. The comparison simply shows what experts can do."[95]

In these preliminary demonstrations of psychological expertise, it turned out that slightly more than 3 percent of immigrants from northern Europe were judged defective compared with almost 9 percent from the southern part of the Continent. Goddard termed even the lower of these figures an "appalling percentage . . . an enormous proportion" in comparison with the estimate of three or four per thousand in the United States in general. Despite the regional differences, he still saw no evidence "that any one race or nationality is more inclined to mental defectiveness than another."[96]

Goddard consequently seemed genuinely shocked at the results of his own first attempt to apply mental tests to samples of immigrants from specific nationalities. Though these immigrants had been "highly selected" to exclude both "obvious" defectives and the few who were "obviously" intelligent, he emphasized that the resulting samples were "representative of their respective groups." The test scores for these representative groups showed that 83 percent of Jews, 80 percent of Hungarians, 79 percent of Italians, and 87 percent of Russians were feebleminded. Apparently anticipating skepticism over these results, Goddard warned against "discard[ing] a scientific result because of apparent absurdity" and assured the public that "a fair and conscientious analysis" of the data offered only one conclusion: "the intelligence of the average 'third class' immigrant is low, perhaps of moron grade." The practical implication of these results was also clear to Goddard: mental tests could and should be used to exclude "feeble-minded aliens." In fact, he noted with some satisfaction that the number of immigrants deported because of feeblemindedness had increased almost sixfold since psychologists had turned their attention to the problem.[97]

More systematic and well-controlled studies were soon carried out, most of them using as subjects not the immigrants themselves but their children in the schools. Although these studies did not yield the same huge proportions of feeblemindedness Goddard found, they reached similar conclusions about the general inferiority of specific European subgroups. An influential textbook published in 1923 by Rudolph Pintner, a professor at Columbia Teachers College, reviewed all the studies that had been conducted and concluded "the races from the south and east of Europe seem inferior in intelligence to those from the north and west." Pintner elaborated on the "social significance" of these results: "Mental ability is inherited. The population of the United States is largely recruited by immigration. The country cannot afford to admit year after year large numbers of mentally inferior people, who will continue to multiply and lower the level of intelligence of the whole nation. Our tests, although inconclusive, would seem to indicate that the level of certain racial groups coming to this country is below that of the nation at large. Increased vigilance is, therefore, required."[98]

Of particular interest to these early investigators were Italians—Pintner acknowledged the existence of more data on their children than on any other foreign group—and especially "Southern Italians." Social scientists of the time stressed the racial gulf between Milan and Palermo: northern Italians, they claimed, were often fair-haired and blue-eyed from infusions of Nordic blood and had given the world poets and painters, while the southern regions were, as the sociologist Edward Alsworth Ross put it, "*utterly sterile in creators of beauty.*" Unfortunately, Ross observed, it was the southern area, "the backwood and benighted provinces from Naples to Sicily that send us the flood of 'gross little aliens,'" the mental and moral inferiors, who "utter untruths without that self-consciousness which makes us awkward liars."[99] All the mental test data confirmed this judgment: the children of Italian immigrants often scored as low as blacks,[100] even when the test was "completely independent of language." Moreover, as one psychologist observed, both the foreign-born Italians and their American-born descendants lived in the worst slums, suggesting that "inferior environments is an effect at least as much as it is a cause of inferior ability."[101] The conclusion was inescapable: slums were not the problem; genetically inferior Italian immigrants were. Their prolific birthrate only compounded the problem. The nationally known psychologist Lewis M. Terman calculated that if the current differential continued, in two hundred years a thousand Harvard graduates would produce only fifty descendants, while a thousand southern Italians would generate one hundred thousand.[102] A. Bartlett Giamatti's family might have been pleased at this prospect, but the social scientists were terrified.

"Not Theories or Opinions but Facts"

These early studies produced only driblets of information compared with the ocean of data that resulted from the army's testing program. In 1917 Robert M. Yerkes, Harvard professor, president of the American Psychological Association, and chair of the Eugenics Research Association's Committee on Inheritance of Mental Traits, became Major (soon to be Colonel) Yerkes, chief of the army's Division of Psychology. In this capacity he assembled the leading mental testers of the time—Terman, Goddard, and others—to prepare three tests of intelligence: the Alpha, a group test for those who could read and write English; the Beta, a nonverbal group test, in which the instructions were "pantomimed" for those who were illiterate in English; and an individually administered examination for those who failed the Beta. Each recruit tested received a grade between A and E, with some plusses and minuses for marginal cases: A and B were for those with very superior or superior intelligence; C+, C, and C- represented medium ability; D and D- indicated poor or very poor mental ability; and E was for the dregs. Under Colonel Yerkes's direction these tests were administered to 1.75 million recruits during World War I, producing an official report published in 1921 that contained close to 900 pages and 750 charts and figures.[103]

The testing procedure, however, was so poorly implemented and controlled that, as Stephen J. Gould has remarked, the entire effort was "something of a shambles, if not a disgrace." Standards for assigning men to the Beta test varied tremendously from one location to another. Many of those who scored low on the Beta, especially among the black recruits, were not recalled for the individual examination, a clearly prejudicial error since performance on the latter produced an improvement in test score in the overwhelming majority of cases. Moreover, the conditions of testing were so "draconian" that Gould has concluded that "most of the men must have ended up either utterly confused or scared shitless."[104] In some camps overcrowding was so bad that men near the back of the room could probably not hear the instructions. One writer reported at the time an instance in which, during the pantomimed instructions for the Beta, "the negroes fell asleep while the examiner was gesticulating."[105] The gigantic number of zero scores on almost every section of these tests should have suggested that the examination was a fiasco because many of the recruits just did not understand the instructions. Instead, the zeros were statistically "corrected" so that many of them became negative scores under the assumption that the test scale did not extend low enough for accurate measurement and that for some examinees a zero score was consequently a "bonus" of some kind.

Nevertheless, the results of the army tests were offered as authoritative in scores of publications, both professional and popular, with no sense that there had been any problems in administering them. One scientist allayed any concern about the pantomimed instructions with the earnest explanation that "the use of language is not a necessary condition to psychological experimentation. Proof of this rather obvious dictum may be had from the animal experiments, which have, to date, been carried on without any satisfactory community of discourse between the human experimenter and the animals."[106]

Unsurprisingly, there was particular interest in racial differences. In the *Atlantic Monthly,* for example, Yerkes noted that whites had scored, in general, considerably higher than blacks, four-fifths of whom were graded D or below. Yet the test score distribution of blacks from the northern states resembled that of the whites much more than it did the distribution of southern blacks, an effect that he attributed to selective migration: the "more energetic, progressive, mentally alert members of the race have moved northward." Of greater interest to Yerkes were the differences "between white racial groups": 69.9 percent of "natives of Poland" scored D or lower compared with only 8.7 percent of those from England, while 0.5 percent of the Polish but 19.7 percent of the English were graded A or B. Another foreign group singled out for a "tragically poor showing" was the Italians, 63.4 percent of whom scored D or lower with only 0.8 percent in the A and B grades. No matter how Yerkes analyzed the data, the northern Europeans from England, Scotland, Holland, Germany, and the Scandinavian countries were at the top; Greece, Russia, Italy, and Poland continuously brought up the rear.[107] Naturally Yerkes concluded with the standard plea for selectively restrictive immigration.

Undoubtedly the most important discussion of the army data occurred with the publication of Carl C. Brigham's book *A Study of American Intelligence*. Brigham, a professor of psychology at Princeton University, had worked under Yerkes in the army testing program, and the mentor contributed the foreword to his protégé's effort, praising the "trustworthiness and scientific value" of the work: "The author presents not theories or opinions but facts. It behooves us to consider their reliability and their meaning, for no one of us as a citizen can afford to ignore the menace of race deterioration or the evident relations of immigration to national progress and welfare."[108]

In the 210 subsequent pages, including 85 tables and figures, Brigham did indeed present facts—three of them—together with some fascinating interpretations. First, when he categorized the foreign-born by number of years of residence in the United States, the data showed "a very remarkable" fact: the average test score increased with an increase in the years of residence until the foreign-born group with over twenty years in the country attained an average slightly above that for the native-born. Brigham was certain that these score differences associated with different periods of residence had nothing to do with linguistic, cultural, or educational factors; they were real differences in innate intelligence, indicating "a gradual deterioration in the class of immigrants" who had arrived in this country over the preceding twenty years. Nor did Brigham allow the admittedly oppressive test conditions to affect this conclusion; on the contrary, he managed to convert them into *support* for the procedure's validity. "The adjustment to test conditions," he wrote, "is a part of the intelligence test. . . . If the tests used included some mysterious type of situation that was 'typically American,' we are indeed fortunate, for this is America, and the purpose of our inquiry is that of obtaining a measure of the character of our immigration."[109] Brigham's second fact was the same observation made by Yerkes, that the Scotch-English-Germanic-Scandinavian groups on average were superior to the immigrants from southern and eastern Europe, and no reasonable opponent could face the supporting charts and figures without conceding this point. Finally, Brigham cited data showing the change in the pattern of immigration between 1887 and 1917: in general, the high-scoring groups had declined as a percent of total immigration, while the low-scoring groups had increased.

Brigham was now ready to tie his three facts into a neat eugenic package using the then common racial trichotomization of Europeans into the tall, blue-eyed, fair-haired Nordics; the stocky, hazel-eyed, brown-haired Alpines; and the short dark-eyed, brunet Mediterraneans.[110] He provided racial estimates of the "present blood constitution" for each European country from which U.S. immigrants had originated: Sweden, for example, was judged 100 percent Nordic; England was 80 percent Nordic and 20 percent Mediterranean; Ireland was only 30 percent Nordic and 70 percent Mediterranean; Russia, Rumania, and Poland were from 90 to 100 percent Alpine; Turkey had no Nordic blood at all, but Asian Turks were 90 percent Mediterranean, while European Turks were only 40 percent Mediterranean (60 percent Alpine) and "unclassified" Turks were 80 percent Mediterranean. Jews did not appear as a separate nationality in this analysis, but in a footnote Brigham observed that based on head form, stature, and coloring, the Jew was an "Alpine Slav." Inspecting these proportions, Brigham concluded that the national differences in intelligence were strictly a racial matter: "At one extreme we have the distribution of the Nordic group. At the other extreme we have the American negro. Between the Nordic and the negro, but closer to the negro than the Nordic, we find the Alpine and Mediterranean type."[111]

The order of intelligence among the various immigrant groups was thus a reflection of the racial ordering: those immigrants with the largest proportions of "Nordic blood" scored the highest. Naturally Brigham concluded that "the Alpine Slav . . . is intellectually inferior to the Nordic," though he felt it necessary to account for the "popular belief" that Jews were intelligent. "The able Jew," he explained, "is popularly recognized . . . because he is able and a Jew" (something like the recognition accorded a horse that can count).[112] In Brigham's analysis the correlation between length of American residence and increase in "innate intelligence" had not been caused by any process of assimilation but by the change in the underlying racial composition of immigrants, from the more capable Nordics of the late nineteenth century to the inferior Alpines and Mediterraneans of the early twentieth. He warned that American intelligence, which had already declined as a consequence of this new immigration, would be further threatened by the accelerating "racial admixture" with blacks and inferior immigrants unless the proper steps were quickly taken to reverse this trend.

Of course, such measures were, Brigham stressed, to be "dictated by science and not by political expediency. Immigration should not only be restrictive but highly selective." But even the immediate cessation of all immigration could not halt the "inevitable" decline in American intelligence, Brigham feared; "the really important steps" involved "the prevention of the propagation of defective strains" already here.[113] Science had decreed the importance of a future uncontaminated by inferior aliens, and thus their entry into American society—whether through immigration or procreation—had to be stopped.

Social scientists had mixed reactions to Brigham's work. Some showered it with praise; the *Journal of Educational Psychology,* for example, shared his concern over the deterioration of Nordic stock from mixing with the inferior newcomers, and it urged that the book be read not only by scientists and educators but "by all thoughtful men and women who have the future of this country at heart."[114] Though other opinions were somewhat less favorable, even the critics typically remained members of a loyal opposition. William C. Bagley, a professor from Columbia University, noted that recruits from the immigrant states of the Northeast had scored higher on the army tests than those from the long-established families of the Southern Appalachian states, and he even calculated a substantial negative correlation between the percent of Nordic blood in a state and its average army intelligence test score. With amusing sarcasm Bagley suggested that

> the Irish, Italian, Hungarian, Greek, Portuguese and French-Canadian elements in Massachusetts and Connecticut may be Nordics in disguise. The tall, long-headed, blue-eyed whites that people the Southern Appalachian uplands may . . . be transformed overnight into stubby Alpines or swarthy Mediterraneans, and thus save the "Great Race" from the stigma of illiteracy and low Alpha scores. The negroes who came north, and whose children trained in North- ern schools made as a group better Alpha scores than many of the Southern whites, may have been pale negroes with strong admix- tures of real Nordic blood.[115]

At the same time, however, Bagley expressed no desire to "quarrel with the facts" of racial difference: blacks would never produce the "highly gifted persons" of the white race, and some white strains were "more prolific in talent and genius" than others. Despite his criticisms, Bagley praised Brigham's "message" as "salutary and timely," acknowledged the "undesirable quality of much of our recent immigration," and supported an education that would advocate "the ideal of race purity" and the prevention of "undesirable blends of blood."[116]

Another critic, the well-known social scientist Kimball Young, com- plained about Brigham's reliance on some of the nonscientific racists in the eugenics movement as authorities on the subject of racial differences, but this "anthropological innocence" seemed to annoy Young *not* because it had led Brigham astray in any way but because Young feared it would compromise the effectiveness of more sober scientific arguments for "eugenic reform" of the immigration laws.[117] Indeed, Young was just then publishing his own work on racial differences. In one study of southern Italian, Portuguese, and Spanish-Mexican children Young found these "Latin" groups mentally inferior to northern Europeans, a result he attributed to the influence of "a negroid strain and other exotic mixtures" in their background.[118] In another article he concluded that southern and eastern Europeans were "decidedly inferior" to Nordics and that racial mixture between the older and the more recent stocks might be "damaging to the welfare of the country."[119] The real basis of Young's annoyance appeared to be resentment that Brigham had overlooked *his* scientific research in favor of the writings by amateurs; there seemed to be little substantive difference between them.

Only one review in the scientific literature offered a truly blunt critique of Brigham's work. "We regret that it is so," wrote Maurice Hexter and Abraham Myerson in a professional journal, "but since it is so, we say it deliberately": "One of the latest developments in psychology, the intelligence test, has in America been overrated as a means of passing judgment upon the unfortunate subjects who are tested. But this is not so important as the danger *that these tests might be used—and in fact are being used, we believe, by certain people—not to advance science or in the scientific spirit, but for race discrimination and in the spirit of propaganda.*"[120] Since Hexter was identified at the beginning of the review as executive director of the Federated Jewish Charities of Boston and Myerson was a well-known Jewish neurologist, criticisms of the sort expressed in their review were often dismissed at the time as the defensive reaction of individuals from a group judged inferior. One enthusiastic adherent to the doctrine of Nordic superiority described a Jewish scientific critic as "naturally" reluctant to "take stock in any anthropology which relegates him and his race to the inferior position that they have occupied throughout recorded history."[121] In general, few of Brigham's scientific peers found serious fault with his conclusions.

The Englishman's "Orders to His Wife"

Although the scientific study of immigrants (as well as the larger field known as race psychology) was predominantly concerned with differences in intelligence, social scientists did not completely neglect other traits. Their treatment of other traits, however, tended more toward a kind of ethnic mysticism rather than the obsession with empirical measurement that characterized the investigation of intelligence; essentially social science offered a sophisticated version of ethnic stereotypes. The primary exponent of this trend was William McDougall, probably the most eminent social psychologist of his day, who had left his native England to take a professorship at Harvard. McDougall insisted that all personality traits were racial in origin and had been "formed and fixed during long ages of the pre-historic period." As a result of this process, he claimed, blacks were not only vastly inferior to all the white races but also (fortunately) very submissive. As evidence for their submissiveness, McDougall cited a "typical and significant incident": after treating a "Negro maid . . . with great forbearance for a time, in spite of shortcomings," a northern mistress finally turned upon the servant and "scolded her vigorously. The maid showed no resentment, but rather showed signs of a new satisfaction, and exclaimed: 'Lor', Missus, you do make me feel so good.' "[122]

Like the Social Darwinists of a few years earlier, McDougall proclaimed blacks a biological threat to American civilization, but unlike his predecessors, he had no inclination to wait for the salutary effect of the natural competition between the races. Instead, anticipating the South African solution by half a century, he maintained that the only sensible way to deal with the menace posed by blacks was a policy of "thoroughgoing segregation," one that went beyond the insufficient measure of confining them to a "ghetto" and provided an "ample territory" where all blacks would be confined.[123] McDougall even devoted an entire book to the argument that the moral principles informing relations between individuals within the white race would inevitably produce destruction if extended to members of other races. Traditional Western moral precepts were for in-house use only; the humane treatment of other peoples would lead, he predicted, to the practical extinction of the white race in all the world except Europe, where they would be "but a dwindling remnant." Fortunately, McDougall observed, many Americans understood this principle instinctively. For example, he noted, despite the influence of the Judeo-Christian ethic and the federal government's insistence on political equality for blacks, "the good sense of the southern white man still steadily forbids him to obey these precepts."[124]

Within the white race McDougall characterized the Nordics as instinctively curious, and thus great explorers throughout history, but also taciturn and individualistic—strong, silent types. The Mediterraneans, on the other hand, he described as weak in curiosity but strongly afflicted with Galton's old source of complaint, the herd instinct, and consequently they derived greatest satisfaction from "just being together *en masse.*" The Alpines he judged somewhere between the two extremes on these traits. In addition, only the Nordics were marked by an exceptional degree of self-assertion, the trait, McDougall explained, that was at the root of "all manifestations of will-power, all volition, resolution, hard choice, initiative, enterprise, determination." This analysis made religion, too, a derivative of race for McDougall: the Mediterranean and to a lesser degree the Alpine traits he found suitable for Catholicism, a religion of authority and public (i.e., social) ritual, but only the individualistic and independent Nordic was temperamentally suited to be a Protestant, who would traverse oceans to maintain his own creed and to "read his Bible in his closet and commune alone with God."[125]

McDougall's analysis also allowed the Harvard professor to offer an account of history in which race was the primary explanatory factor. For example, he explained, the "orderly and successful government of the three hundred millions of India by a mere handful of British" for over a century was a result of British "character or will-power," a trait the non-Nordic natives of India lacked. Indeed, maintained McDougall, if the two groups had been reversed in this respect, "a few Indians would at the present time be ruling over and administering the affairs of all Europe, and perhaps of America as well." Nor could these political differences be attributed to economic development, which McDougall demonstrated by comparing France with England. Although both nations had been "in the van of Western civilization," France had miniscule influence throughout the world compared with Britain, which administered the affairs of one-fifth of the people of the world, controlled immense territories, and had populated North America and Australia. It was no historical accident, the psychologist explained, that the Frenchman, who "deliberates with his wife upon everything that he proposes to do," had been bested in every rivalry with the Brit, who "at breakfast coldly gives his orders to his wife" and then leaves the house to take control of the world. Nordic independence and curiosity, the key to this difference, had spread British influence over the surface of the earth, while the sociable French were handicapped as pioneers and colonists by the predominantly Alpine gregariousness that held them together and thus inhibited independent exploration; the herd instinct had struck again.[126]

The United States, McDougall's adopted country, he described as an originally Nordic land, whose inhabitants displayed the typical traits: "hopeful, bold, enterprising, adventurous, even fierce, yet gentle, self-controlled, cautious, sedate, and imperturbable." He saw this fine Nordic character now threatened by the "disharmonies" of constitution and the "race of submen" that was resulting from mixture with alien blood. A particular cause for concern was the Roman Catholicism of the newcomers, which McDougall had shown to be a function of their race. Even after the restrictive immigration law was passed, he noted with approval that the Ku Klux Klan, "composed in the main of solid, serious minded, pious and patriotic Americans," was still working to oppose the power and influence of the Catholic church.[127]

Extolling the Great Race

Although many of these scientists proclaimed the policy consequences of their racial studies, in fact they could claim little credit for the actual passage of the Immigration Act of 1924. This was not for lack of effort on their part but rather because they joined the issue late. By the time scientists took an interest in immigration, a powerful coalition of forces had made restrictive legislation inevitable.

One of the most significant components of this coalition was those old-line, generally wealthy elements that opposed the newcomers for racist reasons. From Brahmin backgrounds that stressed the importance of "good breeding," these people were naturally drawn to eugenic beliefs, and despite having little formal scientific training, some of them became well-known eugenicist authorities. The primary organization representing their views was the overtly anti-Semitic and anti-Catholic Immigration Restriction League (IRL), founded in 1894 by a number of recent Harvard graduates, among them the prominent New Englanders Robert De Courcy Ward and Prescott F. Hall. Seventeen years later, when Charles Benedict Davenport, as secretary of the Committee on Eugenics, began to organize the various eugenic subdivisions, he named Hall and Ward, his two old Harvard classmates, to head a committee on immigration. The two IRL founders now spoke not as mean-spirited racists and immigrant baiters but as representatives of geneticists and other scientific types. With the obvious advantages of such association in mind, Hall even tried to have the IRL renamed the Eugenics Immigration League, though the organization's board refused to support the idea.[128] Nevertheless, the mantle of science conferred a new respectability on the IRL's positions, and their anti-immigrant polemics became scientific addresses, to be reprinted in such scholarly publications as the *Journal of Heredity.*[129]

Another particularly influential member of the IRL was Madison Grant, proud descendant of a family that had lived in New York City since the colonial period. Though he held a law degree from Columbia, Grant never practiced the legal profession, preferring instead to dabble in zoology and anthropology. A vice president of the IRL, an official of numerous eugenics organizations, president of the Eugenics Research Association for a year, chairman of its Committee on Selective Immigration, and, most important scientifically, cofounder and charter member of the Galton Society, that select inner circle of the eugenics movement that included Davenport, Brigham, the psychologist Edward L. Thorndike, the geneticist Raymond Pearl, and other eminent researchers, Grant was actually regarded as a peer by many of these elite scientists. Though the scientists themselves might have had little direct influence on policy, many of their own conclusions provided legitimacy for others' claims of Nordic superiority. Just as important, by sharing their prestige with the IRL leadership, the scientists further confirmed the public perception of these racists as scientific authorities.

By combining Social Darwinism with simplistic genetics, the "Nordicists," like McDougall, offered a totally racial account of history and politics, past and present. Though somewhat more scientifically sophisticated, they were, in essence, the ideological heirs of Joseph Arthur de Gobineau, the nineteenth-century French count who had first maintained that race was the primary explanatory mechanism for all history, but in place of Gobineau's preferred term—"Aryans"—for the silver and gold threads in the human tapestry, the American group substituted "Nordics."[130] All the white stocks had greater genetic worth than the various "colored races," they claimed, but within the ranks of the former only the Nordic was, as Grant called him, "the white man par excellence": "The Nordics are, all over the world, a race of soldiers, sailors, adventurers, and explorers, but above all, of rulers, organizers, and aristocrats. . . . The Nordic race is domineering, individualistic, self-reliant, and jealous of their personal freedom both in political and religious systems, and as a result they are usually Protestants."[131] Every great civilization, he maintained, had been led by an aristocracy of Nordic blood and had declined because that blood became contaminated by intermixture with inferior types or was depleted through the disproportionate losses in war sustained by the more daring Nordic warriors, who had always led both sides of the conflict. For example, Germany, Grant noted, had been left totally in the hands of "brutalized" Alpine peasants after the Thirty Years War, though he happily saw a Nordic aristocracy beginning to reassert itself there.

Members of this superior race were generally recognized by their large dolichocephalic skull, wavy brown or blond hair, blue-gray eyes, high-bridged "Roman" nose, thin lips, fair skin, and great stature, a sufficiently broad set of characteristics so some evidence of Nordic heritage could usually be found whenever it was needed. Even if all the Nordic markers were absent, however, modern genetics had (happily) shown that dark hair and eyes were Mendelian dominant traits, producing dark coloration in an otherwise pure Nordic strain from, say, a single brunet great grandparent. Membership in the "Great Race" could consequently be regularly claimed for many historical figures on no basis other than their typically Nordic accomplishments. For example, the "huge blond princes" who led both the Trojan and Greek armies (though not the bulk of soldiers, those "little brunet Pelasgians," on either side), Philip and Alexander, the Spanish conquistadores, the Frankish dynasties, the Norman conquerors, the patricians of early Rome (though not the Plebeians, who were Mediterranean, making the contemporary southern Italians the descendants of slaves), Dante, Raphael, Titian, Michelangelo, da Vinci, and "practically every one of the Forty Niners in California" all were Nordics, according to Grant.[132] To this list of individuals belonging to the race of blond, blue-eyed giants, Grant's friend and fellow activist Henry Fairfield Osborn, president of the Second International Congress of Eugenics, added, among others, Galileo, Cervantes, Garibaldi, and even Napoleon. The point, Osborn explained, was not to deprive a group of rightful credit; it was to prevent other races from including within their ranks men who did not belong there. Such erroneous inclusion, he observed, was the basis for those who believed that the United States should admit the Alpine and Mediterranean immigrants from Poland and Italy because two famous Poles had fought in the Revolution and an Italian had discovered America; in fact, Osborn insisted, Kościuszko, Pulaski, and Columbus were all Nordic.[133]

In his best-selling book *The Passing of the Great Race,* Grant detailed the threats faced by Nordics in the United States. War continued to have a deteriorating effect, he claimed: "No one who saw one of our regiments march on its way to the Spanish War could fail to be impressed with the size and blondness of the men in the ranks as contrasted with the complacent citizen, who from his safe stand on the gutter curb gave his applause to the fighting men and then stayed behind to perpetuate his own brunet type." Much more threatening to the Great Race, however, was the presence of all those new immigrants, "the weak, the broken and the mentally crippled" Mediterranean elements together with the "hordes of the wretched, submerged populations of the Polish ghettos," Grant's reference to Jews. Nor did he believe that an improved environment could have any salutary effect on these undesirable newcomers. The country had taken fifty years to learn that good clothes and an education could not "transform a Negro into a white man," he wrote, and it would "have a similar experience with the Polish Jew, whose dwarf stature, peculiar mentality and ruthless concentration on self-interest are being engrafted upon the stock of the nation." Although he found the Jews more personally detestable, Grant was especially disturbed that "the Church of Rome has everywhere used its influence to break down racial distinctions."[134]

Grant was particularly concerned about the imminent biological danger to the Nordics from intermixture with the newcomers. He once even expressed outrage at a famous World War I Liberty Loan poster of a "Christy girl," a young blond woman—"of pure Nordic type," as Grant put it—posed next to an "Honor Roll" of "Americans All!" Along with names like Cejka, Pappandrikopolous, Andrassi, Levy, Kowalski, Chriczanevicz, Gonzales, and other challenges to the Nordic tongue, there appeared one lonely "Smith," producing "shock" on Grant's part at the "implied suggestion that the very beautiful lady is the product of this remarkable melting pot."[135] Any racial combination, he explained for the genetically unsophisticated, always reverted to the "lower" type: "The cross between a white man and an Indian is an Indian; the cross between a white man and a Negro is a Negro; the cross between a white man and a Hindu is a Hindu; and the cross between any of the three European races and a Jew is a Jew." To prevent this kind of deterioration, he urged the recognition of intermarriage as a "social and racial crime of the first magnitude."[136] In fact, Grant assisted in drafting Virginia's antimiscegenation statute, which became a model for similar laws in many other southern states.

Not only might these inferior newcomers intermarry with the Nordic stock, Grant complained, but also their presence had led to a rapid decline in the birthrate of the older Americans, who now refused to bear children that would have "to compete in the labor market with the Slovak, the Italian, the Syrian and the Jew." The native American, that is, the Nordic, Grant observed, was being literally crowded out of the land he had conquered and developed by the swarms of immigrants who "wear his clothes, . . . steal his name, . . . take his women, but . . . seldom adopt his religion or understand his ideals."[137]

Despite all of his references to the current scientific evidence, underlying Grant's racial analysis was a strange twist on Marx, a view of history as class conflict, but one in which the ruling class was always composed of heroic Nordics while the lower sectors of society were always the inferior races. He saw World War I again destroying the aristocratic blood on both sides, while, at the same time, universal suffrage in the United States was facilitating the transfer of power from the Nordic aristocrats to the lower classes of Alpine and Mediterranean origin. This extension of citizenship and the ballot to those who "have never succeeded in governing themselves, much less anyone else," observed Grant, would only result in the selection of mediocrity rather than the man qualified "by birth" for public office. Throughout history, he insisted, "it is only the race of the leaders that has counted and the most vigorous have been in control and will remain in mastery in one form or another until such time as democracy and its illegitimate offspring, socialism, definitely establish cacocracy and the rule of the worst and put an end to progress."[138]

Although there were a few critical reviews, *The Passing of the Great Race* received high praise from many scientists. In fact, according to the geneticist Frederick Adams Woods's "Review of Reviews" at the time, nearly all the unfavorable responses to Grant's book appeared in "other than scientific journals," and these, claimed Woods, were usually "personal resentments from individuals not belonging to the Great Race."[139] (Woods was probably thinking in particular of Franz Boas, the well-known Jewish anthropologist, who had called the work "a modern edition of Gobineau" in the *New Republic.*)[140] But whether the reactions were favorable or critical was not as instructive as the fact that *The Passing of the Great Race* was regarded as a work of science. One prestigious academic journal considered it in an essay review together with books by the geneticists Thomas Hunt Morgan and E. G. Conklin, concluding that it was a "lesson of biology . . . that America is seriously endangering her future by making fetishes of equality, democracy and universal education . . . we must drastically revise our immigration policy."[141]

Soon after the first edition of *The Great Race* was published, World War I and the Russian Revolution occurred, both conflicts with enormous eugenic significance according to the Nordicists, and Grant's friend and protégé T. Lothrop Stoddard presented a scientific analysis of these events. Stoddard was a lawyer and historian with Harvard degrees in both areas and, like Grant, a member of the Galton Society. In *The Rising Tide of Color against White World-Supremacy* he explained that World War I was a white civil war, "a headlong plunge into white race-suicide" that was fracturing racial solidarity while the world of color stood by, watching, unscathed, with "the light of undreamed-of hopes" in their eyes. Despite conflicts between the superior Nordics and the other white stocks, Stoddard emphasized the importance for them all to unite now to maintain "white political domination" in the face of the colored threat—not so much from the blacks, whom he dismissed as inferior savages, but from the Asiatics, the yellow race, which he saw as the main danger in an impending Social Darwinist struggle over who would control Africa and presently "mongrel-ruled" Latin America. With some outrage Stoddard also observed that Bolshevism—"the renegade, the traitor within the gates"—refused to recognize white superiority and, even worse, was encouraging "discontented colored men" to overthrow white domination. Such thought "must be crushed out with iron heels," he declared; "if this means more war, let it mean more war."[142] In a subsequent work Stoddard offered a more scientific consideration of the Bolshevist threat. Led by alienated Jews, the mass of Bolsheviks, he explained, were hereditary defectives—paupers, degenerates, and criminals produced by bad germ plasm—all of whom bore an hereditary hatred of civilization. Thus, he concluded, Bolshevism was not a political issue but a scientific one; such hereditary degeneration could be eliminated only by preventing the "degenerates and inferiors . . . [from] breeding like lice." This, of course, was a problem that could be resolved by "the young science of applied biology," that is, eugenics.[143]

Through activists like Grant and Stoddard the racist wing of the eugenics movement exerted enormous influence. On the one hand, they were recognized as authorities on race by major scientists. In an address to the Galton Society McDougall referred specifically to both men as "serious students" of race, in contrast to the numerous "Bolsheviks and Jews" who were biased against racial psychology.[144] While planning the Second International Congress of Eugenics, Davenport stressed the necessity of keeping out crackpots; only scientists like Grant and Stoddard should be allowed to speak on race.[145] In *A Study of American Intelligence* Brigham excerpted lengthy passages from *The Great Race* on the characteristics of various races, noting with great deference that the passages "do not do justice" to Grant; "the entire book should be read," Brigham urged, "to appreciate the soundness of Mr. Grant's position and the compelling force of his arguments."[146] Even the occasional voice of disagreement suggested a difference between equals, the kind that occurs between one scientist and another. The geneticist Edward M. East, for example, quibbled with the biological accuracy of Grant's placement of a hybrid in the "lower" of the component races, but he still contributed a chapter to *The Alien in Our Midst,* a racist anti-immigrant polemic edited by Grant and charmingly subtitled *Selling Our Birthright for a Mess of Pottage.*

On the other hand, Grant, Stoddard, and others from their clique enjoyed much greater public visibility and influence than any of the scientists. It was *their* work that the public purchased in large numbers (*The Great Race,* for example, went through four editions and numerous reprints between 1916 and 1923). The *Saturday Evening Post* editorialized that *The Passing of the Great Race* and *The Rising Tide of Color* "are two books in particular that every American should read" and emphasized that both works were based on "recent advances in the study of heredity and other life sciences."[147] Legislators quoted passages from *The Great Race* during congressional discussions on immigration, and Theodore Roosevelt praised the book for its "grasp of the facts our people must need to realize . . . it is the work of an American scholar and gentleman, and all Americans should be immensely grateful to [Grant] for writing it."[148] In a campaign speech just prior to the 1920 presidential election, Senator Warren Harding referred to the "abundant evidence on the dangers which lurk in racial differences," though he cited no authority on the subject;[149] but a year later, when Harding, then president, told a Birmingham audience of his "uncompromising" stand against "every suggestion of social equality" between blacks and whites, he referred to "Lothrop Stoddard's . . . 'The Rising Tide of Color' " as evidence that "our race problem here in the United States is only a phase of a race issue that the whole world confronts."[150] In *Good Housekeeping* Harding's vice president, Calvin Coolidge, informed the public that "biological laws tell us that certain divergent people will not mix or blend. The Nordics propagate themselves successfully. With other races, the outcome shows deterioration on both sides."[151] No scientific authority was mentioned, but it was unmistakably the Nordicists' voodoo genetics.

The "Expert Eugenics Agent"

Although all sectors of the eugenics movement agreed on both the scientific fact of Nordic genetic superiority and the consequent need to restrict less capable immigrants, there were differences of opinion over the best way to attain this goal. The racists had little interest in any procedure that would consider immigrants one at a time; they wanted quotas based solely on country of origin, in other words, racial background. The scientists, despite their conclusion that the non-Nordic groups were generally inferior, favored some sort of assessment of the merits of each individual. The biologists usually preferred a study of family lineage to ensure that no defect was lurking in the germ plasm of a normal appearing immigrant, and the psychologists naturally advocated use of their favorite instrument to select only the more intelligent foreigners, whatever their background. These differences did not prevent extensive cooperation between the different groups. Davenport, Yerkes, Brigham, and McDougall all worked closely with the IRL leadership, organizing conferences on immigration restriction, corresponding with government officials, and planning legislative strategy.[152]

The congressional hearings that produced the final act took place before the House Committee on Immigration and Naturalization chaired by Albert Johnson. The congressman and the eugenicists were an ideal match for each other. Known for crude anti-immigrant prejudice—he favored not only an immediate cessation to new arrivals but also the denial of citizenship to many of the immigrants' children[153]—Johnson was pleased to find his own untutored opinions in accord with the latest pronouncements of science. At the same time, a congressman with the good sense to recognize the importance of science for immigration policy was an invaluable ally, and the eugenicists did not hesitate to exploit such an asset, opportunistically naming the not particularly well-educated Johnson president of the Eugenics Research Association for the year prior to passage of the 1924 act.

The committee was besieged with reports and presentations, many of them submitted by the IRL clique in one of their many guises—the Allied Patriotic Societies, the Committee on Selective Immigration, the IRL, and the like. The most influential single witness, however, was probably Harry Hamilton Laughlin, superintendent of the Eugenics Record Office and second in command to Davenport, its director. A history teacher who became interested in animal and plant breeding, Laughlin obtained a doctorate in science from Princeton while he was at the record office. More than any other eugenicist, he was the movement's administrator and its most energetic public lobbyist, devoting himself tirelessly to legislative efforts for the cause.

Laughlin first testified at the hearings in April 1920, and Chairman Johnson was so impressed by his report on the "biological aspects of immigration" that he appointed the witness "expert eugenics agent" to the committee, with the responsibility of conducting scientific studies of immigration under its auspices. In this capacity Laughlin returned at regular intervals with the latest evidence for the decline in genetic quality of immigrants. In 1922 he presented an "analysis of the metal and the dross in America's modern melting pot," documenting the disproportionate rate of "inborn social inadequacy"—crime, insanity, feeblemindedness, and epilepsy—among the new arrivals. Having affected some eugenical expertise by this time, Chairman Johnson announced to his committee, "I have examined Doctor Laughlin's data and charts and find that they are both biologically and statistically thorough, and apparently sound." Laughlin's testimony focused principally on the necessity for a cautious investigation of each prospective immigrant's "individual physical mental and moral quality." This, of course, suggested the significance of mental tests, especially for the detection of those most dangerous and hard to recognize cases, the "upper level feebleminded," and Laughlin pointed out that their use would have excluded almost half of the recently admitted "aliens." Even more essential was thorough knowledge of an immigrant's "biological pedigree," information whose importance he illustrated with an exposition of the fine points of genetic theory for the committee. "Individuals who, in person, may appear perfectly normal, may carry in their blood the hereditary potentialities for producing degenerates," Laughlin explained. Such persons might be "individually good mongrels in reference to mentality," he continued, but American society was still threatened by their defective offspring. That is, even when immigrants appeared healthy and competent, danger and degeneracy were often lurking in their germ plasm. A thorough family history for each individual was clearly imperative.[154]

Shortly before the final bill was written, the committee's expert eugenics agent returned, now carrying with him the additional credential of six months of firsthand observations in Europe as a Department of Labor immigration agent. Laughlin again lectured the congressmen that immigration was, first of all, "a biological problem," but this time his focus was different. Despite an allusion to the usefulness of intelligence tests and the importance of family history, race was now the dominant motif in Laughlin's testimony. There was, he maintained, an "American race," not "a single pure stock" but nevertheless a race of white people from northern and western Europe. The immigration question was thus clearly framed. "We can continue to be American," Laughlin observed, "to recruit and to develop our racial qualities, or we can allow ourselves to be supplanted by other racial stocks" that were "not assimilable." The latter prospect he considered "more insidious" and perhaps even more harmful than military invasion, since "military conquest by a superior people would be highly preferable to a conquest by immigration by peoples with inferior" hereditary traits. From this point of view individual assessment was important specifically for "would-be immigrants of blood distantly related to the average American"; such persons would have to possess genetic value "on an especially high order, to compensate for distance in blood."[155]

Laughlin did not consider his testimony politically partisan. When one committee member alluded to criticisms of the data, the eugenicist quickly ran for the scientific high ground, insisting that he had done nothing more than present the "scientific facts," while the critics, who had collected no data and had done no studies, nevertheless complained that his work was "biased . . . because its conclusions are displeasing." The committee's chair rushed to support his star witness. "Don't worry about criticism," Johnson reassured Laughlin. "You have developed a valuable research and demonstrated a most startling state of affairs. We shall pursue these biological studies further."[156]

With the assistance of such expertise the final bill, passed in 1924, contained nationally selective (i.e., "racial") quotas, restricting immigration from each country in proportion to its residents in the United States according to the 1890 census, exactly the proposal supported by Madison Grant.[157] Since relatively few Americans before the turn of the century had been born in the Alpine and Mediterranean areas, immigration from these countries was, for all practical purposes, terminated. (Temporary legislation had been enacted in 1921, basing the maximum percentage of new immigrants on their country's representation in the 1910 census, a policy the Nordicists found unfair to the Great Race.) The national basis for the restrictions was attractive for its simplicity; the proposals for assessment of every prospective immigrant's family background or intelligence were, of course, utterly impractical. Even though the scientists' specific suggestions were not adopted, their claims about racial differences were at the heart of the legislation.

In general, however, the scientists themselves were *not* racists, at least not in the sense of being bigoted (though McDougall and Laughlin might have been exceptions). They *did* believe in judging others as individuals and claimed no great satisfaction at the discovery of racial differences in ability; sadly, they insisted, the data had forced them to this conclusion. Their lack of prejudice, of course, made the scientists more persuasive; their assertions could not be discounted as the result of an ideological agenda like Grant's or Stoddard's. The best evidence of this sincerity on the scientists' part was that a number of them later repudiated their earlier claims. Seven years after publication of *A Study of American Intelligence* Brigham, for example, decided that his own work, "one of the most pretentious . . . racial studies" was, in fact, "without foundation" (though by this time the recantation had no practical effect—not only had the immigration issue been settled but, appearing in the final paragraph of an obscure technical article in a professional journal, Brigham's belated realization was barely noticed).[158]

Though perhaps not motivated by overt racism, the eugenical scientists were guilty of a kind of "sciencism," a Baconian belief that the findings of science should be used not only to attain certain social goals and values but to define them. Although they frequently claimed their research to be apolitical, this was usually a confusion between separating their science from politics and proffering it as a replacement. Instead of offering refuge to the huddled masses and the wretched refuse, science had decreed a preference for Nordic aristocrats while denying that this was in any way an intrusion into the political process. As one president of the Eugenics Research Association remarked, the organization's work on immigration "immediately took the whole question out of politics and placed it on a scientific or biological basis."[159] This contradiction did not seem to trouble the scientists. Indeed, they continued to insist on their political innocence while proposing even more repressive domestic policies as a consequence of science.

Social Science vs. Individual Rights

To the eugenicists, the influx of inferior immigrants also exacerbated an already existing problem, the presence of so many "feebleminded" in the United States. The social scientists had concluded that feeblemindedness was, as one psychologist called it, a "menace . . . to the social, economic and moral welfare of the state," the chief cause of "crime, pauperism, alcoholism, prostitution and the spread of venereal disease."[160] Moreover, they were certain that in the great majority of cases this defect was due solely to heredity. They were therefore horrified to see "nests" of such hereditary feebleminded proliferating throughout the country.

The most important evidence that feeblemindedness was a simple hereditary trait, transmitted like any other Mendelian unit character, was Henry H. Goddard's 1914 study of the "Kallikaks," a fictitious name composed of the Greek words for beauty (*kallos*) and bad (*kakos*). According to Goddard, the scion of an old colonial family with a reputation for honor and respect had, "in an unguarded moment," strayed from "the paths of rectitude" to dally with a "feebleminded" tavern girl, beginning a line of descendants marked by mental defectiveness of all kinds; he later married a woman "of his own quality" and with her carried on the more traditional, respectable stock of his ancestors.[161]

These two backgrounds had supposedly produced six generations of each type, and Deborah Kallikak, the latest member of the defective line, had been placed in the Vineland Training School for Backward and Feeble-minded Children, where Goddard was the director. According to the institution's staff members, she was "quick and observing, has a good memory, writes fairly, does excellent wood-carving," and could read music on the cornet; in fact, one expert on mental retardation actually mistook her for the teacher.[162] Despite this "seeming normality," Deborah had a low intelligence test score (one contemporary scholar believes that her performance would be diagnosed today as a learning disability),[163] and Goddard predicted a lifetime of institutionalization for her. He was correct: Deborah would spend the last eighty-one years of her life in confinement.

Goddard sent Elizabeth Kite, his field-worker, to investigate Deborah's family background, and it was she who first claimed discovery of the bifurcated ancestry. On the only occasion that she described the evidence for her conclusion, it was somewhat less than definitive, however. "I can get no one who remembers her," Kite remarked of that nameless tavern girl who had supposedly originated the defective Kallikak line, "though I found several people who remember that their mothers recognized something about her different from other women and they talked about her a great deal."[164] Not only was the "diagnosis" of feeblemindedness questionable, but with such little information there seemed no reasonable basis for believing that the original Kallikak had fathered the tavern girl's child.

Nevertheless, Kite went on to assess the mental condition of both the living and deceased members of the defective branch. The word *feeble-minded* appeared in her judgments with the persistence of a hiccup. Diagnoses of the living were made solely on their appearance, in most cases merely a glance at their faces being sufficient to establish degeneracy. One girl of twelve "was pretty, with olive complexion and dark, languid eyes, but there was no mind there." In a different home "three children . . . stood about with drooping jaws and the unmistakable look of the feeble-minded." For another child in the same family, "a glance sufficed to establish his mentality which was low." In still another case a woman's appearance showed her "to be criminalistic, or at least capable of developing along that line." On the rare occasion that children looked normal, there was "good reason to believe that they will develop the same defect as they grow older."[165]

Clinical judgments of the deceased family members were based on second- and third-hand descriptions of their appearance. "After some experience," Goddard explained, "the field worker becomes expert in inferring the condition of those persons who are not seen, from the similarity in language used in describing them to that used in describing persons whom she has seen." Using such a hard-nosed method of classification, Goddard had "conclusive proof" that 143 descendants of the illegitimate child were feebleminded, while only 46 were found to be normal; in addition there were 36 illegitimate children, 33 "sexually immoral persons," 24 alcoholics, 3 epileptics, 3 criminals, and 8 who kept "houses of ill fame." The evidence offered for these judgments was again less than compelling. In a typical diagnosis one woman was proven feebleminded by the fact that "she had at least one feeble-minded brother, while of her mother it was said that 'the devil himself could not live with her.' " There was occasional evidence for a strong environmental effect: two children of feebleminded parents, for example, were "adopted into good families and brought up under good surroundings," and "they proved to be normal and their descendants normal." Goddard interpreted these cases as "high-grade morons, who, to the untrained person, would seem so nearly normal, that at this late day, it would be impossible to find any one who would remember their traits well enough to enable us to classify them as morons." In contrast to this crew of defectives and degenerates the legitimate side of the family had produced nothing but good citizens—"doctors, lawyers, judges, educators, traders, landholders, . . . men and women prominent in every phase of social life."[166]

Despite its obvious flaws Goddard's report of this "natural experiment" was generally acclaimed by the scientific community (though an exception some twelve years later was the disbelieving sarcasm of Abraham Myerson, the neurologist who also scored Brigham's work).[167] It not only furnished conclusive evidence for the hereditary transmission of mental defectiveness but also provided what Goddard called "a living demonstration of the futility of trying to make desirable citizens from defective stock through . . . compulsory education." Moreover, the data were so perfect, the results so neat and clear. As Edward M. East noted in a moment of unintentional insight, "The correspondence between theoretical expectation and actual result is so good as to be almost suspicious."[168]

"We Should Hardly Miss Them"

To the eugenicists, the Kallikak study represented not so much a scientific discovery of great significance but a confirmation of their worst fears: the country was in danger of being inundated by genetic defectives. Indeed, the situation was even worse than the Kallikak study would suggest. Most of that well-known family were diagnosed as "imbecile," the middle level of feeblemindedness, or "idiot," the lowest.[169] The more serious threat to American society, according to the social scientists, was the "moron," that highest level of feeblemindedness, which, unlike the other categories, was not marked by physical stigmata of degeneration and hence was recognizable only by "trained observers" like Goddard and his field-workers; such "high grade defectives," Goddard warned, were "often mistaken for intelligent people and placed in responsible positions."[170]

To avert impending social disaster, the first important step was to curtail the rapid increase of so many feebleminded by preventing their reproduction. The eugenicists generally agreed that a simple surgical procedure would be the most efficient method for accomplishing this goal, and they embarked on an ambitious campaign to sterilize all those people "whom society would be better off without," not just the institutionalized imbeciles and idiots but the millions of citizens who were "bungling their work, existing meagerly when times are good, and living off the rest of the population when times are bad."[171] Numerical estimates of the size of this group varied. Laughlin calculated them as that 10 percent of the population "so meagerly endowed by nature that their perpetuation would constitute a social menace";[172] another eugenicist judged that "we should probably be disposing of the lowest fourth of our population, and . . . we should hardly miss them."[173]

Always the movement's consummate administrator, Laughlin spearheaded this effort also. As secretary to the Committee to Study and Report on the Best Practical Means of Cutting Off the Defective Germ-Plasm in the American Population, he submitted its two-volume report in 1914, a typically thorough analysis of sterilization in the United States that included the complete text of every law passed, the briefs and court decisions from all relevant litigation, and, of particular importance for other activists, a model eugenical sterilization law, which was elaborated in an even larger compendium on the subject by Laughlin eight years later; the report also proposed a year-by-year schedule for sterilizing fifteen million people over the next two generations.[174] (An interesting personal sidelight is that the model law included epilepsy, a condition afflicting Laughlin himself, as one of the grounds for sterilization since it was "often associated with feeble-mindedness, crime, inebriety and insanity." "Even when associated with sterling traits in worthy persons," Laughlin wrote, no doubt with himself in mind, "epilepsy is a deteriorating factor."[175] Probably to meet the desired goal without the prescribed treatment, Laughlin, a married man, chose to remain childless.)

In 1924 Virginia enacted its own statute patterned along the lines proposed by Laughlin, but when eighteen-year-old Carrie Buck, an inmate of the State Colony for Epileptics and Feebleminded (where four thousand people would be involuntarily sterilized over the next half-century) was chosen for the first sterilization, the law was challenged and upheld, first by the local circuit court, then by the Virginia Supreme Court, and finally by the Supreme Court of the United States. Laughlin testified as an expert witness at the circuit level. His "scientific analysis" of material collected by a eugenics field-worker indicated that Carrie, her mother, and her seven-month-old illegitimate daughter all suffered from "mental defectiveness": the first two had scored poorly on an intelligence test, and the infant had been observed by the field-worker, who reported that "there is a look about it that is not quite normal, but just what it is, I can't tell." Laughlin's telling elaboration of the Buck family background furnished additional evidence for the court. "These people belong to the shiftless, ignorant and worthless class of anti-social whites of the South," he explained. Carrie's mother had been "maritally unworthy, having been divorced from her husband on account of infidelity," and the illegitimate child established Carrie's "immorality, prostitution and untruthfulness."[176] This account was the received wisdom about Carrie Buck at the time. A typical description of the case in a popular book promoting sterilization noted that she "took to immorality" in spite of the "good environment" provided by the foster home, and "when Carrie became pregnant that was the last straw. . . . The girl had demonstrated that she was . . . incapable . . . of self-restraint."[177] Unmentioned in any of the descriptions was the fact that her pregnancy was the result of rape by a relative of Carrie's foster parents, who had subsequently committed her to an institution not because of mental deficiency but to hide her condition and protect her assailant.[178] Nevertheless, Laughlin testified that her behavior presented "a typical picture of a low-grade moron," whose feeblemindedness and moral delinquency were hereditary. He concluded that she was a "potential parent of socially inadequate offspring," the statutory definition of a person who could be subjected to mandatory sterilization.[179] When the United States Supreme Court upheld the Virginia law, Justice Oliver Wendell Holmes agreed with Laughlin. "In order to prevent our being swamped with incompetence," Holmes wrote, "society can prevent those who are manifestly unfit from continuing their kind. . . . Three generations of imbeciles are enough."[180]

Despite the eugenicists' ambitious plans, the state laws fortunately were very selectively enforced, and instead of that inadequate lowest tenth of the population only about forty-five thousand persons were surgically deprived of potential parenthood. Though no other case furnished the extensive record of *Buck v. Bell,* many of the court decisions summarized in Laughlin's own analyses suggested that Carrie Buck was not the only victim of some sort of prejudice. In one instance sterilization was ordered for an "habitual criminal" who had "a strain of negro blood in his veins and . . . a lustful and disgusting appearance." In another the court acknowledged that an immigrant laborer, found guilty for the theft of food, had been "forced to steal to prevent [his children] from starvation," yet it recommended sterilization, apparently on the assumption that at least it would prevent his situation from getting any worse.[181]

Coping with a Moron Majority

The feebleminded menace became even more threatening after analysis of the army mental test scores. In addition to the inferiority of blacks and immigrants, the army data showed almost half (47.3 percent) of the white draftees had a mental age of less than thirteen years, the criterion that many psychologists regarded as the upper limit of feeblemindedness. To the social scientists, it seemed that the country was heading for a moron majority. (Since the standard definition of a moron was someone with a mental age between seven and twelve, it was unclear whether the upper limit should have been exactly twelve or anything less than thirteen; obviously it was the latter interpretation that produced the "almost half" estimate offered by many scientists.)[182] Of course, the logic behind this claim was suspect. As the journalist Walter Lippmann pointed out in a famous debate in the *New Republic* with the mental tester Lewis Terman, the army tests, administered to the largest and most representative sample ever, must have created their own norms: they defined "average" American performance. The social scientists were thus enunciating a reverse Lake Woebegon effect, arguing that the average adult test score was *below* average. A strangely uncomprehending Terman continued to insist that the standards for the army tests had been "established independently."[183] With little regard for such technical issues, however, this new evidence of mass mediocrity made clear that sterilization was an inadequate response (not to mention the logistic impossibility of sterilizing almost half the population). Instead, the social scientists now began to raise questions about the viability of democracy.

The eugenics movement had always been fundamentally elitist, of course. Faced with the onslaught of non-Nordic newcomers, the racist wing opposed universal suffrage as the "barbarism of number" and favored the imposition of a fee as well as an educational criterion before permitting exercise of the franchise.[184] It was the social scientists, however, who really led the movement's opposition to democracy. Even before the results of the army testing, the Columbia professor Edward L. Thorndike, charter member of the Galton Society and probably the most influential educational theorist in the country, had complained in the mass media of the "public danger" from those incompetents who did "not 'know [their] place'" and foolishly desired "to understand the specialist instead of obeying him." The safer course was to rely on the "experts . . . to do the thinking for us," Thorndike advised, especially in those areas too complex for the average person, such as "the choice of occupation for one's children, the planning of a city's government, . . . the expenditure of public money, or the regulation of public morals."[185] Ordinary folk were not to be entrusted with such decisions—for their own good. "The abler persons in the world," wrote the Columbia professor, were also "the more clean, decent, just, and kind," and thus, he concluded, "it has paid 'the masses' to be ruled by intelligence . . . the world will get better treatment by trusting its fortunes to its 95- or 99-percentile intelligences than it would get by itself."[186]

The army test results provided yet further reason for excluding the masses from the democratic process: the science of individual differences had now produced empirical evidence of their unfitness to participate. As Bertolt Brecht once wrote, "Those who lead the country into the abyss call governing too difficult for the common man." With this latest proof in hand that the society's basic political principles were scientifically unrealistic, the social scientists began to insist on what Terman called "a less naive definition of the term democracy," one that would "square with the demonstrable facts of biological and psychological science."[187] In most cases this meant some sort of political caste system based on intellect. Goddard, for example, had initially favored "segregation" of the feebleminded—placing them in institutions—to prevent their reproduction instead of having them sterilized, which he feared would produce a group of people "free to gratify their instincts" without fear of pregnancy.[188] (In fact, this concern was the real motivation for Deborah Kallikak's lifelong confinement; on occasion she was permitted a "venture into community life," only to be quickly reinstitutionalized at the first sign of heterosexual interest.)[189] Once the army tests had established "beyond dispute" that "half the human race [was] little above the moron," the segregation of tens of millions of incompetents was clearly not feasible, though. It was also now clear to Goddard that the traditional approach to democracy was "manifestly absurd" and that reform of the voting laws was necessary: "we have been too free with the franchise and it would seem a self-evident fact that the feeble-minded should not be allowed to take part in civic affairs; should not be allowed to vote. It goes without saying that they cannot vote intelligently, they are so easily led that they constitute the venial vote and one imbecile who knows nothing of civic matters can annul the vote of the most intelligent citizen."[190]

Yet Goddard did not despair completely of democracy, provided it was applied in a properly scientific manner, that is, with due regard for differing mental levels. As the director of an institution for the feeble-minded, he had observed that "the morons and imbeciles . . . would select and do obey the superintendent and his helpers because they are working unselfishly to make the morons and imbeciles happy." Here in an institution, Goddard decided, was "the truest democracy" of all, "and it is an aristocracy—a rule by the best." Thus, he concluded, it *was* possible for the moron majority—all those "children of thirteen"—to participate in the political process, but only by putting the superior in command, by "*selecting* the wisest, most intelligent and most human to tell them what to do to be happy." If the feebleminded could not all be institutionalized, then the society should be restructured in the institutional image.[191]

In such a scientifically organized society, Goddard explained, it would be the responsibility of the intelligent few "to recognize the limitations of those of arrested development," which included not just the moron majority but all those only "slightly above . . . the high grade feeble-minded," the millions of "laborers, . . . who must be told what to do and how to do it; and who . . . must not be put into positions where they will have to act upon their own initiative or their own judgment." The resulting hierarchy of intellect would be "a perfect democracy . . . based on an absolute knowledge of mental levels." It would have a "perfect government—Aristocracy *in* Democracy." Indeed, Goddard asserted, "a society organized on this basis would be a perfect society."[192]

Such a psychometric paradise would also indicate the proper distribution of society's material resources. There were, Goddard acknowledged, those idealists who believed in improving conditions for the poor: "For example, here is a man who says, 'I am wearing $12.00 shoes, there is a laborer who is wearing $3.00 shoes; why should I spend $12.00 while he can only afford $3.00? I live in a home that is artistically decorated, carpets, high-priced furniture, expensive pictures and other luxuries; there is a laborer that lives in a hovel with no carpets, no pictures and the coarsest kind of furniture. It is not right, it is unjust.'" However, to his fellow superiors, "to which group all readers . . . must modestly admit they belong, for the simple reason that a 'C' intelligence or less could not be interested in these topics," Goddard explained the fallacious logic underlying any attempt to raise living standards. It assumed, he wrote,

> that if you were to change places with the laborer, he would be vastly happier than he is now, that he could live in your house with its artistic decorations and its fine pictures and appreciate and enjoy those things. . . . Now the fact is that *that workman* may have a ten year intelligence while you have a twenty. To demand for him such a home as you enjoy is as absurd as it would be to insist that every laborer should receive a graduate fellowship. How can there be such a thing as social equality with this wide range of mental capacity? The different levels of intelligence have different interests and require different treatment to make them happy, and we are committing a serious fallacy when we argue that because we enjoy such things, everybody else could enjoy them and ought to have them.[193]

In a scientifically organized society a worker *belonged* in a hovel.

Another call for an aristocracy of intellect came from George Barton

Cutten, a clergyman, a social scientist, and the president of Colgate University, for whom democracy was just "out of the question." The army testing had disclosed too many "mentally subnormal" for universal "manhood suffrage" to be realistic, and yet we were about to double "our greatest . . . failure," wrote Cutten, contemplating imminent passage of the Nineteenth Amendment. Though it might be "a wise course to treat the people like children and let them play at governing themselves," he observed, what the country really needed was not elected "leaders" but "rulers"—intelligent autocrats who would "rule and rule well." Like Goddard, Cutten also found the new science of mental levels a reason to be hopeful. He anticipated that mental tests would produce "a caste system as rigid as that of India," on the one hand, depriving "at least 25 per cent" of citizens of the ballot while, on the other, returning "the burden and responsibility of government where it belongs, . . . to the rule of . . . the real and total aristocracy." This caste system, Cutten emphasized, would not depend on any accident of birth, wealth, or favor, however; it would have a "rational and just basis."[194]

The most specific program for reorganizing the political process came from William McDougall. The error of traditional democracy, he noted, was the unscientific assumption underlying the one man, one vote concept, that different individuals (not to mention different races) were of equal value. Since it had now been proven that not all individuals were genetically fit to exercise the ballot, McDougall proposed a different principle, one that would solve Terman's concern over how to square democracy with the results of science: "one *qualified* citizen, one vote" (emphasis added). To implement this principle, the population would be divided into three classes: A, the class of full citizens; C, the class of citizens unenfranchised due to mental defectiveness or lack of education, perhaps 25 to 33 percent of the adult population in the United States (McDougall estimated that in a country like Mexico or India the same plan would place 80 or 90 percent in class C); and B, the class of candidates for admission to A. Children of the members of A would be born into class B and, unless found to be unfit, would automatically graduate to A upon attaining majority. Children born to parents either of whom was a member of C would start life in that class but, after passing a qualifying test, could be admitted to B, where they would have to spend twenty years in probationary status before being considered for admission to A. Moreover, to discourage the squandering of sound heredity in a foolish mixture with an inferior, any member of A who married a member of C would automatically revert to the latter class. McDougall saw no cause for controversy in this plan. After all, most blacks and Indians were already in class C status, he observed, and thus his program would be merely "the explicit recognition and legal regulation of a state of affairs already existing in disorderly fashion."[195] Science would not create injustice; it would organize it.

All these proposals assumed that scientific evidence was, or ought to be, the prerequisite for political and moral conclusions. For the social scientists, there were no self-evident truths; all men (and most certainly women) were not born equal, nor were they endowed with any inalienable rights unless science could establish their existence. All "social and political institutions," proclaimed James McKeen Cattell, the psychology professor who had coined the term *mental test,* had to be "based on the truths determined by science," and "no social system, no political theory ... can be maintained when it is not in accord with science." The Declaration of Independence was therefore to be honored in the same manner as other outmoded scientific theories—"as the dead bodies over which we have advanced."[196]

"The Limit of Their Educability"

Even if the army test data were valid, a citizenry worthy of participation in the political process might still be produced through education. Such a belief had long been part of the American creed. As Thomas Jefferson had written to William Charles Jarvis, if the people were "not enlightened enough to exercise their control with a wholesome discretion, the remedy is not to take it from them, but to inform their discretion by education."[197] The social scientists, however, had sealed off all the exits. They agreed that attempts to enlighten the moron majority were hopeless. "No amount of education," proclaimed Goddard, "can change a feeble-minded individual into a normal one, any more than it can change a red-haired stock into a black-haired stock."[198] Indeed, the mental tests had demonstrated that some persons were destined for leadership roles while others were only fit for menial labor, and the expenditure of educational resources on the latter group was considered largely a waste. As chair of the National Education Association's Subcommittee on Use of Intelligence Tests in Revision of Elementary Education, Lewis Terman concluded in the subcommittee's official report that it was "of greater value to society to discover a single gifted child and aid in his proper development than to train a thousand dullards to the limit of their educability."[199] The political process was not the only institution in need of restructuring by science.

The scientific organization of education according to mental levels would necessitate the measurement of every schoolchild's "innate" intelligence, a program whose most vigorous advocate was Terman, the nation's foremost expert on the development and use of intelligence tests.

(Though his beliefs might not have been informed by venal interest, the sale of his tests helped make Terman a wealthy man. The published version of the NEA subcommittee's report contained advertisements for a number of standardized tests that he had helped construct, including the Terman Group Test of Mental Ability, of which he was the sole author.) One major purpose of such mass testing was the identification of children who did not belong in school beyond the sixth grade because "by that time they have gotten all they can get," and any further attempts to educate them would be useless.[200] Terman was particularly concerned that without the tests teachers would be unable to detect these limitations in their students. In his influential 1916 textbook *The Measurement of Intelligence* he proudly announced that through the use of tests "we have often found one or more feeble-minded children in a class after the teacher had confidently asserted that there was not a single dull child present." These were cases whose mental deficiency was "almost never recognized without the aid of a psychological test." Because teachers were so frequently deceived by the acceptable schoolwork done by morons, Terman maintained that all promotions should be made on the basis of intelligence tests rather than on the school's mere "test of information."[201]

Nor were all the overlooked dullards to be found only in the public schools. In an article contemptuously entitled "Adventures in Stupidity: A Partial Analysis of the Intellectual Inferiority of a College Student" Terman described the inadequacy of "K," a Stanford freshman whose IQ test score placed him in the high-grade moron category. Terman did emphasize, however, that K was "stupid only by contrast" with his fellow university students; his moron performance made him an average specimen, and compared with blacks or southern Italians, he was almost "gifted."[202] But K's presence at Stanford was certainly a blunder, the kind that could be avoided by greater reliance on test scores.

Another important purpose of universal intelligence testing was "vocational guidance," the direction of each child toward an appropriate political and socioeconomic future. Terman's 1916 text, for example, explained that some children, whose "dullness" was "racial," were destined to be "the world's 'hewers of wood and drawers of water' . . . [and] should be segregated in special classes and be given instruction which is concrete and practical. They cannot master abstractions, but they can often be made efficient workers." One such child, a Portuguese boy, was described as "perfectly normal in appearance and in play activities . . . liked by other children . . . thoroughly dependable both in school and in his outside work." Nonetheless he tested as a high-grade moron, and Terman had no doubt that "the tests have told the truth": the boy was "uneducable beyond the merest rudiments of training. No amount of school instruction will ever make [him an] intelligent voter or capable citizen." Though K, the Stanford student, was more capable than such children, on the basis of K's test performance Terman predicted an uninspiring future for him too: K would never manage a business, would never comprehend the principles of credit, would never understand what a bond is, and could never aspire to a profession, though some thirty blue-collar vocations or routine clerical positions were possible for him; he might be a respectable citizen but never a leader in his community or an intelligent voter.[203]

Since a child's "limits" could be "fairly accurately predicted by means of mental tests given in the first school year," Terman urged the beginning of vocational training and guidance as early as possible; any unrealistic hopes for higher education should be eradicated no later than age ten. Such early assistance would prevent "the saddest as well as the most common failures in life," those that occurred when aspiration exceeded ability. In addition to protecting students from their own ambitions, vocational guidance would ensure that bright students did not "waste" their abilities in an occupation requiring "mediocre intelligence."[204] At the same time that children were directed toward appropriate vocations, however, the basis for these decisions was to be kept secret. Terman emphasized that neither the students nor their parents were to be granted access to the test scores that would have such influence on their lives.[205] Presumably, they were not sufficiently knowledgeable to appreciate this evidence of their limitations or, even worse, might balk at their scientifically prescribed future.

This viewed education not as an opportunity for the development of each individual's potential but rather as a mechanism for matching persons to the role for which they had been "conditioned by . . . nature." As the University of Chicago educator Frank N. Freeman explained, education was not "a gift by the state to the individual for the benefit of the individual. The only valid conception of public education is that it is for the purpose of fitting the individual to take his place in the life of the community."[206] In fact, the school's function in this process was to provide more than just the appropriate training; "sorting the students" by test score was to prepare them for life by facilitating the acceptance of their designated position. Perhaps "my neighbor," Freeman wrote,

> has a better house than mine . . . wears better clothes . . . receives promotion in his profession or his business more rapidly . . . has more fame and more prosperity than I have. I may even suffer the pain of losing my position or of being forced to accept a considerably poorer one than I had expected. All of these facts constitute an aspect of life to which one must adjust oneself. . . . It is the business

of the school to help the child to acquire such an attitude toward the inequalities of life, whether in accomplishment or in reward, that he may adjust himself to its conditions with the least possible friction.[207]

A scientifically structured educational system was to be the servant of a scientifically structured society, fulfilling Charles Spearman's dream of giving to each "a fitting place in the state" while ensuring social harmony, especially among those whose place would not be enviable. Maximal efficiency was to be combined with minimal discontent.

Science or Sentiment

The eugenical scientists did not consider themselves in any way politically partisan; their agenda had been informed by neither personal opinion nor vested interest. In his debate with Walter Lippmann, Terman sarcastically remarked that "there ought to be a law passed forbidding the encroachment of quantitative methods upon those fields which from time immemorial have been reserved for the play of sentiment and opinion. For example, why should one not be allowed to take his political or social theory as he takes his religion, without having it all mixed up with IQ's, probable errors and coefficients of correlation?"[208] The message was clear: there was a difference between the scientist's facts, derived from impartial and objective methods, and the journalist's opinions, based on nothing other than emotion. Moral superiority was clearly with the former; the scientists stood for knowledge and enlightenment, while their opponents represented ignorance, superstition, and fear of scientific truth.

Thus while some scientists, like McDougall, had undeniably fascist tendencies, others could proclaim genuinely liberal sympathies, even while producing support for the most reactionary policies. It was not their fault that the exercise of pure reason produced invariably oppressive recommendations. When Terman, for example, was publicly referred to in 1948 as a conservative, he took umbrage at the classification, emphasizing his liberal voting record, support for socialized medicine, and personal donations to the Spanish Loyalists. "Most of all," he wrote, "I believe in civil liberties of the kind supposedly guaranteed by the Bill of Rights. Our failure to ensure those rights to minority groups I consider a national disgrace. Nothing disturbs me more than our widespread racial and religious discrimination. I believe in universal suffrage without regard to race, property or political faith."[209] Yet Terman's apparently sincere belief in civil liberties had not prevented him from pronouncing democracy inconsistent with the findings of science, from terming "the least intelligent 15 or 20 percent of our population . . . democracy's ballast, . . . always a potential liability" since they only "vote blindly or as directed by political bosses," or from warning of those "distinctly inferior" immigrants from southeastern Europe and the "racial . . . dullness" of so many Hispanics and blacks who could never be "intelligent voters or capable citizens" yet posed a eugenic threat to the rest of society "because of their unusually prolific breeding."[210] The public had no idea that Terman was a closet libertarian; it only saw his scientific conclusions, those ineluctable facts based on "probable errors and coefficients of correlation." The country's recognized expert on mental ability—not some disgruntled Willkie supporter complaining of the masses who voted for FDR—had concluded that millions of Americans were mentally incapable of exercising the franchise.

Although eugenical science won some modest victories over sentiment, in general the ambitious plans for reorganizing society according to mental levels went unfulfilled. Masses of people were not systematically disenfranchised because of low intelligence (though other reasons were often found). The obsession with mental tests, however, left a scientific legacy that would continue to exert substantial influence on the field of education—the belief that "intelligence" was biologically innate and hence unchangeable, that its growth ended at biological maturity, that it could be directly assessed by performance on a series of tricky little problems that must be solved as rapidly as possible, and that this assessment determined not only what one *did* know but also what one *could* know. This reluctance to explore the modifiability and diverseness of intellectual accomplishment has been partly responsible for the quasi-eugenic role that education still plays, channeling individuals, often from an early age, toward futures determined appropriate for them by the results of an IQ test.

Inspiration from Abroad

By the early 1930s the eugenics movement's influence had substantially diminished. Once the immigration restriction law had been passed, resolving the policy question, there was no longer interest in differences in the intelligence of European races; it had never been a scientific issue of any significance. Then, too, the Great Depression was no respecter of superior genes. The standard textbook on eugenics continued to insist that unemployment was an hereditary trait and that those who lost their jobs were morons, fit only "to push a single lever on a single machine."[211] But when many of the finest Nordic specimens found themselves unemployed even though they possessed an impeccable pedigree, it became much less credible to maintain that wealth and status were indications of genetic fitness. Despite the declining interest at home, the U.S. movement found new reason for optimism in the rising popularity of "political biology" in Germany.

"Courage Enough to Make Ready"

As in the United States, German eugenics tended to pay lip service to the Galtonian ideal of encouraging proliferation of the fit while concentrating, in practice, on elimination of the unfit. In 1904 Ernst Haeckel, an influential biologist and pioneer of eugenical thought in Germany, had maintained that the "destruction of abnormal new-born infants" should be considered not murder but a beneficial practice for both the child and the community. He also objected to medical practices that prolonged the "sickly existence" of the diseased, malformed, and mentally disordered, and he advocated the creation of a commission to determine which "utterly useless" lives should be eliminated, a decision that would be implemented "by a dose of some painless and rapid poison."[212] The recognized founder of eugenics in Germany, however, was Alfred Ploetz, who coined the term *Rassenhygiene*—literally "racial hygiene"—for a medical policy based on eugenical principles, one concerned with the health of the race as well as that of the individual. In 1904 Ploetz established the *Archiv für Rassen- und Gesellschaftsbiologie* (Journal of Racial and Social Biology), which over the next two decades developed an international scientific reputation, and the following year he founded the Gesellschaft für Rassenhygiene (Society for Racial Hygiene), which soon became a prestigious organization whose membership included some of Germany's most distinguished scientists and physicians.[213]

Then at the end of World War I the newly established Weimar government, as part of its program for postwar social reconstruction, turned to science for a systematic evaluation of the war's "racial hygienic" legacy. In contrast to the Imperial regime, which had rejected the value of *Rassenhygiene,* the more scientifically progressive Weimar administration wished to take advantage of the latest technical expertise and provided considerable support for eugenics by establishing major research institutes on *Rassenhygiene* and including eugenicists, predominantly researchers in genetics and anthropology, as members of official state councils on public health.[214]

As a consequence, genetics came to be viewed in Germany as an applied rather than a basic science, whose significance derived largely from the expected application of its results to the medical and social problems of national reconstruction; that is, eugenics was essentially indistinguishable from genetics. This fusion was clearly reflected in the title of the most important German textbook on genetics at the time, *Menschliche Erblichkeitslehre und Rassenhygiene* (Human Heredity and Racial Hygiene), a massive two-volume work by the internationally recognized scientists Erwin Baur, Eugen Fischer, and Fritz Lenz. Translated into English as *Human Heredity,* the first volume was hailed by scientists in the United States and England as "a masterpiece of objective research" and "the best existing book on human inheritance."[215] The second volume, entitled *Menschliche Auslese und Rassenhygiene (Eugenik)* (Human Selection and Racial Hygiene [Eugenics]), was authored solely by Lenz, a University of Munich professor of *Rassenhygiene,* but was never translated. The purpose of genetics/eugenics in this context was to elevate the discussion of social problems above partisan political wrangling by providing scientific solutions based on scientific values. Thus, despite its late start, German eugenics soon enjoyed higher scientific status and greater official recognition than did the American movement.

Unsurprisingly, the German geneticists concluded that their nation's decline in eminence was primarily due to biological degeneration, which was mainly the result of medical advances and welfare institutions that had impeded the normal operation of the laws of natural selection. Whatever its scientific merits, this explanation took on increasing economic appeal during the 1920s as Germany experienced a series of financial crises. With much of the working class impoverished by a combination of mass unemployment and skyrocketing inflation, there was greater resentment at the state's expenditures on the biologically unfit; in addition to being a eugenic liability, they were also very expensive citizens. One solution to their presence was offered by Karl Binding and Alfred Hoche, two distinguished German professors, in *Die Freigabe der Vernichtung lebensunwerten Lebens* (The Permission for Destruction of Life Unworthy of Life), a closely reasoned argument for the official, therapeutic killing of "worthless" people, among them the mentally ill, the feebleminded, and the deformed. Binding, a psychiatrist, explained that most of these individuals were already "mentally completely dead" so their elimination was a scientifically defensible, indeed "useful," act, "not to be equated with other types of killing." Hoche, a jurist, argued that any errors in diagnosis or judgment would be inconsequential compared with the resulting social benefits.[216]

As in the United States, the German eugenicists' major proposal for preventing any further national decline, however, was sterilization of the biological undesirables. Noting, with some admiration for their American colleagues, that the United States was further advanced in the implementation of this important measure, the German scientists hoped to follow the lead of the American movement. In *Menschliche Auslese und Rassenhygiene (Eugenik)*, the second volume of the Baur-Fischer-Lenz work, Lenz described with approval Harry Hamilton Laughlin's plan for sterilizing the least capable 10 percent of each generation but recommended an even higher percentage in his own country, where he estimated the undesirables at about twenty million people, including six million in the category of "physically weak or infirm." It would be "without doubt in the interest of our overpopulated country," Lenz wrote, "if the least competent third of the population would have no descendants"; not only would the state be spared the greater expense involved in their care and education, but "space could be opened for the millions of competent" who were being crowded out by the inferiors.[217] Weimar law at the time, however, did not consider advancement of the nation's racial health sufficient justification for sterilization. This concern for the rights of the individual was particularly galling to Lenz, who considered the genetic quality of the race to take precedence over the rights of any individual. In his thesis a few years earlier he had maintained that the state's purpose was essentially to enforce just such a biological goal: "not . . . to see that the individual gets his rights, but to serve the race. . . . All rights must be compatible and subordinate to this end."[218]

Although the large number of individual incompetents was considered the major cause of biological decline—and their sterilization a first priority—the Weimar scientists also emphasized the importance of racial purity for the nation's eugenic health. This concern had nothing to do with the inferiority or superiority of one race to another, Lenz explained, but was merely a consequence of the scientific fact that "the hereditary traits of every race have been uniquely adapted to them through thousands of years of natural selection, and this harmony would be destroyed by racial mixture." Here again German scientists saw the United States with its antimiscegenation statutes leading the way, though Lenz noted that legal prohibition would not be of much practical value unless it was accompanied by "strict . . . social separation."[219] He was also concerned about the insufficient attention these laws paid to the value of Nordic purity—they protected only "whites" in general from genetic encroachment by other races. "The Nordic race," Lenz wrote, "marches in the van of mankind," providing great discoveries and excelling all others "in constancy of will and foresight." The other European races, though clearly superior to peoples of color, were lacking in the Nordic capacities for genius, truth, honor, and, most of all, that special talent for self-control, which produced the "Nordic gift for civilization." Moreover, within the ranks of this favored race, Lenz found the Teutonic Germans to be an especially favorable combination of the slender blond Nordics and the heavier blond "Atlantics," and when the leadership and boldness of the former were coupled with the steadfastness and trustworthiness of the latter, he proclaimed, "we get figures of megalithic proportions," truly the racial crème de la crème.[220] Any serious consideration of racial purity had to take account of these fine points of racial analysis.

Of particular practical importance to German society was the effect of any mixture with Jews, a people Lenz characterized as a "mental race," that is, a group marked not so much by physiognomic indices—especially since, he explained, their "instinctive desire not to look singular" had produced sexual selection for physical similarity to their "hosts"—but more by certain fundamental similarities of mind, genetic characteristics that had developed through Darwinian mechanisms over the course of thousands of years. Since, according to Lenz, Jews, as outsiders, had been generally excluded from a society's productive occupations, only those with a "special aptitude for acting as intermediaries in dealing with the goods produced by others, and in stimulating and guiding others' wishes" were likely to prosper and reproduce. Through natural selection Jews had thus developed (racial) traits of "shrewdness and alertness . . . but also . . . an amazing capacity for putting themselves in others' places and for inducing others to accept their guidance," causing them to gravitate toward such professions as merchant, trader, moneylender, lawyer, writer, politician, and doctor, all callings in which success depended largely on an ability to exert "mental influence over . . . fellow human beings." As a consequence, he noted, even though Nordics and Jews alike were characterized by "a strong desire to get their own way," the Nordic was "inclined to seek his ends by force, the Jew rather by cunning." Moreover, Lenz observed, the special "Jewish talent for living among purely imaginary ideas as if they were concrete facts" made them persuasive both as merchants and as revolutionaries, thus providing a biological foundation for the seemingly contradictory assertions that Jews were, at the same time, both capitalist profiteers and Marxist revolutionaries. Although "it would be wrong," he remarked, "to suppose that the Jews are *merely* parasites" (emphasis added), his analysis of their genetic traits left little possibility for them to play any other role, and despite whatever "intermediating" economic contribution they might make, "still, it is true," he pointed out, "that whereas the Teutons could get along fairly well without the Jews, the Jews could not get along without the Teutons."[221]

Although Lenz did not judge Jews substantially less intelligent than Nordics, he concluded that the racial differences between them were nevertheless genetically disharmonious: unlike that "favorable mingling of blood" between Nordic and Atlantic, which had produced the superior Teuton, "the crossing of Teutons and Jews is likely . . . to have an unfavorable effect." According to science, Lenz maintained, racial mixture would not be in the interest of the Germans or the Jews.[222]

Much to his dismay, however, Lenz found that Jews tended to deny the "Darwinian fact" of "unbridgeable" racial distinctions in the hope that "by living in a Teutonic environment and by adopting a Teutonic culture, . . . [they] could be transformed into genuine Teutons." This notion was, of course, an illusion, he explained; Jews could not make themselves into Teutons "by writing books about Goethe." Advising his "Jewish fellow citizens . . . not to get the wind up" whenever "the Jewish race" question was mentioned, Lenz emphasized that only "a tranquil and objective discussion of the Jewish problem would serve the true interests of both sides." The main consideration for Lenz was that "race"—that is, the Nordic or Teutonic race—was "the first and indispensable condition of all civilisation," the ultimate criterion of value to be preserved at all costs—indeed, the reason for the scientific study of racial differences. Any resolution of the Jewish question had to be informed by this concern.[223]

Such analyses by Lenz, Baur, and Fischer, Germany's most distinguished scientists in race, genetics, and anthropology, not only exerted enormous influence in their own right but also conferred scientific respectability on Germany's rising "Nordic movement," led by Fischer's former student Hans F. K. Günther, the social anthropologist who provided the theoretical foundation for Nazi racial theory and was widely regarded as its official ideological spokesman. In books that sold well over half a million copies, an enormous readership for scientific works, Günther presented a German version of Madison Grant's analysis, offering the usual litany of praise for Nordics as the bearers of all true culture and civilization and the ideal racial type—smarter, bolder, and more independent and creative than either the lazy, childish Mediterranean or the slow, narrow-minded Alpine. For Günther all history could be explained as class conflict between a ruling group that was always Nordic and "lower orders" always of an inferior race. "Nordic blood," he maintained, had characterized the ruling class of every great civilization—Persian, Greek, Roman, and even Chinese—and each of these civilizations had fallen when that blood had been depleted through war or intermixture. Moreover, in the modern era he saw an additional danger from wealth in the hands of inferiors, which was used to acquire power and influence, allowing moneyed "upstarts" to attain an undeserved equality with their Nordic superiors.[224]

Despite these threats to Nordic dominance, Günther found the situation not yet irredeemable since, happily, the loss of Nordic blood had made "least way" among the Germanic peoples. To safeguard their hereditary endowments, however, the Germans had to purge their ranks of all non-Nordic elements and protect themselves from any further intermixture, especially with the Jews, themselves a racial mixture in which non-European elements were predominant. This alien wedge of "ferment and disturbance," as Günther termed the Jews, posed "the very greatest danger for the life of the European peoples and of the North

American people alike," threatening to force these biologically superior groups "off those paths which their own genius has marked out for them."[225] To prevent such a tragic outcome he exhorted Germany to follow the U.S. example, where eugenic research had become a "patriotic preoccupation" and compulsory sterilization laws had made the country a "model for the future." In particular, he paid homage to Grant and Stoddard for their efforts toward passage of the restrictive immigration law, "only the first step," Günther hopefully called it, "to still more definite laws dealing with race and eugenics." The United States was well on the path to Nordic revival, and Germany could do the same, he concluded, if "we have courage enough to make ready for future generations a world cleansing itself racially and eugenically."[226]

The scientists of *Rassenhygiene* recognized Günther's Nordic movement as a natural extension of their own work and an important contribution to it. After all, Ploetz himself many years earlier had termed the Aryan (i.e., Nordic) race "the race of culture *par excellence,*" whose progress was "synonymous with the advancement of all mankind," and Lenz speculated that without Ploetz's work there might never have been a Nordic movement and certainly not a "Professor of Social Anthropology in Jena," a reference to the position then held by Günther. (Though Lenz was clearly referring to the establishment of this chair as a consequence of Ploetz's ground-breaking thought, the founder of *Rassenhygiene* had also played a more direct role in the process, soliciting support from Nazi officials for Günther's appointment.) Lenz and Eugen Fischer, Germany's premier anthropologist of the time, had high praise for Günther's efforts to promote *der nordische Gedanke* (the Nordic concept), an ideal that in Lenz's opinion not only had been extremely beneficial for the German people but also had made material contributions to the spread of race-hygienic thought. Indeed, Lenz noted, the later editions of Günther's book were "more and more oriented toward *Rassenhygiene.*"[227]

Thus, while Hitler was still imprisoned in Landsberg am Lech fortress and just beginning *Mein Kampf,* renowned university scholars like Lenz and Fischer and cruder race theorists like Günther had already provided the intellectual and scientific foundation for much of what would become the Nazi program. Indeed, Lenz would later boast of how, in 1917, he had presented "all of the important features of National Socialist policy."[228] All these scientists agreed that Germany's problems were primarily biological and needed biological solutions at both the individual and racial levels. In particular they agreed that racial purity was important for national progress and that the Jews were the major threat to that purity.

"The Political Expression of Our Biological Knowledge"

Despite the Weimar administration's official support for eugenic research and application, the scientists' conclusions had not yet been translated into policy as the decade drew to a close, amidst increasing social and economic chaos. Though disappointed at this lack of progress, they pinned their hopes for the future on the growing Nazi movement and especially its charismatic leader, who seemed to understand the importance of putting eugenical concepts into practice. Hitler had written passionately of his intention, "by preserving the best humanity, to create the possibility of a nobler development of these beings."[229] As soon as the Nazis had achieved some regional control, one of their first official acts, in 1931, was to have Günther elevated to an important university chair in the newly established area of racial research, over the opposition of the faculty; Hitler himself attended Günther's inaugural lecture.[230] There was reason for the scientists to be hopeful.

Nazi literature further confirmed this impression of the party as the standard-bearer for science. In 1930 the first volume of the *National-sozialistische Monatshefte* (National Socialist Monthly), for example, honored Ploetz for his contributions as "the founder of German *Rassen-hygiene*" and featured a cover article entitled "Der Nationalsozialismus als politischer Ausdruck unserer biologischen Kenntnis" (National Socialism as the Political Expression of Our Biological Knowledge). Declaring that "National Socialist methodologist is strictly scientific," the article explained that the party's program was solidly based on countless studies from anthropology, anatomy, genetics, and other areas of research and that the resulting knowledge of a people's genetic structure, including how to make changes in underlying genotypes by eliminating the present dynamic of "contra-selection," "finds its most consistent expression in National Socialism." In the National Socialist state, the article continued, scientific results would be "directly and continuously applied to national reconstruction." Most important, National Socialism would teach the German people to " 'think in generations.' "[231]

A year later a conference of the National Socialist Pharmacists and Physicians declared racial purification of Germany one of the prime Nazi objectives. To aid in accomplishing this task, the conference proposed that the German population be divided into three groups: the highest, the Nordic—described by one speaker as "the finest flower on the tree of humanity"—was to be nurtured; the middle group would be tolerated; and the lowest group was to be eliminated through compulsory sterilization. To implement this policy, the conference called for the establishment of special race bureaus that would keep track of every citizen and prevent marriages that would not promote Nordic predominance.[232]

Such scientifically sound directions made National Socialism particularly appealing to the leading German geneticists. In his volume of the Baur-Fischer-Lenz text Lenz noted that the official party program explicitly named *Rassenhygiene* as a goal, declaring the "Nordification" (*Aufnordung*) of the population the highest priority, and he observed that National Socialism could be viewed as "applied biology, applied ethnology." Despite his obvious approval of the Nazi program, Lenz maintained that the scientist's place was not to meddle in politics but only to point out the path to progress. "Pursuit of this path," he wrote, "is the business of the statesman for whom we are waiting."[233]

By 1931, however, it was clear that the wait was over. In one of the most important German biological journals Lenz acclaimed the Nazis as "the first political party, not only in Germany but overall, which presents racial hygiene as a central priority of its program," and he lavished praise on the eugenical wisdom expressed in *Mein Kampf*. Hitler, Lenz noted, had read the Baur-Fischer-Lenz genetics text while in prison and, despite having only a secondary school education, had developed a deep appreciation for the basic concepts of *Rassenhygiene*. In fact, Lenz seemed flattered to observe, many passages from his text were reflected in Hitler's own writing. This was probably not an idle boast; much of *Mein Kampf* did indeed sound like a direct reprise of the geneticist's ideas. Hitler, too, viewed the state's purpose as service to the race and maintained that in pursuit of this goal it had to prevent those not "physically and mentally fit" from reproducing their kind. Moreover, his estimate that such defectives numbered in the millions led Lenz to infer, with unconcealed approval, that Hitler intended sterilization "not just for extreme cases, which would be meaningless for improving the health of the race, but ... [for] the entire inferior portion of the population." Lenz also remarked favorably on Hitler's special interest in advancement of the Nordic racial elements, though he noted that the politician preferred the term *Aryans* for these creators of all great culture as an antithesis to the parasitic Jews. Though Lenz found Hitler's observations on "the Jewish question" occasionally exaggerated, he reminded his fellow scientists of Hitler's own words, that "the speech of a statesman to his people" had to be measured " 'not by the impression it leaves on a university professor but by the effect it exerts on the people.' " This leader of "a great movement," concluded the geneticist, "is the first politician of really significant influence who has recognized racial hygiene as a central task of all politics and is ready to fight for it energetically."[234]

Lenz's optimism was not misplaced. When Hitler seized power early in 1933, National Socialism proclaimed its policies nothing more than "applied biology," an assertion that already bore the imprimatur of some leading scientists. Many eugenicists were given positions in the new administration, and all Nazi officials (and eventually Hitler Youth) were expected to understand basic genetic principles. The reign of science had begun.

Only months after the Nazis took control, Reichsminister of the Interior Wilhelm Frick (who would eventually be tried at Nuremberg and sentenced to death by hanging) addressed the first meeting of the newly appointed Sachsverständigenbeirat für Bevölkerungs- und Rassenpolitik (Expert Advisory Council for Population and Race Politics), an elite group that included Ploetz, Günther, Lenz, and a number of other prestigious scientists and physicians. Citing estimates as high as 20 percent for the genetically defective proportion of the German population, Frick denounced that "exaggerated care for the single individual," which, by disregarding "the principles of heredity, selection and *Rassenhygiene*," had burdened the state with so many "sick, weak and inferior." He observed that the means to solve this problem was now available, however:

> The scientifically derived knowledge of heredity, based on the progress of the last decades, gives us the opportunity to recognize the principles of heredity and selection as well as their significance for the *Volk* and the state. It gives us the right and the moral obligation to prevent genetic defectives from reproducing. No misunderstood charitable or religious scruples, based on the dogmas of past centuries, should prevent us from meeting this obligation; on the contrary we must consider it an offence against Christian and social charity if, in spite of this knowledge, we were to allow hereditary defectives to produce offspring.[235]

In addition, Frick warned of the "racial deterioration" in the German population caused by miscegenation with other peoples, especially the Jews. "We must have the courage," he emphasized, "to rate our population for its hereditary value."[236]

At about the same time another Nazi official declared that every individual should be examined for biological worth and then assigned a position according to the results; those whose genetic value did not indicate a productive assignment should be eliminated. The meaning of a "biological state" was clear: biology *should* be destiny, and under the Third Reich it *would* be.

National Socialism's deeds quickly lived up to its words. Only two weeks after Frick's address the new government enacted the Law for the Prevention of Genetically Defective Progeny. Drafted by Frick, but also reflecting the best scientific advice from members of the Expert Advisory Council, it allowed the involuntary sterilization of individuals judged to suffer from any of a number of "hereditary diseases": "weakmindedness," schizophrenia, insanity, epilepsy, blindness, deafness, bodily deformities, alcoholism, and others. The actual decision to sterilize was to be made by the Genetic Health Court, consisting of a judge and two physicians, at least one of whom had a background in genetic theory. (Fischer served as a judge in one such court in Berlin, and both Fischer and Lenz helped evaluate the "genetic health" of individuals being considered for sterilization.)[237] Although official estimates projected the immediate sterilization of some 400,000 persons, Lenz nevertheless complained that the law was not broad enough because it applied only to those with evident (i.e., currently identifiable) hereditary defects. Since such traits could also be transmitted to offspring by persons who themselves showed no signs of the defect, Lenz found it advisable also to sterilize those healthy persons who might produce defective progeny. "As things are now," he told a meeting of the Expert Advisory Council, "only a minority of our fellow citizens . . . are so endowed that their unrestricted procreation is good for the race."[238]

National Socialism also quickly moved to create a more enlightened approach to health care by the medical profession, one that would replace the unscientific concern for each individual's welfare with the more scientifically enlightened view that the physician's primary responsibility was to the genetic health of the state and the race. Only a few months after enactment of the sterilization law the Reich announced the establishment of two state medical academies, which would provide training in racial biology to prepare all physicians in public service for their new duties as "genetic doctors." Within a year the leading German medical journal, now under Nazi control, began publication of a new supplement, *Der Erbarzt* (The Genetic Doctor). In the first edition of *Der Erbarzt,* its editor Otmar Freiherr von Verschuer, another prominent German researcher in genetics and director of the Frankfurt Institute for *Rassenhygiene,* explained that a patient must be treated "as one part of a larger whole or unity: his family, his race, his *Volk.*"[239] According to science, the good of the *Volk* was to take precedence over the health of the individual. Even before *Der Erbarzt* appeared, Gerhard Wagner, the führer of the Nazi Physicians League and a member of the Expert Advisory Council, proudly observed that "knowledge of racial hygiene and genetics has become, by a purely scientific path, the knowledge of an extraordinary number of German doctors. It has influenced to a substantial degree the basic world view of the State, and indeed may even be said to embody the very foundations of the present state."[240]

After years of toiling in relative obscurity, the scientists of *Rassenhygiene* were now delighted by a regime ready to make their own claims and slogans the basis for state policy and to enact the measures they had been clamoring for as essential to the biological salvation of the state. Clearly elated by such wisdom at the highest levels of government, the scientists showered praise on Nationalism Socialism in general and its führer in particular. This was not the intimidated acquiescence of scientists in Lysenkoist Russia but genuine enthusiasm, a wholehearted embrace of Nazi ideology, which they readily agreed really *was* merely "political biology." Eugen Fischer, for example, Germany's foremost anthropologist, praised the "new leadership" for

> deliberately and forcefully intervening in the course of history and in the life of the nation, precisely where this intervention is most urgently, most decisively, and most immediately needed. To be sure, this need can only be perceived by those who are able to see and to think within a biological framework, but it is understood by these people to be a matter of the gravest and most weighty concern. This intervention can be characterized as a biological population policy, biological in this context signifying the safeguarding by the state of our hereditary endowment and our race, as opposed to the unharnessed processes of heredity, selection, and elimination.[241]

Dissent from such scientifically well-grounded policies could obviously originate only out of ignorance.

In an address to the German Society for *Rassenhygiene* Ernst Rüdin, a professor of psychiatry who was one of the organization's original members and now its head, recalled the early, fruitless days when the racial hygienists had labored in vain to alert the public to the special value of the Nordic race as "culture creators" and the danger of "unnatural" attempts to preserve the health of heredity defectives. Now *Rassenhygiene* was finally receiving the attention it deserved, and Rüdin virtually slavered over the man whose efforts had produced this change: "The significance of *Rassenhygiene* did not become evident to all aware Germans until the political activity of Adolf Hitler and only through his work has our 30 year long dream of translating *Rassenhygiene* into action finally become a reality." Terming it a "duty of honor" (*Ehrenpflicht*) for the society to aid in implementing Hitler's program, Rüdin proclaimed, "We can hardly express our efforts more plainly or appropriately than in the words of the Führer: 'Whoever is not physically or mentally fit must not pass on his defects to his children. The state must take care that only the fit produce children. Conversely, it must be regarded as reprehensible to withhold healthy children from the state.' "[242]

Other scientists involved with the *Archiv für Rassen- und Gesellschafts-biologie*, Germany's leading eugenical journal, also fawned over the new order. When Frick's address to the Expert Advisory Council was published in the *Archiv*, it was prefaced with a passage labeled "Motto," a lengthy quotation from *Mein Kampf* on improving the genetic quality of the race in the "Volkish State." An editorial comment at the end again praised Hitler for ushering in "an age of revolution in racial biology."

Written by "one of the oldest pioneers of German *Rassenhygiene*," the unsigned comment viewed "the proud emergence [of *Rassenhygiene*] with great delight and profound hopes. The fate of German eugenics, the Third Reich and the German people will remain firmly linked to one another for a long time."[243] Though many of these scholars later became members of the party, the truth was that they did not join the National Socialist movement; it had joined them.

Within the next two years the new government passed the so-called Nuremberg Laws to implement further the "national biologic measures," particularly with respect to the *Judenfrage* (the "Jewish question"). The Reich had emphasized the necessity for sound research on this issue, and Nazi scholars dismissed crudely anti-Semitic literature out of the concern that mere prejudice, lacking scientific evidence, would discredit National Socialism.[244] Fortunately, there was clear agreement on the facts among the most prestigious scientists in the country: the Jews were a *Gegenrasse* —a counterrace, genetically inimical to the Germans. One medical researcher even argued, in the same tradition as Charles Benedict Davenport's concern with genetic disharmonies, that racial miscegenation produced disease because the offspring's various organs would degenerate at different rates.[245] The new legislation, based on scientific consensus, forbad marriage between a Jew and an Aryan—as well as any "extramarital congress" between them. It also excluded "non-Aryans" (i.e., Jews) and anyone married to a non-Aryan from government office, university professorship, pharmaceutical operation, and the practice of medicine.[246] The courage Günther had called for was certainly not in short supply.

"Towards a Biological Salvation"

As science and National Socialism became such harmonious companions in the years prior to the Nazi takeover, the American eugenicists took increasing interest in this "progress" in Germany. Clearly in recognition of the German emphasis on *Rassenhygiene,* the *Eugenical News,* the newsletter of the Eugenics Record Office edited by Harry Hamilton Laughlin, added the subtitle *Current Record of Human Genetics and Race Hygiene* to its masthead in the late 1920s. Then, only weeks before Hitler's victory, the *News* presented a detailed analysis of the German movement, praising the scientific contributions of Lenz, Fischer, Günther, and others. Noting Hitler's attraction to the "Nordic idea," the article predicted "new race hygienic laws and a conscious Nordic culture" as soon as the Nazis took control.[247] The American eugenicists were eagerly anticipating the establishment of biological reform in Germany.

When the Reich actually passed its first piece of eugenical legislation—

the sterilization law—the American eugenicists were positively exultant, seeing at last the realization of their fondest dream: a state that would translate their science into official policy. The *Eugenical News* immediately dismissed any possibility that the new statute could be "deflected from its purely eugenical purpose" into an "instrument of tyranny," and it praised Germany for leading "the great nations of the world in the recognition of the biological foundations of national character. It is probable that the sterilization statutes of the several American states and the national sterilization statute of Germany will, in legal history, constitute a milestone which marks the control by the most advanced nations of the world of a major aspect of controlling human reproduction, comparable in importance only with the states [sic] legal control of marriage." Though unsigned, the article was undoubtedly written by Laughlin, who also noted, with obvious pride in his own contributions, that "the text of the German statute reads almost like the 'American model sterilization law.' "[248] This was no exaggeration on his part; Laughlin's work was highly regarded in Germany, and in 1936 he was awarded an honorary medical degree by the University of Heidelberg.

The biologist Paul Popenoe, author of the most widely used American eugenics text and editor of the *Journal of Heredity*, also reviewed the new German law. Noting that Hitler had read the definitive German work on heredity by Baur, Fischer, and Lenz, Popenoe judged the führer's program to be based "solidly on the application of biological principles to human society." Filled with quotes from *Mein Kampf* to illustrate Hitler's grasp of science, the review offered praise for "a policy that will accord with the best thought of eugenicists in all civilized countries." The Nazi government, Popenoe concluded, had gathered about it the recognized leaders in eugenics, had depended largely on their counsel, and thus had "given the first example in modern times of an administration based frankly and determinedly on the principles of eugenics."[249]

Leon F. Whitney, another sterilization activist, also saw the Nazi law as a vindication of the American scientists' efforts to attain the same goal. Germany's greater commitment to the study of heredity had put the United States "to shame," he observed, with the result that "while we were pussyfooting around," the Germans were setting an example for the world by forcibly sterilizing 400,000 defectives. By such "foresight," Whitney wrote, "Germany is going to make herself a stronger nation," and he declared it imperative that the United States do the same. Although he acknowledged the possibility for abuse when such immense power was granted to the state, Whitney judged it extremely unlikely since "the only persons who ought to be given this power of decision are scientists—trained to arrive at judgments without fear or favor . . . and scientists are not going to risk making mistakes."[250]

As National Socialism progressed further toward becoming the biological state, the American eugenicists continued to cheer wildly from the sidelines, pining for the day when the United States would follow the German example. When the Nazis announced establishment of the first "race bureau" in Germany, which would help administer the laws against "alien races" and sort families "into those whom the State would want to have children and those whose breeding appears undesirable,"[251] one of Laughlin's staff members at the Eugenics Record Office suggested that Hitler "should be made honorary member" of the organization.[252] The *Eugenical News* regularly published articles filled with praise for the Reich's scientific policies. In 1934 it devoted an entire issue to the latest advances in Germany, featuring Wilhelm Frick's address to the Expert Advisory Council,[253] followed by a detailed account of the structure of political biology in Germany—the institutes, professors, journals, and laws. The Nazi policy of "Race-Hygiene and Eugenics," observed the overview hopefully, was being received "everywhere . . . with the greatest interest, particularly since . . . Dr. Goebbels has done his utmost to spread ideas on heredity and biology." Another article praising the Nazi effort to disseminate scientific ideas reprinted a leaflet in current use by the Reich. Though the science of heredity was not new, the leaflet noted, only one man had made its doctrine into a "State Cause," and for this achievement Germany was "the first to thank this one man, Adolf Hitler, and to follow him on the way towards a biological salvation of humanity."[254] Then, at the end of National Socialism's second year in power, the *Eugenical News* summarized the regime's accomplishments as a triumph of "biological . . . thinking," placing the nation well on the road to genetic redemption: "In no country of the world is eugenics more active as an applied science than in Germany. The state has taken over the responsibility for building up the German population, in both numbers and quality. . . . As practical statesmanship for effecting the announced ideals, Germany is the first of all the great nations of the world to make direct practical use of eugenics."[255] Germany might be the first to thank Hitler, but the American eugenicists were not far behind.

The Americans were gratified, no doubt, to find their own achievements regularly acknowledged by the Germans as such significant contributions to the theory and practice of "political biology." When, for example, the Reich announced the beginning of university lectures on "race hygiene for physicians," the doctor in charge of the program stated that he was following "American pathfinders Madison Grant and Lathrop [sic] Stoddard" and cited "race legislation" in the United States as a "model" for the new Germany.[256] Having complained some years earlier in *The Great Race* that "a sentimental belief in the sanctity of human life" was blocking scientific attempts to eliminate "defective infants,"[257]

Grant was understandably eager to lend further assistance to a state that refused to succumb to such an unscientific principle. He instructed the publisher of his latest book, *Conquest of a Continent,* a racial history of the United States that included praise for Hitler's concern for racial purity, to forward copies with the "Compliments of the Author" to Eugen Fischer, Fritz Lenz, and Alfred Rosenberg, one of Hitler's closest scientific advisers. After disappointing sales in the United States and England, which Grant attributed to Jewish influence, the book did much better in Germany, where it was published with a special foreword by Fischer.[258]

Nor was the American eugenicists' enthusiasm for the biological state dampened by National Socialism's increasing oppression of Jews. Although the Americans had not themselves attempted to pass anti-Semitic legislation, there was no shortage of scientific opinions in the United States on the genetic undesirability of Jewish immigrants. Even a seemingly liberal biologist like Raymond Pearl, who publicly denounced the race prejudice of the Nordicists, had privately encouraged "discrimination against the Jew in our universities"—for scientific reasons, of course: in the struggle to determine "whose world is this to be, ours, or the Jews?" the Jews enjoyed the advantages of "the nearly complete absence ... of any inhibiting sense of morals or decency" and the "Jewish" traits of "versatility and superficiality," which "will win out ... over [gentile] thoroughness and depth."[259] Less tolerant scientists did not confine their professional conclusions to private correspondence. One Ellis Island physician had maintained that their persistent and deliberate refusal to practice sound eugenics had produced all sorts of congenital "Jewish psychopathology."[260] Jews were so repulsive, the sociologist Edward Alsworth Ross had written, invoking what was doubtlessly in his opinion the most damning comparison, that when they moved into a neighborhood, the blacks would flee in search of "a more spotless environment." Carl C. Brigham also complained that Jews ("Alpine Slavs") were receiving preference in immigration, despite having an intelligence level below that of Nordics.[261] Ugliest of all, Kenneth L. Roberts, one of the scientists' journalistic allies, traveled through Europe to study the immigration problem firsthand and returned to warn the country that hordes of Jewish "slime" were waiting to threaten the germ plasm of America's solid Nordic base. One interview with Roberts resulted in a feature article in the *Boston Herald* entitled "Danger that World Scum Will Demoralize America."[262]

A number of scientists on both sides of the Atlantic had long concluded that the Jews were "parasites." The revered Galton had written that they were "specialized for a parasitic existence."[263] His protégé, the eminent statistician Karl Pearson, who praised Hitler's racial policies, had warned England that the inferior Jewish immigrants, "hastening to profit from the higher civilization of an improved humanity," might well develop into a "parasitic race."[264] Ross had described the condition of Jews in the United States as "prosperous parasitism," a result of their ability to cheat and lie. Though Davenport had not specifically uttered the "*p*" word in a "quantitative" study of hereditary traits, he concluded that Jews ranked highest of all racial groups on "obtrusiveness, . . . the tendency to intrude into matters, or groups of persons, where not invited."[265]

With such opinions common among the American eugenicists, they viewed the Nuremberg Laws as yet another sign of German scientific progress; it was only good biological sense to protect a "host" from parasites. When criticisms of the biological state arose after passage of the Nuremberg Laws, C. G. Campbell, then president of the Eugenics Research Association, denounced the "irresponsible and hysterical charges" that had obscured "the correct understanding and the great importance" of the Nazi measures. The German policy of "biological improvement" was not a political creation, he explained; it was merely "the integration of the well-considered conclusions of its anthropologists, its biologists, and its sociologists, the latter of whom, in contradistinction to many in other countries, take full cognizance of the biological basis of collective life. No earnest eugenicist can fail to give approbation to such a national policy. Indeed it goes to realize the hopes that eugenicists have entertained for many years, but have despaired of ever seeing adopted in the present generation."[266]

Even as Nationalism Socialism became more and more oppressive, some American scientists still looked to Germany as a model. In 1938 Jews were legally prohibited from attending German theaters, concerts, lectures, cabarets, and other cultural events; they were banned from work in medicine, real estate, and a number of other occupations; and they were barred from attending German schools.[267] At the same time, Harry Hamilton Laughlin was promoting a film in the United States entitled *Eugenics in Germany.*[268] The following year T. Lothrop Stoddard traveled through Germany, returning with great praise for the high-ranking officials he had interviewed—Goebbels, Himmler, and Hitler—and with special admiration for the fairness and rationality of the sterilization courts. Though Stoddard found the plight of the Jews—now confined in ghettos, their property confiscated—"hard and distressful," he had no doubt that National Socialism was pursuing a biologically sound policy. If Germany had to tolerate a certain amount of opposition from an "unscientific" public abroad unable to understand the importance of racial purity, in Stoddard's opinion that was a small price to pay.[269]

The American eugenicists even made their own modest contribution to the plight of Jews in the Reich. In the late 1930s there were last-ditch attempts to waive some of the restrictions in the 1924 Immigration Act in order to grant asylum to a few eventual victims of the Holocaust. These efforts were vigorously opposed by the eugenicists, especially by Laughlin, who submitted a new report, *Immigration and Conquest,* reiterating the biological warnings against the "human dross" that would produce a "breakdown in race purity of the . . . superior stocks." While almost one thousand German Jews seeking to immigrate waited hopefully in a ship off the coast of Florida, Laughlin's report singled them out as a group "slow to assimilate to the American pattern of life," and he recommended a 60 percent *reduction* in quotas, together with procedures to denationalize and deport some immigrants who had already attained citizenship. For the eugenicists, Nordic purity was as important in the United States as it was in Germany.[270] The ship was sent back to Germany.

"I Endeavored to Serve Only Science"

The eventual effects of eugenic logic under National Socialism are only too well known. First came the euthanasia program, a practical method for ridding the society of its biological deadweight in the simplest and most efficient manner. Though sterilization might *eventually* have produced the desired result, in the meantime an enormous number of "useless eaters" were draining scarce resources. The unfit and inferior were enjoying a parasitic existence at the expense of the healthy and strong, a situation, the scientists pointed out, with dire consequences for the health of German society. Konrad Lorenz, later to be awarded a Nobel Prize for his work in ethology, noted the similarity between the "necessary measures" for treating two conditions: "On the one hand, bodies with a cancerous tumor, and, on the other hand, a people with unfit individuals among them. Just as in cancer . . . the best treatment is the earliest possible recognition and eradication of the growth as quickly as possible, the racial-hygienic defense against genetically afflicted elements must be restricted to measures equally drastic." If this "inferior human material" were not properly eliminated, Lorenz stressed, then "in the same way as the cells of a malignant tumor spread throughout the larger organism," it would "pervade and destroy the healthy social body."[271]

First to be euthanized were all those social inadequates whose presence had so troubled many American scientists: the mental patients, the feebleminded, the epileptics, the diseased, the institutionalized, and the criminally insane. Soon added to the list were children—at first, under three years but later up to seventeen—with such problems as bedwetting and difficulties in education.[272]

The final extension of scientific logic in the Reich produced the Final Solution. The most eminent scientists in Germany had concluded that the Jews were a "parasitic" race, a genetically unassimilable group posing a biological danger to the German people, and one leading zoologist even included members of "alien" races in his textbook chapter entitled "Parasitic Diseases."[273] Whether the scientists had intended these conclusions to be taken metaphorically, to Hitler they were literal, biological discoveries, and the man the scientists had supported as the most knowledgeable practitioner of applied biology set out to become the biological savior of the German people by eradicating the Jewish "bacillus," a "germ carrier" that thrived in "purulent infection centers" and provided a "breeding grounds of blood mixing," in order to rescue the host organism.[274] Although less radical measures—deportation, mass sterilization, confinement to reservations—were proposed to prevent contamination of the German gene pool by Jews, eventually they were subjected to the same fate as the lives "unworthy of life."[275]

During the late 1930s and early 1940s, while legal discrimination was giving way to mass murder in the Reich, leading German scientists continued to provide the imprimatur of science for National Socialist ideology and policy. In an effort to confer scientific and legal legitimacy on the practice of euthanasia, for example, Lenz and a number of other professors and physicians attempted to draft a law permitting it well over a year after the killing of the unfit had actually begun. Lenz himself proposed that the decisive article should read: "The life of a patient, who otherwise would need lifelong care, may be ended by medical measures of which he remains unaware."[276] Von Verschuer remained a regular contributor to the scientific literature on the *Judenfrage,* maintaining always that National Socialist policy was biological, "rooted in the science of heredity . . . in the knowledge of the alien racial nature [*Fremdrassigkeit*] of the Jews."[277] In 1944, while the Nazi effort to make Europe *Judenrein* was in full swing, von Verschuer observed that the biological danger posed by Jews and Gypsies had been now eliminated by National Socialism but that a larger effort extending across all of Europe was required to protect Germany from "foreign racial elements."[278] In the *Archiv für Rassen- und Gesellschaftsbiologie* Rüdin celebrated ten years of National Socialist rule by congratulating Hitler and the Nazis for "such brilliant race-hygienic achievement . . . putting into practice the theories and advances of Nordic race–conceptions . . . the fight against parasitic alien races such as the Jews and the Gypsies . . . and preventing the breeding of those with hereditary diseases and those of inferior stock."[279]

Fischer was perhaps the most outspoken of the scientists. In a 1939 speech he stressed that "in order to preserve [their] hereditary endowment," the German people "must reject alien elements, and when these have already insinuated themselves, it must suppress them and eliminate them." Though he did not "characterize every Jew as inferior as Negroes are," he insisted that "the Jew is an alien and . . . must be warded off"; it was a matter of biological "self-defence."[280] As a scientific authority,

Fischer was also invited to be a guest of honor along with Günther at the opening ceremonies of the Institute for Research into the Jewish Question in 1941, where various "solutions" to the presence of Jews were discussed. In 1944, with the Holocaust in progress, Fischer was invited, again along with Günther, to a planned international anti-Jewish congress. Although the congress was never held, Fischer's response to the invitation called it "high time" for the creation of a "scientific front line" against Jewry and pronounced it "an honour" for him to chair the workshop on "race-biology."[281]

All these scientists were extremely proud of their contributions to state and people—not in the petty, egotistical sense that they themselves were of great importance but in the more earnest and high-minded sense that their *science* had proved of value—and they realized how fortuitous the emergence of Nationalism Socialism was in providing this opportunity for their scientific efforts to be of service. As von Verschuer told the Kaiser Wilhelm Institute in 1939, "We geneticists and racial hygienists have been fortunate to have seen our quiet work in the scholar's study and the scientific laboratory find application in the life of the people."[282] Fischer expressed similar sentiments in 1943. "It is a rare and special good fortune," he wrote "for a theoretical science to flourish at a time when the prevailing ideology welcomes it, and its findings can immediately serve the policy of the state. The study of human heredity was already sufficiently mature to provide this, when, years ago, National Socialism was recasting not only the state but also our ways of thinking and feeling. . . . the results of the study of human heredity became absolutely indispensable as a basis for the important laws and regulations created by the new state."[283]

The highest levels of the Nazi party found no reason to take exception to the scientists' assessment of their own significance. "I am convinced," wrote Heinrich Himmler, head of the Gestapo and architect of the Holocaust, concerning Fischer and Lenz, "that through their scientific work, they have both made a considerable contribution, in the last few years, to the theoretical basis and the scientific recognition of the racial components of National Socialist ideology."[284] There was agreement between the scholars themselves and the officials that German scientists had played an instrumental role in the creation and acceptance of Nazi doctrine. The Nazis had merely designed and implemented the mechanisms to attain the goals proclaimed scientifically necessary by the geneticists and anthropologists.

When the full extent of the Nazi atrocities was discovered after the war, the Reich's policymakers, together with the doctors and medical professors who had actually planned and supervised the mass killing, were held predominantly responsible. Many of the latter group were not academic small-fry or Nazi puppets but distinguished contributors to their field, often with international reputations.[285] In his revealing study of *The Nazi Doctors* Robert J. Lifton, a Yale psychiatrist, found a particular "attraction of the Nazi biomedical vision for a certain kind of biologically and genetically oriented scientist." These doctors were frequently characterized by their friends and colleagues as decent, reliable, and dedicated professionals. One of the leaders of the Nazi euthanasia program was described as "a highly ethical person, . . . one of the most idealistic physicians," who had been ready earlier in his life to work with Albert Schweitzer in Africa. Such idealism was converted to brutality through what Lifton calls "an embrace, even worship, of scientific-medical rationality." As another Nazi doctor explained to Lifton, "We wanted to put into effect the laws of life, which are biological laws. . . . We understood National Socialism from the biological side—we introduced biological considerations into [party] policies."[286]

Although a number of these doctors stood trial for their crimes, the geneticists and anthropologists, clearly the intellectual accomplices to mass murder, were generally not called to account for their actions. Only scientists who had pointed out the implications of their research, they had not personally participated in the bloodletting. Indeed, most of the "racial hygienists" retained their positions as professors and researchers at leading German universities and institutes. Otmar Freiherr von Verschuer, for example, not only had provided scientific legitimacy for the most oppressive aspects of National Socialism but also, as director of Frankfurt University's Institute for Hereditary Biology and Racial Studies, had regularly received from his protégé, a young scientist named Josef Mengele, the results of research carried out at Auschwitz—eyes of various colors and blood samples of individuals deliberately infected with typhoid bacteria to study racial differences in disease.[287] Nevertheless, at the war's end von Verschuer received a slap on the wrist—a fine of six hundred Deutschmarks imposed by a denazification tribunal—and was appointed to a prestigious chair in human genetics at the University of Münster, soon becoming the head of a large research center there. In 1956 the German Society for Anthropology dedicated a special issue of its journal *Homo* to von Verschuer on his sixtieth birthday, discreetly omitting any mention of his publications on the *Judenfrage* in the accompanying bibliography.[288] Eventually reminded, in 1962, that he had once praised Hitler as "the first statesman who has wrought the results of genetics and racial hygiene into a directing principle of public policy," von Verschuer was admittedly "shocked" at his own earlier statements but still maintained that he had not been involved in any political activity: "I endeavored to serve only science."[289]

In 1946 Fritz Lenz, too, was appointed to a chair in genetics at the prestigious University of Göttingen. Though he published little after the war, in 1953 he wrote that "the persecution of the Jews was fostered by political fanatics who knew little of genetics."[290] When his complicity with National Socialism was also mentioned in 1962, he refused to express even von Verschuer's modicum of contrition. Lenz, who had called for sterilization of one-third of his compatriots, provided the scientific explanation for Jewish "parasitism" reiterated by Hitler, and praised the führer for putting science into practical action, now professed total lack of responsibility for the Reich's policies because "I . . . did not participate in the drafting" of the laws.[291]

Eugen Fischer was perhaps the most politically compromised scientist, continuing to publish anti-Semitic literature during the war and attending various Nazi conferences on the Jewish question that produced the Final Solution.[292] Yet after the war he became a professor at the University of Freiburg and was made an honorary member of the reorganized German Anthropological Association.

Apparently having learned little from the Nazi experience, many German scientists continued to emphasize the importance of race and eugenics. Hans F. K. Günther was not reappointed to a university position, but after being exonerated from responsibility for war crimes, the major scientific ideologue of Nazi racial theory carried on as if nothing had happened, continuing to espouse the same ideas and participating in the formation of postwar groups devoted to Nordic supremacy. Lenz and Fischer both went on record with criticisms of a statement on race drafted by a number of internationally recognized scientists under UNESCO sponsorship. The statement pointed out the obvious: all human beings belonged to a single species, they were all entitled to equality of opportunity and equality in law as an ethical principle not predicated on equal endowment, and no racial intermixture had been proven to produce any biological disadvantage. Lenz complained that the statement "runs counter to the science of eugenics" and warned of Western civilization's decline and fall as a result of ignoring the principles of eugenic selection. Moreover, he insisted, different races did *not* belong to a single species and the "psychical hereditary differences [between races] are much more important than physical differences"; Jews, he still maintained, were a race distinguished by the former.[293] In a nice touch, Fischer now opposed the UNESCO statement out of his "conviction that freedom of scientific enquiry is imperilled [sic] when any scientific findings or opinions are elevated, by an authoritative body, into the position of doctrines."[294] Another German anthropologist sought to refute the assertion on racial intermixture by noting that "half-castes always try to win recognition as members of a higher race," and "in defence of prohibiting marriage between persons of different races" he asked "which of the gentlemen

who signed the Statement would be prepared to marry his daughter
... to an Australian aboriginal."[295] Though the Reich was gone, its
science lingered on.

• • •

Although there had been acts of extreme barbarism before, the Holocaust was truly unique, but not because of its cruelty or even the size of
the slaughter; mass extermination, unfortunately, has occurred more
than once in human history.[296] What made the Nazi program different
was the sophistication of both its perpetrators and their methods. The
Holocaust did not take place in a "backward" nation; Germany was one
of the most civilized countries in the world, modern and technological,
with the most highly class-conscious working class and the largest socialist party in the advanced industrialized nations. Moreover, in the early
twentieth century Germany enjoyed an unsurpassed scientific tradition,
especially in medicine and bacteriology, where such Nobel laureates as
Rudolph Virchow, Robert Koch, Emil von Behring, and Paul Ehrlich
were world renowned for their accomplishments. Most significant, although
there had been no dearth of prejudice against Jews in Germany during
the nineteenth century, it did not approach the influential ideology of
anti-Semitism in tsarist Russia, Poland, or even France, where the Dreyfus
affair in the 1890s had made Jews a vulnerable target. Indeed, Germany
had long been a haven for Jews seeking relief from the pogroms farther
east, and German Jews, living in relatively amicable integration with
their gentile neighbors, were among the most assimilated in the world.

In this sophisticated society with the least traditional anti-Semitism,
National Socialism converted the "Jewish question" from a religious to a
genetic issue. Unlike the former traditional view, in which a Jew could be
redeemed by accepting Christianity, the biological outlook made Jews a
threat to the state by birth, not by belief. It was for this reason that the
Nazis sponsored so much research on *Mischlinge* (mixtures), scrutinizing
everything from various features to posture in order to determine who
was *really,* that is, genetically, Jewish. This transformation of anti-Semitism
from an irrational, emotional basis to a more intellectually respectable,
scientific basis helped lead to a program of mass murder carried out not
so much with passion as with efficiency. As a pathetic Adolf Eichmann
testified during his trial in Israel, he was "neither a Jew-hater nor an
anti-Semite" but was acting on orders from Himmler based on "natural
selection": "Since the ultimate survivors [of the concentration camps] will
undoubtedly constitute the most resistant group, they must be treated
accordingly [i.e., killed] since this natural elite, if released, must be
viewed as the potential germ cell of a new Jewish order."[297] For Eichmann
and probably many others mass murder was not personal, just science.

Treatment of the sick and the weak was similarly grounded in biological morality, as the Nazis carried the dire predictions of Social Darwinist scientists on both sides of the Atlantic to their logical policy conclusions.[298] The thousands of persons who participated in the medical extermination of the handicapped, feebleminded, and mentally ill could thus assuage whatever personal reservations they must have harbored with the knowledge that scientific authority had decreed the necessity of these actions to realize a future uncontaminated by the retarded, the diseased, the crippled, and the immoral. With this utopian vision in mind, they could view the number of deaths as a direct measure of progress toward the goal. One mental institution actually held a special ceremony on the cremation of the ten-thousandth patient, and all the staff members from doctors to secretaries celebrated the occasion with beer. The head of this institution, who personally opened the gas containers that killed many of the children and other patients, acknowledged being "torn" by his victims' agonies, but he continued, "reassured to learn what eminent scientists partook in the action."[299]

The Holocaust has commonly been conceived of as a revolt against reason, the ultimate example of the "irrational," designed and executed by the pathologically insane. But if reason was the object of the revolt, it was also the chief ally, a dialectic so monstrously rational that it could override all the traditional bounds of morality. The Holocaust was not so much the overthrow of reason as its triumph over morality. It allowed a scientific ultrarationality—what Hitler called "ice cold logic"—to provide murder with rational justification.

It would be foolishly simplistic, of course, to blame the Holocaust all on science; whatever role science played was only the hem of a much larger garment. Germany experienced a series of devastating humiliations in the fifteen years prior to the Nazi takeover—the terms at Versailles, which reduced the nation to a second-rate power; French seizure of the Ruhr industrial area in 1923 to enforce payment of war reparations; the subsequent hyperinflation that devalued the mark to less than a billionth of a penny, wiping out many families' life savings; the world economic slump of the early 1930s that produced unemployment rates greater than 25 percent in Germany—all of which made the country fertile ground for a strong leader who would reassert national pride and unity. This Hitler did by reifying the *Volk*, providing a biological definition for citizenship that made national health and survival a consequence of biological—in other words, racial—purity and intermixture the cause of national decline. But the fact that Germany's greatest experts on race and biology had been making similar claims for some time provided Nazi ideology with the patina of scientific respectability. Scientists might not have loosed the dragon, but they had certainly done their share to feed it.

To Each according to His Worth

By the mid-1930s, no longer obsessed with the immigration problem so prominent only a decade earlier, the eugenics movement in the United States began to turn its attention to another significant racial problem in need of scientific solution: the growing concern for the political rights of blacks. The 1933 edition of the most popular eugenics textbook found biology still an insurmountable obstacle to any attempts to end discrimination against blacks; science allowed the possibility that they might serve in southern legislatures as a representative of their own people but certainly not of whites, who would not stand for "Negro political domination."[300] Such assertions made eugenics increasingly attractive to individuals like Dr. Hiram Wesley Evans, Imperial Wizard of the Ku Klux Klan, who began to cite Harry Hamilton Laughlin and other scientists in support of his own position.[301] In the *Eugenical News* Madison Grant's protégé Earnest Sevier Cox, another well-known Klansman who had urged the repatriation of all blacks of "breeding age" back to Africa, was praised as a "greater savior of his country than George Washington." Cox himself later contributed a lengthy report to the *News* on the repatriation movement.[302]

These associations caused increasing embarrassment for scientists who were otherwise in agreement with the eugenics cause. For example E. A. Hooten, a Harvard professor and an ex–Galton Society member, praised those "persons sincerely interested in human welfare . . . [who] are striving to improve the quality of the human animal by biological measures," and he insisted that scientists "ought to be in the forefront" of such activity. His observation that "democracy is making the world safe for morons" also suggested sympathy for some of the oppressive measures advocated by eugenical science. Nevertheless, he could no longer bring himself to participate actively in the movement because of its "vicious racial propaganda, especially the nonsense of Nordicism." "If eugenics is going to command the support of disillusioned anthropologists," declared Hooten, no doubt thinking of himself, "it will have to divest itself entirely of its Ku Klux Klan regalia."[303]

This call for a more moderate approach to eugenics, one that would eschew overt racism and calls to emulate foreign fascists, found one last ambitious prewar response from a major social scientist. In 1940 the Columbia University professor Edward L. Thorndike, the country's most prominent educational psychologist for the previous forty years and an original member of the Galton Society, produced *Human Nature and the Social Order,* a 963-page tome espousing a system of social ethics based on "impartial scientific truth." Although he had been a participant in the scientific warnings against immigration two decades earlier, here Thorndike described the underlying assumptions of eugenics unconfounded by issues of race and immigration. He saw modern society in genetic decline, its citizenry largely composed of inferior masses, most of whom were robbers "deep down in their nature," classic authoritarian personalities instinctively desirous of having "other human beings step out of the way, bend the knee, lower the glance and obey the command" yet simultaneously eager to submit "*to the right kind of man.*" He also, however, saw the world blessed with a small number of great thinkers, "men" who were not only intelligent but also benevolent, impartial, and "sympathetic . . . toward all that is good."[304]

The problem, from Thorndike's point of view, was that traditional ethics had displayed a sentimental prejudice in favor of equal treatment of persons. In place of this outmoded belief he offered a more rational approach based on the scientific study of individual differences: greater weight was to be accorded to the desires of superior individuals. Indeed, he proposed a system of precise mathematical weights appropriate to an individual's ability: an average person's wants would count for 100, the truly superior person's for 2,000, and an idiot's for 1; other adjustments would be made for age, "racial stock," and personality traits; and even animals would not be forgotten, the needs of a "useful domestic animal" receiving 1/500th of a human weight and the needs of other animals 1/10,000th. It was true, Thorndike acknowledged, that some "men of genius" had also been ruthless, but he found this all the more cause to grant them power so they would have no reason to "extort it by force." Even if they sometimes sought "eccentric, ignoble or ruthless satisfactions," he wrote, their contributions would more than compensate for these minor peccadilloes, and consequently the society's "most prudent investment" was to identify superior individuals early and "give them whatever they need . . . [and] one good clue to what they need is what they themselves desire."[305]

While genetic superiority entitled a few people to "acquire pecuniary, political, and persuasive power," Thorndike judged the less capable masses overpaid at four dollars a day, an inflated wage resulting from the "generosity" of their employers; indeed, he maintained, it was the employers who deserved even more than the admittedly sizable rewards they already received, and working people should be "grateful" to them for the "gift" of a job. The one scientific prospect for a reduction in such gross economic inequality, according to Thorndike, was "eugenic advance," which alone could produce a decrease in the underlying cause of material differences—*innate* inequality; only after society had achieved genetic equality would it be possible to consider greater equality of "pecuniary rewards." Under the present genetic circumstances, however, the concept of social justice was in Thorndike's view a misleading euphemism designed to reduce feelings of inferiority in the poor.[306]

If eugenic improvement was to be realized, "ownership" of the society's genetic resources could not be entrusted to just anyone, and Thorndike proposed that a woman's uterus and a man's spermatozoa be placed "at the disposal of the state or some board of trustees" that would ensure their use for the general welfare. "There is nothing very radical in such a reform," he observed: "Women today bear children to be maimed and killed at the pleasure of rulers. It is only a step further to have children born to serve the state in more useful ways. Children are taken away from parents considered unfit to rear them and given to others. It is only a small step further to prevent such from being born."[307]

Devoid of racist or nativist rhetoric, Thorndike's scholarly work made the underlying assumptions of eugenics clearer than ever. From *Mein Kampf* to *Human Nature and the Social Order* every eugenical work, whether by demagogue or respected scientist, had been obsessed with the political implications of biological inequality—with the perceived contradiction between the maxim that all individuals are created equal and the biological facts. A scientifically derived morality and social policy therefore had to recognize the necessity of privilege for those few who were born with greater value and restriction for others. Complete democracy, political rights for all, and, of course, any attempts at reducing material inequities were an artificial enforcement of the equality of biologically unequal persons. To the eugenicists, failure to appreciate this view suggested an inability to abandon sentimentality and accept modern science.

Because eugenics had so often been intertwined with pseudoscientific assertions about race and nationality, the inaccuracy—indeed, the plain foolishness—of many of these claims became the principal focus of criticism, leaving the underlying assumptions unchallenged. The real problem of eugenics was not the commission of scientific errors, though these were certainly committed in abundance. The attention given to empirical questions largely overshadowed consideration of the more important error, however, the conviction that sociomoral tenets could appropriately be derived from science. Concepts of liberty, justice, and equal rights are neither determined nor justified by scientific results but flow from agreements among human beings based on constitutional, religious, and moral principles. The intrusion of science into this domain only impeded the Enlightenment's promise to free individuals from the coercive power of church and superstition, moving them out of the religious frying pan and into the scientific fire. Of course, this does not suggest that science has no role in social policy, but it is not in defining goals or rights;

it is in developing techniques and methods for achieving principles that have been defined elsewhere. The failure of many scientists to appreciate this distinction would produce a replay of the same conflict in a different context twenty years later.

4

Science Giveth and It Taketh Away: The Scientific Controversy over Integration

THE COMPARATIVE ability of different immigrant groups, a matter proclaimed for years to be of monumental significance for science and society, declined as a scientific priority in the mid-1930s, reflecting the decline of the social controversies that were going to be resolved by such knowledge. The earlier assertions of Polish, Italian, and Russian inferiority had had only political purposes—to halt immigration or to deprive immigrants of their rights in one way or another—and as soon as these political campaigns disappeared, interest in the scientific issue also vanished.

In addition to this altered political context, a different kind of scientific transition was taking place during the 1930s and 1940s, catching the whole field of "racial science" in a paradigm shift that replaced evolutionary development with cultural differences as the preferred explanatory construct for the diversity of human behavior. With this change in emphasis from Charles Darwin to Franz Boas, from the dominance of instincts to the importance of learning, human beings were now viewed as the creatures as well as the creators of culture. Most scientists agreed that the differences between various groups, in both intelligence test scores and cultural achievements, could be explained by the history of their cultural experiences rather than by any innate differences in mental abilities. A postwar UNESCO conference of social scientists, for example, issued a statement maintaining that when races were "given similar degrees of cultural opportunity to realize their potentialities, the average achievement of the members of each group is about the same."[1] Another group of scientists—geneticists and physical anthropologists—also convened by

UNESCO took a slightly more agnostic position, acknowledging that it was "possible . . . that some types of innate capacity for intellectual and emotional responses are commoner in one human group than in another" but concluding that "available scientific evidence" provided no basis for any belief in such innate differences.[2]

Despite being crafted by scientists, these statements were also primarily political documents—scientific conclusions are not reached by proclamation—issued in response to the racially based policies of the Third Reich. Although each statement noted that equality as an ethical principle was not dependent on a demonstration of equal endowment, only a single sentence of each four-page declaration was devoted to this point, making it seem that the scientists were responding to the implicit syllogism, "if there are innate differences between groups, then that legitimates differences in their rights," chiefly by denying the precedent rather than by challenging the validity of the implication. Perhaps this was not completely unreasonable on their part. They were, after all, scientists with expertise on human differences and thus uniquely qualified to speak to the premise. Then, too, insisting on the separation of abilities and rights as a moral postulate had not been notably successful in the past. Maybe in some more humane future such a position would have greater appeal, but immediate historical experience had indicated that the linkage between biological and political equality was popular in principle and devastating in practice. If scientific support for biological equality between groups was an effective, practical method for reducing oppression based on race and ethnicity, perhaps that was more important than abstract philosophical argument. As Thomas Hobbes had observed in *Leviathan*, "If nature therefore have made men equal, that equality is to be acknowledged; or if nature have made men unequal, yet because men that think themselves equal will not enter into conditions of peace but upon equal terms, such equality must be admitted."[3] Biology is *not* destiny; the problem was what to do in a world where many people still believed it should be.

At the same time that the UNESCO statements were being drafted in Europe, the second reconstruction was already visible on the social horizon in the United States, and some American social scientists, eager to support the movement for black equality, embarked on a similar strategy. Instead of dismissing the question of racial differences as scientifically meaningless and politically irrelevant, they insisted that there were no significant differences in intelligence between blacks and whites. The purpose of this claim was also unabashedly political; one of its major spokespersons, Otto Klineberg, a professor of psychology at Columbia University, would later note that a major obstacle to the realization of human rights was "the belief, widely and stubbornly held, that some races and peoples are inferior."[4] What better way could there be for scientists to help achieve the admirable goal of human rights than by removing the obstacle? The scientists also argued that segregation should be struck down because it had produced demonstrable psychological harm. Both these assertions again predicated political rights on scientific results. The segregationists would eventually fasten on the scientists' claims as the supposed linchpin of the argument for integration and launch a furious counterattack against what they called the "equalitarian dogma" in an attempt to change the terms of the political debate from the abstract issue of equal constitutional entitlements to the more empirical issues that had been raised by the scientists.

Of course in the American South, soon to become the major battle-ground in the civil rights struggle, a combination of statutes and "custom" had enshrined the remnants of America's original sin, maintaining a system of white supremacy that kept blacks separate and unequal—politically disenfranchised, relegated to inferior facilities in public transportation, education, and health care, and completely excluded from many public recreational facilities and libraries; in some cities they were not even permitted to operate a motor vehicle.[5] For the sophisticated southerner, underlying this accepted fact of daily life was the Social Darwinist belief that blacks occupied a lower rung on the evolutionary ladder. Blacks were not just intellectually inferior to whites; they had a distinctly different set of mental characteristics. This fundamental difference erected certain natural limitations to any attempts at reform or improvement since, as one University of Virginia professor had explained in 1913, it was not possible "to deprive the Negro of his own racial mental characteristics, and to substitute our own in their place," because "no matter how much we educate him, no matter how much we better his position in society, he will remain a Negro psychically as long as he remains a Negro physically."[6] At the time this view was not confined to the South. In a 1921 speech on blacks President Warren Harding had declared that "a black man cannot be a white man . . . and should not aspire to be as much like a white man as possible in order to accomplish the best that is possible for him. He should seek to be, and he should be encouraged to be, the best possible black man, and not the best possible imitation of a white man."[7] Only in the South was this belief still encoded into law after the war, however.

Whether its citizens appreciated the fine points of Social Darwinist theory, the South instinctively recognized the importance of the white woman as the perpetuator of racial superiority and thus the necessity of ensuring that she remain absolutely inaccessible to contact with males from the lower race.[8] As W. J. Cash explained in *The Mind of the South,* from abolition on, "any assertion of any kind on the part of the Negro" constituted a threat to this holiest of taboos: "in destroying the rigid fixity of the black at the bottom of the scale, in throwing open to him at least the legal opportunity to advance, . . . [it] inevitably opened up to the mind of every Southerner a vista at the end of which stood the overthrow of this taboo. If it was given to the black to advance at all, who could say . . . that he would not one day advance the whole way and lay claim to complete equality, including, specifically, the ever crucial right of marriage?"[9] The danger of a mulatto posterity had therefore been raised in opposition to every movement for the rights of blacks. Even before emancipation southern journals had defended slavery as necessary to prevent the United States from becoming "a decaying population of perhaps twenty millions of idle, quarrelsome, effeminate, and vicious half breeds." Calls for greater black equality at the turn of the century typically elicited a similar response, now informed by a substantial dose of Social Darwinism, that the real question was whether whites "shall . . . blend . . . Caucasian, world-ruling, world-conquering blood with the servile strain of Africa."[10] In the modern era this obsession with miscegenation had not diminished. In Alabama, for example, there were efforts to remove from the public libraries *The Rabbits' Wedding,* a children's book about two rabbits who married and lived happily together in the forest, because the accompanying illustration portrayed one rabbit as white and the other black.[11] The South's peculiar institution was thus necessary to ensure what Cash described as "the right of their sons in the legitimate line, through all the generations to come, to be born to the great heritage of the white race."[12]

The *Brown* Case

In 1954 the Supreme Court issued its decision in *Brown v. Board of Education of Topeka, Kansas,* a historic line of demarcation between the Jim Crow past and the desegregated future. Actually *Brown* was a consolidation of four cases—one from South Carolina, one from Virginia, and one from Delaware, as well as the Kansas case—all being appealed from rulings in the lower courts that had upheld segregated schools.[13] According to Justice Tom Clark, the Supreme Court deliberately chose Kansas to head the consolidation and thus provide the decision's name in order to avoid the appearance that the issue was a purely southern one.[14] Social scientists were prominently featured in this lengthy judicial battle. They testified in each of the four lower court proceedings and furnished an appendix to the brief submitted to the Supreme Court by the NAACP legal team, which represented all the plaintiffs.

"Supported by Modern Authority"

Even before the *Brown* cases began to work their way through the judicial system, the scientists were obviously eager to enter the fray. In the late 1940s Max Deutscher and Isidor Chein, two prominent social psychologists, conducted a survey of social scientists on "the psychological effects of enforced segregation" in open anticipation that "social science evidence may be a significant if not crucial factor in any Supreme Court decision on segregation." Specifically, the pollsters expected expert opinion on the "detrimental *effects*" of segregation to be important "since," they maintained, "the court decision will be based on whether enforced segregation is considered to be a violation of the *rights* of citizens" (emphases added).[15] This was a non sequitur: rights and effects have no necessary relationship, and for that matter some whites might legitimately claim that integration had "detrimental effects" on *them*. (Three decades later a white sanitation supervisor in Louisville, Kentucky, did indeed attribute his bout of depression to the stress of being forced to work with blacks, and the state Workers Compensation Board upheld his claim and awarded him benefits.)[16] The results of the survey showed that an overwhelming majority of the 849 scientists believed enforced segregation to be psychologically harmful, although a number of their individual comments inspired little confidence in the respondents' objectivity. Noting a supposed paucity of good literature created in the South, one psychologist concluded that segregation "narrow[ed] the interest and psychological freedom of the enforcing group"; another commented on the costly and wasteful duplication of separate educational facilities. Though motivated by a commendable desire for justice, such self-appointed literary critics and economists hardly qualified as expert scientific opinion.[17] Although Chein acknowledged that the survey was an opinion poll and not a factual demonstration, he argued that "if there is widespread agreement and conviction among scientists concerning an issue of fact, this cannot be a simple accident. There is probably no other group of people as accustomed as are scientists to distinguishing between their biases and pertinent evidence."[18] This was extremely, and personally, ironic since the previous generation of social scientists had reached "widespread agreement and conviction" that Polish Jews, like Chein's own family, were racially inferior and should be kept out of the country.

Two years later the court battles began in earnest. The social scientists who actually testified for the plaintiffs were such distinguished researchers as Otto Klineberg from Columbia, Jerome S. Bruner from Harvard, David Krech from Berkeley, M. Brewster Smith from Vassar, and many others, perhaps twenty-five to thirty in all.[19] Their testimony emphasized two points: first, segregation had a harmful impact on the developing personality of black children and their motivation to learn; and second, racial differences on intellectual tests were caused by environmental handicaps stemming from segregation, discrimination, and prejudice since there were, in fact, no significant differences in innate intelligence or learning ability between the races.

Only one of the many professionals to take the stand offered any empirical data. Kenneth B. Clark, a black psychologist at the City College of New York, had devised a technique referred to as the "Dolls Test" for studying racial attitudes in young black children. Clark would show a child four dolls, two of them brown skinned and black haired, the other two white skinned and blond. The child was then asked to choose one of the dolls in response to each of a number of requests, like "Give me the doll you like best; the doll that is a nice doll; the doll that looks bad; the doll that looks like a white child; the doll that looks like a Negro child; the doll that looks like you." In the South Carolina case Clark had performed this test on sixteen black children from the plaintiffs' educational district: eleven had picked a brown doll as "bad," ten had chosen a white doll as "nice," and seven had selected a white doll as the one that looked like themselves. From these results, in his testimony Clark concluded that "these children . . . have been definitely harmed in the development of their personalities."[20]

In addition to the expert testimony in the lower courts, three psychologists—Clark, Chein, and Stuart Cook, a professor of psychology at New York University—drafted a paper entitled "The Effects of Segregation and the Consequences of Desegregation: A Social Science Statement." This document summarized the fragmentary testimony of the social scientists scattered throughout the lengthy transcripts from the trial courts and cited the Deutscher and Chein survey to show that the statements by the witnesses were indeed representative of opinion in the field. To allay any fear that "an intellectually inferior group may jeopardize [sic] the education of the more intelligent," the three psychologists again emphasized that "the available scientific evidence indicates that much, perhaps all, of the observable differences among various racial and national groups may be adequately explained in terms of environmental differences."[21] The "Statement" was then circulated to several dozen leading researchers, along with a request for their signature if they were in substantial agreement, and the final document, bearing thirty-five of the most eminent names in American social science as coauthors (including both Allports—Floyd and Gordon—Hadley Cantril, Else Frenkel-Brunswik, Robert Merton, Gardner Murphy, Theodore Newcomb, and Samuel Stouffer) was submitted to the Supreme Court as an appendix to the appellants' brief.

To their credit the social scientists had changed teams in the struggle over rights, but though they were now on the "good" side, their position still suggested linkage between human rights and (the latest) scientific conclusions; science now supported the extension of rights, whereas in the 1920s it had justified their restriction. In fact, none of the scientific testimony had any proper bearing on the fundamental issue—whether segregated schools were offensive to the constitutional guarantee of equal rights. Neither the infliction of psychological harm nor the intellectual equality of blacks and whites was in any way relevant to this question.

In addition, the only empirical data submitted to the court to support the scientific assertions turned out to be of questionable validity. Clark had interpreted the results of his Dolls Test as evidence of psychological damage because a majority of the sixteen black children tested had chosen the white doll as "nice" and the brown doll as "bad." However, in a previous and much larger study comparing 134 black children from segregated Arkansas schools with 119 black children from desegregated schools in Massachusetts he had found that the northern children were consistently more pronounced in their preference for the white doll, selecting it as "nice" and the brown doll as "bad" substantially more often than the southern children did.[22] If such a choice did indicate damage, one could legitimately conclude that integration had produced more of it than segregation had. This contradiction between Clark's testimony in court and his published research was overlooked by the inept opposition at the lower levels, but by the time oral argument took place before the Supreme Court, the defense was much better prepared. John W. Davis, the 1924 Democratic candidate for president and a magnificent advocate—"irresistible," one observer called him—made the South's case with wit and eloquence. He termed Clark's responses from the sixteen South Carolina children "a sad result [which] we are invited to accept . . . as a scientific conclusion." "But I am reminded of the scriptural saying, 'Oh that mine adversary had written a book,'" declared Davis, who then smoothly noted for the Court the exact results of Clark's published research and inquired rhetorically what had become of the "blasting influence of segregation."[23] The injustice of segregation lay in its official subordination of blacks to second-class status, an effect not necessarily discoverable by science; the attempt to provide scientific proof of its cruelty had come close to exculpating it.[24]

One could, however, certainly understand the social scientists' desire to align their profession with the forces of freedom and, even more, the NAACP legal staff's use of every possible weapon in an adversary procedure. Let the defendants claim some evidence was irrelevant or misleading; the plaintiffs' responsibility was to represent one side as vigorously as possible, particularly when that side had clear moral authority. Besides, who knew what might influence the courts, especially when in quest of a ruling that would run counter to a century-long tradition. The NAACP attorneys thus took the chicken soup view of the social science evidence: maybe it wouldn't help, but it couldn't hurt. In the long run this would turn out to be a misguided tactic.

Of course, in the final analysis it was the Supreme Court's responsibility to support its decision on an appropriate basis, one that did not make constitutional entitlements dependent on the contemporary fashion in social science. In oral argument the Court made clear that the expert testimony would be of little significance to the eventual ruling. When Thurgood Marshall, head of the NAACP legal team, alluded to the scientific testimony, he drew a frank response from the bench:

> Justice Frankfurter: Of course, if it is written into the Constitution, then I do not care about the evidence. If it is in the Constitution, then all the testimony you introduced is beside the point, in general.

> Mr. Marshall: I think, sir, that so far as the decisions of this Court, this Court has repeatedly said that you cannot use race as a basis of classification.

> Justice Frankfurter: Very well. If that is a settled constitutional doctrine, then I do not care what any associate or full professor in sociology tells me. If it is in the Constitution, I do not care about what they say. But the question is, is it in the Constitution?[25]

Law, however, is also a conservative enterprise, bound to the decisions of the past, and every previous legal consideration of the "separate but equal" fiction had found it defensible. The most recent of these was the Supreme Court's 1896 ruling in *Plessy v. Ferguson* that enforced segregation of passengers on interstate railroad cars was permissible. The *Plessy* decision had been recognized as authoritative for sixty years, and the *Brown* justices, sensitive to precedent, were no doubt reluctant simply to call it callous, stupid, and wrong and to summarily overrule it, although this may well have been their personal opinion. To resolve this dilemma, the Court stressed the present significance of public education as a distinguishing factor from the *Plessy* era, when some half the states did not even have compulsory education laws. In the middle of the twentieth century public education had become "perhaps the most important function of state and local governments," noted Chief Justice Earl Warren, writing for a unanimous Court, and the opportunity for such an education "is a right which must be made available to all on equal terms." Segregated schools were clearly in violation of this right. Although he cited the Fourteenth Amendment as the constitutional basis for this finding ("No State shall make or enforce any law which shall abridge the privileges or immunities of citizens of the United States; nor shall any

State deprive any person of life, liberty, or property, without due process of law; nor deny to any person within its jurisdiction the equal protection of the laws"), some of the opinion's ensuing explanation fell back on the language of the social scientists. Separation of black children "solely because of their race," Warren wrote, "generates a feeling of inferiority as to their status in the community that may affect their hearts and minds in a way unlikely ever to be undone," and, quoting the Kansas court's opinion, itself taken almost verbatim from one of the psychologists who had testified there, he stressed the effect of this sense of inferiority on a child's motivation to learn. "Segregation with the sanction of law," the Kansas judge had said, "has a tendency to [retard] the educational and mental development of negro children and to deprive them of some of the benefits they would receive in a racial[ly] integrated school system." Finally, in what seemed like an attempt to justify further the break with tradition, Warren noted that "whatever may have been the extent of psychological knowledge at the time of *Plessy v. Ferguson,* this finding is amply supported by modern authority," and a footnote—the famous footnote eleven—cited seven works by contemporary social scientists, among them a paper by Kenneth Clark, the Deutscher-Chein survey, and the Swedish sociologist Gunnar Myrdal's mammoth work on race relations, *An American Dilemma.* [26]

There were several possible motivations for these psychological observations and the oblique concluding reference. One likely reason was the Court's desire to find every additional source of support for a decision that was certain to provoke intense resistance. Then, too, the *Plessy* opinion, which had claimed legislation "powerless to eradicate racial instincts,"[27] had obviously been informed by the Social Darwinist beliefs of its time, and the *Brown* Court might have wished to suggest that the scientific assumptions underlying the earlier decision were no longer considered valid. Edmond Cahn, a law professor at New York University, suggested at the time that the final allusion to "modern authority" was merely a gracious gesture to acknowledge the efforts of the scientists, a kind of consolation for having largely ignored their contributions in the final opinion, as well as a recognition of their altruism and dignity in the face of what were sometimes personally insulting experiences in the lower courts. In the Virginia case, for example, instead of concentrating on the testimony elicited during direct examination, the defense attorney launched an undisguised personal attack on Chein and Clark through a series of offensive questions about their place of birth, ethnic background, religion, skin color, and opinions on interracial marriage. Whether the allusion was intended as acknowledgment, consolation, or balm, it was still no more than a courtesy; once it had been paid, Cahn noted, "the Court was not disposed in the least to . . . base its determination on the expert testimony."[28] When queried almost two decades later, Warren himself recalled the list of references as an intended response to the *Plessy* opinion's callous observation that segregation degraded blacks "not by reason of anything found in the act, but solely because the colored race chooses to put that construction on it."[29] Whatever the Court's actual intentions at the time, it is certain that the scientific evidence had absolutely nothing to do with the constitutional basis for the decision.

Nevertheless, several observers gave social science significant credit for the Court's decree. The headline in the *New York Times* called it "a sociological decision," and James Reston wrote that the "Court's opinion read more like an expert paper on sociology than a Supreme Court opinion. It sustained the argument of experts in education, sociology, psychology and anthropology. . . ."[30] Will Maslow, director of the Commission on Law and Social Action of the American Jewish Congress, noted that the NAACP had struggled for sixteen years to convince the Court that segregation was unconstitutional but was unsuccessful until it turned to the psychologists. "When the final decision was handed down," declared Maslow, "it rested not on conceptual legal principles or the legislative history of the Fourteenth Amendment or even on the sociological demonstration that in practice segregation results in inferior schools but on the psychological finding of thwarted intellectual development."[31]

Some of the social scientists themselves offered very immodest assessments of the role they had played. Even before the *Brown* decision had been rendered, Clark, for example, was announcing that "proof . . . that segregation itself is inequality . . . had to come from the social psychologists and other social scientists" and that the testimony of such professionals had "push[ed] forward the frontiers of constitutional law and legal precedence."[32] After the decision he proudly observed that "ethics cannot stem from the law alone but must be fed to it through the ceaseless struggles of . . . scientists,"[33] a view that would have received the wholehearted support of every eugenicist. Although Clark seemed to realize that what social science could contribute to ethics with one hand, it could remove with the other, it did not dampen his enthusiasm for science's moral relevance. Instead he called for professional organizations to establish "machinery which will prevent social scientists from . . . offering with equal certainty contradictory testimony";[34] apparently scientifically derived ethics was not opposed to censorship. Eighteen years after *Brown* Clark finally arrived at a different position. In 1972, when a number of studies questioned the educational benefits of integration, Clark responded that the courts "should decide questions of school spending and integration, not on the basis of uncertain research findings, but on the basis of the constitutional and 'equity right of human beings.' "[35] This was undeniably correct, just as it had been in 1954.

Other scholars in social science and even in law expressed views similar to Clark's. The University of Chicago law professor Philip Kurland also claimed that the Supreme Court had "follow[ed] the lead of scientists such as Dr. Clark. . . . [and] there is nothing that a lawyer can add to this social science presentation."[36] In an analysis published some years later the social scientist Paul L. Rosen maintained that the Court had "deferred to the authority of modern social science," which not only had "confirmed that all significant achievement disparities between Negroes and whites could be explained in environmental . . . terms" but also had actually revealed "new meaning" to the equal protection clause of the Fourteenth Amendment.[37] Behind all these exultant claims lay the danger of basing rights on a foundation as flimsy as scientific testimony. As Edmond Cahn pointed out, contemporary psychologists were "liberal and egalitarian" in their views, but "suppose, a generation hence, some of their successors were to revert to the ethnic mysticism of the very recent past; suppose they were to present us with a collection of racist notions and label them 'science.' What then would be the state of our constitutional rights?"[38]

Particularly ironic was the Supreme Court's decision to ignore totally Clark's recommendations where his scientific expertise was singularly appropriate. In the original *Brown* opinion the Court postponed any decree on the process of implementation, inviting all parties to submit their ideas on whether desegregation should take place gradually or be mandated forthwith. This was precisely the point where social scientists should have played a prominent role; the goal had been set for clear constitutional reasons, and the question was now one of technique—how best to achieve it. Clark carefully assembled the data on numerous case studies of desegregation around the country and from this thorough review extracted a number of principles for the accomplishment of efficient desegregation with a minimum of racial disturbance. A common theme of these principles was the importance of a resolute attitude by authorities, a clear statement of policy that specified a date for the mandated change, firm enforcement, and no tolerance for violation, evasion, or subterfuge.[39] Clark's evidence, both empirical and theoretical, suggested that gradualism would likely be interpreted as indecision and thus lead to increased resistance and opposition. Despite the benefit of Clark's expertise—as relevant in this instance as it had been irrelevant to the first ruling—when the Court issued its second opinion in *Brown* a year later, the justices caved in to pressure from the southern states and remanded supervision to the individual district courts so that desegregation could be implemented, in those famous oxymoronic words, "with all deliberate speed."[40]

"Talking Anthropology"

Southern segregationists, outraged by the *Brown* Court's departure from previous rulings, were no more disposed than so many of the academics to recognize the decision's constitutional basis; they too preferred to give the credit for the *Brown* decision to—or more appropriate from their viewpoint, to blame it on—the social scientists. Their first response to the scientists' putative role was the time-honored tactic for discrediting defenders of human rights: redbaiting. Senator James Eastland from Mississippi filled the pages of the *Congressional Record* with the left-wing affiliations of the Court's "modern authorities": Myrdal's book *An American Dilemma* had been sponsored by "the Carnegie-Foundation-of-Alger-Hiss fame"—one word in Eastland's speeches; the well-known Columbia anthropologist "Frank" Boas (Eastland chose to Americanize Franz Boas's name even while complaining of his subversive politics), who had participated on Myrdal's project, was associated with some twenty petitions and organizations, all alleged to be under Communist "influence"; Clark had received his undergraduate degree from Howard University, "a socialistic Negro College"—no mention was made of his doctorate from Columbia.[41] Many other southern leaders followed the same tactic; Eugene Cook, Georgia's attorney general, noted that one of Myrdal's advisers had sent a message of condolence upon the death of Joseph Stalin.[42]

Even at the height of the McCarthy era, however, redbaiting was not going to produce a reversal of a Supreme Court decision, and, having decided that the scientists were the chief culprits, the segregationists turned to the expert evidence itself, both the direct testimony and the references listed in the footnote. The scientists had been trumpeting their contributions as the basis of the decision, and the segregationists would now join them in a strangely symbiotic concurrence over the significance of this evidence but, of course, with a different view of its validity. Although Jim Crow laws had always been based on the putative inferiority of blacks, the original southern strategy in the lower courts had been largely to ignore the scientific testimony as irrelevant to the central issues of states' rights and legal precedents. This approach was now considered a serious error, if an understandable one, and to rectify it, the segregationists were only too willing to accept the premise that science should play the pivotal role in legal decisions about the rights of black people. They thus embarked on a campaign to overturn *Brown* or prevent its implementation by revealing to the Court and the public what science had *really* proven about the effects of integration and the ability of blacks. The Supreme Court's citation of three works by authors who had not even testified in any of the cases made such a strategy even more appealing since the segregationists could claim that they had been deprived of the opportunity to cross-examine these "witnesses" under oath and disprove or impeach their "evidence."

This approach was most forcefully proposed by Carleton Putnam, who agreed that the Supreme Court had no right to overturn segregation but insisted that the South was sabotaging its own cause by focusing on legal and constitutional issues. Desegregation, he explained, had resulted from a subversive movement, both within and outside the academic world, whose purpose was to denounce heredity and insist that nothing was innate, thus making environment responsible for all human differences. Instead of harping on states' rights, southerners "should be talking anthropology," a subject they had avoided so far, according to Putnam, out of "instinctive human kindness," a sensitive reluctance to make a public issue out of black inferiority.[43] The time for kindness had passed, however; this was now a matter of survival.

The scientific testimony in *Brown* was therefore not a *harmless* irrelevance; it would provoke a sustained attack on integration by a handful of racist scientists. If the Court wanted scientific data, the segregationists would supply the data with a vengeance. Since the plaintiffs' experts had testified that segregation was damaging to the personality and self-esteem of black children, the opposing scientists would marshal their own evidence to show that integration was even more harmful to the young black psyche. In response to the scientists' claim that racial differences in scholastic performance were environmentally based, they would offer numerous IQ studies "proving" that the differences were hereditary. "Science" would once again be proffered as the justification for oppression, but this time many scientists who had opposed such tyranny were, themselves, partly to blame for having first framed the issue of rights within the scientific domain.

Moreover, the plaintiffs' emphasis on segregated schools as an inherent obstacle to the learning process also strongly implied that desegregation per se would produce immediate improvement in black educational achievement. Besides confusing moral triumph with technical solution, this view was extremely naive; such a complex problem would certainly not yield to such a simple remedy. When the predicted improvement was not immediately achieved, the segregationists had yet more reason to cry that the Supreme Court had been hoodwinked by biased evidence.

In addition to the issues directly raised in the *Brown* case, the segregationists would introduce one other "scientific" concern that they insisted was the core of the controversy—the necessity to prevent miscegenation. To discourage the "unthinkable," the southern states had all enacted antimiscegenation laws, many of which imposed penalties of up to ten years imprisonment. The statutory definition of a "Negro" varied from "any ascertainable trace of Negro blood," whatever that meant, to such specific fractions as one-sixteenth or one-thirty-second. (As Mark Twain wrote of Roxy, she was "as white as anybody, but the one-sixteenth of her which was black outvoted the other parts.") A person legally defined as black in Georgia could therefore become white by crossing the border into Florida.[44] Such laws were not declared unconstitutional until 1968, well after *Brown* and the civil rights legislation, in the wonderfully entitled *Loving* case.[45]

Despite the existence of these punitive sanctions, the strict enforcement of segregation, especially among impressionable schoolchildren, was still considered an essential prophylactic measure, and when the *Brown* decision threatened to demolish the wall of racial separatism, horrified southern defenders envisioned widespread "amalgamation" rising from the ruins. As one southern writer explained, even though race preference was a "universal instinct," it was not active in the very young, and, consequently, only a few years of integrated education could produce, *horribile dictu,* "large numbers of indoctrinated young Southerners free from all 'prejudice' against mixed matings."[46] (Needless to say, these fears were not assuaged when the very first black student at the University of Georgia, admitted only after a legal battle, married a white classmate, a fact not revealed until they had moved to New York. Georgia's attorney general warned that the couple would be arrested and prosecuted should they return, and the white groom's father announced that "this is the end of the world.")[47] Besides correcting the misinformation already on the record in *Brown,* the segregationist scientists thus found it necessary to warn the country of the dire genetic effects certain to result from what one leading southern anatomist called the "protoplasmic mixing of the White and Negro races."[48]

The Scientific Counterattack

The Supreme Court's observation on the harmfulness of segregation to the hearts and minds of black children, by implication, struck at the central tenet of Social Darwinism—that different races were incapable of living together harmoniously. In response a number of right-wing social scientists still wedded to that theory insisted that racial prejudice was an inevitable characteristic of human beings, and, suddenly solicitous of the sensibilities of black children, they maintained that segregation sheltered them from the greater injuries certain to result from integration. Ernest van den Haag, a New York University professor who was a well-known conservative, for example, worried that the experience of being "resented and shunned personally and concretely by their white schoolmates throughout every day" would be much more humiliating to blacks than "a general abstract knowledge that they are separately educated because of white prejudice."[49] At the World Court's hearings on apartheid van den Haag would later explain that science had proven intergroup prejudice capable of reduction only through the enforcement of physical and social separation, a finding he offered as justification for apartheid in South Africa, segregation in the United States, and even denial of the ballot to blacks.[50]

A. James Gregor, a professor of social and political philosophy, was another social theorist with newfound concern over the welfare of blacks. According to Gregor, whenever Europeans had come into contact with darker-skinned peoples, the latter had always suffered extermination, enslavement, or subordination, a result he attributed to the inevitable preference of every "dominant" group for its own kind. Thus, he concluded, racial discrimination was "an elementary social fact," a problem "beyond the power of men to resolve," and past attempts "to accommodate peoples of visibly different race" in the same society had only produced great tragedy.[51] Integration, according to Gregor, was about to add yet another disastrous chapter to this record: it would create "insurmountable tensions" for the black child and—in words obviously chosen for their similarity to the Court's description of *segregation's* harm—"impair his personality in a manner never likely to be undone." As a model for a minority group's healthy development, Gregor offered the Guatemalan Indians, who suffered no impairment of personality even though segregated into an inferior status, because they had the good sense not to "attempt to identify with the upper caste and consequently do not suffer status frustrations, self-rejection, and its attendant liabilities."[52] To attain the same happy outcome for blacks, Gregor urged that they be "insulated in an all-Negro environment."[53]

The claim that integration would be injurious to blacks was the less important front in the counterattack on *Brown;* the major thrust was aimed at the social scientists' assertion that racial differences in scholastic performance were due not to innate intellectual differences between whites and blacks but to environmental handicaps inflicted on blacks, chief among them segregation. The first salvo in this assault was fired in 1956 by Frank C. McGurk, a professor of psychology at Villanova University, in *U.S. News and World Report,* which, during the struggle over integration, consistently featured articles written by or sympathetic to the scientific racists. An editor's introduction to McGurk's article called it "one of the few scientific studies in the field of psychology" on the subject of race differences. In fact, it was not a "study" at all; it was a review, a highly polemical one, of six actual studies of test performance conducted between 1935 and 1951. Comparing the differences between blacks and whites in these six cases with the difference in the World War I army tests, McGurk found no substantial reduction despite what he claimed were considerable intervening improvements in social and economic opportunities for blacks, and he concluded that environmental "manipulation" was of little value: "there is something more important, more basic, to the race problem than differences in external opportunity." Instead of facing these scientific facts, he continued, society had pursued a policy based first on wishful thinking and then on "distorting propaganda," and "when that, too, failed, we appealed to the legal machinery to do what nature what was not content to do."[54]

The McGurk article did not go unanswered, but the response persisted in the erroneous assumption that integration was, properly, a scientific issue. Just five weeks later *U.S. News and World Report* published a statement by eighteen prominent social scientists, many of whom had been involved in the desegregation cases, quoting expert opinion on racial differences in ability from both the UNESCO declaration and the appendix submitted to the Supreme Court.[55] Public discussion of the integration controversy now had at least one foot on the scientific turf, and again segregation's opponents had helped cooperate in this small victory for its defenders.

Exposing the "Equalitarian Dogma"

The McGurk article was just a skirmish; the full-scale offensive began a few years later, led by Henry E. Garrett, the most eminent scientific spokesman for segregation. Chair of the Psychology Department at Columbia for sixteen years before accepting a professorship at the University of Virginia, Garrett had also been president of the American Psychological Association, the Eastern Psychological Association, and the Psychometric Society; a fellow of the American Association for the Advancement of Science; and a member of the National Research Council. Garrett was the chair at Columbia when Kenneth Clark was a graduate student there, and the professor's opinion of the black doctoral candidate provides an interesting metaphor for the controversy over racial differences in IQ. Garrett judged Clark "none too bright . . . he was about a C student, but he'd rank pretty high for a Negro." Despite this dubious praise the C student would achieve much greater distinction than his chairman. Though author of a number of textbooks and unimaginative articles, Garrett made no lasting impact in his field and is virtually unknown to contemporary students, whereas Clark went on to write prizewinning books of enduring significance and to receive numerous honors, including the American Psychological Association's first Award for Distinguished Contributions to Psychology and two Gold Medal awards for Contribution by a Psychologist in the Public Interest.[56]

Though he had always believed blacks to be genetically less intelligent than whites, prior to *Brown* Garrett had expressed his views in the subdued language appropriate to professional journals. Test score differences between races, he acknowledged, were "subject to a number of interpretations," though the consistently lower performance of blacks made it "extremely unlikely" that "environmental opportunities can possibly explain *all* the differences."[57]

After the *Brown* decision, however, Garrett discarded all signs of moderation, his style changing from the cautiously professional to the intemperately polemical, as he championed the "scientific" defense of segregation. "No matter how low ... an American white may be," he now wrote in one of the leading scientific journals, "his ancestors built the civilizations of Europe, and no matter how high ... a Negro may be, his ancestors were (and his kinsmen still are) savages in an African jungle."[58] American blacks, he warned, were the "blood brothers" of Africans, who "grew up without towels, handkerchiefs and toilet paper."[59] Given this biological chasm between the races, Garrett decreed it completely "unsound" to treat "persons ... strictly as individuals"—it might seem "high-minded and tolerant," but "one simply cannot do this: a person is one thing or another, a Negro or a white man."[60] Segregation, he explained, was therefore a necessity, in part to protect the inferior blacks, many of whom were still "only a cut above savagery,"[61] but, more important, to prevent "widespread amalgamation," the real goal of the civil rights movement. The latter prospect was no less an obsession for Garrett than it was for less scientific segregationists. "The Negro has nothing to offer the white man," he exclaimed, and "should American whites under the emotional goading of various pressure groups become convinced that it is their 'duty' to absorb the Negroes now living in this country, our country would inevitably deteriorate intellectually, morally and materially. It is too great a risk to take in the name of abstract kindness. In fact, it could ... spell the difference between survival and destruction."[62] In response to such a threat Garrett predicted with approval that white parents would "teach their children to hate Negroes."[63]

At the moment, however, many people did not seem to appreciate these elementary truths, and in an article entitled "The Equalitarian Dogma" Garrett sought to unmask the systematic manipulation of science that had confused so much of the country and had culminated in the Supreme Court's decision. He began by recalling that not long ago a scientific consensus had judged "the Negro ... less intelligent and more indolent than the white, and ... lacking in the fundamental traits of honesty and reliability." Nevertheless, he observed, modern social scientists in alliance with sentimentalist humanitarians, social reformers, and "crusaders" had turned their backs on these common sense conclusions and now insisted that all races were potentially equal in ability. This shift had been accomplished, according to Garrett, by a massive barrage of propaganda that had pervaded the fields of psychology, anthropology, and genetics along with most of the media. As the primary source of this misinformation he named Franz Boas, a Columbia University professor of anthropology for almost forty years and one of the most influential voices in the discipline's change of emphasis from the importance of evolution to that of culture.[64] (Long the favorite villain of scientific racists, Boas had also been a personal target of Madison Grant's anti-Semitism.)[65] Additional sources of influence were "Jewish organizations," which exhibited a "preoccupation with racial matters," and "Communists and their frontmen in government, in entertainment, in radio and television." The "Equalitarian Dogma," concluded Garrett, was "at best . . . a misguided effort . . . [and] at worst . . . the scientific hoax of the century."[66]

First appearing in the *Mankind Quarterly,* a newly created and relatively unknown journal of ethnology published by and for racist social scientists, the article originally circulated to a very small and sectarian readership. It did, however, come to the attention of Dwight J. Ingle, chair of the Department of Physiology at the University of Chicago and editor of the prestigious journal *Perspectives in Biology and Medicine.*

Ingle had already publicly expressed his opposition to "the random mixing of races in schools and housing . . . [as] neither scientifically sound nor morally right." Then in his autobiography published two years later he described his personal experiences living in an integrated neighborhood near the university. His black neighbors were poor and uneducated, and Ingle himself detailed how absentee landlords would illegally subdivide large single houses into tiny apartments with exorbitant rents, bribing building inspectors to overlook violations. Nevertheless, he maintained that blacks purposely "crowd together to save rent money in order to drive a Cadillac." Moreover, after a neighborhood outcry over police brutality in the shooting of a black man, Ingle complained of the community's sympathy for criminals; having personally observed the incident, he explained that the officer had (justifiably) fired only because the suspect continued to yell after being ordered to keep quiet.[67] (*U.S. News and World Report* excerpted these few pages from Ingle's obscure autobiography and featured them in an article entitled "After Negroes Moved In . . . The Trials of a Community";[68] actually blacks had been living in the area for many years before the university decided to "redevelop" it.) Pinpointing the origin of these problems in the genes, Ingle proposed allowing only those few blacks with demonstrated character and intelligence into white neighborhoods and schools. Somewhat later, also fearful that interbreeding was being "encouraged as a means of solving racial problems," he warned of the "biological consequences" and possible "risk to civilization" from intermarriage between even "culturally and intellectually compatible" blacks and whites.[69] (Ingle's autobiography also suggested his scientific opinion on gender differences. With great compassion he described the "tragedy of a gifted girl," a graduate student with outstanding ability, respected and admired by everyone: she "would have preferred to be a wife and mother" but had decided instead to become a scientist because she was "devoid of breast development.")[70] Ingle's statements were later offered in evidence by Virginia's attorney general when that state's antimiscegenation law was challenged in court.[71]

Though more willing to make exceptions for a few extraordinary blacks, Ingle obviously shared many of Garrett's sentiments about the desirability of integration, and he purposefully moved to give the "Dogma" article greater exposure, publishing a slightly revised version in his own journal and providing it to *U.S. News and World Report* for reprint.[72] This segregationist screed seemed strangely out of place in the staid *Perspectives,* a periodical typically devoted to much more technical issues, but in an accompanying editorial Ingle explained that he had "invited and accepted" the essay, though its publication did not constitute endorsement. This pose enabled Ingle to have it both ways: the issue of genetic differences between blacks and whites and their relation to blacks' civil rights could be raised yet disowned, affording him the luxury of playing the detached mediator, who was only allowing all viewpoints to be heard.

If Garrett's rhetoric was too strident, however, it might not be possible for Ingle's (feigned) moderate posture to remain untarnished by the association; not even the disingenuous disclaimer of endorsement would shield him from censure for publishing racist extremism. So even while, as he would later admit, Ingle agreed with many of Garrett's points, he insisted that the "tone" be made more "dispassionate." (After two revisions by Garrett, Ingle was still not completely satisfied but "decided to go no further in requesting an author to say what I wanted him to say.")[73] A revised version thus appeared in *Perspectives* (and in *U.S. News and World Report*), omitting, for example, the references to "oversensitized" Jews and extensive Communist influence. Most important, Garrett added a qualification to the meaning of "equalitarian" so that it now referred only to the doctrine of *genetic* equality: "I do not intend the broader meaning: that of belief that all men should have equal political and social rights, a concept not debated here."[74] This conveyed the erroneous impression that Garrett believed in equal rights for all and only wished to raise the scientific question as a separate issue, when, of course, he was actually interested in the latter to justify deprivation of the former. Perhaps Garrett intended the rather oblique construction that the belief in equal rights, though debatable, would not be debated *here*—in his

article—but naive readers certainly assumed the more charitable interpretation. They were further encouraged to do so by Ingle's introduction,
which observed that "almost all scientists accept the principle of equal
legal and moral rights for the individual regardless of race," something he
knew to be absolutely untrue in Garrett's case.[75]

The controversy that ensued over the "Dogma" article in Ingle's own
journal rendered his position less credible. He continued to insist that
Garrett had only "called for continued debate and research," even in the
face of a new statement by Garrett that integration of "the black African,
over most of his history . . . a miserable creature, . . . would . . . level society down to a dead level of mediocrity."[76] To all questions about his own
motivation in soliciting the "Dogma" article, Ingle responded that only
unfettered research would produce the "fuller information about genetic
differences among races," which was the key to solving the nation's racial
difficulties.[77] The only specific example he offered of the usefulness of
such knowledge, however, was in dealing with the problem of "forced
desegregation," a phrase which in 1961, long before the controversy over
court-ordered busing, was no more than a euphemism for opposition to
blacks' rights to attend "white" schools or live in white neighborhoods.
These were moral and legal rights, unrelated in any way to the outcome
of research (and supposedly accepted by all scientists, according to
Ingle). Despite his distaste for Garrett's immoderate rhetoric, Ingle clearly
shared the belief that racial differences in ability should preclude blacks'
constitutional entitlements. Indeed, he would later drop much of the
pretense, terming integration an infringement on the right to "freedom of
association" and calling the increased percentage of blacks resulting from
integration of the Washington, D.C., public schools an "affront," which
the nation should not tolerate.[78]

Race and Reason Day in Mississippi

The equalitarian science behind integration was further exposed in 1961
by Carleton Putnam's book *Race and Reason*. In many ways a latter-day
Madison Grant, Putnam had studied history and politics at Princeton
before receiving a law degree from Columbia, had been an airline
executive for many years, and had authored a well-received biography of
Theodore Roosevelt's early years before turning his interest to anthropology.
In the latter area, like Grant, he viewed race as the key to history, with
Anglo-Saxons ranking first in the racial hierarchy. Unlike Grant, however,
Putnam saw the contemporary necessity of ignoring distinctions between
groups higher up on the racial pyramid in order to unite against the
blacks at the base.

Just as the immigration issue had been the catalyst for Grant's scientific efforts, the Supreme Court's ruling provoked Putnam's sudden activity. By his own account Putnam knew immediately and instinctively that the *Brown* decision was wrong; though himself a northerner, he realized that southerners loved blacks and had instituted "a way of life with the Negro that took his limitations into consideration with great kindness." He took no action personally until four years later, when he wrote a lengthy letter to President Dwight Eisenhower that was eventually printed in newspapers throughout the country as a paid advertisement from the "Putnam Letters Committee." The letter opposed all social, political, and legal equality between the races on the grounds that blacks had done nothing to "earn" these privileges. As further support for his position, Putnam cited Abraham Lincoln's desire to have "the superior position assigned to the white race" and his opposition to allowing blacks the ballot, service on a jury, or eligibility for public office.[79]

Although Putnam claimed that the thousands of responses drawn by his letter were overwhelmingly favorable, he was more interested in the 5 percent of the replies that disagreed with such self-evident wisdom. Most of the dissenters based their opposition on " 'modern' anthropology," and it was not until reading their comments that Putnam first grasped how cleverly the equalitarian "movement" had proceeded in its subversion of academia as well as government, "infiltrating first the sciences that surround anthropology, moving next into the more strictly social sciences, enthroning itself at last in the Supreme Court's desegregation order."[80]

In *Race and Reason* Putnam, like Garrett, identified the source of equalitarian thought as Franz Boas and "his disciples," all of them "members of a minority group."[81] The latter term the racist scientists reserved for Jews more than for blacks, as a kind of code phrase used to avoid accusations of overt anti-Semitism while still blaming integration on a Jewish, left-wing conspiracy. Supporters of the rights of blacks, wrote Garrett in a typical example, "mostly members of minority groups, seem willing to destroy Anglo-Saxon civilization because of real or fancied grievances."[82] Putnam regularly stressed the "minority" background of the major equalitarian scientists, noting that just a "cursory inspection of their names"—Chein, Dobzhansky, Hershkowitz, Klineberg, and others—"suggested the nature of the forces acting on most of these individuals." He even tracked down the marriage license for the anthropologist Ashley Montagu, the principal force behind the UNESCO statements who had long claimed that the whole concept of race was a social myth, finding, suggestively, that his original name was Israel Ehrenberg and his mother's name was Mary Plotnick.[83]

Putnam described how "Boas's group" had immigrated to the United

States in the late nineteenth century after "centuries of failure" in their struggle for freedom abroad, and not easily assimilated here either, they set out to demonstrate their own worth "by proving that *all* races were equal in adaptability to our white civilization." Settling largely in the urban centers of cultural dissemination in the Northeast, where they bred prolifically "not only in children but in ideas," they had "taken over" important academic positions and had achieved enormous influence in entertainment and mass communications. Impelled by what Putnam called the "double drive" of "out-group" resentment and socialist ideology, they had used their vantage points to mislead the nation into a policy that was "bound to weaken the white race as a whole." Only in the South, which could still claim a "purer concentration of those stocks . . . schooled in the Protestant Ethic," did Putnam see any hope for a bulwark against equalitarianism.[84]

Though it was predominantly Jews who furnished the ideology, they had an even more dangerous ally, according to Putnam—"the mulatto who was bent on making the nation a mulatto," whose disharmonic mixture of ambition and inadequacy made him unhappy with his own lot and a nuisance to everyone else. Putnam described the alliance between the mulatto and the "minority group" equalitarian as a coalition of "men who had nothing in common save a belief that they had a grudge against society." Nevertheless, he pointed out, almost every scientist who had influenced the Supreme Court had been from one of these two groups. To expect an impartial report on race from such people, Putnam wrote, was "like expecting a saloon keeper to prepare an impartial study on prohibition."[85]

Putnam had little to say about actual scientific details; the biological inferiority of blacks was, for him, just a matter of common sense, something that "any man with two eyes in his head" could observe. But if the truth was so obvious, how did such an overwhelming consensus to the contrary arise? Could not some scientists see what was so apparent to Putnam? In fact they could, he explained, but had been prevented from speaking out by equalitarian intimidation that had produced a virtual academic police state:

One prize-winning Northern scientist, whom I visited at his home in a Northern city asked me . . . whether I was sure I had not been followed. Another disclosed in the privacy of his study that he had evidence he was being checked by mulattoes at his lectures. All when first approached, were hesitant, withdrawn and fearful, and the reason was not far to seek. The employers on whom their livelihood depended—the universities, the museums, the foundations—were either controlled by equalitarians or intimidated by the race taboo. The scientists whom these institutions employed, if they were ever to hint at the truth, must do so deviously, under wraps over wraps, half seeming to say the opposite.

Though unwilling to divulge the names of any of these timid souls, Putnam, as "a man entirely independent of control," saw his own unavoidable obligation to broadcast the truth.[86] As he announced shortly after publication of *Race and Reason*, he was not himself an anthropologist but was speaking on behalf of "a muzzled group of scientists."[87] Such paranoia was obviously unfounded: McGurk, Garrett, and Ingle had encountered intense opposition from their fellow scientists, but no one ever threatened their "livelihood." Indeed, they would all escalate their attacks on equalitarianism without any occupational repercussions.

Of course, most important to Putnam were the social implications of these suppressed scientific truths, that blacks were not victimized by political oppression but by biology: "It is what he is that makes the average Negro a second class citizen, not segregation." Though Putnam acknowledged the existence of some intelligent blacks, he found these exceptions typically the result of "white genes" in their background. "A man may be as black as the ace of spades," he explained, "and still be a mixed blood with . . . relatively high intelligence, and other white attributes." When it came to the exercise of rights, however, "a race must be considered as a race," he insisted; "there is just no alternative to building the system around the average." This completely ruled out not only integration but also extension of the franchise to blacks, and in a later work Putnam noted with horror that some people actually proposed "to inject into the bloodstream of the body politic, without any control whatever, a virus of Negro votes which . . . is absolutely certain to undermine our 'constitution.' "[88]

Race and Reason sold sixty thousand copies within six months,[89] and many public officials in the South were quick to see the validity of Putnam's argument. In Louisiana the State Board of Education, referring to Putnam as an "eminent anthropologist," made the book compulsory reading for all college faculty and deans and for all students enrolled in anthropology, sociology, psychology, and a required course on "America vs. Communism." Recognizing that the sciences were being "distorted and perverted," the board's resolution took steps to squelch any equalitarian influence in Louisiana by mandating the content of science professors' courses. The Virginia legislature was also inspired by *Race and Reason* to introduce a resolution supporting segregation on the basis of scientific evidence of black inferiority. In Mississippi Governor Ross Barnett was so impressed by Putnam's work that he officially proclaimed October 26, 1961, "Race and Reason Day," an occasion to be observed throughout the state "by reading and discussing Race and Reason . . . and by participating in appropriate public functions." Quick to heed the governor's call, the (Jackson, Mississippi) Citizens' Council sponsored a film of Putnam's speech at a banquet held in his honor and soberly announced its distribution as part of "Project Understanding." In addition, southern senators, such as Georgia's Richard B. Russell and South Carolina's Strom Thurmond, endorsed the book, and Senator Harry F. Byrd from Virginia sent out free copies accompanied by a personal note of support.[90]

Putnam's book was not received quite as favorably by most scientists. One leading geneticist termed it a "murky tide" of pseudoscience pandering to race prejudice,[91] and two major professional organizations for anthropologists issued formal statements of condemnation. At its 1961 meeting the Council of the American Anthropological Association unanimously passed a resolution that "repudiates statements now appearing in the United States that Negroes are biologically and in innate mental ability inferior to whites, and reaffirms the fact that there is no scientifically established evidence to justify the exclusion of any race from the rights guaranteed by the Constitution. . . . All races possess the abilities needed to participate fully in the democratic way of life and in modern technological civilization."[92] This seemingly vigorous statement of opposition, in fact, implicitly accepted the scientific racists' underlying premise. An observation that "there is no scientifically established evidence" justifying the denial of a group's rights implied that science properly had some role in deciding who qualified for constitutional entitlements. If the Council of the American Anthropological Association maintained that "all races possess the abilities needed," while Garrett, Putnam, and others disagreed, then the issue remained an empirical rather than a moral question, thus prolonging the debate by focusing attention on the quality of each side's evidence.

The American Association of Physical Anthropologists adopted a resolution more to the point, deploring "the misuse of science to advocate racism. We condemn such writings as *Race and Reason* that urge the denial of basic rights to human beings . . . and we affirm . . . that there is nothing in science that justifies the denial of opportunities or rights to any group by virtue of race."[93] Putnam claimed that when asked for a show of hands, only three members of the association out of the more than seventy who voted on this resolution acknowledged having actually read his book.[94] If his account of this incident was accurate, the condemnation of a specific work by scientists unfamiliar with its contents was troubling, though the more general point in the resolution—the attempt to disavow any relevance of science to political equality—was appropriate even if no one had read Putnam's book.

Evolving Last, Evolving First

Only months after the publication of *Race and Reason* another assault on integration was launched by the retired medical professor Wesley Critz George, a distinguished scientist and former head of the department of anatomy at the University of North Carolina Medical School as well as president of the North Carolina Academy of Science. George was the recipient of a $3,000 grant from Alabama's Governor John Patterson—who had telegrammed President John Kennedy that the federal government would have to "invade" Alabama before a black would be admitted to its state university—in order to conduct a study of the scientific facts of race.[95] George began his resulting report, *The Biology of the Race Problem*, with the segregationists' standard framing of the issue: the Supreme Court had "based their decision in *Brown vs. Board of Education* upon 'science' and the opinions of 'authorities,'" thus making "the validity of their ruling dependent upon the truth and validity of their scientific material." More than the other scientific racists, however, he offered a detailed account of the "pertinent evidence" that the Court had neglected. Prior to his discussion of the facts, George reported having read in a UNESCO pamphlet the "dogmatic statement [that] 'such biological differences as exist between members of different ethnic groups have no relevance to problems of social and political organization,'" but he quickly dismissed this assertion as an "unproven and almost certainly untrue . . . thesis . . . supported mostly by tricks of writing, not by scientific investigation and the presentation of established facts."[96]

Some of the most important neglected evidence, according to George, came from his own area of expertise—research on brain anatomy, the physical bases for intellectual differences—and the most significant of these studies, he claimed, was a lengthy technical paper by Robert Bennet Bean published in 1906. In the tradition of the nineteenth-century craniometricians who had searched for the physiological indications of presumptive black inferiority, Bean claimed to have found such incredibly clear-cut racial differences in a number of measurements related to the size of the frontal lobe that he reported an error rate of only 6 per cent in determining race from an examination of an "unknown" brain. He also reported that on each measurement the blacks ranked just about midway between whites and "ourang-outangs." The "races are evidently opposites in cardinal points," Bean had concluded: "The one is subjective, the other objective; the one frontal, the other occipital or parietal; the one a great reasoner, the other emotional; the one domineering, but having great self control, the other meek and submissive, but violent and lacking self-control, especially when the passions are aroused, or any sudden danger appears; the one a greyhound, the other a bulldog."[97]

Despite such dramatic results, Bean must have felt a little self-conscious at the relatively trivial difference he found in overall brain weight between blacks and whites—a larger white brain was a cardinal tenet of craniometric thought at the time—and he explained in an "addenda" that the sample was composed predominantly of "high-class Negroes," including a number of "mulattoes and mixed bloods" but "low class" whites.[98]

The practical implications of Bean's work did not pass unnoticed at the time. An editorial in *American Medicine* immediately announced that blacks had been proven "more animal in type," suited more to the jungle than to civilization, and saw no likelihood of improvement, since "no amount of training will cause that brain to grow into Anglo-Saxon form." "It seems dreadful that we did not know these anatomical facts," continued the editorial, "when we placed a vote in the possession of this brain which cannot comprehend its use," but "now . . . it may be practicable to rectify the error."[99] In a popular magazine Bean himself concluded that it was "useless to try to elevate the negro by education," especially those blacks with "projecting masses of fat about the buttock," who had "the smallest brain of all human beings."[100]

The "perfection" of Bean's data had led Franklin P. Mall, his superior at the Johns Hopkins Anatomical Laboratory, to collect the same measurements on a large number of brains, many of them from the original sample. Mall, however, employed an important change in the procedure: "in order to exclude my own personal equation," he made all measurements *before* identifying the race of the specimens from laboratory records. Using this "blind" method, he obtained considerably different results, finding no racial distinction in the weight or size of the frontal lobe, even on the same specimens that had been previously measured by Bean.[101] Mall's refutation, published in 1909 in the same scientific journal in which the original article appeared, produced little change in the opinion of those who had found such practical significance in Bean's data. It certainly made no difference to George, who noted Mall's failure to confirm the earlier results but attributed it to an unrepresentative sample of blacks that probably included mulattoes.[102] This was rather ironic in view of the fact that Bean had blamed the small racial difference in brain weight on the excessive number of mulattoes in *his* sample.

When George came to discuss the origin of racial differences, however, he could cite a much more impressive and contemporary authority. Only months after completion of the anatomist's report, Carleton Putnam's cousin, Carleton S. Coon, professor of anthropology at the University of Pennsylvania and president of the American Association of Physical Anthropologists, would publish a book claiming that different portions of *homo erectus,* the immediate ancestor of *homo sapiens,* had evolved into the latter state at different times, as each of the five main subspecies or races crossed the genetic threshold separately. According to this theory, the Caucausoid race, the forerunners of contemporary whites, passed this critical point some 200,000 years prior to the ancestors of modern blacks, the Congoids, who only became *sapiens* some 40,000 to 50,000 years ago. Since the group that had crossed the evolutionary threshold earliest had thus evolved the most, Coon suggested a correlation between the amount of time a subspecies had actually existed as *homo sapiens* and the level of civilization attained by its members.[103] Though it contained no allusion to contemporary social problems, this new work arrived at a convenient moment for the segregationists. (Putnam implied that his cousin was sympathetic to the South's cause but did not join the struggle because "his position as dean of the world's physical anthropologists deserved detachment.")[104] Even before its publication Putnam issued a new pamphlet—which George then summarized in his own report— explaining Coon's proven "fact" that whites had an evolutionary lead of 200,000 years over blacks.[105] Few other scientists, however, found the evidence for this speculative thesis persuasive, and reviewers pointed out numerous inaccuracies and inconsistencies in the argument. (The fossil evidence since then has strongly suggested an African origin for both *homo sapiens* and *homo erectus,* and "restriction mapping" analysis of mitochondrial DNA has traced the origin of the human gene pool to a sub-Saharan African female.)[106]

Aside from the scientific merits of Coon's theory, George's use of it provided a nice example of the racists' flexibility. Robert Bennet Bean, whose 1906 investigation of the frontal lobes had been so dispositive for George, went on to publish a more comprehensive racial study, including not only brain comparisons but also new observations on emotional and behavioral differences. He found, for example, that the "finely modulated expressions of the White Race denote a responsive neuro-mechanism, well differentiated muscles, and thin elastic skin," in contrast to the "less differentiated, coarse bundles of facial muscles . . . in the Black Race as well as the great thickness of the lips and skin," which only allowed "contractions of a primitive type." To illustrate the latter, Bean presented an incredible photograph of a mugging face entitled "Laughing Negro," in which "the bulky lips are pulled upward and outward, the large teeth are exposed in contrast with the black face, and instead of a graded smile or laugh we notice the broad grin characteristic of the Black Race." The primitiveness of these expressions, along with the differences in frontal lobe development and other indications of blacks' inferiority, he attributed to their *earlier* evolutionary development.[107] For many scientists of Bean's era this had been the commonly accepted explanation: having evolved long before whites, blacks were biologically more similar to their anthropoid predecessors and were thus "more primitive" mentally and physically.[108] There was little doubt that George could just as easily have offered the older theory as compelling evidence for black inferiority, had Coon's new thesis not presented the opportunity to exploit the anthropologist's prestige.

Unsurprisingly, George found the social implications of his evidence inescapable: it was of the utmost importance to avoid integration, a program that would endanger the society by commingling "the genes of the Negro race with those of the White race." He acknowledged that there were "some fine and able Negroes" but, in stylish prose, stressed that "one swallow does not make a summer, and a few intelligent Negroes do not make a race." This implied no reluctance on George's part to recognize the worth of those few, though. "To be sure," he observed, "we should value every man according to his merit—within his own race," that is, as long as blacks were not admitted into "those areas of Caucasian life where mates are chosen." For George, however, if a black was dissatisfied with such a restriction, there was "a question as to whether he honestly wants legitimate 'opportunity' or actually wants racial amalgamation."[109]

George concluded his "impartial study" with a description of the Boas school and its pervasive influence on modern thought. In particular, he noted, all freshmen at the University of North Carolina were enrolled in a course whose first required reading was a "race tract" by the well-known social psychologist Otto Klineberg, "one of the principal producers of shoddy integration propaganda." With an air of vindication he reported finding three full shelves of this work on reserve in the library to begin the mass indoctrination of unsuspecting freshmen. Just to be certain about the matter, George even decided to read the article, only to have his worst fears confirmed: Klineberg's paper was "without scholarly merit and without literary charm or virtue."[110]

In response to George's report the American Association for the Advancement of Science's Committee on Science in the Promotion of Human Welfare issued a statement emphasizing that racial differences in ability were irrelevant to "axiomatic" political principles. It was also severely critical of George's decision to eschew publication of his work in the scientific literature, where it could be subjected to the scrutiny of his peers, in favor of preparing it for an obviously partisan political agency. The committee did not, however, rule science out of the civil rights controversy altogether; it still maintained that the Court had relied on scientific evidence for its finding of injury to the "hearts and minds" of black children, and it suggested that "contrary evidence regarding the *effects* of segregation on Negroes" was indeed relevant to the constitutional question.[111] This was an unfortunate concession. The segregationists had no scarcity of "facts" on this issue either.

Rehearing the Evidence

With the release of George's report to the governor of Alabama in October 1962, the segregationist scientists felt ready for their day in court. Despite what Putnam called "all the power of the educational establishment, all the massive and saturating influences of a vast Negrophile news and entertainment media, all the cunning of politicians," the segregationists were hopeful that the "truth" would still prevail if the "deceitful" evidence offered to the Supreme Court was exposed and the decisive scientific proof presented.[112] Putnam produced a new open letter—this time to President Kennedy—which was displayed in a full-page ad in the *New York Times*. At a time when federal troops had been required to allow a Mississippi black man to enroll in his own state university, the letter blamed "the cause of our trouble [on] . . . the incomplete and partisan nature of the evidence on which the Supreme Court's decision in 1954 was based," and it asked Kennedy to read George's report personally and "clear the way to the Supreme Court for a new case based on it, as well as upon voluminous other evidence now being assembled in various cases soon to be initiated in the lower courts. Meanwhile, fairness would seem to demand that, until such a case has been heard, enforcement proceedings under the 1954 decision be kept as charitable as possible."[113]

The first and most important judicial challenge to *Brown* came in *Stell v. the Savannah Board of Education*. Over eight years after *Brown* the public schools in Savannah, Georgia, were still completely segregated, and the NAACP filed suit requesting a federal court order that would compel immediate desegregation. After this action had been initiated, a group of white parents entered the case as "intervenors," claiming that the defendant board of education did not adequately represent their children's interests. According to their own petition, the intervenors were "Whites, sharing a common biological origin, cultural heritage and consciousness of kind," who charged that their children would be "forcibly compelled to associate with plaintiffs and others of their ethnic group" in the public schools.[114] It quickly became clear that use of this third party was the tactical device for a presentation of the scientific opposition to *Brown*.

The *Stell* case became a warped mirror image of *Brown*. This time the segregationists based *their* position on the alleged educational impairment of both black and white children and the psychological harm resulting from integrated schools, while the plaintiffs objected to the introduction of testimony on these points, claiming that the issues had already been decided in *Brown*, which was binding on the present case. The segregationists, however, had carefully chosen *Stell* for intervention, knowing that Frank M. Scarlett, the presiding judge, was one of their strongest allies on the bench. To rule on the plaintiffs' position, he found it "essential to consider the legal parameters" of the *Brown* decision, and his review of the exact language in that opinion led Scarlett to the conclusion that the determination of injury caused by segregation had been a finding of fact: the Supreme Court's conclusion that separate schools adversely affect the learning process had been based on evidence, not case law. In Scarlett's opinion, it was therefore appropriate to treat a similar claim in *Stell* as likewise subject to proof or disproof by the introduction of evidence, and he overruled all the NAACP's objections.[115] If one accepted the significance of the social science evidence in the original decision, the judge's position was not completely unreasonable. Though informed by different sympathies, it was the logical extension of the claims made by so many vigorous supporters of the *Brown* decision who had agreed—even boasted—that the Court had accepted scientific testimony as the definitive evidence for the fact of segregation's harmful effects.

The resulting testimony in *Stell* was remarkably devoid of the segregationists' usual invective, omitting any mention of interracial mating, accusations of equalitarian conspiracy, or references to blacks as savages. Instead, the expert witnesses for the intervenors presented a systematic and relatively unemotional attack on every one of the allegations that had been made by the social scientists in the *Brown* cases. R. Travis Osborne, a professor of psychology at the University of Georgia, began with a series of test score comparisons between black and white students at various grade levels in the rigidly segregated Savannah school system, all of which showed that the black students scored lower than their white peers. Garrett followed Osborne with testimony that these differences in educability were inherent and could not be substantially altered by environmental changes of any kind. Then George reviewed the brain anatomy studies from his report for the governor of Alabama and cited Coon's thesis for the genesis of racial differences. Finally, van den Haag testified that prejudice would increase rather than decrease as a result of "non-voluntary" contact between racial groups, creating a tension in the classroom that would multiply disciplinary problems and harm the educational process for everyone. Even more severe, the social theorist claimed, was the injury that integration would inflict specifically on blacks, who would develop a "collective neurosis" from failure to establish an appropriate and healthy identification with their own group. If schools were structured by educational achievement so that only the superior black children, whose existence was acknowledged even by Osborne and Garrett, were placed in integrated classes, that would be the worst solution of all in van den Haag's view, leading to "pathological disturbance" in these few capable black students and intensified feelings of rejection among the rest, now deprived of their "natural leadership."[116] Viewed as a whole, the testimony of the expert witnesses not only provided a rebuttal to the scientific evidence in *Brown* but also precluded every possible scheme for allowing a white child and a black child into the same classroom.

Judge Scarlett's opinion was predictably favorable to the segregationists. He quoted extensively from their witnesses and included their charts and references—the Bean study, Coon's book, the McGurk article, and many others. His findings were almost identical with their own conclusions: integration would seriously injure both black and white students and adversely affect the public school system.

Despite this favorable outcome for their side, the segregationists were not entirely pleased with the result in *Stell*. Putnam had looked forward to seeing the equalitarians squirm when faced with the "evidence" of their own deceit, and he seemed deeply disappointed that no scientific witnesses appeared for the plaintiffs, an omission he interpreted as a "confession . . . that cross examination . . . under oath was something they dared not risk." He also complained about the lack of press coverage: only one national magazine, *U.S. News and World Report* (ever sympathetic), covered the case in detail, printing the entire text of Judge Scarlett's conclusions. Aside from the ruling itself, there was, however, one other moment of satisfaction for Putnam. As George rendered his testimony on "just *what it was* the Negro inherited," Putnam suddenly realized that Constance Baker Motley, the NAACP's "mulatto lawyer," was "weeping audibly."[117]

Of course, the United States Court of Appeals for the Fifth Circuit would not allow Scarlett to stand *Brown* on its head and ordered him to implement the Supreme Court's decision, notwithstanding his personal conclusions about the facts or the law of the case. It also clarified for him that segregated schools had been proscribed in *Brown*, not on the basis of the scientific facts but because racially separate schools constituted a violation of the equal protection of the law guaranteed by the Fourteenth Amendment.[118] The Supreme Court's subsequent refusal to hear *Stell* on appeal was anticlimactic.

Although there were other court battles before sympathetic southern judges, none of them dared to uphold segregation after the reversal of Scarlett's ruling and the reprimand for his abuse of discretion. In the *Evers* case, for example, named for the daughter of slain civil rights leader Medgar Evers, another set of intervenors presented a scientific attack similar to the testimony in *Stell* to a Mississippi district court. Judge Sidney Mize's subsequent opinion agreed with all the segregationist assertions and noted that "the facts in this case 'cry out' for a reappraisal and complete reconsideration" of the *Brown* ruling, but he was not rash enough to permit this conclusion to affect his own decision. Even though Mize judged integration of the Jackson schools to be contrary to the facts and the law, he had no choice but to order it.[119]

Having been soundly defeated in the court system, some of the scientists still attempted to make their case directly to the public through hateful leaflets. Much of this literature was authored by Garrett, who would spend the remaining years of his life spewing out a series of ugly pamphlets distributed by various anti-integration organizations. In one the psychologist claimed that a "normal" black resembled a European after frontal lobotomy.[120] Another, entitled *How Classroom Desegregation Will Work,* was sent to half a million public schoolteachers in 1965–66. Along with the usual warnings against intellectual deterioration and intermarriage, it included a photograph of a smiling, white elementary schoolgirl surrounded by cheerful black playmates. This innocuous image of racial harmony was captioned "Will YOUR Child Be Exposed to THIS?"[121] In a *Newsweek* interview about the pamphlet Garrett denied that he was a racist or hatemonger, observing, in dubious support of his claim, that "those black Africans are fine muscular animals when they're not diseased."[122] In *Breeding Down,* yet another Garrett booklet distributed gratis to hundreds of thousands of teachers, the former president of the American Psychological Association explained that the civil rights movement's strategy for blacks to attain equality with superior whites was to make whites "Negroid" through mongrelization.[123] Even in the year of his death, almost two decades after the *Brown* decision, Garrett was still trying to turn back the civil rights clock with a pamphlet entitled *IQ and Racial Differences,* which was advertised two years later in the *Boston Globe* at the height of that city's strife over school busing.[124] In addition to the old arguments about black inferiority, he attacked the "one-man one-vote" principle as another unscientific, equalitarian device, ensuring "that the vote of the feeble-minded person counts as much as that of an intelligent man." Garrett's language was almost identical with Henry H. Goddard's observation sixty years earlier that "an imbecile who knows nothing of civic matters can annul the vote of the most intelligent citizen."[125] Democracy, like integration, could not withstand scientific scrutiny.

The Recrudescent Right

The scientific campaign against integration was more than just an attempt to preserve American apartheid; it also provided the first opportunity since the prewar period for far-right-wing scholars and scientists to promote essentially Nazi ideology—though with a distinctly American flavor—by focusing primarily on blacks' inferiority while retaining a more Machiavellian role for Jews behind the scenes. A cornerstone of National Socialist thought had been that Jews wished to deny the existence of racial differences. According to Lenz, their desire that "there should be no unbridgeable racial distinctions" would allow Jews to participate in Aryan civilization without being "looked upon as aliens."[126] Hitler's more sinister interpretation had claimed that the Jew preached the "equality of all men without regard to race and color" in order to "mask his activity and lull his victims" while pursuing his "real aim of ruining the hated white race, . . . throwing it down from its cultural and political height, and himself rising to be its master."[127] The equalitarian conspiracy described by Garrett and Putnam—a group of Jewish scientists had spread a myth of racial equality to foster the integration and acceptance of blacks, inevitably producing the decay of American society and culture—followed nicely in this tradition. Indeed, Putnam's *Race and Reason* would become a part of the American Nazi canon, a "classic" work that would influence the thought of such new extremists as David Duke and Tom Metzger and is still highly recommended by contemporary Nazi publications.[128] Much of the scientific opposition to *Brown* thus saw the debate over black inferiority as a wedge for the introduction of a broader agenda involving race and eugenics.

From Preserving "Freedom of Choice" to
Advancing "Ethnology and Eugenics"

In 1959 a number of scientists with this Radical Right perspective moved to give it organizational form. A key member of the group was Robert E. Kuttner, a researcher trained in zoology and biochemistry but also a prominent member of the Liberty Lobby, an umbrella organization for neo-Nazi politics, founded in 1955 by one of the most influential figures in Far Right politics, Willis A. Carto, who considered "Hitler's defeat . . . the defeat of Europe and America." Liberty Lobby's theory was based on Francis Parker Yockey's view of the Jews as "culture distorters," conspiring to destroy the racial basis of Western civilization; Yockey's *Imperium,* dedicated to "the Hero of the Second World War" (i.e., Hitler) and published by Carto's Noontide Press with an introduction by Carto himself, has been called the "neo-*Mein Kampf* for neo-Nazis." The Lobby's initial political program was based on Klansman Ernest Sevier Cox's plan to send blacks back to Africa, a proposal Carto termed "the strongest blow against the power of organized Jewry."[129]

It was as a spokesman for the Liberty Lobby that Kuttner appeared before the House Committee on the Judiciary in 1963 during its discussion of impending civil rights legislation. Reminding the committee that he was testifying "as a scientist," he described how "compulsory tolerance" of a racial group had always produced hostility. As an example of this inevitable result, Kuttner cited the treatment of "European minorities" by the Germans, resentful at being forced to accept people whose presence they had previously tolerated without compulsion; and "perhaps we should consider," he concluded, "that they had justice on their side."[130] The implication was clear and ominous: civil rights legislation would justifiably turn white benign neglect into a holocaust.

On other occasions Kuttner seemed intent on encouraging such an unhappy outcome. In an address to the New Orleans Leadership Conference, for example, he explained how integration promoted the use of "white girls . . . [as] *the major economic resource of the ghetto male*":

> If you have a drug habit costing $60 or $80 a day, you can survive only if you catch a white girl. And if you want to keep her, you better put her on a habit too, because when she wakes up, she'll run back to mother with her brown baby, if mother will take her. . . . Believe me, no Black male can steal enough color TV's out of hotels to support a drug habit. You can't rob pension checks off senior citizens except one day a month, when the mail brings the check. . . . You can't rob liquor stores and grocery stores forever. . . . The only answer is to catch a white girl, and integration makes that much easier today.[131]

Moreover, soon after the Liberty Lobby acquired *American Mercury* — which replaced *Western Destiny, Northern World, Folk,* and *Right,* all recently "suspended" Lobby publications dedicated to Nordic superiority[132] — turning it into what one historian called a "blatantly Hitlerian" periodical, Kuttner, a member of the new editorial staff, contributed an article describing how whites had once endured the harshest slavery but had earned their freedom through use of "the White man's brain and stamina and determination." In contrast, he noted, blacks had "enjoyed a slavery unparalleled in history for mildness and humanity" but still could not gain their own freedom and had to wait "passively" for liberation until it was "handed" to them.[133]

Another central participant in creating the new scientific organization was A. James Gregor (previously Gimigliano), then professor of philosophy and political science at the University of Hawaii but later to become a well-known political scientist at Berkeley and the Hoover Institute. At the time he had just published an article filled with glowing praise for the "last phase" of National Socialism, not the earlier "tragi-comic image of hysterical Nordicism" but the "far more profound theory" of the late 1930s, "all to [sic] little known outside the immediate intellectual circle which fostered it." According to Gregor, this more mature approach to race instituted by Hitler was a "scientifically sound and emotionally satisfying" philosophy, no longer concerned with superiority or inferiority but rather with the creation of a racial ideal "as an archetype for an entire civilization." A Mediterranean could thus be, for example, just as courageous as a Nordic but in a "Mediterranean fashion," not in a "Nordic fashion." With obvious exuberance Gregor discussed the implications of this racial ideal for its "political expression, . . . Nationhood": for Germany there was a "Nordic mythos"; for Italy, "an animating devotion of Romanita." He did not speculate on what this "scientifically sound and emotionally satisfying" theory had offered for Jews or Gypsies.[134]

In February 1959 Kuttner, Gregor, Henry Garrett, and some half-dozen others, including the Liberty Lobby attorney Alfred Avins, filed a certificate of incorporation in Queens, New York, for an organization called the Association for the Preservation of Freedom of Choice. Listed as the purposes of this group were the promotion of an individual's right "to associate with only those persons with whom he desires to associate" and the provision of aid and encouragement for scientific research on intergroup relations, ethnic characteristics, and their implications for freedom of choice. Approval for the certificate was denied by Queens County Supreme Court Judge J. Irwin Shapiro, who characterized the avowed purposes as "the negation of a whole series of fundamental and basic rights . . . vouchsafed to *everyone* by the United States Constitution." Terming the "Aesopian language" of the certificate a "cloak" for the real aim of the organization—to deny to certain segments of the population the right to ride, work, play, eat, study, or worship where they desired—he ruled that the law should not be used to further such "malevolent purpose." As the association's lawyer, Avins submitted a response, claiming that only "unreasonable" discrimination based on race or creed was offensive to public policy and offering the refusal to rent an apartment to an individual for reasons of race as an example of discrimination that was both reasonable and desirable. Citing Avins's response as the proof for what had at first been only an inference, Shapiro concluded that the association was nothing more than a "hate group."[135]

Having been rebuffed in its attempt to form an organization, substantially the same group, again with Avins as its counsel, tried in a different venue, this time incorporating in Maryland as the International Association for the Advancement of Ethnology and Eugenics (IAAEE). The formal statement of purpose now omitted all language concerning free association, stressing instead the desire to "effectuate a betterment and enhancement . . . of the various peoples, stocks, races, ethnic and cultural groups" by applying the findings of eugenics, ethnology, history, prehistory, archaeology, and a host of other sciences. According to its charter, to accomplish this purpose, the IAAEE would publish and disseminate appropriate writings and would provide assistance "in any lawful manner" to others with an interest in such problems.[136]

The IAAEE literature listed a thirty-four-person "Executive Committee." In addition to Kuttner, who became the association's president, and Gregor, its secretary, the committee included Garrett and every other scientist who would later appear as an expert witness in the *Stell* case. European and South African scientists were also members, reflecting an alliance between American segregationists and neo-Nazi elements abroad. Another well-known committee member was Charles Callan Tansill, a professor of history at Georgetown University who had delivered such a vehement denunciation of Abraham Lincoln in 1947 that even some die-hard segregationists were embarrassed.[137] Tansill had also opposed U.S. entry into World War II and even after the war continued to blame that "slippery" politician in the White House for involving the United States in the struggle against Hitler, who, according to the historian, only wished to halt the spread of communism.[138] Though Tansill had not been involved in the IAAEE's incorporation effort, after his death in 1964 his name was strangely elevated from membership on the Executive Committee to prominent display as the association's "founder." As other members of the committee passed away during the next few years, they too were posthumously elevated to a similar status, and soon the IAAEE boasted five "founders," all conveniently deceased.[139]

In addition to his role as an incorporator and a member of the Executive Committee, Garrett was probably instrumental in obtaining financial assistance for the association. At the time of its creation he was also a member of a committee (along with Francis E. Walter, chairman of the House Un-American Affairs Committee, and Mississippi's Senator James O. Eastland) that distributed grants for the Pioneer Fund, a private trust fund established in 1937 by the Massachusetts textile millionaire Wycliffe Preston Draper to promote "race betterment" by funding research and also by providing aid for the education of children "descended predominantly from white persons who settled in the original thirteen states . . . and/or from related stocks."[140] Along with Draper, the original directors of the fund had been Harry Hamilton Laughlin, the old "expert eugenics agent" for the House Committee on Immigration, and Frederick H. Osborn, another virulently anti-immigrant eugenicist, who had contributed the preface to Madison Grant's *Passing of the Great Race.* By the time of the IAAEE's founding, however, the immigrant invasion had been replaced by the civil rights movement as the major threat to "race betterment," and Draper himself offered grant money to a number of leading geneticists for studies that would prove the inferiority of blacks and promote their repatriation to Africa.[141] Garrett acknowledged having placed several grants himself, explaining that they were necessary because "objective" research was not possible in equalitarian-controlled university departments. It was highly probable that one of those grants went to the IAAEE, an organization that had the stated aim of "restoring freedom of inquiry to . . . the study of race and race relations" and that Garrett himself had helped create.[142] Moreover, the foundation had expressed special interest in the racial incompatibility of blood transfusions—not a topic considered worthy of serious concern by the medical research community—and the very first volume of a journal sponsored by the IAAEE published a study concluding that blood donors should only come from the same ethnic group as the patient's.[143]

"A Free and Open Discussion"

The IAAEE's first and most significant activity was promotion of the *Mankind Quarterly*, a new professional journal in the field of race and ethnology. In his announcement of the *Quarterly*'s creation, Gregor, the IAAEE secretary, explained that its purposes were to "permit a free and open discussion of racial and related problems" and to "re-open the American academic world . . . to European scientific and speculative thought." Behind this scholarly sounding rhetoric would be a journal devoted to the ideology that different racial groups were not "scientifically" entitled to the same rights. The *Mankind Quarterly* thus provided a respectable academic platform for opinions that were previously more likely to be expressed in the Ku Klux Klan or the Nazi party.

The *Quarterly*'s editor in chief was the Scottish physical anthropologist and member of the IAAEE Executive Committee Robert Gayre of Gayre, a name implying some kind of baronial background. (Fittingly, Gayre was also a herald—a specialist in the family pedigrees, genealogy, and art history underlying coats of arms.) In the midst of the war he had authored a book filled with photographic examples of the European races taken directly from "Professor Hans F. K. Günther's authoritative work on German racial science" to assist in distinguishing "Nordic types" from other races so the boundary between Germany and Poland could be redrawn to achieve "*racial* stability." The revised boundary, Gayre had explained, would make the "Slav states . . . basically more Alpine [and] the Germans . . . considerably more Nordic."[144] While editor of the *Mankind Quarterly*, Gayre was also involved with the Northern League, an organization founded as a postwar rallying point for Nazi intellectuals.[145] When the league's founder, Roger Pearson, translated some of Günther's writings on "Aryan religion," Gayre rendered fulsome praise on the posthumous work and boasted of his own prewar acquaintance with the great German "expert."[146] Actually, Gayre tended more toward Strasserist nazism, named after Hitler's opponents within the Nazi movement, Gregor and Otto Strasser, which emphasized the "socialism" in National Socialism, rejecting both communism and capitalism as Jewish-dominated systems that had to be overthrown in favor of an approach based on white racial solidarity. Although he bristled over any attempt to link his journal to nazism,[147] Gayre once commented on the unfortunate general perception of the term "Nazi" as synonymous with "Hitlerian Nazi," an observation that readers unaware of these fine distinctions on the Right must have found somewhat puzzling.[148]

Under Gayre's editorship the *Mankind Quarterly* listed Gregor and Kuttner as assistant editors (among others) and two "honorary associate editors"—Garrett and R. Ruggles Gates, a British geneticist who had been involved in the eugenics movement for over forty years and had contributed to the prewar German literature on *Rassenhygiene*. Although he had been well respected for his work in cytology, Gates had squandered much of his career on an unsuccessful attempt to convince his discipline that the different races were actually five separate species. With such a view, naturally he opposed race crossing and in the 1920s had promoted all the warnings of disharmonic mixture.[149] A decade later he was often cited as the scientific authority for "biology's warning against intermarriages between Jews and those of Germanic . . . race."[150] After the war he promoted the baseless claim that the Rh-negative gene, "which is responsible for the deaths of countless Caucasian infants and foetuses," was a result of "prehistoric crossings between the Basques and people speaking the Indo-European languages."[151] Gates died only a year after the *Mankind Quarterly*'s appearance (thus becoming a founder of the IAAEE), and the Italian sociologist Corrado Gini replaced him as an honorary associate editor. A fascist sympathizer and former scientific adviser to Mussolini, Gini, like Gates, had been active in eugenics since its early days and had also contributed to the Reich's journals on *Rassenhygiene*.

The first volume of the *Mankind Quarterly* left no doubt about its ideological posture. Gayre's introductory editorial noted with regret the neglect of "racial aspects of man's inheritance . . . during the last two decades," the period since the Nazi writings on race. One article explained that the presence of "different races . . . in the same community . . . automatically provoked" hostility because "each group is endangering the genetic integrity of the other."[152] Particularly unusual for a scientific journal, another article was a reprint of a work originally published fourteen years earlier at the end of World War II by E. Raymond Hall, a vice president of the American Association for the Advancement of Science, occupant of an endowed chair as Distinguished Professor of Zoology, director of the Museum of Natural History of the University of Kansas, and coauthor of the two-volume *Mammals of North America,* the standard reference on the topic. At the time Hall had desired to apply his knowledge of zoology to "racial and international problems at the peace table." Noting the law of nature that whenever two "subspecies" attempted to exist in the same geographic area, the one from the smaller land mass suffered extinction, he concluded that "permitting the immigration of Orientals, and . . . granting citizenship . . . to Orientals . . . violates every biological law . . . that relates to harmonious existence. . . . To imagine one subspecies of man living together on equal terms for long with another subspecies is but wishful thinking and leads only to disaster and oblivion for one or the other." As a consequence, Hall proposed the "deportation of 'invaders' " and the restriction of "citizenship rights to one subspecies only," a policy, he observed, that had already been sensibly implemented for American Indians by the establishment of reservations.[153] Immediately after the first issue appeared, the Yugoslavian anthropologist Bozo Skerlj, who had been named to the *Quarterly's* honorary advisory board, resigned from the position, explaining that the abuse of anthropology in the interest of racial prejudice was offensive to him not just as a scientist but also as a former prisoner at Dachau. In accepting the resignation, Gates noted that Skerlj would never have been considered for membership on the board had the journal known of his "harrowing experience," which "naturally had such an effect on [his] mental outlook."[154]

The *Mankind Quarterly* churned out a steady stream of scientific racism. The largest number of articles, of course, concerned blacks in the United States. One complained of the "Negrophile . . . perversion of history and the social sciences," which "palm[s] off colored mediocrities as statesmen and geniuses";[155] another proposed restricting the participation of blacks in the polity because it was "obvious that the Negro in the United States is . . . inferior" and "even if . . . of adequate intelligence he may be temperamentally unsuited for citizenship";[156] yet another contrasted the Western commitment to exploration and the pursuit of knowledge with the essence of "Negritude," expressed in a "cry" from Martinique: "Hurray for those who have never invented anything, Hurray for those who have never explored anything, Hurray for those who have never conquered anything."[157] Some contributors, however, took a larger view of racial conflict in the world. A reprise of T. Lothrop Stoddard's warning in *The Rising Tide of Color* predicted an inevitable "ultimate conflict" for "world dominance" between "the White and Yellow races," in which "the other races and mixtures will be used by one side or the other when to do so will bring benefits and . . . [will be] annihilated by one side or the other when they become an obstruction." To prepare for this impending struggle, the author urged the immediate reunification of Germany—over the opposition of those "selfish minority interest[s]"—so that the vast "white" forces on each side of the Iron Curtain could be freed for more sensible deployment.[158]

In addition to its own articles, the *Quarterly* heaped praise on every racial extremist. When Ku Klux Klansman Ernest Sevier Cox's thirty-year-old book *White America,* containing a proposal to send all blacks back to Africa, was reissued after his death by the Liberty Lobby's Noontide Press, the *Mankind Quarterly* called it "a classic book by this truly great man" and noted that the book's "greatest contribution" was its "practical solution" for keeping the United States white.[159] The Englishman H. B. Isherwood, himself a Northern League member and author of a number of ugly pamphlets on race, warmly recommended Geryke Young's *Two Worlds—Not One,* a book dividing all humans into Eastern "Subjectives"—including "Mongoloids, Negroids and Semites"—and Western "Objectives"—the "White" world—finding the former unfit by their "innate nature" to associate with the latter on equal terms.[160] "A Japanese or Indian conducting Beethoven or Verdi, a Chinese playing Chopin, or . . . Negro opera singers should offend our sense of truth," Young had written, "because of the underlying cultural incompatibilities." (Only months after the publication of Young's book, the South African Broadcasting Company did indeed bar four nonwhites from a Beethoven contest there on the grounds that "different races perform best in their own idioms.")[161] Occasionally, however, the sharp-eyed Gayre could find some fault in an otherwise commendable work. For example, in his review of *Christianity and the Survival of the West* by Revilo P. Oliver, a founding member of the John Birch Society who eventually became too anti-Semitic even for that organization, Gayre generally praised the book for demonstrating Christianity's roots among Nordics—all the disciples except Judas Iscariot had fair skin, according to Gayre—yet he found some of Oliver's claims "too sweeping"—like the observation that "there are some non-Europeans who are sincere Christians."[162] In the *Mankind Quarterly* race, not grace, was the route to all salvation.

Sharing Science

In addition to its promotion of the *Mankind Quarterly,* the IAAEE was involved in two other projects at the time: publication of a series of monographs and reprints of articles, many of which had originally appeared in the *Quarterly,* and sponsorship of one other, more sophisticated, collection of essays, *Race and Modern Science.* When Gregor announced the association's founding in 1961, he noted that its principal project at the time was the compilation of a symposium on race, resulting in a book that was to appear later that year.[163] Though *Race and Modern Science* was not published until 1967—and with no mention of the association—there was little doubt that it was the work alluded to by Gregor: it was edited by Kuttner, the IAAEE president; included sixteen invited contributions, all but three of which came from members of the Executive Committee; was advertised for the next decade in the *Mankind Quarterly;* and was dedicated to R. Ruggles Gates, who "proposed and helped plan this book." (It was probably Gates's unexpected death that had caused the delay.)

In the introduction to *Race and Modern Science* Kuttner, citing such "eminent" authorities on race as Fritz Lenz and Eugen Fischer, explained that the book was a reaction to UNESCO's attempt to combat racism with science, one that provided a "fuller understanding" of the evolutionary value of race prejudice "as an isolating mechanism favoring group survival and genetic variability."[164] As the geneticist L. C. Dunn noted, if the UNESCO statements were indeed "a veritable bible for egalitarians"—as they had been called by one scientist quoted by Kuttner—then *Race and Modern Science* was conceived of as a balancing volume—a bible for nonegalitarians.[165] One writer after another then insisted that prejudice was innate, inevitable, and served an important biological purpose. Gini, for example, explained that because of the "innate disposition" to racism, nations tended naturally toward biological homogeneity and that National Socialism in Germany had thus been an understandable attempt "to eliminate heterogeneous socio-cultural as well as anthropological elements." Gregor found general agreement among "specialists" that prejudice was "rooted in the nature of man" and pointed to the ubiquitous "repugnance to outbreeding" as evidence, though he noted that such groups as Jews and Communists had been taught to suppress their natural tendencies. Yet another contributor pointed out the biological consequences of such suppression—"the rising number of racial and subracial crossings whose human products will increasingly present their unique problems to society."[166]

Despite the content of these essays, their tone was devoid of the kind of rancor and epithets that had characterized so much other work sponsored by the IAAEE, providing the book with a more sophisticated, scientific image. There was little doubt about its nature or its intended readership, however. *Race and Modern Science* was advertised and distributed by the Liberty Lobby's Noontide Press, appearing on its literature list between such offerings as *The Hoax of the Twentieth Century,* a revisionist debunking of the Holocaust "myth," and *The Iron Curtain over America,* described as a "brilliant" documentation of the "traitorous conspiracy" between the Russians and the Jews, who "controlled . . . the machinery of the United States government."[167]

The IAAEE quickly became the Far Right's major intellectual authority, and its publications provided scientific support for the preachments of various racists and Nazis. IAAEE literature was cited, advertised, and sometimes even reprinted in such sources as the *Citizen,* the official magazine of the (Jackson, Mississippi) Citizens' Council, the organizational center of the southern opposition to integration; the *Northlander,* the Northern League's magazine; and a series of racist booklets produced by Britons Publishing Company, which specialized in republishing (over eighty times since 1920) *The Protocols of the Learned Elders of Zion,* the infamous forgery that purported to document the Jewish conspiracy for world domination.[168] When there were internal disputes in the neo-Nazi ranks, it was perceived as no small advantage to be able to cite an IAAEE publication as support for one's position.[169]

Despite their authoritative role among the already converted, the scientists had had little effect on the broader public during the 1960s. Searching for a reason to be optimistic in the face of segregation's demise, one right-wing theoretician anticipated that the breakdown of "America's traditional apartheid" would at least produce "a surge of hatred for the Negro."[170] Suddenly there was new reason for the scientific racists to be hopeful, however, as interest reemerged in the thesis of black intellectual inferiority and its political implications, this time on the part of some very prominent researchers untainted by an obviously ideological agenda.

5

"Unaided by Eugenic Foresight": The Controversy over Jensenism

AT LEAST through the mid-1960s the civil rights movement, untainted by political or ideological entanglements, maintained an overwhelming moral authority. The nation could no longer tolerate the contradiction between its professed ideals and a sociolegal system refusing millions of citizens access to schools, neighborhoods, restaurants, and even water fountains. As the most blatant forms of segregation disappeared, the movement's emphasis began to shift from struggling for equal rights to improving the conditions of life for the society's poor, a concern auspiciously echoed by Lyndon Johnson's War on Poverty. This temporary confluence of the civil rights movement's goals with the president's domestic agenda produced the Great Society programs, landmark social welfare legislation providing many of the most impoverished citizens with new access to health care, nutrition, and education.

Although these measures were intended to benefit not just blacks but *all* of that "other America" that Michael Harrington had so forcefully brought to the nation's attention, some scientists, again claiming blacks to be genetically inferior, opposed the War on Poverty by using the same logic that the segregationists had employed against *Brown.* "The feasibility of producing any significant change in the position of minority racial groups," wrote Robert E. Kuttner in *Perspectives in Biology and Medicine,* "rests on the assumption that genetic capacity is approximately the same for all groups."[1] That is, programs of medical care, better food, and educational assistance for blacks and other minorities were justified only if they were genetically equal to whites.

Underlying this claim was the logical extension of early Social Darwinist thought that had unregretfully predicted—indeed, even relished—an imminent demise of the black race. This prognosis had scientifically precluded any social assistance to blacks on the grounds that it would artificially interfere with the natural termination appropriate for an inferior group. As one Social Darwinist had put it early in the century, there was "nothing in the history of the Negro to suggest great fecundity, ... as the standard of living rises, as cómpetition sharpens, his economic 'well-being' will find it harder and harder to keep pace, his family will shrink more and more, his race will dwindle faster and faster into insignificance."[2] During the eugenics era this laissez-faire approach to the elimination of biological inferiors gave way to government intervention on the side of the "superior stocks," although such policies were informed by concern about the flood of undesirable immigrants more than about the black population, still confined largely to the South at the time and subject to vigorously enforced legal segregation. By the 1960s, however, it had long been evident that blacks were not going to succumb to the evolutionary struggle, and the contemporary eugenicists were horrified to see that government now intended to intervene on behalf of genetic inferiors: the War on Poverty would allow—perhaps even encourage—poor blacks, as well as less competent whites, to have larger families. Even if the oppressive measures of an earlier era were no longer acceptable, there was an enormous difference between tolerating the existence of inferiors and aiding in their proliferation.

One of the most controversial elements of the new legislation was the attempt to improve the cognitive abilities of the poor; in addition to its programs of humanitarian aid, the War on Poverty provided resources for educating the "disadvantaged," on the grounds that improved skills would better enable the children of the poor to compete in the job market. This belief in education as a major route to socioeconomic mobility had long been part of the American creed. As nineteenth-century industrialization produced a rising demand for skilled employees, education had become increasingly viewed as, in Horace Mann's words, "the great equalizer."

During the earlier eugenics era, however, education for the masses had been impugned as a foolish waste of resources; learning was to be reserved for the elite, the select few who were genetically equipped to benefit from it. The biologist Paul Popenoe even reported a sizable *negative* correlation between achievement and intelligence in the Los Angeles schools—the brighter students were supposedly achieving a lot less than the duller ones—and he described how the few capable children were being intellectually abused while teachers devoted most of their efforts "to goading the moron into a little more speed than he is built for."[3] Public education, Popenoe concluded, was just not compatible with eugenics. A number of other early eugenicists explained that education was of limited value because its benefits could not be genetically transmitted. Albert E. Wiggam, for example, declared that "a thousand years of educating . . . the parents will never improve the children . . . [who] are born not from the improved body cells but from the unimproved germ cells." Education was useless in the face of Wiggam's concluding aphorism: "Wooden legs are not inherited, but wooden heads are."[4]

Although this obsession with the "germ cells" soon passed and education was once again considered a worthy route to self-improvement, there remained the inaccurate belief that "heritable" meant "fixed." The concept of mental ability as a largely heritable trait still suggested to many people that the education of those children unable, "by nature," to benefit from it was a waste of expenditures. In fact, geneticists had abandoned such thinking long ago. In 1939 the English scientist Lancelot Hogben, one of the most distinguished geneticists of his time, remarked that complaints about students' innate inabilities should "not engage the sympathy of educationists who take their job seriously. . . . If knowledge is the keystone of intelligent citizenship, the fact that many people do not benefit from existing provisions for instruction is less a criticism of themselves than a criticism of educational machinery."[5] Yet in the 1960s a number of scientists rediscovered inherited wooden heads as genetic roadblocks in the educational path of many black children. These researchers were not the simpleminded eugenicists of an earlier era, and in place of unit characters they constructed models of much greater sophistication. Nor were they segregationists in the Garrett mold; instead, they stressed the importance of judging each individual on his or her merits. Nevertheless, the latest research on mental ability led them to many of the old eugenical conclusions.

Opposing "Genetic Enslavement"

While Henry E. Garrett, A. James Gregor, Robert E. Kuttner, Ernest van den Haag, and the other IAAEE scientists were persevering in their losing battle against integration, Dwight J. Ingle, a University of Chicago physiologist, resurrected the fecundity of the genetically inferior as the major justification for scientific concern with racial differences in intelligence. Unlike his predecessors, however, Ingle professed concern for the welfare of blacks and noted with great solicitude that "the very high birth rate among indolent incompetent Negroes is a threat to the future success of this race." To improve their prospects, he recommended sterilization or some other method of "conception control . . . for all who, either because of genetic limitations or because of poor cultural heritage, are unable to endow children with a reasonable chance to achieve happiness, self-sufficiency, and good citizenship."[6] At the same time, to protect society from the present effect of defective genes and harmful culture, Ingle proposed quarantining the carriers of such social ills in specific complexes—low IQ housing—where they would be provided with "an intensive program of birth control."[7]

In his later writing Ingle outlined specific programs for the genetic improvement of blacks that would exercise social control over their right to bear children. Preferring to avoid "coercive methods" if possible, he proposed that a group of professionals—physicians and scientists—pass judgment on the "genetic, . . . social, economic and behavioral fitness of the individual for parenthood." If the judgments of such experts were not followed voluntarily—and Ingle believed that they would not—more "forceful methods" would be necessary. A century earlier Francis Galton had vaguely threatened that the poorer stock would forfeit all claims to kindness if they continued to produce inferior children, but Ingle was prepared with specific details. He suggested the mandatory implementation of an "anti-fertility agent" under the skin of every woman of child-bearing age and the subsequent requirement of a license, granted only after appropriate review of the applicant, to have the substance temporarily removed. Such methods of "biological engineering" were, for Ingle, the "means necessary to true equality for the Negro."[8]

A Return to the Past

Ingle did not have to carry the eugenical banner by himself for long. In 1965 the physicist William Bradford Shockley, occupant of a named chair in engineering at Stanford, entered the controversy, bringing with him the instant authority of that ultimate scientific credential, the Nobel Prize, which he had received jointly with two colleagues for their invention of the transistor. Invited as a laureate to address a Nobel conference on "Genetics and the Future of Man," Shockley chose the occasion to launch a eugenical program right out of the 1920s. He began by acknowledging a lack of formal training in genetics but claimed that he had long been concerned with overpopulation (indeed, as a student thirty years earlier he had written a paper on population control, suggesting that women who had many children because they did not take the "proper precautions" should not receive the same "level of obstetric care" as more responsible mothers).[9] Sometime ago he had come to the conclusion that relief from famine in Third World countries would only exacerbate the problem in the long run. Nevertheless, he emphasized, when a famine occurred in India that prompted the U.S. government to send surplus wheat, he did not publicly object because "at this time" he was not yet completely confident in his "reasoning ability as to future developments."[10] The point of this introductory anecdote was to impress on the audience that, as a careful thinker, Shockley would not recommend withholding food from the starving until he was fairly certain that such a policy was eugenically constructive.

Turning from the quantity of human beings to their quality, the topic of his lecture, Shockley explained that one of the greatest threats to the future was the "genetic deterioration" of the human race: improvements in medical technology, together with the "abundant American society," were assuring "to all the privilege of reproducing their kind," even those suffering from "genetic defects" that would not have allowed them "to survive to the stage of reproduction in a more primitive environment." The seriousness of this trend had first occurred to Shockley when he read of a businessman who had been blinded by a teenaged acid-thrower, "one of approximately a dozen illegitimate children of an irresponsible and destitute woman." (In later versions of this incident Shockley increased the number of children to seventeen and claimed the mother capable of remembering only nine of their names.) Such individuals were no longer being eliminated by the evolutionary dynamic, he observed, and in place of survival of the fittest, the selective proliferation of genetically defective, large, and often illegitimate families was producing evolution in reverse. The major culprit in this reversal, according to Shockley, was the War on Poverty's social programs, which were attempting to achieve "the most happiness for the most." Such a goal he termed an absurdity; "thinking people" knew that only evolution could produce real improvement.[11]

Despite the sense of personal discovery that marked Shockley's presentation, it was largely an unimproved reprise of earlier eugenical thought. Just as Herbert S. Jennings had urged in 1927 that every person be "his own hormone factory" rather than have to depend on clinical treatment for diabetes, Shockley, too, complained of biochemical techniques "like those available for diabetes, for patching up genetically defective offspring so that they may be successful citizens in a progressively more artificial environment. I believe this is a possibility which appeals to few thinking people. It does not appeal to me." Just as Edward M. East had conjectured in 1929 that a war of annihilation might be necessary to reverse "organic retrogression," Shockley, too, found nuclear war a grim possibility for resuming evolutionary progress by forcing society to select from the survivors those with undamaged genes to perpetuate the race. He even extolled Oliver Wendell Holmes's opinion upholding the compulsory sterilization of Carrie Buck and complained over the changes in state legislation and institutional medical policy that had caused a decrease in the number of sterilizations performed.[12]

Shockley's Nobel address, delivered in St. Peter, Minnesota, received little attention from the media, but, once again, a notable exception was *U.S. News and World Report*, which interviewed him and published a lengthy feature on the increasing reproduction of the "inferior strains." To place society back on the evolutionary track, he proposed another idea from the past in the interview: government should change sides in the War on Poverty; the rich should receive larger income tax exemptions for their children than the poor.[13] As Paul Popenoe and Roswell Johnson had observed in their textbook forty years earlier, for poverty to have a eugenic effect, society should create deliberate economic burdens to parenthood. In response to the interviewer's query about heredity and race, a topic not mentioned by Shockley in the original speech, the physicist also disclosed his fear that, especially among blacks, the genetically least capable were producing the largest number of offspring.

This interview was reprinted in the *Stanford M.D.*, the medical school's alumni magazine, and it quickly produced an angry response signed by all seven members of the university's Department of Genetics, among them Joshua Lederberg, also a Nobel Laureate. The geneticists called Shockley's statements the "kind of pseudo scientific justification for class and race prejudice [that] is so hackneyed that we would not ordinarily have cared to react to it. However, Professor Shockley's standing as a Nobel Laureate and as a colleague at Stanford, and now the appearance of his article with a label of Stanford medicine, creates a situation where our silence could leave the false impression that we share or acquiesce in this outlook which we certainly do not." Shockley's colleagues went on to deplore "the tone of his entire discussion about 'bad heredity,'" a concept they termed "myopic," and they wondered why he did not "trot out the 'scientific documentation' of the . . . Kallikaks."[14] (Their sarcasm turned out to be prescient: a short time later Shockley did indeed cite the Kallikak study as serious evidence.)[15] Even if Shockley's premises were valid, wrote the genetics faculty, it was more important to develop those techniques of medical care, education, and social organization "that can create incentives and useful careers for the whole wonderful variety of human beings." In response Shockley accused the geneticists of attempting "to dictate permissible channels of thinking." This was a tactic he would employ regularly during the controversy to come—claiming that those who criticized his proposals as an infringement on individuals' rights were attempting to suppress his free speech, a task as impossible in Shockley's case as it would be undesirable. He also took issue with the geneticists' reference to the "wonderful variety" of human beings; to Shockley there was nothing wonderful about the feebleminded.[16]

"Sound Methodology rather than Emotionally Based Racism"

Criticism, for Shockley, always produced an evangelical reaction, motivating him to seek vindication in the support of others. If the Stanford geneticists thought his position ridiculous, he would appeal "above their heads" to the National Academy of Sciences, and, beginning in 1966, he would make an annual, and urgent, plea to the Academy for the study of racial aspects of the "heredity-poverty-crime" nexus. His first proposal coyly suggested that an "ethnic composition index" might, by showing a positive correlation between performance and "fraction of Negro genes," demonstrate blacks "surpass" whites.[17]

The 1967 Academy meeting took place only months after the Stanford geneticists' condemnation, however, and the time for subtlety had passed. Shockley began his quest for support by defending the ethics of his proposals. Citing widespread popular sentiment for depriving some individuals of the right to produce children, he claimed that scientists who opposed such policy and the research on which it could be based expressed "an undemocratic contempt for public wisdom that is quite in keeping with totalitarian regimes and wholly out of harmony with the free speech and free principles of our constitution." The opponents of eugenics, the basis of policy in the Third Reich, were suddenly converted into the real totalitarians. "The lesson to be learned from Nazi history," Shockley lectured his colleagues, was "the value of free speech, not that eugenics is intolerable." No doubt he meant that the Holocaust would not have been possible in a more open society in which the true purpose of the concentration camps was widely known.[18] (Shockley would later clarify the point, observing that "only the most anti-Teutonic racist can believe the German people to be such an evil breed that they would have tolerated the . . . gas chambers if a working First Amendment had permitted exposure and discussion of Hitler's final solution.")[19] Whether this was true, repressive actions prior to the Final Solution were hardly carried out in secret. The hundreds of legal measures enacted against Jews before 1938—their termination from professional and academic positions, their confinement to ghettos, confiscation of their businesses, prohibition of their marriage to Aryans—were all part of a program well publicized to the German people and justified on the basis of science. These measures, too, had enjoyed the popular support that Shockley now pointed to as proof of his critics' "undemocratic contempt" for "public wisdom."

Shockley then considered the issue of race, offering statistical evidence for an "orderly relationship" in which whites achieved comparatively greater "eminence" than blacks, while blacks were disproportionately represented in the statistics on illegitimacy and crime. In a nice Galtonian touch he converted the data from twelve different measures to a common scale, discovering that in each case blacks were lower than whites by about 1.2 "social capacity units." Given such striking results, only a "thought-block," Shockley concluded, had prevented the pursuit of the "simplest case" model, that genetic disadvantage was the reason for poverty and crime among blacks. He estimated that within a decade and at a cost of less than ten million dollars science could determine whether blacks' "genetic inheritance [will] produce such a low social capacity index" that environmental improvements would be of no benefit to them. In the meantime, Shockley maintained, if there were a genetic cause to these "social capacity" differences, the vast expenditures on social programs would only exacerbate the problem by assisting those least capable to reproduce.[20]

The implication was clear: Medicare and food stamps were doing more harm than good; a true war on poverty demanded not the care and feeding of the poor but their systematic elimination through sterilization or other methods of birth control. Under the present system of aid the proliferation of genetically less capable blacks would lead to what Shockley termed their "genetic enslavement," an ingeniously Orwellian phrase implying agreement with the humanitarian observation that blacks had been the victims of oppression but suggesting a different twist on its source. Just as morally enlightened Americans had fought to liberate blacks from chattel slavery, they were now called on to oppose genetic slavery. Those who insisted on a social policy predicated on black inferiority were thus converted into freedom fighters, while those who disagreed would only be complicit in their further persecution by the internal oppressor. Shockley would later explain that "genetic enslavement" was occurring because "those Negroes with the fewest Caucasian genes" were "the most prolific and also the least intelligent";[21] to free blacks from their genetic shackles, it would thus be necessary to prevent the reproduction of the relatively "pure" black population. Even if it turned out that Shockley was wrong about black inferiority, he believed that exposure of the error would help overcome "*unreasonable* prejudice" (emphasis added).[22] This was not an idle adjective that the physicist had chosen; if blacks were indeed genetically disadvantaged, he saw nothing unreasonable about prejudice against them. As he had pointed out to the Stanford geneticists, Shockley saw nothing wonderful about inferior human beings.

The Academy was not particularly impressed with Shockley's call for research. One official response, prepared by three of the Academy's most distinguished geneticists, noted that the complex polygenic nature of intellectual traits and the unavoidable inequality of environments made any attempts to assess the relative roles of heredity and environment in racial differences hardly more than guesswork, easily biased by political and social views; and in any case, it concluded, major social decisions would not depend on such information.[23] Nevertheless, Shockley continued at meeting after meeting to introduce resolutions and make presentations on race and the specter of genetic deterioration. But as one Academy president put it, "Our members simply refuse to be used for his purpose.... there is no more reason why the Academy should serve to sponsor the study which he proposes than there is for us to sponsor any of 10,000 others."[24] Shockley was infuriated by this rejection and railed at what he perceived as scientific suppression, comparing himself with Galileo and the Academy with Lysenkoites. He was, however, always treated with respect at meetings and never denied the floor from which to launch his polemics; he was never suppressed, merely ignored.

Being told that racial differences were not capable of definitive scientific analysis seemed to remove all doubt on Shockley's part concerning the genetic inferiority of blacks. The "objective examination of relevant data" now led him "inescapably to the opinion that the major deficit in Negro intellectual performance must be primarily of hereditary origin and thus relatively irremediable by practical improvements in environment." Quite apart from the questionable nature of the first conclusion, the second, offered as a consequence of the first, was in fact a non sequitur; many highly heritable traits are easily manipulated through environmental intervention—such as glasses to improve vision. In Shockley's analysis, however, an enriched environment could do nothing to overcome genetic inadequacy. Nor did he feel that any assistance or enrichment was necessary, even in the most oppressive surroundings, to ensure the emergence of true innate ability. As evidence for this belief, he frequently related an unreferenced and wildly improbable anecdote about an unnamed scientist who "until age six ... was an Aztec Indian at a blow-gun and stone-axe level, isolated from modern civilization for four centuries [sic]." After escaping from slavery, the child did not enter school until age ten, according to Shockley, yet acquired a master's degree in physics by twenty-one and went on to a distinguished career in engineering.[25]

More serious than Shockley's disdain for the Academy's scientific caveat was his disregard for its assertion of the genetic issue's irrelevance for social policy. In fact, he maintained, the Great Society programs were *already* based on an assumption of equal genetic ability among ethnic groups. The proof of this supposed link came from two little-known government publications. A 1965 report entitled *The Negro Family* issued by the Department of Labor's Office of Policy Planning and Research had stated that "there is absolutely no question of any genetic differential: Intelligence potential is distributed among Negro infants in the same proportion and pattern as among Icelanders or Chinese or any other group." A year later an article on the Armed Forces Qualification Test in a journal published by the Office of Education had asserted it was "a demonstrable fact that the talent pool in any one ethnic group is substantially the same as that in any other ethnic group."[26]

For the next decade this strange notion that the War on Poverty had been based on a genetic assumption would become the mantra of justification for scientific attempts to prove blacks at a genetic disadvantage. Of course, this putative link between science and policy, supported by only two obscure observations in bureaucratic publications, was even less credible than the segregationists' discovery of *Brown*'s scientific premise. The more vulnerable members of society have always levied a moral, and increasingly a political, claim on the rest of us for additional resources, whether the source of their greater vulnerability is social, physical, or genetic. An affluent society bears a moral obligation to ensure minimal levels of health, shelter, and nutrition for its poorest citizens regardless of their IQ scores. Moreover, the antipoverty measures designed to attain these levels were implemented only after large-scale demonstrations and political campaigns. The tens of millions of people whose demands for social justice finally produced the legislation could hardly have cared one whit about the genetic controversy had they even been aware of its existence; nor could the legislators themselves have found it a relevant matter. By positing genetic equality as the "dogma" underlying government policy, however, Shockley could then argue, with some logic, that a demonstration of the former's flawed nature would naturally raise doubts about the soundness of the latter.

In addition, Shockley insisted, an established innate difference in intelligence between the races would provide "sound methodology, rather than emotionally based racism," as a basis for "social action." While he did not elaborate at the time—beyond proclaiming that antipoverty programs were "doomed to fail because they are against nature"[27]—it sounded as if the methods of science and the malevolence of racism would point in the same direction, though an appeal to the former would provide the more respectable justification absent from the latter. This impression was strengthened by his remarks on IQ scores. When Shockley's research proposals were severely criticized, the philosopher Michael Scriven came to his defense, at the same time pointing out "that the worth of people and their rights do not depend on IQ." Shockley immediately attacked Scriven because "the word 'depend' discounts the significant positive correlations that exist between IQ and all other quantitative or orderable traits that have been studied—correlations that have significantly lower correlation coefficients for Negroes than whites."[28] That is, in Shockley's opinion, IQ was a measure not just of intelligence but of overall human worth—for whites. Blacks he found to be an exception to this general relation between IQ and other "high-quality" traits; even when they were intelligent, their ability was unassociated with these other useful characteristics. For Shockley, this analysis provided a justification for the racial gap in earnings that still existed after controlling for IQ. "An IQ increment for a white," he explained, "pulls up with it other personality traits valuable for earning power to a greater extent than does an equal IQ increment for a Negro."[29] Thus, even when "intelligence" was ruled out as a factor, scientifically derived explanations could justify lower black wages, nicely eluding any taint of discrimination or prejudice.

Nature's Color Coding

Shockley's conflict with the scientific community had two important consequences for the physicist. Rebuffed by his mainstream colleagues, he moved toward closer alliance with those scientists naturally most sympathetic to his claims—the IAAEE members and other opponents of integration. Although Shockley did not share all their political goals, he found the segregationists' belief in genetic differences between the races a refreshing contrast to the Academy's "thought blockage." Particularly impressed by Robert E. Kuttner's "ingenuity,"[30] Shockley submitted a paper by the IAAEE president to the National Academy of Sciences, reporting that American Indians achieved higher average scores than blacks on scholastic tests despite greater socioeconomic disadvantage and questioning whether antipoverty programs could possibly "uplift" blacks without regard for genetic determinants[31] (Kuttner spared the Academy his observation that such programs made it easier for black men to maintain a drug habit by "catching a white girl"). Shockley eventually arranged for Kuttner, a biochemist at a Chicago hospital, to obtain a research position in the Stanford University electronics laboratory. He also began to recommend the racial analyses of such authors as Carleton Putnam[32]—eventually gracing the book jacket of Putnam's *Race and Reality* with his own writing—and, even more extreme, Wilmot Robertson,[33] a Far Right theoretician whose book, acclaimed by Kuttner in the *Mankind Quarterly,* had praised Hitler and advocated the physical separation of all the "unassimilable" minorities into their separate territories—not just blacks but also Hispanics, Jews, southern Italians, and others.[34]

Understandably, Shockley was given a hero's reception by the segregationists. Actually, concentrating on the antipoverty measures, he had little to say about the *Brown* decision, though he did once note an increase in crime beginning in 1964 and proposed case studies of criminals to determine whether integration had "provided training experiences in school for what later develops into criminal violence."[35] Moreover, his specific eugenical proposals were always framed in terms of individuals rather than races. Nevertheless, Shockley's unyielding assertion of blacks' genetic inadequacy made him the segregationists' newest scientific champion, a role he made no effort to disavow. The *Citizen,* the official publication of the all-white Citizens' Council in Jackson, Mississippi, featured frequent coverage of his "noble" and "courageous" efforts to force integrity upon the "conglomeration of moral cowards" that constituted the National Academy of Sciences.[36] *White Power,* the paper founded by the American Nazi party leader George Lincoln Rockwell, praised him as a "modern Galileo who is knocking down the whole Jewish equality swindle."[37] Shockley occasionally expressed some reservations about his prominence in "white supremacist" publications whose views "conflict with my version of the golden rule," but on balance he found these sources valuable for their lack of the hypocrisy, which, in his opinion, marked the rest of the U.S. press. Besides, he claimed to feel no more responsibility to correct any misuse of science by Nazis and Klan members than he would to stop the reckless use of his car by someone who had stolen it.[38]

Another, more important consequence of Shockley's unsuccessful attempts to enlist scientific support was his decision to bypass his colleagues; if all they could offer was "mindless derogation," then he would take his case directly to the American people. The major route to the public was, of course, through the media, and Shockley, ever the verbal freight train, candidly admitted that it was his "intention to use significant members of the American press as the blocks or pulleys . . . and the First Amendment as a line upon which I shall endeavor to exert a force so as to deflect the rudder of public opinion and turn the ship of civilization away from the dysgenic storm that I fear is rising over the horizon of the future."[39] He thus set out to become an "operator," as it is called by reporters, a person who cultivates the press to enhance his personal publicity or political cause.[40] Obsessed with public visibility, Shockley became a one-man public relations firm and lobbyist for his eugenical views. Each new lecture was carefully orchestrated to achieve maximum coverage from the media, especially from those members he knew to be sympathetic; each new proposal or idea was announced through a press conference or news release. Even unfavorable exposure could prove useful if handled correctly, and Shockley would turn a critical magazine article or newspaper column into the starting point for a contentious exchange that would provide his crusade with additional publicity for the publication's next three or four issues.

Although Shockley actively sought interviews that would allow him to elaborate on his views, he also instituted an elaborate screening system to prevent any waste of time with a journalist not intellectually capable of appreciating his arguments. Prospective interviewers had to study a considerable amount of material on Shockley's scientific theories and ethical beliefs and then pass a rigorous set of quizzes before being deemed worthy to meet personally with the physicist. Since these examinations were sometimes administered over the phone, there were at least two instances in which he "approved" a journalist before finding out that he was black. On one occasion that information was eventually volunteered over the phone, leading Shockley to change the agreed site of the interview from his home to his office so that two student assistants could be present—he seemed to feel the need for protection from the associate editor of *Christian Century*.[41] On the other occasion no mention was made of race beforehand, and the journalist arrived accompanied by a white photographer, whom Shockley immediately assumed to be the writer. When apprised of the facts, Shockley insisted on yet a final test constructed on the spur of the moment before proceeding with the interview.[42]

Like Dwight Ingle, Shockley emphasized his personal concern for the supposed victims of genetic enslavement in his media campaign. He presented himself to the public as not only a Galileo, steadfastly opposing the "theologico-scientific delusion" that had caused "unsearch dogmatism" and "thought blockage" in the scientific community, but also a Schweitzer, the blacks' real friend. He alone was concerned enough to diagnose the true cause of their poverty, crime, and educational failure and to offer the only solution that would rescue them from the internal oppressor. "There is no one," he insisted, "who is currently more likely to reduce Negro misery in this country in the next generation than myself."[43] Those who refused to look into Shockley's telescope were thus the real culprits, their foolish emphasis on discrimination and other environmental disadvantages producing a "cover-up" that he compared with German ignorance of the Final Solution.[44] Once again Shockley had converted those who opposed discrimination into the real Nazis and those who justified it into freedom fighters.[45]

Despite his tone of moral elevation, there was no doubt that Shockley desired to encourage blatantly discriminatory practices. On a number of occasions he declared that "nature has color-coded groups of individuals so that statistically reliable predictions of their adaptability to intellectually rewarding and effective lives can easily be made and profitably be used by the pragmatic man in the street."[46] Elaborating on such profitable usage, he once explained to an interviewer that prejudice was only "illogical" when not supported by "strong facts," but when "based on sound statistics, [it] really shouldn't be called prejudice." Thus, for example, the refusal to hire blacks solely because of their race was not really prejudice, because "the pragmatic man-in-the-street has had experience and knows what to expect from blacks." When pressed about his personal experiences with blacks by the interviewer, Shockley suggested a position for which they were particularly well-suited by nature's "color-coding." While recuperating in the hospital after an automobile accident, he had found the black nurses much more "comforting" than the whites and their "quality of care" superior; indeed, he emphasized, "they were the only ones who cleaned my rear end properly."[47]

Shockley was more concerned, however, with the genetic improvement that would result from preventing the birth of all those unfortunates "disadvantaged by an unfair shake from a badly loaded parental dice cup."[48] To aid in accomplishing this goal, he proposed that "bonuses . . . be offered for sterilization. . . . At a bonus rate of $1,000 for each point below 100 I.Q., $30,000 put in trust for a 70 I.Q. moron potentially capable of producing 20 children might return $250,000 to taxpayers in reduced costs of mental retardation care. Ten percent of the bonus in spot cash might put our national talent for entrepreneurship into action."[49] After first outlining this "Voluntary Sterilization Bonus Plan" in an address to the American Psychological Association in 1971, Shockley rarely gave an interview or made a speech without plugging "The Plan." It received some immediate attention, but after consulting with sympathetic journalists, Shockley made a sensational addition designed to increase The Plan's publicity value. Since "those who are not bright enough to hear of the bonus on their own are the most important ones to reach," Shockley suggested that "bounty hunters attracted by getting a cut of the cash part of the bonus might then persuade low IQ, high-bonus types to volunteer."[50] Though he typically referred to The Plan as only a "thinking exercise," Shockley's recommendation of "some test cases" implied his hope that it would receive more serious consideration.[51]

Shockley did make one other specific proposal, but since it did not receive the attention accorded The Plan, he mentioned it much less frequently. Like Dwight Ingle's suggestion, it involved the subcutaneous implantation of a contraceptive device that could be removed only upon presentation of childbearing certificates issued by the state. A woman would initially receive certificates for two children but could purchase more on the "open market" from other women who had decided not to become pregnant.[52] By converting children into another commodity available in greater abundance to those with more money, Shockley expected genetic improvement to result, since the more affluent were assumed to be genetically superior.

To facilitate his public relations campaign, Shockley formed the Foundation for Research and Education on Eugenics and Dysgenics (FREED), with himself as president and R. Travis Osborne, a member of the IAAEE's Executive Committee and one of the segregationists' expert witnesses in their attempts to overturn *Brown,* as FREED's "adviser." Founded, according to its charter, "solely for scientific and educational purposes related to human population and quality problems,"[53] FREED functioned in practice as a lobbying agency for Shockley's ideas, disseminating a newsletter with the details of his latest public appearances, his press releases, and copies of newspaper articles by and about him—everything from college publications to the *Times* of London, and especially from the Manchester, New Hampshire, *Union Leader*, where that famous conservative curmudgeon William Loeb provided him copious space. All responses to FREED were saved and even microfilmed "for . . . historical reasons," noted Shockley, apparently anticipating a future in which his campaign would be retrospectively viewed as the beginning of eugenical solutions for social problems. Like any other lobby, FREED was eager to find new "recruits." Recipients of the newsletter and sympathetic respondents were asked for permission to have their written support circulated "to other people who live in your neighborhood."[54] If he could, Shockley would build a new eugenics movement door-to-door.

In 1977 a *New York Times* investigation divulged that Shockley had received over $179,000 from the Pioneer Fund during the preceding decade,[55] and it is likely that FREED was subsidized from this source. Pioneer, founded on a belief in the superiority of "white persons who settled in the original thirteen states," must have been delighted by a Nobel Laureate who proclaimed this prejudice to be a scientific conclusion. In Shockley's opinion "the most competent population in terms of social management and general capacity for organization" was the first European settlers in America, whose superiority resulted from "the most brutal selective mechanisms" of early American life—there had been no antipoverty programs in the colonial period to help inferiors survive and reproduce. In fact, Shockley suggested that in addition to producing a general resumption of the evolutionary process, a more specific salutary effect of worldwide nuclear war would be the probable survival of the foresighted and well-organized Swedes and Swiss, thus returning genetic dominance to some of that early American stock.[56]

Shockley was popular with the segregationists, but his campaign produced little public support (though it did elicit the approval of the *Wall Street Journal*, whose editor agreed that programs to aid the disadvantaged were "futile or even self-defeating" because they could not "repair genetic damage").[57] Quite apart from the unappealing nature of the proposals themselves, his irascible and condescending personal style was no small disadvantage. When, for example, a television host once attempted to rescue Shockley from his own fiasco by tactfully interrupting a confusing technical presentation to suggest a change of direction, the physicist would have none of it, insisting that he "would like to reach those few who *can* understand."[58] An element of buffoonery was eventually added to Shockley's image when he announced that he had, on more than one occasion, made a personal contribution to genetic improvement by donating to the Repository for Germinal Choice, a sperm bank intended to produce gifted children through the artificial insemination of highly intelligent women with genetically superior sperm. As a *New York Times* editorial observed, in an obviously personal comment on the seventy-year-old Shockley, "Can it be that women who want exceptionally smart children will end up with offspring who are merely bald and near-sighted?"[59]

The Firestorm over Arthur Jensen

When Shockley's initial presentations to the National Academy of Sciences provoked little enthusiasm—at times, even disparagement—he began to work behind the scenes, feverishly attempting to mobilize support from other scientists. For example, he telephoned Jerry Hirsch, a well-known behavior geneticist from the University of Illinois, in an attempt to "recruit" him shortly before Hirsch was to deliver a paper at an American Association for the Advancement of Science symposium on race. (Notably unaffected by Shockley's arguments, in the symposium Hirsch called the "notorious nature-nurture" controversy a "pseudoquestion.")[60] During the conversation Shockley informed Hirsch of discussions he had been having with Arthur Jensen, a University of California, Berkeley, psychologist, who was spending the 1966–67 academic year as a fellow at the Center for Advanced Study in the Behavioral Sciences on the Stanford campus.[61] The subsequent enlistment of Jensen in Shockley's campaign added the credibility of the psychologist's ongoing research program in the relevant fields of intelligence and education.

Unlike Shockley and Ingle, Jensen could not be perceived as some outsider meddling for personal or political reasons in a scientific area where he had no demonstrated expertise. In fact, in earlier work Jensen had argued that the low socioeconomic status of blacks and Hispanics "cannot be interpreted as evidence of poor genetic potential" because "powerful racial barriers to social mobility" existed. These severe "socioeconomic and cultural disadvantages" had led him to the "reasonable hypothesis that [blacks'] low-average IQ is due to environmental rather than to genetic factors."[62] When Jensen did arrive at a genetic explanation for racial differences, he could therefore point to his conversion as evidence of a genuine scientific temperament, influenced not by a priori prejudices but "by the research of others and the results of my own investigation, which . . . have involved the testing . . . of more than 15,000 children."[63]

Arthur Jensen had begun his scientific career in the area of clinical psychology but quickly became disenchanted with the soft style that dominated that field. Finding the quantitative approaches of the English psychologist Hans J. Eysenck more appealing, he obtained a postdoctoral fellowship at Eysenck's research department in the University of London's

Institute of Psychiatry at Maudsley Hospital. Author of dozens of books and hundreds of articles, the Englishman was a world-renowned scientist, particularly well known as a severe critic of environmentalism and a champion of hereditarian explanations. Almost in awe of Eysenck, Jensen "felt lucky to be at the Maudsley" with this "great professor," whom he described as a man of "exceptionally quick, incisive intelligence, a greater verbal and ideational fluency than I'd seen in anyone else, and a vast erudition, seemingly always at his fingertips."[64] While in England, Jensen also attended the Walter Van Dyke Bingham Memorial Lecture entitled "The Inheritance of Mental Ability," given by Eysenck's mentor, Sir Cyril Burt.[65] Proclaiming Burt "England's greatest and most famous psychologist," Jensen found his presentation "the best lecture I have ever heard."[66] The talk itself was the culmination of more than a half-century's work on Burt's part, much of which later turned out to be fraudulent, that demonstrated heredity was the predominant cause of both individual and class differences in intelligence.[67]

When Jensen returned to the United States, his own work on learning led to research on ethnic minorities and the poor—it was the mid-1960s, and Head Start and Title I programs had just been proposed amidst great enthusiasm. At the beginning of his year at the Center for Advanced Study Jensen embarked on a review of all of Burt's articles on the genetics of intelligence and proceeded to "the total world literature" on the subject.[68] Though he was convinced at the time that individual and class differences in ability were largely genetic in origin, he was passionately opposed to the view that "culturally disadvantaged children" with low IQs were

> destined for intellectual and occupational mediocrity. This widespread belief gives rise to various plans for watered-down, less intellectual, and less academic educational programmes tailored to the apparent limitations of a large proportion . . . of low socioeconomic status children. . . . This is a harmful and unjust set of beliefs. . . . Failure to distinguish between hereditary retardation and cultural retardation, as well as being a social injustice, results in a waste of educational potential and talent. The consequences are especially damaging to the social progress of minority groups, and the costs are borne by our whole society.[69]

During the year on the Stanford campus, however, Jensen's position changed dramatically. Not only did he begin to find the genetic explanation for racial differences much more plausible, but he also suddenly expanded his interests from intelligence and educability—his area of professional expertise—to the problem of eugenic decline caused by the proliferation of poor blacks. It was certainly possible that Jensen's review of "the total world literature" on the topic had influenced his thinking, but it was also not coincidental that his pronouncements suddenly became a more finely nuanced version of Shockley's. Where Shockley had proposed a " 'simplest cases' approach" to explain racial differences in poverty and crime, Jensen now lectured his professional colleagues that "it is good scientific strategy to begin with the simplest possible hypothesis": the difference between blacks and whites "in tested intelligence is caused by the same factors, operating in the same degrees, that cause differences in intelligence between individuals"; that is, blacks were genetically less intelligent than whites. Though only a few months earlier he himself had labeled such an explanation harmful and unjust, Jensen now discovered that the real reason for neglect of this "simplest hypothesis" was the "official decision" expressed in the same two obscure government publications cited by Shockley. He now concluded that not only were these premature dismissals of the genetic explanation without "factual basis" but also "the actual acceptance of them may unwittingly harm many Negro children born and unborn."[70]

After centuries of first slavery and then enforced segregation, both justified by the claim that blacks were inferior, there would seem to be a Swiftian irony to the claim that a belief in genetic equality would now inflict terrible harm on them, but Jensen's clarification of this assertion proceeded on the same logic that had informed Shockley's prediction of "genetic enslavement." If the inverse relationship between socioeconomic class—itself to a great degree genetically determined, according to Jensen—and family size were more pronounced among blacks than whites, then the racial gap in ability would be increasing. "The policy of ignoring this problem," he warned, "might well be viewed by future generations as our society's greatest injustice to Negro Americans";[71] in particular, "future generations of Negroes . . . could suffer the most from well-meaning but misguided and ineffective attempts to improve their lot in life."[72] Though such ominous predictions were vaguely phrased, there was no mistaking Jensen's point: antipoverty programs, "misguided and ineffective attempts" to improve the quality of life, were providing the inferior black poor greater opportunity to reproduce their kind. Instead of well-baby clinics and child-development programs, the real need was for a different kind of government assistance, one that would give priority to sterilization and conception control.

At the same time that Jensen was dropping these eugenic hints, the major thrust of his research was in his own area of specialization—learning and intelligence. He had found that many "disadvantaged" children with low scores on standard IQ tests were much "brighter" than their IQ would lead one to expect. Such children, with IQs "as low as 60," would enter a new class, "learn the names of 20 or 30 children in a few days, quickly pick up the rules and the know-how of various games on the playground and so on," an adjustment Jensen found to be in striking contrast to the inept performance of middle-class children with similar IQs. To verify this playground effect, he had even devised special tests that "show how fast a child can learn something relatively new and unfamiliar, right in the test situation," and again poor and minority children with low IQs performed much better than middle-class children in the same IQ range.[73] Upon confirming this result, Jensen had been initially exultant at its implications for the potential of slum children and had anticipated the discovery of widespread latent genius suppressed by cultural disadvantage and social injustice—potential IQs "of 130, or 140, or 150 among the groups whose measured IQs are 70 to 90."[74]

When such dramatic improvements were not immediately in evidence, however, Jensen concluded that there were two separately inherited, underlying cognitive processes: one, "not . . . an intellectually important function," involving the simpler abilities of memory and association; the other, a more conceptually complex capacity for abstract thought and problem solving. According to Jensen, the traditional methods of education in the United States, which required mainly the latter abilities, had evolved "in relation to a relatively small upper-class segment of Anglo-European stock" and thus were not as successful with a new student population that was less "homogeneous in genetic and cultural background."[75] (The historical observation was another ironic note since, only a generation earlier, leading social scientists had found Anglo-European stock to be anything but genetically homogeneous; the old mental testers had proven the non-Nordic elements lacked exactly that intellectual mettle upon which Jensen now claimed their education had been based.) Jensen, however, offered reason to be optimistic about the education of the "new" groups, if only the schools would reorient their methods to take advantage of these children's strengths. Though unable to comprehend principles and concepts, they could be "trained" using "operant conditioning techniques." The practical conclusion Jensen drew from his research was conceptual education for the more traditional students and training through rote association for most of the "disadvantaged."[76]

THE Article

In mid-1968 Jensen's work was known to few people outside the small number of professionals who read the educational research literature. Among this group, however, were the editors of the *Harvard Educational Review,* who now invited him to submit an expanded discussion of heredity and intelligence as a lead article, to be followed by commentaries from a number of psychologists with different perspectives. The letter of solicitation proposed an outline that, among other topics, included "a clear statement of your position on social class and racial differences in intelligence."[77] In response Jensen produced the most explosive article in the history of American psychology, triggering one of the most bitter scientific controversies since Darwin and catapulting him from relative obscurity to national prominence and, in some quarters, notoriety. "How Much Can We Boost IQ and Scholastic Achievement?" took up almost the entire winter 1969 issue of *HER*, the longest article in the journal's history. Its title reflected Jensen's concern with genetic limitations—not "how?" but "how much?"—and 123 pages later he concluded that scholastic achievement could be considerably improved by using the "Level I" abilities of rote memory found in such abundance among the disadvantaged but that little could be done to change "intelligence," a trait dependent on those "Level II" abilities of conceptualization and abstract reasoning in which the disadvantaged were genetically deficient.

The article began with a very short fuse: "Compensatory education has been tried and it apparently has failed." A brief introduction went on to explain that these compensatory efforts had been based on the belief that almost all children were capable of normal educational progress and that, as a consequence, the poor academic performance of minority students was mainly due to "social, economic and educational deprivation and discrimination." The resulting programs had therefore attempted to provide them the same kind of cultural enrichment and additional instruction in basic skills enjoyed by middle-class "majority" children. Even with "unprecedented support from Federal funds," Jensen maintained, educational improvement for minorities had been "utterly unrealized," a fiasco that provoked a rhetorical flurry on his part. "Why has there been such uniform failure of compensatory programs?" he inquired: "In other fields, when bridges do not stand, when aircraft do not fly, when machines do not work, when treatments do not cure, despite all conscientious efforts on the part of many persons to make then do so, one begins to question the basic assumptions, principles, theories and hypotheses that guide one's efforts. Is it time to follow suit in education?"[78] Maybe, he implied, deprivation and discrimination were not the real problem; maybe the problem was the assumption that disadvantaged children could be taught by the same methods that had proven successful with the white middle class.

This hasty dismissal of compensatory education was based on two reports, the first a Commission on Civil Rights evaluation of a number of public school projects. Though Jensen named two specific examples discussed by the commission, he provided no details. The actual report was quite instructive. Its description of the Banneker Project in St. Louis clearly stated that the program had not involved the expenditure of federal money and that it had attempted to raise motivation rather than provide instructional assistance for students. Banneker was thus completely irrelevant to the model that Jensen had claimed was unsuccessful. His other example, the Higher Horizons Program in New York, had been patterned after an experimental project in Harlem, in which additional per pupil expenditures of 80 dollars a year in junior high and 250 dollars a year in high school had produced phenomenal gains in a selected group of students. When Higher Horizons attempted to apply the demonstration project to a broader group, however, it reduced the additional per pupil funding to 50–60 dollars a year. Even more important, as the program expanded over time, the number of support personnel dwindled in comparison with the number of children. Sometimes administrative checkerboarding—in which, for example, a Higher Horizons reading improvement teacher would be hired at the same time a regular class-room teacher was dropped—provided the image of additional assistance when, in fact, there had been none. The commission's description of these maneuvers suggested the opposite of Jensen's conclusion: an apparently successful compensatory model had failed because of improper implementation on a larger scale.[79]

At the time of Jensen's article there was also mounting evidence that many school districts receiving federal money for compensatory education had failed to comply with the statutory criteria for appropriate use of these funds. According to the legislation, federal aid was to be used only for "supplementary" assistance to the "educationally deprived" and was not to "supplant" in any way the expenditures of the local district; that is, the money was to provide additional assistance for eligible students only *after* the local board had funded a program for them comparable to that offered to other children. Nevertheless, in addition to the kind of person-nel shuffling found in Higher Horizons, federal funds were often used merely to enlarge the local operating budget and finance normal expendi-tures on teacher salaries, libraries, sports equipment, and even new construction. In some cases the money allocated for compensatory educa-tion was used to provide black schools with services already provided to white schools through local funds. Other school systems subsidized spe-cial projects having nothing to do with educationally deprived children—for example, swimming pools in a Louisiana district and a 2.5 million dollar educational television station in Fresno, California. Such clear violations of the law resulted in the misexpenditure of tens of millions of dollars until more careful monitoring forced an end to these practices and ordered some school systems to repay substantial amounts to the government.[80]

Jensen's other source of evidence for compensatory education's failure came from early evaluations of Head Start, the federal project designed to assist preschoolers living in poverty. These programs had generally produced only modest gains in IQ, which then tended to diminish shortly after the child entered elementary school. This should have come as no surprise to Jensen, who had emphasized only a few years earlier that "pre-school intervention without adequate follow-up in the first years of elementary school is inadequate, because the culturally disadvantaged child does not go home after school, as does the middle-class child, to what is essentially a tutorial situation."[81] Yet it was the children who now seemed inadequate to him rather than the lack of follow-up.

Head Start, however, had never been designed as a solution for the educational problems of the disadvantaged; it was intended as the first payment on a long-overdue moral debt to the poor, a humanitarian response to the plight of children in the richest country in the world who had never seen a dentist or doctor, never enjoyed a balanced diet, or never played with art materials and children's books. Though the opportunity for educational enrichment was one purpose, comprehensive health examinations, improved nutrition, other support services for the pre-schoolers' families, and the "maximum feasible participation" of parents were all goals of equal importance. Moreover, when the availability of federal money for Head Start was first announced—only a few months prior to the scheduled implementation date—it produced a frantic rush of applications by school boards, civic groups, churches, colleges, sororities, and local action agencies, none of whom wanted their community to be left out.[82] The result was a helter-skelter of programs hastily thrown together in most cases—no two of them the same, each independently developed and administered, each concentrating on whichever goal seemed most important in its community. Even those few that chose to emphasize cognitive development had no illusion that a brief and hastily planned intervention would produce large, sustained increases in IQ. Jensen's judgment of the program's inadequacy was thus based on the failure to attain a goal for which it had not been primarily designed. The most controversial article in the history of American psychology had begun with an assertion based on data that were for the most part irrelevant.

Longitudinal studies of Head Start would later conclude that it was one of the most successful Great Society programs, producing perhaps not increased IQ scores but definitely improved performance in school and a better chance for a more satisfying and productive life. The Perry Preschool Project in Ypsilanti, Michigan, for example, one of the more educationally intensive programs, was specifically cited by Jensen because the average IQ gain of 8.9 points, which it had initially produced, dwindled to a mere 1.6 points by the end of the second grade, "a nonsignificant gain," he emphasized. A study of the Perry children sixteen years later, however, showed that they had much higher rates of high school graduation, employment, and participation in college and vocational training and a much lower incidence of welfare, delinquency, crime, and teenage pregnancy than similar children who had not been experienced the preschool intervention.[83] In fact, Head Start became one of the few Great Society programs to survive the cut-and-slash Reagan years, and it was subsequently increased 40 percent by the "kinder, gentler" Bush budget.

Having passed judgment with such certainty, however, Jensen could now spend the next hundred pages on a genetic explanation for compensatory education's putative failure, dependent largely on the claim that the "heritability of intelligence" was 80 percent. Much of this discussion was highly technical in nature, making it intimidating to some and impressive to others, who assumed that such an immense methodological apparatus must necessarily indicate a profound intellectual endeavor.

Near the end of this complex presentation Jensen turned to the cause of racial differences in intelligence. He began with the strongest reminder that decisions involving the selection of persons—for college, graduate or professional school, employment, promotion—were always made about individuals and that

> the variables of social class, race and national origin are correlated so imperfectly with any of the valid criteria on which the above decisions should depend, or, for that matter, with any behavioral characteristic, that these background factors are irrelevant as a basis for dealing with individuals—as students, as employees, as neighbors. Furthermore, since, as far as we know, the full range of human talents is represented in all the major races of man and in all socioeconomic levels, it is unjust to allow the mere fact of an individual's racial or social background to affect the treatment accorded to him. All persons rightfully must be regarded on the basis of their individual qualities and merits, and all social, educational and economic institutions must have built into them the mechanisms for insuring and maximizing the treatment of persons according to their individual behavior.[84]

After expression of such an admirably liberal credo, a discussion of racial differences might have seemed of little practical importance, but Jensen quickly supplied a compelling rationale: since the civil rights movement was citing the "disproportionate representation of different racial groups in the various levels of the educational, occupational and socioeconomic hierarchy" as evidence of unfairness and discrimination in the society, scientists were "forced" to examine all the possible explanations for such inequities. Perhaps the disproportion had nothing to do with unfairness, he speculated; perhaps there were real differences among the races in characteristics "indisputably relevant to educational and occupational performance."[85] That is, maybe genetic differences—not discrimination, deprivation, or economic exploitation—were the real reason that blacks had the highest rate of unemployment and the dirtiest and lowest-paying jobs when they were hired. Jensen was suggesting, stripped of euphemisms, that blacks were poor because they were dumb.

Jensen offered this genetic explanation in cautious, scientific language, noting that there were "various lines of evidence, no one of which is definitive alone, but which, viewed all together, make it a not unreasonable hypothesis that genetic factors are strongly implicated in the average Negro-white intelligence difference."[86] Such verbal gymnastics did not indicate any real doubt on Jensen's part, however. As the Harvard geneticist Richard Lewontin pointed out, if taken at face value, Jensen's conclusion was "guilty of the utmost triviality," a waste of journal space. "Like all cant," as Lewontin termed it, "the special language of the social scientist needs to be translated into common English,"[87] and when properly decoded, Jensen's real meaning was clearly that blacks were genetically inferior in intelligence. Indeed, not long after sticking this cautious toe in the water, Jensen would ignore all the reservations, estimating "that something between one-half and three-fourths of the average IQ differences between American Negroes and whites is attributable to genetic factors."[88] He even offered a possible explanatory mechanism—"a biochemical connection between skin pigmentation and intelligence" linked to their joint development in the embryo's ectoderm.[89]

Jensen recommended eugenic measures as the long-term solution for the presence of so many persons with genetically substandard intelligence—whether black or white. Even though some retarded parents admittedly produced children of average and even superior IQ, who, he rhetorically inquired, would wish upon these well-endowed children the kind of environment provided by such parents? As Leon F. Whitney, an activist in the earlier sterilization campaign, had observed, whether a "useless" life had been caused by bad genes or bad environment, in either case the parents of such a child *ought never to have produced him.*"[90] While the civil rights movement had not seemed to stir Jensen's conscience, the plight of children born to retarded parents moved him deeply: "Have we thought sufficiently of the rights of children—of their right to be born with fair odds against being mentally retarded, not to have a retarded parent, and with fair odds in favor of having the genetic endowment needed to compete on equal terms with the majority of persons in society? Can we reasonably and humanely oppose such rights of millions of children as yet not born?"[91] Of course, to champion the rights of these nonexistent children meant to ensure that they remained that way—by preventing adults labeled inferior by test scores from reproducing.

Moreover, Jensen noted—in an argument identical with Shockley's—the proliferation of children of incompetent parents was a particular threat to the black population, where lower-class families were reproducing much more rapidly than middle- or upper-class families, and then, in perhaps the single most inflammatory observation of the article, he posed the question, using Shockley's favorite phrase: "Is there a danger that current welfare policies, unaided by eugenic foresight, could lead to the genetic enslavement of a substantial segment of the population?"[92] More socially sensitive than Shockley, Jensen avoided specific proposals for sterilizing large numbers of blacks with low IQs or otherwise preventing their reproduction (though in an interview he once asserted that people with low IQs were "a burden on everyone, a disservice to themselves," and he urged that "we should prevent their reproducing").[93] Such a leading question made it unnecessary to point out the obvious, however. After all, in what other way would eugenic foresight aid current welfare policy? Distribution of assistance according to genetic desirability?

Finally, Jensen concluded with the implications for improving the education of minorities. He was "reasonably convinced" that basic skills could be mastered by all disadvantaged children with normal "Level I" abilities for memory and association, which were generally their strengths, provided that the methods of instruction were not based on those "Level II" conceptual abilities, which were generally lacking "in these children's genetic and cultural heritage." The problem, Jensen feared, was that most classroom instruction relied on the latter. Indeed, he wrote, "if a child cannot show that he 'understands' the meaning of $1 + 1 = 2$ in some abstract, verbal, cognitive sense, he is, in effect, not allowed to go on to learn that $2 + 2 = 4$."[94] (Though Jensen's assertions were typically well documented, this one seemed to be mere speculation; every year millions of children memorize "times tables" just as they have always done, with little deeper understanding of the principles of the number system. For that matter, there are many college courses—statistics, for example—in which some students attain conceptual insight while many others memorize techniques with only a marginal appreciation of the underlying theory.) The practical implications of Jensen's article were therefore both educational and social: rote memorization to improve the scholastic skills of all those low IQ black children unable to understand abstract principles and some sort of eugenic program to reduce their numbers.

The Politics of Jensenism

The *HER* article was published in late February 1969 and became an immediate cause célèbre, something everyone was discussing, though few people had actually read it. The mass media pounced on the work, giving it unprecedented publicity for an article appearing in an academic journal. This instantaneous reaction occurred, at least in part, because Jensen had released a copy to *U.S. News and World Report* prior to *HER*'s publication, though he offered two differing accounts of how this had came about. In one, a writer from that magazine, who "knew nothing" of the forthcoming article, was visiting Berkeley to interview various faculty members about campus unrest. Jensen took the opportunity to volunteer information and give the writer a copy, informing him that *HER* had already released it to other members of the media. It sounded like a hint that the writer would have to act quickly or his magazine would trail the rest on this story. In this version, written in a context in which Jensen was emphasizing the speed of media response, he noted that the feature in *U.S. News and World Report* appeared only two weeks after the interview.[95] When a critic "accused" Jensen of releasing the article to gain publicity, however, he responded that the magazine had interviewed him "*after* learning about the article" (emphasis added) and that "they requested a prepublication copy," which he provided. In this account he stated that the story was published "almost a month" after the interview.[96] Whichever the true version, Jensen hardly seemed reluctant to respond to the media's interest; few scientists offer advance copies of their articles to journalists under any circumstances.

Though there had been local newspaper attention, particularly in the Boston and San Francisco areas—the home bases of *HER* and Jensen—the national coverage did begin with *U.S. News and World Report*'s feature story entitled "Can Negroes Learn the Way Whites Do?" a fairly accurate summary of the main points of Jensen's article.[97] Within a few weeks *Time* and *Newsweek* followed suit, and eventually every major publication and a host of smaller ones would profile the controversy.[98] But it was Lee Edson, science writer for the *New York Times Magazine,* who coined the term *Jensenism,* and his discussion of theory and theorist produced more letters to the editor than any other article ever published in that periodical.[99]

The media's focus, of course, was on race differences, and their unsubtle treatment of Jensen's conclusions often caused him to complain that his work was misrepresented to the public. He was particularly outraged by the title of the *Newsweek* story—"Born Dumb?" Yet the *New York Times Magazine* interview, which he called "the most thorough, thoughtful, and well-balanced story" of all the press coverage, "eminently fair and of meticulous accuracy,"[100] quoted Jensen as stating that "there are intelligence genes which are found in populations in different proportions, somewhat like the distribution of blood types. The number of intelligence genes seems to be lower, over-all, in the black population than the white."[101] The message underlying this more scientific language did not seem all that different from *Newsweek's* less sophisticated headline. At any rate, to the public, Jensenism became synonymous with black inferiority.

Because of the publication lag in academic journals, the scholarly controversy took longer to peak, but its duration was much greater than the relatively short attention span of the popular press, lasting throughout the 1970s. In an appendix to a 1972 book Jensen presented a list of 117 references written in response to the *HER* article, and this bibliography was hardly exhaustive.[102] On a 1978 list of the hundred most frequently cited social science articles from the previous ten years, Jensen's contribution to *HER* placed sixth. Unlike the other papers, which tended to be "seminal" works in their respective fields, Jensen's article was cited so often because it was an object of great controversy, though.[103]

For an academic debate the controversy was unusually bitter and personal. One social scientist accused Jensen of having done "injury to children" by "help[ing] to abort" compensatory education; major psychologists termed his work "academic manure," "obscene," and "abominable"; and there were ad hominem attacks on him as a racist.[104] Jensen was anything but reluctant to continue the fray; every adverse article received a rebuttal, every challenge a reply, every trivial criticism a letter to the editor. One observer calculated that over a five-year period Jensen produced an average of three hundred published words per day in the professional literature, a count excluding, of course, his numerous responses to critics in the mass media.[105] Nor were the reactions confined to print. Professional associations in anthropology and psychology circulated petitions and passed resolutions condemning conclusions of racial inequality, specifically naming Jensen as the latest offender.[106]

"Gusting through the Capitol"

It might have seemed surprising that Jensen's ideas caused such a storm when other scientists with overtly racist agendas had drawn relatively little attention. Only three years earlier Henry Garrett, a former president of the American Psychological Association, had authored a series of murky hate pamphlets and tracts opposing enforcement of the Constitution because blacks were allegedly inferior, yet he produced nothing close to the uproar over Jensen, who had made no explicit suggestion that anyone be deprived of rights. It was true that his article was published in *HER*, an influential publication despite having no more than twelve thousand subscribers, but in the very same journal a few years earlier Frank McGurk had claimed black inferiority to be an obstacle to integration, and he was hardly noticed.

The major reason for the intense reaction to Jensen was the timing of his work. The period just prior to the *HER* article had been a time of transition in the civil rights movement and the nation's response to it. As long as the movement had concentrated on equal rights—in polling places and public accommodations—it had enjoyed an unquestioned moral authority. These were "safe" issues: the movement's gain entailed no loss for whites. As the focus of civil rights activity shifted toward improving services and conditions for the poor, however, its agenda contained many issues where a victory for the movement was perceived to involve a cost for middle-class whites: compensatory education meant higher taxes; affirmative action might deprive others of jobs. Feelings of prejudice that had been suppressed while blacks braved fire hoses and police dogs to vote now needed a new and reasonable foundation.

Then, only months before publication of the *HER* article, Richard Nixon won a presidential election by stealing George Wallace's thunder and waging a campaign based, at least in part, on the country's increasing impatience with the civil rights movement's new direction. An ugly undercurrent of intolerance was rising to the surface in regions previously thought to be too sophisticated for racial prejudice. The original reports of Jensen's work in his own metropolitan area shared newspaper coverage with stories of physical assault on people attending a local school board meeting on integration and threats to board members and their families.[107] As John Ehrlichman, Nixon's adviser on domestic issues, would later acknowledge, many of the president's policies, especially in education and housing, were specifically designed to appeal to this emerging antiblack sentiment.[108] On the same day that Lee Edson coined *Jensenism* in the *New York Times,* the newspaper also reported a slowdown in administration attempts to enforce desegregation in the South, prompting a "rebellion" by half the civil rights lawyers in the Justice Department and producing the first break in open court between the Justice Department and the NAACP's Legal Defense Fund since the pre-*Brown* days.[109] According to Ehrlichman, Nixon even discussed upcoming cases on desegregation with Chief Justice Warren Burger, a clear breach of ethics.[110]

In such a political climate Jensen's article was much more threatening to the movement's supporters. It was perceived—correctly—as a scientific encoding of the shifting political impulses of the time, a signal that the Second Reconstruction had begun to decline. Moreover, its practical implications did not go unnoticed among policymakers. A *Life* magazine story quoted Daniel Moynihan, then a presidential adviser, remarking that "the winds of Jensenism were gusting through the capitol at gale force." It also cited a "high government official" who acknowledged the article as *"secret knowledge"* in the Washington bureaucracy, something not widely discussed but highly influential.[111] Edward Zigler, a professor of psychology at Yale and the director of the Federal Office of Child Development at the time, later observed that the "important decision-makers" might not have understood the technical portion of Jensen's paper, but they certainly did not miss his "clear statement that compensatory education is a failure."[112] At the very moment a new administration was balking at continued funding of educational assistance to the poor, a Berkeley professor had conveniently appeared, proffering a batch of IQ scores, to announce that these programs were a waste of the taxpayers' money. Though Jensen's name was not mentioned, Nixon's first major statements on education, delivered shortly after his veto of an educational appropriations bill, were highly critical of compensatory efforts and stressed the need for research on why some students learn more easily than others before investing additional public funds in projects that did not work.[113]

In private discussions the president remarked that federal programs could not benefit blacks because they were genetically inferior to whites, though, again, he referred to no specific scientific authority for the belief. The comment in a White House policy meeting most likely to have come directly from Jensen's article was made by Spiro Agnew. According to Ehrlichman, in a discussion on race and education Agnew stressed the distinction between *racial* discrimination and discrimination based on the fact that "people have different IQs, talents and other legacies."[114] This was almost identical with Jensen's claim that discrimination based on intelligence might appear to be racial due to the relation between race and IQ. Pat Buchanan, a White House aide at the time, submitted a memo to Nixon questioning the value of "all our efforts and expenditures not only for 'compensatory education' but to provide an 'equal chance at the starting line' " and suggesting that, because of genetic differences in intelligence, "a lot of what we are doing in terms of integration of blacks and whites . . . is less likely to result in accommodation than it is in perpetual friction . . . as the incapable are played [sic] consciously by government side by side with the capable."[115] Jensen himself noted with satisfaction the influence of his ideas in the new administration, observing that "the kind of research being funded and some of the appointments being made reflect in subtle ways some of the ideas in my *Harvard Review* article."[116]

Another cause of the controversy over Jensen was the radical student movement of the 1960s, then in its last moments of activity prior to self-destruction. Despite the internecine conflicts in Students for a Democratic Society, the "struggle" against racism had been a central tenet of every faction, and Jensen now provided an inviting target around which to mount a new campaign. Within days of *HER*'s publication a sound truck traversed the Berkeley campus blaring "Fight racism; fire Jensen."

In addition to the demand that he be fired, students were urged to boycott his classes, his lectures were interrupted, and he received hate mail and threatening phone calls.[117]

Such normally inexcusable acts drew some condemnation but not nearly the kind of indignation that might have been expected from the academic community. One social scientist compared the activists' campaign against Jensen with the behavior of antiwar protesters, noting that both groups saw their actions as a "moral choice" in which civility was abandoned on behalf of a higher value.[118] In perhaps the frankest refusal by a scientist to become exercised over Jensen's plight, the well-known researcher Ethel Tobach privately wrote that "I feel quite strongly that the hooliganism that disrupts Jensen . . . is something that one must expect in view of the fact that the indignities done to people are no longer being tolerated. I don't think that violence changes the things that are wrong with society, but I understand them very well. Therefore, I can hardly say that I deplore them; I just think that they are wasting their time."[119] Tobach might not have been so blunt had she anticipated publication of her remarks, but a lot of academics who expressed themselves more diplomatically in public probably harbored similar private sentiments.

A final factor contributing to the controversy was the very sophistication and scholarly nature of Jensen's presentation. He was not easily dismissed as just another die-hard segregationist or obvious bigot like the hysterically ranting Garrett. He could legitimately claim to have embarked on his research not only without a political agenda but also with a clear predisposition toward a finding of racial equality, thus suggesting the image of a scholarly mind only gradually freeing itself from an erroneous assumption through the influence of carefully collected data. No one pointed out Jensen's sophistication as a reason for the bitterness of the debate—his opponents did not wish to concede such praise for the article, and many of his most ardent supporters were segregationists, for whom acknowledgement of Jensen's greater scholarliness would be a tacit admission of the true nature of their other experts, such as Garrett and McGurk.

The difference was instinctively recognized, however. Although Shockley often mentioned Garrett as a major psychologist who believed in black intellectual inferiority, he would never have risked the ridicule certain to result from distributing one of Garrett's fulminations to his scientific peers as expert opinion. Immediately after publication of Jensen's article, however, Shockley sent a copy of the entire 123 pages to every one of the approximately seven hundred members of the psychology, anthropology, sociology, and genetics sections of the National Academy of Sciences.[120]

New Support for Segregation

The racists immediately sensed that Jensen could confer a new respectability on their position and a vindication of their claims. Even before the *HER* article made Jensen's name a household word, segregationists were already lauding the then unknown psychologist's conclusions as an indication of "renewed interest" in the thinking of Carleton Putnam. Probably alerted to Jensen's work by Shockley, who had close ties to the anti-integration activists, an editor of the *Jackson* (Mississippi) *Daily News,* a center of resistance to integration, predicted that "the courts will have to rule on educational matters along the lines which educational experts indicate . . . [and] that is why the report of Dr. Jensen is so important."[121] In keeping with this prediction, only days after the article's publication it was offered as evidence by the defense in a Virginia desegregation suit.[122] The entire article was also inserted into the *Congressional Record* by John R. Rarick, a Democratic representative from Louisiana and easily the most rabid reactionary in the House, a featured speaker at the national convention of the Liberty Lobby's Board of Policy, and a man reported to have links to the Ku Klux Klan.[123] The Klan itself began to circulate a pamphlet entitled *Race and Integration: Scientists Speak Out,* devoted largely to Jensen's research and conclusions.[124]

Jensen might have lanced the boil of racism by a simple dissociation of his own scientific interests from their use by reactionary political elements. It would not have been a difficult matter to denounce unequivocally all those who cited his work as support for segregation or other racially repressive policies, especially since he was already on record in favor of treating every individual on his or her merits, but even when challenged to do so, he refused.[125] When asked whether he was concerned that racists might quote his research out of context for their own purposes, Jensen replied, "I don't want to give these people the power of censorship over my research"—a strangely oblique response since the question contained no suggestion of any change in his work, only the problem of its political misuse.[126] Perhaps there was no scientific imperative for Jensen to repudiate the racists, but it was widely perceived as a moral responsibility; as the Talmud observed, a person who can protest injustice and does not becomes an accomplice in the act.

However, having suffered intense criticism from the same quarters that had opposed the racist scientists, Jensen seemed to feel some degree of sympathy, even kinship, for them. Only weeks after publication of the *HER* article the Society for the Psychological Study of Social Issues, a division of the American Psychological Association, released a statement to all the major news services and a number of professional journals, a portion of which was an almost verbatim repetition from its statement of opposition to Henry Garrett issued eight years earlier.[127] The one-size-fits-all mentality suggested an inability to distinguish between Garrett's hate polemics and Jensen's scholarship. Instead of emphasizing the differences between Garrett's work and his own, however, Jensen's response complained about the Society's "long history of reprimanding persons" like Garrett and McGurk and "censur[ing]" them for articles asserting the existence of racial genetic differences.[128] In fact, there had been little criticism, much less censure, of these scientists until they had sought to use their conclusions as a basis to overturn desegregation.

In addition, Jensen reserved the term *racist* only for those who did not "recognize the overlap between racial groups" and thus assumed all whites superior to all blacks.[129] By this definition almost nobody had ever been a racist—certainly not Putnam, Garrett, or McGurk, all of whom viewed racial differences as a matter of relative frequency; not the *Mankind Quarterly* contributor who acknowledged "exceptional" blacks with abilities superior to those of many whites even while insisting that they were "unsuited for citizenship in a democracy" and should not be allowed to vote;[130] not the early Social Darwinists, who looked forward to blacks' extinction yet conceded that "some Negroes are better than some Whites . . . mentally," a fact one writer judged of no greater relevance to their rights than the fact that "some dogs are superior to some men";[131] not even Josiah Nott, who had waged a vigorous campaign against the abolitionists yet did "not doubt that *individuals* of inferior races, as Indians and negroes, are capable . . . when compared with the whites."[132] According to Jensen's definition of the term, none of these rabid opponents of blacks' rights was "racist."

Nor was Jensen reluctant to participate in the segregationists' ongoing political campaign against the implementation of *Brown*. A year after the *HER* article the House Subcommittee on Education held hearings on the Emergency School Aid Act, a bill designed to provide financial assistance to school systems actually undergoing the process of integration. Seizing on the bill's reference to desegregation as a route to educational improvement for students attending "racially isolated" schools, the scientists who had opposed *Brown*—Garrett, Osborne, McGurk, van den Haag—again insisted that integration was based on science, this time on the assumption that it would produce educationally beneficial effects. To refute this assumption, they submitted statements to the subcommittee, repeating their evidence on black inferiority from the *Stell* case and concluding that the inherent intellectual differences between black and white children could not be altered by a change in the school's racial composition or, for that matter, by any other intervention. As Osborne noted in his statement, desegregation was "destructive" to the education of blacks and whites alike. This latest rendition of the decade-old theme was now part of a new strategy: since the bill under consideration also allowed funds for "evaluation," the segregationists urged the subcommittee to utilize this provision "to find out once and for all" whether integration did indeed improve the quality of education.[133] Clearly, they hoped that a negative answer to this question would provide new leverage to turn public schools from the integrationist path.

To the experts from *Stell* were added two new authorities. William Shockley submitted a statement asserting a "hereditary origin" for the "deficit in Negro intellectual performance" and suggesting, like the others, that the proposed legislation's evaluation component should be used to determine whether integration had any educational value.[134] Arthur Jensen also testified. He was one of only two scientists to appear in person before the subcommittee; the other was Ernst van den Haag, who delivered yet another attack on Kenneth Clark's twenty-year-old data from the Dolls Test. In his prepared statement, which Congressman Rarick reprinted in the *Congressional Record,* Jensen, too, claimed that the Emergency School Aid Act was based on the "premise" that "racial isolation . . . has an adverse effect on education," thus joining in the segregationists' contention that desegregation was in fact based not on constitutional entitlement but on empirically demonstrable assertions. From this point of view, his next logical step was to suggest "an essential preliminary inquiry . . . [which] relates to the truth or falsity as a scientific matter of the basic factual assumption underlying this bill," although he left little doubt about what he expected such an inquiry to demonstrate. "I do not believe that this premise alone can be regarded as adequate justification," Jensen told the committee, because "the educational abilities and needs of the majority of white and Negro children are sufficiently different at this present time in our history."[135] The implication was clear: in the face of these differing needs and abilities, desegregation would only harm both groups. Whatever Jensen's personal opinion of segregation, he was a participant in the segregationists' latest attempt to offer science as an obstacle to integration.

In the ensuing discussion between the two witnesses and the members of the subcommittee, Jensen stressed the importance of identifying the large number of black children who needed special education—in other words, classes for the retarded—explaining that in integrated schools such children were likely to be denied this placement because they would be mistakenly "treat[ed] like the average white child."[136] After listening to both Jensen and van den Haag raise objections to the possible success of integrated education, the subcommittee's chair latched onto the segregationists' strategy: if the evaluation, which all these experts had urged, did sustain their claims that integrated schools were an educational disaster, then "the courts would have no recourse but to take another look at *Brown.*" Was it possible, the chair inquired, "that this legislation conceivably could shoot down *Brown?*" Van den Haag quickly replied that an evaluation might indeed lead the courts to approve greater "freedom of choice." Jensen maintained a discreet silence.[137]

Institutionalizing Inequality

To all the controversy produced by his work Jensen pleaded if not ignorance at least innocence, maintaining that he was just a scientist pursuing a scientific question. As he told a reporter for the *Times* of London, "I take a non-political view. I'm almost embarrassed by my lack of political involvement in this issue. That whole side of the thing is beyond me." It was his critics, he claimed, whether scientists or not, who insisted on approaching this purely scientific issue on a political, an "ideological" level.[138]

If Jensen had begun as a political naif, he was certainly a quick study. In addition to all his media interviews, polemics in nonscientific periodicals, and congressional testimony, he quickly went on record asserting that research on the question of racial differences should be "widely discussed by the scientific community *and the general public as well*" (emphasis added).[139] To invite the public to participate in a genuinely scientific debate was unusual to say the least (contrast this "invitation" with scientists' response to the public's desire to participate in the debate on recombinant DNA research), and it suggested a Shockley-like intention to appeal beyond the scientific community to a larger constituency.

Moreover, the profession of a totally apolitical stance left Jensen in a rather paradoxical position. He had explained in the *HER* article—and he would continue to emphasize—that the scientific question of racial differences in ability derived meaning only from the political context of disproportionate black poverty. It was the civil rights movement's claim of discrimination as a major obstacle to vertical mobility for blacks that had "forced" Jensen to examine the genetic explanation for their socioeconomic inequality. The sole raison d'être for this line of research was its potential to disprove the movement's claim and relocate the cause of black impoverishment in their genes. There could be little doubt about the existence of racial discrimination in employment in 1969: a U.S. Labor Department survey of four large cities had recently found not a single black apprentice among union plumbers, steamfitters, sheet-metal workers, stonemasons, structural ironworkers, operating engineers, lathers, painters, or glaziers.[140] Low IQs were hardly the reason that no blacks were employed in these fields; nor would higher IQs have gained them entree. But if science could demonstrate that blacks were clustered preponderantly at the economic nadir merely as a reflection of their genetic merit, then the country could ignore all the unfounded complaints about alleged discrimination. This was hardly an apolitical position. In the profusion of scientific articles and books produced by Jensen after the *HER* article, the rationalization of inequality between blacks and whites was a frequent subtext and often the only practical implication. *Educability and Group Differences*, for example, was a four-hundred-page attempt to prove blacks genetically inferior to whites in intellectual ability through a point-by-point refutation of environmentalist explanations for the racial difference in IQ. At the end of this tome Jensen presented the "educational implications" of his genetic hypothesis: not all children respond to the same instructional method at the same time; they have to be treated as individuals. After two pounds of detail from a review of hundreds of studies, this seemed an incredibly banal outcome, one that appeared to have little to do with race. But, Jensen explained, to treat black children as individuals meant to recognize their genetic limitations—to realize that their poor performance was "not mainly the result of discrimination and unequal environmental conditions." The false emphasis on environmental factors, he declared, would only generate "social paranoia" resulting from the myth of discrimination, a belief in "mysterious hostile forces" as the cause of inequality.[141] In a subsequent article Jensen elaborated on the psychological dynamics of this myth. The "failure to succeed," he explained, "is less apt to be perceived as personal failure if one identifies with a group which is claimed, justifiably or not, to be discriminated against. Having the status of an unprivileged caste, real or imagined, makes personal failure more tolerable."[142] The social role of the genetic explanation was thus to strip away this self-deception and force blacks to face their inherent shortcomings; if only blacks could be persuaded of their intellectual inferiority, presumably they would accept their justifiably lower socioeconomic status and stop complaining of imagined mistreatment.

Having scientifically rationalized the disproportionate representation of blacks among the poor, Jensen insisted that their appropriate education had to be based on the same genetic facts. Since it was not "realistic" to expect the schools to change "basic intelligence," he opposed all compensatory programs as a waste of "limited resources on misguided, irrelevant and ineffective remedies." Besides its practical ineffectiveness, Jensen regarded compensatory education as an attempt to replace the liberal ideal of "equality of educational input"—a goal that, he maintained, had already been achieved—with "unequal input" in order to provide special advantages to minorities that were not available to the middle class.[143] Even more serious, according to Jensen, the public school system generally suffered from the same erroneous assumption underlying compensatory efforts—that all children could be taught by the "usual methods

of instruction," dependent largely on "thinking" and "conceptualizing"—
and he saw the presence of a substantial number of pupils genetically
incapable of such learning as a threat to the very survival of universal
public education.[144]

Jensen continually insisted that there was only one productive intervention: the sole hope—not just for improving education for minorities
but also for maintaining the viability of compulsory education in the face
of so many genetically handicapped students—was to provide *"a diversity of conditions suited to the diversity of individual abilities and needs
of the pupil."*[145] For Jensen, this was the true definition of equal educational opportunity, one that went beyond irrelevant concerns with equal-
izing expenditures, facilities, or equipment to the core of the problem—the
need to institute different instructional methods and goals that would
place that mass of children genetically incapable of benefiting from the
traditional curriculum into a program oriented toward their abilities to
associate and remember, while only the more "intelligent" students would
be taught to understand principles and concepts. This procedure would,
by Jensen's own calculation, relegate the great majority of blacks to the
associative track. Indeed, that would be its purpose—to salvage their education by relieving blacks of the burden of understanding. An educational
version of the attempt to save Vietnamese villages by destroying them,
Jensen's proposal would soon resegregate most blacks into the lower tier
of an educational caste system, channeling them into correspondingly
menial occupations and thus perpetuating their position in the underclass.
After all, what employer seeking to fill a position of any responsibility
would consider an applicant certified by the schools as too unintelligent
to learn except through rote memorization? Though perhaps not as rigid
as *Brave New World*'s plan to program "Gamma, Delta and Epsilon"
embryos for a lower-class role, Jensen's concept of educational equality
proceeded from an implicit recognition that blacks as a group were
genetically deficient in the higher conceptual abilities necessary for true
success in contemporary society. It was consequently necessary to create
remedial programs for them that would really work, capitalizing on their
associative strengths and, in the process, preparing them for the social
niche appropriate to their "Level I" abilities. Rather than reduce socioeconomic inequality, the schools would institutionalize it.

Jensen also opposed affirmative action as the political corollary of
racial differences in intelligence. Though less outspoken than Shockley,
who claimed that court rulings in favor of affirmative action were based
on the "national egalitarian lie,"[146] Jensen believed that the policy was
consciously predicated on the assumption that blacks and whites were
intellectually equal and that scientific evidence for racial inequality
should thus render it untenable. From his analysis of racial differences

Jensen concluded that five to six times more whites than blacks were genetically qualified for the better colleges and professional schools—in other words, had IQs above 115—making the unequal representation of races in higher education and the professions again merely a social reflection of biology; according to science, there *should* be disproportionately more whites than blacks in professional positions. (At the time of the *HER* article there was a total of 783 black medical school students, a number that would rise to 3,456—out of 53,000 medical students altogether—in the next eight years. Even if Jensen's estimate of five to six times more qualified whites than blacks were correct, there would still be a large underrepresentation of blacks.) Because of this genetic disparity, Jensen considered affirmative action programs not just unfair to "borderline" whites "crowded out" by the preference for minorities but, more serious, a source of incompetence, unavoidably producing "the accountant who cannot calculate or the surgeon who has not learned anatomy." It was not that he could cite any example of an "affirmative action" doctor who had not learned anatomy; it was unnecessary to identify actual incompetents when the fact of their existence was deduced from genetic differences between the races. To Jensen, affirmative action was thus scientifically disproven.[147]

This insistence that policy had been predicated on some underlying scientific assumption was, once again, erroneous. There have been numerous statutes enacting affirmative action at various levels of government and numerous court cases, some favorable and some unfavorable depending on the particular circumstances and the venue, but in no instance has a legislative action or a judicial decision ever concerned itself in any way with the issue of genetic equality. There are some powerful and persuasive arguments to be offered in opposition to affirmative action, but they have nothing to do with biology.[148]

Despite his claims of political innocence, Jensen was proposing, as a consequence of his research, a highly political agenda, almost all of it unfavorable to the aspirations of blacks. To do so was certainly Jensen's right as a citizen, a right he should not have had to forfeit just because his political ideology was informed by his scientific conclusions. But like the eugenicists in the anti-immigration campaign, Jensen sought to have it both ways: while proposing a political agenda, he attempted to use his status as a scientist to deny any political interest or involvement, fending off critics with the charge that it was *they* who insisted on making a political response to his purely scientific conclusions.

The Science of Jensenism

Despite the fact that the political implications were, according to Jensen himself, the only reason for interest in the question of racial differences, it was, of course, possible to evaluate the scientific merit of his work entirely apart from any political considerations. For all its scholarly nature and technical sophistication, his argument for a genetic difference in intelligence between the races was remarkably weak, based not on any new evidence but on the putative inability to explain the difference in any other way. Yet because the argument was clothed in what was, for many psychologists, the daunting mathematical regalia of behavior genetics, many of the initial responses by well-known social scientists were rather inept, creating the impression that Jensen's case must have been fairly solid.

A particularly severe early critic, for example, was Martin Deutsch, a professor of psychology at New York University who first claimed to have found seventeen errors in Jensen's *HER* article—a number he later increased to fifty-three—"all of them unidimensional and all of them anti-black."[149] The few examples offered by Deutsch for these implications about Jensen's objectivity and perhaps even his integrity were trivial at best, though: a "68%" that was transposed as "86%" or a study cited by Jensen that was based on data from only eight subjects.[150] Because of the seriousness of Deutsch's charge, Jensen brought the matter to the American Psychological Association's Committee on Scientific and Professional Ethics and Conduct, which, after almost two years of repeated demands, finally obtained the complete list of supposedly malignant errors. Deutsch's full evidence again proved so trivial that *Jensen* attempted to distribute the list to the public; clearly he felt vindicated.[151] Moreover, the image of his critics waving around a changing set of undisclosed errors as Joseph McCarthy did with his list of State Department Communists gave Jensen the moral high ground.

Intelligence and Jelly Rolls

Actually, instead of reporting any recent research, the scientific portion of the *HER* article had been almost entirely devoted to a restoration of two psychological antiques, old concepts that had been gathering dust in psychology's basement until Jensen's attempt to refinish them and set them out for the public as if they were new. The first was the "factor analytic" definition of intelligence—originally proposed in 1904 by the English scientist Charles Spearman—as the theoretical, mathematical construct necessary to account for the fact that those who score high on one kind of test tend to score high on others; that is, intelligence was the single underlying factor explaining the correlation between different tests of mental ability.[152] Since intelligence was conceptualized as unidimensional, it implied that all individuals could be ranked on one linear continuum of intellectual ability. Indeed, Jensen would soon extend the scale's range at both ends until this "purely mathematical, theoretical construct" became "an interspecies concept" relating every organism's intelligence to its respective phylogenetic status, a notion that the Harvard palentologist Stephen J. Gould termed "the most naive bit of writing about evolution . . . in years."[153] The intellectual worth of every earthly creature, from the lowest amoeba to the highest human, could once again be placed on a single continuum; the great chain of being had been discarded in the nineteenth century only to be resurrected a hundred years later.

Whether intelligence should be considered a unidimensional or multidimensional construct had been debated by psychologists since their initial interest in the concept at the beginning of the century. A temporary truce between the two positions was obtained in 1923 when the Harvard psychologist E. G. Boring offered his famous tautology, "Intelligence is what the tests test." Less well remembered, however, is his very next observation that although "the ordinary connotation of intelligence is much broader . . . no harm need result if we but remember that measurable intelligence is simply what the tests of intelligence test, until further scientific observation allows us to extend the definition."[154] That is, psychology had to recognize that its definition of intelligence was but a first approximation that had to be greatly expanded before it could better represent common usage, which was the standard. To defend his unidimensional model, Jensen claimed the derivation to have taken the opposite path, that is, *intelligence* originated as a technical term in psychology for the "general factor common to standards tests of intelligence" before "filter[ing] down into common parlance."[155] Actually, *intelligentia*, a Latin word meaning the capacity for understanding—*intelligence*—was frequently used in Cicero's orations and by medieval philosophers; the contemporary term is traced back some centuries by standard unabridged dictionaries and was discussed in Darwin's *Descent of Man and Selection in Relation to Sex.* Quite apart from his inaccurate account of linguistic history, Jensen was calling for a public discussion of racial differences in "intelligence" at the same time that he insisted that this commonly used term had a scientifically idiosyncratic meaning.

Reliance on the factor analytic definition, however, made it possible for Jensen to assess mathematically the degree to which any test or task was "loaded" with "g," the underlying general intelligence factor. Though some standard IQ tests were "purer" measures of g than others, he found them all to be generally g laden, thus confirming some empirical relationship between intelligence and its most commonly used—and frequently criticized—operational definition. The *im*perfection of the relationship between IQ tests and *g* in some cases also proved useful to Jensen, allowing him to account for an increase in IQ scores obtained by some compensatory programs without having to acknowledge any change in intelligence: the curriculum in these programs had reduced the *g* loadings of the IQ test, divesting it of "the same meaning as an index of general intelligence."[156]

A common criticism of standard measures of intelligence has been their quite modest relationship to actual accomplishments, typical correlations with occupational performance being about 0.2.[157] (The correlation between height and weight is about 0.5; thus, selecting persons for job placement on the basis of IQ score would be considerably less accurate than attempting to select the tallest individuals on the basis of their weights.) As the Yale psychologist Seymour Sarason has observed, "Psychology has for too long sought to measure a world of its own contrivance, and this it has done extremely well—so well that for decades it did not have to face the possibility that ingeniously measuring a world of one's own making is a mammoth waste of time."[158] To demonstrate that *g* was much more than just a measure of "academic intelligence," Jensen also assessed the "*g* loadings" of nonacademic tasks. He analyzed the tasks performed by U.S. Army cooks, solemnly reporting that making scrambled eggs had zero loading while the preparation of jelly rolls was much more highly saturated with *g*.[159] His unidimensional construct of intelligence thus largely excluded memory and learning ability while including the skills of jelly roll preparation.

The greatest difficulty with Jensen's mathematically defined construct of intelligence was that it tended to reify the correlation between various tests, that is, to treat the statistical abstraction of a general relationship between scores on two tests as if it were the result of some underlying material reality. A correlation between a pair of tests—say, one of verbal ability and one of quantitative—is based on a general trend for a large number of persons but does not necessarily hold for any single one of them. Even given the correlation, there are still many individuals whose high ability in one area is coupled with mediocre performance in the other. When, for example, specialized aptitude tests were administered to one group of students in place of global measures of intelligence, more than half of them scored in the top 10 percent on a specific ability.[160] Research on so-called geniuses has suggested a similar conclusion. When the psychologist David Feldman studied the development of a number of "child prodigies," he found the unitary notion of intelligence inadequate to account for their high achievement. Although prodigies occasionally have all-around ability, more often they are exceptionally talented in only one domain—"pretuned" to master some specific area of endeavor. In some cases high overall ability may even prove to be an obstacle to prodigious accomplishment since multiple talents tend to "compete" for available time and resources, whereas a child with a single ability is more likely to display the tenacious commitment to it that produces outstanding achievement.[161] To insist that all "intelligent" behavior is rooted in some single underlying general ability is tenable only at the level of mathematical abstraction; to impose the unidimensional construct willy-nilly on the multidimensional domain of behavior conveniently allows the placement of every person in a simple linear ordering of intellect, but it fails as a description of real human beings.

It was not until a decade after Jensen's *HER* article, when much of the controversy over his work had subsided, that research on human intelligence, an area that, after stagnating for years, had been pronounced "dead" by one of its own most well-known experts, finally began to generate some new interest and excitement, largely as a result of discarding the single continuum approach in favor of looking at a variety of skills.[162] Howard Gardner, for example, has proposed a theory of "multiple intelligences," each one having a biological origin and permitting individuals to produce important cultural products. So far Gardner has suggested seven such "intelligences": musical, linguistic, bodily-kinesthetic, logical-mathematical, spatial, interpersonal, and intrapersonal. An individual would thus be characterized by a collection of abilities, each having recognized cultural significance, rather than by a single faculty identified by an intelligence test. The evidence for the biological basis of these abilities has been derived from experimental, not correlational, evidence. For example, damage to a specific area of the brain has been shown to cause impairment of the specific ability controlled by that region. At the same time, the fact that such damage does not affect other faculties is strong evidence that g is a myth.[163]

Heritability: The Pursuit of Irrelevance

The establishment of g as the theoretical construct of intelligence and the IQ score as its appropriate operational definition allowed Jensen to turn to his second antique—the "heritability" of intelligence. Interest in this issue also dated back to the beginning of the century, when early eugenicists, such as Karl Pearson, called for measurement of "the relative shares" of heredity and environment as "the first problem" of their science, although this cry for research could not be construed to indicate any doubt about its outcome. "Nature dominates nurture, . . . inheritance is more vital than environment," Pearson asserted,[164] and Frederick Adams Woods, the "American Galton," concluded—long in advance of any empirical evidence—that heredity "exercised in mental life a factor not far from nine-tenths, while from the moral side it is something over one half."[165]

If Jensen's technical definition of intelligence, a word that psychologists had attempted to appropriate from the colloquial domain, proved somewhat elusive to the public, the concept of heritability brought total confusion. The heritability of a trait is defined as the proportion of observed differences between persons that is due to genetic differences. This concept and the techniques for its estimation had been developed not with human behavior in mind but specifically for the analysis of various traits of farm animals and agricultural crops—the fleece weight of sheep, milk yield of dairy cattle, egg production of fowl, or yield per acre for wheat. The purpose of such heritability estimates was primarily to increase the efficiency or amount of food production by finding to what extent a trait will "breed true" (i.e., the higher the heritability of some characteristic, the more effective would be a selective breeding program in increasing the yield on that trait). To the public, however, Jensen's assertion that the "heritability" of intelligence was 80 percent had little to do with such concerns. The common interpretation of his claim was that an *individual's* intelligence was largely hereditary; that if it was hereditary, then it must have been determined by the genes; and that if it was determined by genes, then obviously there was little possibility for change from environmental intervention. Actually, every one of these conclusions was false.

Since heritability is the proportion of *differences* between persons that is genetic, it is applicable only to groups, not to individuals. Any attempt to partition an *individual's* IQ score into a hereditary and an environmental component would be utter nonsense, similar to asking how much of the weight of a two-hundred-pound man is due to his genes and how much to his environment. Yet such statements appeared often in discussions of Jensen's work. A writer in *Commonweal,* for example, noted that Jensen "assigns a good 80 percent of a person's intelligence to genetic factors and a minority 20 percent to environmental influence."[166] Perhaps some misinterpretation was to be expected in the popular journals, but scientists have made similar contributions to the confusion. It is not unusual to find a biology textbook by university professors explaining that "80 percent of our basic intelligence is inherited and . . . the remaining 20 percent . . . determined by our environment" or even a university textbook on genetics claiming that "from half to three-fourths of intelligence is genetically based, the rest environmentally controlled."[167] Hans J. Eysenck, the world-famous researcher who rushed to support Jensen during the controversy, explained that "the figure of 80% heritability is an average. It does not apply equally to every person in the country. For some people environment may play a much bigger part than is suggested by this figure; for others it may be even less."[168] One social scientist called this observation a "priceless howler,"[169] suggesting, as it did, that one person's IQ might be, say, 90 percent genetic, while another's might be only 40 percent. A geneticist compared it to "a physicist writing about the temperature of a molecule."[170] Nor was this just a careless choice of words on Eysenck's part. A decade earlier he had noted that for some persons "the importance of environment would be very much higher [than 20 percent], perhaps as high as 70 or 80 percent."[171] A decade after the Jensen controversy, still involved in the same debate, he continued to write that from the 80 percent to 20 percent division of variation in IQ between heredity and environment, "it does not follow that these proportions would be the same for a given individual."[172] From a layperson such observations might have been amusing; from a scientist of international rank they were astonishing.

Then, too, heritability is a variable, not a constant, and thus has no fixed or "true" value. An estimate of a trait's heritability is valid only for a particular group at a specific time, a still photo of the sources of variation among those people at that moment. A moment later the picture could change for many reasons. For a group of individuals raised in a rural area unaffected by environmental pollution, the heritability of cancer—the degree to which individual differences in propensity to develop the disease is genetic—would be very high. If, however, the group was dispersed, some remaining in the pristine environment and others relocating near oil refineries or chemical plants, then the heritability of cancer would become very low for these same people; the individual differences in their cancer propensity would now be largely due to environmental factors. In general, a trait's heritability for a group of persons increases as their environment becomes more uniform and decreases as the environment is diversified. Heritability also varies inversely with individuals' genetic similarity: the more genetically homogeneous a group becomes, the lower a trait's heritability is, and the more heterogeneous, the higher the heritability. In the theoretically degenerate case of a group in which the persons were all genetically identical, the heritability of *every* trait would therefore be zero, since all differences between them would be environmental in origin. If a group of genetically distinct individuals was raised in an identical environment, then the heritability of *every* trait would be 100 percent, since all variation would necessarily be genetic.

If the heritability of *any* trait in a genetically identical group is zero, then obviously heritability is not synonymous with genetic causality. The number of legs on a human being, for example, is certainly a matter of genetic determination, but those individuals with less than two legs are generally the result of some kind of environmental intervention, accidental or intentional: the prenatal effects of thalidomide, loss of a limb in war, surgery to treat a circulation problem, and the like. Since all the observed variation is environmental, the heritability of the number of legs is zero. This is not as paradoxical as it may sound once it becomes clear that the object of study is not the individual value of a trait but rather the difference in its value from one person to another. Substituting an analysis of these differences for an analysis of the trait means that genetically determined traits could yield very low heritability and that traits with high heritability could have little genetic cause. Again, however, even a leading university textbook on genetics can offer the misleading observation that "a trait with a heritability of 0 has no genetic basis."[173]

Perhaps the most harmful popular misconception was the belief that a high heritability "fixed" the value of a trait, setting limitations on the possibility for change. According to this thinking, if the heritability of IQ was 80 percent, then there was only 20 percent "remaining" for manipulation, and thus environment could have a very small impact at best. Though sounding logical, such reasoning was specious; heritability and alterability have little to do with one another. Body weight, for example, is a trait with high heritability, but it can be dramatically increased or decreased by fast, famine, or gluttony.

Jensen himself, of course, well understood this distinction, and his technical discussions made the point with clarity. In the *HER* article he cited tuberculosis, once a disease with high heritability, as an example of a trait for which environmental advances had made genetic factors largely irrelevant.[174] (This was a somewhat ironic choice of example since a previous generation of scientists had insisted that, precisely because the disease had high heritability, only the careful selection of genetic stock for parenthood would eventually eliminate it, and some had even opposed TB sanatoriums because of their allegedly dysgenic effect.)[175] In a different article, devoted entirely to the meaning of heritability, Jensen noted the "troublesome misconception . . . that a high heritability necessarily means immutability of the trait in question, implying a hopeless fatalism, against which some people tend to react emotionally. A heritability index simply tells us that in the particular population sampled, for the particular measurement obtained, a certain proportion . . . of the total variance is attributable to genetic factors."[176]

Having acknowledged such points in theory, however, Jensen seemed to feel that they could be ignored as a practical matter. Because IQ showed high heritability, he explained in the *HER* article, "if compensatory education programs are to have a beneficial effect on achievement, it will be through their influence on motivation, values, and other environmentally conditioned habits that play an important part in scholastic performance, rather than through any marked direct influence on intelligence per se. The proper evaluation of such programs should therefore be sought in their effects on actual scholastic performance rather than in how much they raise the child's IQ."[177] That is, despite the obligatory genuflection toward theoretical possibility, in practice Jensen found no hope for intellectual growth; the best that could be expected was to make low-IQ children study harder so that their schoolwork would improve even though their "intelligence" could not. (The last sentence in Jensen's comment was, again, ironic: having detonated the controversy with his opening proclamation of compensatory education's failure because it had not raised IQ scores, he buried much later in the dense text of the article the acknowledgment that IQ scores were not, in fact, the proper basis of evaluation.) Perhaps Jensen's frankest observation occurred in response to the Harvard geneticist Richard Lewontin, who had raised the issue of immutability. After first denying that he had suggested change was impossible, Jensen went on to offer an analogy for the attempt to increase (black) children's intelligence: "With all our technological progress in the physical sciences since the seventeenth century, we have not yet produced the philosopher's stone that can change base metals into gold. Though this was the most highly sought goal of the forerunners of modern chemistry, it was abandoned as soon as scientists discovered the actual nature of matter."[178] As Lewontin observed in response, "How revealing is rhetoric."[179]

In addition to these problems of interpretation, many of the world's leading geneticists have maintained that the entire notion of heritability was misguided for such complex human traits as intelligence—that although the IQ scores themselves might yield uncomplainingly to behavior genetic formulas and computer algorithms, there were just too many unknowns in the different models for estimating heritability, too many indefensible assumptions necessary to reduce the number of unknowns, and too little control over the correlation between genotype and environment for such estimates to have any meaning. Otto Kempthorne, a recognized expert in biostatistics, claimed, for example, that " 'heritability' does not even exist in the human IQ context" and that the controversy over its value was therefore "stupid," an argument "about the magnitude of an imaginary number."[180] The British biologist and Nobel Laureate Sir Peter Medawar insisted it was just "*not* possible . . . to attach exact percentage figures to the contributions of nature and nurture to differences of intellectual capacity . . . for reasons that seem to be beyond the comprehension of IQ psychologists, though they . . . have been made clear by a number of the world's foremost geneticists."[181] These were hardly scientists who could be dismissed as radical environmentalists. Both men had been equally critical of the claim that there was no genetic causation for mental ability—"flat-earthism" Medawar called such an assertion.

Even though there was no scarcity of scientists who believed that the process had some validity, the plethora of statistical models available for estimating the heritability of IQ produced wildly varying results, sometimes even from two different analyses of the same set of data. In one study the researchers acknowledged that the most direct model yielded a heritability close to zero, so they changed models to increase the estimate, still producing only the modest result of 0.38.[182] The University of Illinois psychologist Lloyd Humphreys, another long-time researcher in the field and one of Jensen's strongest supporters, declared that he was "99 percent confident" that the heritability of IQ was somewhere between 0.20 and 0.80, a rather trivial conclusion considering that the limits of heritability are 0.00 and 1.00.[183] After analyzing data from many different models, the Harvard sociologist Christopher Jencks (now at Northwestern) concluded that the most likely estimate was somewhere between 0.25 and 0.65. The Yale psychologist Sandra Scarr obtained values ranging from 0.11 to 0.53, though various statistical "corrections" produced substantial increases. Reanalyses of Jencks's and Scarr's data using different assumptions resulted in yet lower estimates.[184] Nevertheless, Jensen continued to insist that the heritability of IQ was approximately 0.80.

Even if all the conceptual flaws and methodological difficulties could somehow be overcome, an accurate estimate of the heritability of IQ would still be the answer to a nonproblem, an academic triumph with no scientific or practical relevance. While the models and the techniques of analysis have become increasingly more sophisticated, the major substantive achievement of the research has been the rather pointless compilation of a series of heritability estimates from different tests administered to different samples, the psychometric equivalent of a butterfly collection. Moreover, since heritability has no implications for the possibility of change, the bulk of Jensen's *HER* article—a detailed discussion of heritability—was a non sequitur as an elaboration of its opening assertion that compensatory education had been tried and had failed. Whether compensatory education could produce improvement in children's cognitive skills was (and is) an important question, but the value of IQ heritability has no bearing on the answer. As Jencks concluded, after spending a number of years calculating IQ heritabilities, "Mathematical estimates of heritability tell us almost nothing about anything important."[185] Even Lindon Eaves, one of Jensen's strongest supporters among genetic researchers, complained that his emphasis on estimates of heritability was "uninspiring to geneticists and may leave psychologists wondering whether genetics contributes anything really useful to the understanding of behavior."[186]

Though Jensen was forced to acknowledge, at least in theory, that high heritability did not preclude improvement, he insisted that it had one particularly significant consequence:

> If a number of individuals are all given equal opportunity—the same background, the same conditions, and the same amount of time—for learning something, they will still differ from one another in their rates of learning and consequently in the amount they learn per unit of time spent in learning. That is the meaning of heritability. It does not say that individuals cannot learn or improve with instruction and practice. It says that given equal conditions, individuals will differ from one another, not because of differences in the external conditions but because of differences in the internal environment which is conditioned by genetic factors . . . it is true that heritability has nothing to do with teachability. But was this ever really the question? Has anyone questioned the fact that *all* schoolchildren are teachable? The important question has concerned *differences* in teachability—differences both among individuals and among sub-groups of the population. And with reference to the question of *differences,* the concept of heritability is indeed a relevant and empirically answerable question. . . . The degree to which equal conditions of teaching or instruction will diminish individual differences in achievement *is* inversely related to the heritability.[187]

This interpretation, itself debatable (there is nothing in the meaning of heritability that prevents the diminution of individual differences as a result of environmental changes, especially when those changes provide some individuals with the improved conditions already available to others), was Jensen's ultimate answer to those who dismissed the value of heritability. Even though it did not exclude environmental improvement, he claimed that it did prove the inevitability and the constancy of differences: the same individuals would maintain their advantage in performance, perhaps even increase it, no matter how much conditions were improved for everyone. "Superior" genotypes in one environment would remain superior in other environments. A rising tide might elevate the level of all boats, but some craft would still be yachts while others would remain dinghies.

The existence of these supposedly invariant differences had important policy implications, according to Jensen. Increasing the cognitive skills of all students was not society's real concern, he maintained:

> what most educators, government officials, and writers in the popular press who discuss the present problems of education are in fact referring to is not primarily dissatisfaction with some absolute level

of achievement, but rather with the large group differences in educational attainment that show up so conspicuously in our educational system—the achievement gaps between the affluent and the poor, the lower-class and the middle-class, one race and another, the majority and the minority, the urban and the suburban, and so on. Educational differences, not absolute level of performance, are the main cause of concern. Whether we like to admit it or not, the problem of achievement differences today is where the action is, where the billions of dollars of educational funds are being poured in, where the heat is on, and where the schools are being torn apart.[188]

If reduction of differences was the real objective, the "billions of dollars" were being wasted, according to Jensen's analysis; science was placed squarely against all those fuzzyminded liberals with their idealistic beliefs that greater expenditures on education could possibly reduce genetically determined inequalities.

Heritability, Race, and a "Personal Hunch"

The tempest over the heritability of IQ might have remained confined to the academic teapot were it not for Jensen's comments on race. His conclusion, rather tentative sounding at first but soon phrased with less reservation, that the difference in average IQ between blacks and whites had a genetic basis created the real cause célèbre. In fact, this assertion was remarkably devoid of any scientific support, resting entirely on the high heritability of IQ *within* each race. "I don't know of any other evidence that . . . [the difference between races] is genetic," Jensen frankly admitted.[189] The premise of this argument was certainly arguable: in addition to all the problems that beset heritability estimates for the white population, the very few studies on blacks have reported lower values, generally between 0.2 and 0.5.[190] The more serious weakness, however, was in Jensen's logic. The heritability of a trait within two groups bears no necessary relationship to the heritability of the difference between them. It is easily possible for the former to be 1.0 while the latter is 0.0. The heritability of lung cancer, for example, is probably close to 1.0 for both heavy smokers and nonsmokers, but the difference in lung cancer rates between them, almost totally due to the effect of tobacco, has a heritability close to 0.0.

This fundamental error in logic was pointed out by numerous critics, who offered one example after another of similar group differences in highly heritable traits due to environment.[191] Acknowledging the validity of this point, Jensen nevertheless insisted that within group heritabilities had a probabilistic, if not necessary, relationship to a genetic basis for group differences; the latter became "a priori" more likely, "more plausible," as the former increased.[192] There was no logical basis for this assertion either; it was just as likely, a priori, that two such groups were genetically similar but experienced environments systematically differing in some factor of critical importance for the trait in question. As an example of his contention, Jensen often cited the height of Watusis and Pygmies, a trait with high heritability within each population and a genetic explanation for the difference between them. Pointing out the numerous environmental differences between these two groups, he noted that, nevertheless, no one had seriously proffered a nongenetic rationale for the difference in their heights because "no one emotionally *needs* to believe that differences in height are not inborn."[193] This illustration was not even remotely similar to the IQ controversy, though; the environmental differences between Watusis and Pygmies bore no demonstrated relevance to the trait in question, and there was no overlap in their heights—the tallest Pygmy is considerably shorter than the shortest Watusi. Even if there had been greater similarity to the IQ trait, it would have been merely one specific instance in which high within group heritability was conjoined to a heritable difference. A single such example, purposefully selected to illustrate this co-occurrence, would hardly provide the basis for a generalization to other traits, especially when there was abundant documentation of empirical examples indicating a different result.

To bolster his position, Jensen frequently cited the agreement of other "eminent" authorities. In a typical passage he wrote that "the fact of the high heritability of IQ, therefore, makes it a very reasonable and likely hypothesis that genetic factors are involved in the Negro-white difference. No geneticist to my knowledge has argued otherwise."[194] Although scientific conclusions are not reached by referendum, if one claims to be supported by a show of hands, it is important to count correctly. The fact was that almost *no* geneticist agreed with the above statement. Jensen's strongest supporter among internationally known geneticists was probably Lindon Eaves, a professor at the University of Birmingham in England. Although Eaves praised Jensen for a "facility with the literature which is shared by few of his critics," he was

> disturbed by the impression that, whatever Jensen may say to the contrary, he still believes that generalizations from conclusions within populations are helpful and justified. He alludes . . . to . . . an [sic] monotonic increasing relationship between the heritabilities of a trait "within" and "between" populations. For analytical purposes this can be little more than wishful thinking. . . . We may conceive, with equal justification, of models which would predict the reverse

relationship, and indeed, the real world may behave as if there were no relationship at all. Since there are no means for discriminating between such models at the moment the choice still remains a matter of opinion rather than knowledge.[195]

At one point in the controversy Jensen claimed a new source of support for his contention. A reprint of the *HER* article added an allusion to recent work by John De Fries, a geneticist at the University of Colorado who had proven, according to Jensen, the existence of "a definite increasing monotonic relationship" between heritability within groups and between groups.[196] If this had been true, Jensen's position would have been strengthened immeasurably. When the De Fries formulation was eventually published, however, the between groups heritability was a function of within groups only when the genetic difference between the groups was already known; that is, the formula demanded prior knowledge of the very conclusion that Jensen wished to extract from it. De Fries himself made this point unambiguously in a symposium in which Jensen was also a participant: "since no valid estimate of r [the measure of genetic difference between groups] exists for IQ data, it is impossible to choose a particular value of h^2_f [the between groups heritability] at this time. Nevertheless it is abundantly clear . . . that a high within-racial heritability by no means implies a highly heritable racial difference."[197] Seemingly unable to relinquish his misconception, Jensen reacted to this statement by congratulating De Fries for putting "an end to the mistaken notion that there is no connection whatever between within group and between group heritability." Repeating that he had just demonstrated "that the heritability of between group means may be very low, in spite of a high within group heritability," an apparently chagrined DeFries observed that "it *appears* that Professor Jensen now agrees with this conclusion" (emphasis added).[198]

Eventually Jensen was forced to admit that there was "no necessary or logical connection between WGH [within group heritability] and BGH [between group heritability]," but even this concession was accompanied by the testy observation that it "affords considerable comfort to those who wish to avoid seeking a scientific explanation of the white-black differences in IQ";[199] apparently there were emotional needs on *both* sides of this debate. Moreover, when it became no longer tenable to maintain that any geneticist supported his position, Jensen began to imply, Carleton-Putnam style, that they were reluctant to admit the truth. Because race was the "touchiest" topic, he wrote, leading experts would just not publicly acknowledge "the carefully considered scientific views that they would express in private discussions."[200]

Jensen did offer one other argument for a genetic difference in IQ between races, based not on any evidence in support of the hypothesis but on an attempt at proof by default, employing the Holmesian adage that when the impossible has been eliminated, whatever remains, no matter how improbable, must be true. He thus devoted a considerable amount of attention to the systematic investigation and subsequent rejection of environmental hypotheses. When each simplistic variable—socioeconomic status, income, unemployment, and so forth—proved inadequate to account for the racial difference in IQ, Jensen concluded that in this case "whatever remains" was genes.[201] (His level of sensitivity to environmental differences between the races was suggested by the statement to an Australian audience that there was no "cultural difference" between blacks and whites in the United States.)[202] A genetic explanation thus became the repository of scientific failure, a substitute for an admission of ignorance, much as the ancients had ascribed all phenomena not otherwise fathomable to the influence of various deities. As one critic remarked, a genetic attribution on such grounds "was not merely made in ignorance but . . . was explicitly based on ignorance."[203]

Though Jensen's evidence for the genetic hypothesis was largely irrelevant, there *were* more appropriate methods to study the question. While it would still not be possible to control all the important variables, one approximation to scientific rigor would be an investigation of black children adopted into white homes. Such a "controlled program of adoption" had been proposed by Shockley in his 1965 interview with *U.S. News and World Report.* In *The Genetics of Human Populations,* probably the most authoritative text on the subject, the geneticists L. L. Cavalli-Sforza and W. F. Bodmer had also recommended this method as the most adequate attempt, though they acknowledged that it would still not be able to eliminate the effects of prejudice.[204] Jensen himself had even encouraged such a study in his discussion of an earlier finding that white children whose mothers had an average IQ of 85 developed an average IQ of 106 when adopted into "superior" foster homes. At the time he was concerned about the "illegitimate use" of this study that might suggest a similar gain could take place for black children placed in superior adoptive environments. This was "an incorrect prediction," Jensen had explained, because the white children had "regressed" upward toward their mean of 100 even without the influence of the foster home, whereas black children would derive no benefit from a regression toward *their* mean, which was only 85. (Regression is the statistical tendency for a child's measurement to be closer than the parent's to the population average.) He did, however, believe that a parallel study using black children would be "relevant and informative."[205] A few years later the psychologists Sandra Scarr and Richard Weinberg conducted such a study, finding that black children adopted by middle-class white families also obtained an average IQ of 106. This was indeed a relevant and informative result.[206]

Another appropriate method of research was the study of persons varying in known degrees of racial hybridity. A number of such investigations had already been conducted prior to the Jensen controversy but had not provided any evidence of a detectable genetic difference between races. One study had considered the IQs of children fathered by U.S. servicemen and born to unwed German women just after World War II. The average IQ of children with black fathers was virtually identical with the average IQ of children with white fathers even when the two groups were matched for age, sex, socioeconomic status, and other social variables. Another study of black subjects had found no relationship between measures of ability and the presence of blood-group genes more characteristic of white populations. Other studies of black children with exceptionally high IQs had disclosed no evidence of greater white ancestry than in the black population in general.[207] Sometime after Jensen's involvement the most sophisticated study of this type was conducted, again by Scarr and her associates. Based on a number of genetic blood-group markers, estimates of Caucasian admixture were derived for a large sample of black public school students. These estimates showed no association with any of four cognitive tests or with the value of g extracted from them; that is, there was zero correlation between the degree of Caucasian admixture and measures of intellectual ability.[208] (This was essentially a study that Shockley had encouraged for sometime, though in typically sensational style he had publicly requested blood samples from prominent blacks like Roy Wilkins. If their "mental performance was independent of Caucasian ancestry," Shockley had announced, "then this new fact would go far towards convincing ... me that American Negro disadvantages are primarily due to prejudice rather than to genetic causes."[209] Nevertheless, his belief in blacks' intellectual inferiority did not change one iota after Scarr's study.)

Jensen's only comment on the cross-racial adoption study and all the studies of racial hybridity except for Scarr's, which had not been completed, was that their "major findings ... generally come out in the direction one should expect from a genetic hypothesis," though he offered no details to support this seemingly inaccurate summary.[210] He was subsequently invited to contribute a commentary to a collection of Scarr's works that included the above studies on race and intelligence. Scarr had been an outspoken exponent of the importance of heritability estimates for IQ, and Jensen could hardly dismiss her as one of his "ideological" opponents. Indeed, she had been prepared to publish a conclusion of genetic difference between the races if the data so indicated.[211] His commentary on the adoption study explained that "the IQ gain *that is claimed*" (emphasis added) had nothing to do with the adoptive environment since, in this case, the black children were a select group with more high-IQ genes to begin with; many of them, Jensen noted, were interracial children, "predominantly Caucasian, genetically speaking." Having offered this interpretation of the adoption study, naturally he was unconvinced by Scarr's research on intelligence and blacks' degree of Caucasian admixture. Jensen's criticism of the latter work insisted that the Raven's Matrices, one of the cognitive tests administered to Scarr's subjects, was a better measure of intelligence than was the value of g derived from the mathematical, factor analytic approach.[212] The flood of articles he had produced in support of the latter as the true definition of intelligence now seemed less important than the fact that the Raven showed a slightly higher relationship to Caucasian admixture (though still not significantly different from zero) than either the factor analytic definition of intelligence or any of the other cognitive tests. Jensen's refutation of Scarr's clear results was thus attained only by completely contradicting a central tenet of his own work.

Over a decade after the *HER* article Jensen acknowledged that there was, in fact, no scientific evidence for a genetic basis to racial differences in IQ, but he still supported the hypothesis based on "my *personal hunch,* which is really of no general scientific importance." Despite this frank admission, he was "shocked" when Scarr, as a result of her own research, advocated the "reeducation of school personnel . . . on . . . the elimination of any lingering suspicion about genetic racial difference in IQ."[213] Jensen opposed such advocacy, still believing it appropriate to encourage teachers to entertain a hypothesis of questionable value to black students and certain to be personally insulting to them.

Perhaps the most instructive aspect of the scientific debate over Jensenism was its striking similarity to the debates carried on throughout the previous sixty years. The methods of data analysis had become increasingly sophisticated, but the issues and the responses to them had remained exactly the same: whether intelligence was unidimensional or multidimensional; to what extent individual differences in intelligence were "due to" genes; and whether there were genetic differences between races and ethnic groups. If the history of the scientific controversy in this field were a film played continuously in a movie theater, at a certain point one would say, "This is where I came in," and get up and leave.

Of course, just as in the past, the scientific controversy over Jensenism was largely a surrogate for other concerns, whose true nature was typically revealed not by Jensen's critics but by his supporters. Those scientists who still believed that biology was the route to social improvement quickly saw the merit in Jensen's work. For example, R. A. McConnell, a biophysicist at the University of Pittsburgh, hailed the *HER* article as the most important paper in psychology since Pavlov and Freud. In a statement that did little to inspire confidence in the review processes of scientific journals McConnell described the "new revolutionary fact (equivalent to nuclear fission) that . . . intelligence is determined 80% by heredity and 20% by environment." Then he explained the implications of this "fact": differences between people could not be eliminated "regardless of how much money is spent for preschool training, improved teaching, unlimited university admissions, subsidized rent in suburban communities and guaranteed annual incomes." The only real solution, wrote McConnell, was eugenic, and he offered a "homely example" of the consequent principle that should inform national policy: "Suppose a farmer had a herd of cows that was too big for his pasture. Would he reduce the herd randomly or would he remove the less fit?"[214] The most important paper since Pavlov and Freud left little doubt how the less fit would be determined—or who they would be.

Jensen's Scientific Allies

While a number of scientists found some merit to Jensen's concern with heritability, very few, aside from the avowed segregationists, agreed with his position on racial differences. It was not so much that they dismissed any possibility of genetic difference in IQ between blacks and whites but that they distinguished between this possibility and the irrelevance of Jensen's argument. Only two well-known researchers rushed to support him on the racial issue, and both were clearly more interested in pointing out the sociopolitical implications of blacks' inferiority than in quibbling over the validity of the evidence.

Cooperating with Nature

Fastest to take Jensen's side was his former mentor, the English psychologist Hans J. Eysenck, the author of hundreds of articles and dozens of books and a man with a marked preference for hereditarian explanations. For example, when research showed delinquent behavior was more frequent among children from "broken homes," Eysenck interpreted the correlation to be the result of a heritable trait that caused both separation of the parents and criminal behavior in their children; that is, people who obtain divorces were more likely to carry genes for criminality.[215] Almost twenty years after the surgeon general had authorized the placement of health warnings on cigarette packs, Eysenck was still maintaining—in work funded by R. J. Reynolds and the Tobacco Research Council—that tobacco-related diseases were really genetic and that smokers were more susceptible to them because the tendencies to smoke and to develop the illnesses were both the result of hereditary predisposition.[216]

Eysenck also had a long history of obsession with the deleterious consequences of disproportionate proliferation of the inferior. In 1948 he had predicted that at the current rate of loss in the population's average IQ, in fifty years "it is doubtful if civilization as we know it could survive."[217] By 1973, about half the way to the onset of this catastrophe, Eysenck's fears of general social decline had been replaced by a more specific genetic threat: if the average IQ in England "were to sink to that characteristic of American Negroes, then not only would our living standard sink dramatically, but widespread famine would kill off many millions."[218]

Often embroiled in controversy, Eysenck was a furious rival, seemingly determined to win every argument, by underhanded tactics if necessary. Yet at the same time he would accuse opponents of his own worst practices and issue sanctimonious calls for a pristine level of debate. He complained, for example, of smear tactics in the IQ controversy. According to Eysenck, those who had called attention to the genetic role in racial differences "have been accused of following in the steps of Hitler, . . . an absurd attempt to establish guilt by association." But incredibly, only two paragraphs earlier in the same publication he himself had written that Robert Peckham, the federal district court judge in San Francisco who had enjoined the use of standard IQ tests for the placement of black children in classes for the mentally retarded, had "achieved immortality by joining Stalin and Hitler in banning IQ tests."[219]

In the controversy over heritability and race Eysenck became Jensen's dark doppelgänger. In contrast with Jensen's cautious scientific statements and vague hints of dire implications, Eysenck's assertions left little to inference. Where Jensen had emphasized the importance of genetic factors, Eysenck insisted that "the whole course of development of a child's intellectual capabilities is largely laid down genetically."[220] Where Jensen had concluded that compensatory education had not raised intelligence, Eysenck proclaimed that not only were compensatory programs "a lost cause" but also all those other "Left-wing" solutions—"Better Schools, Smaller Classes and More Teachers"—were hopeless in the face of genetic determinism. In fact, he noted, the American educational system had already "compensated up to a point for the innate lower ability of the blacks," and presumably their saturation level had been reached.[221] Where Jensen was usually careful to comment only on differences in IQ scores, Eysenck abandoned even this minimal subtlety, referring to different groups' genetic "superiority" or "inferiority."[222] Where Jensen had enough sense to say little about integration, Eysenck claimed to support it but then offered lurid stories of how even voluntary, indeed "exemplary," integration programs had only produced ghetto behavior among middle-class students—shakedowns, dope-peddling, and sexual assault, with rape occurring on the floor in public while passing students nonchalantly ignored the victim's screams for assistance.[223]

Eysenck first entered the controversy when he published *The IQ Argument*—issued as *Race, Intelligence and Education* in England, where it was publicly disavowed by "the entire editorial staff" of its London publisher[224]—a book produced in such a hurry that it lacked an index and offered no references in the text, both extraordinary omissions in a scientific work. (A brief bibliography was appended, but since it was not keyed to the text, it was of little assistance in tracking down the basis for specific statements.) But then the book did not appear to be intended for the scientific community. Its superficial treatment of the issues and its breezy popular tone seemed aimed at the larger public in an attempt to influence popular opinion—an extremely offensive attempt, made all the more so by its levity.

Eysenck began *The IQ Argument* by relating a personal anecdote:

> I was boxing for my College when one evening our coach came to me and said that I was fighting a Negro. "Watch it," he said, "these niggers have heads made of iron. Never punch him on the chin. Go for the midriff." "Oh yes!" I thought, "there goes Mr. Racial Prejudice. I've heard of these stereotypes; you'd be a fool to believe in that sort of nonsense." . . . However, I said nothing, and went into the fight without paying much heed to the warning. Nothing happened in the first round, but in the second my opponent dropped his guard for a second, and I hit him on the chin with one of the best blows I ever managed. . . . He hardly blinked an eye but my hand seemed to explode. For a moment I thought I had broken a bone.[225]

The point to this inflammatory opening gambit was apparently to suggest that automatic rejection of a stereotype was no more logical than unthinking acceptance. But the medium was probably the message to most readers, a message that was repeated only two pages later when Eysenck emphasized that scientific neutrality was an especially important requirement in the present case since opinions on race were associated with political attitudes: conservative psychologists were more likely to be "racialist," even on purely scientific issues, he noted, while liberals were more likely to be "nigger-loving." Though Eysenck placed both epithets in quotations marks, suggesting they were terms used by others, it was hard not to wince at the latter characterization. If this were not enough, he later illustrated the experimental-design difficulties in research on racial differences by reciting a racist limerick. In real life, Eysenck observed, it was not possible to find "the happy outcome attending the well known Miss Starkey, who foolishly married a darkie; the two for their sins, had three pairs of twins, one white, one black, and one khaki."[226] If a neutral attitude was the first requirement of science, it appeared that Eysenck had just flunked his own test.

Much of *The IQ Argument* was just a verbatim repetition of others' work—usually Jensen's—with lengthy quotes extending over several pages so that it was sometimes difficult to distinguish Eysenck's words from those of an original author.[227] The book's one new contribution to the scientific debate was Eysenck's pseudo-Darwinian explanation for the existence of racial differences in IQ. He suggested that a number of historic circumstances had produced an American black population selected by criteria that had depleted their gene pool of "high-IQ genes." First of all, the "brighter" Africans had used their "higher intelligence to escape [the slavers], so that it was mostly the duller ones who got caught." Then, too, many Africans had been sold into slavery by their own tribal chiefs, who, according to Eysenck, "got rid of their less intelligent followers." In addition, he claimed, even in America "natural selection" continued to reduce black IQ as slaveowners systematically eliminated "uppity" blacks, who naturally would also have been the more intelligent ones. (Either Eysenck did not use *intelligence* in Jensen's technical sense, which the public did not understand, or African chiefs and slaveowners had anticipated the nature of *g* many years before science.) As further evidence that an ethnic subgroup might differ substantially from its parent population, Eysenck referred to the "known" fact that Americans of Italian, Spanish, Portuguese, and Greek extraction had descended from immigrants "less able, less intelligent" than the original populations in the countries of their birth. Finally, perhaps to ensure that no one was left unoffended, he claimed the opposite tendency to have affected the Irish for centuries— because their most able citizens had been attracted to foreign countries, "we might expect a distinctly lower IQ level among the remaining." Triumphantly, he concluded that the "facts seem to confirm these hypotheses; Macnamara found the Irish to have IQ's which were not very different from those observed in American Negroes."[228] (Actually, John Macnamara, an Irish psychologist, had studied only Irish children who spoke English at home but were taught in Gaelic in the schools and had found that they obtained an average IQ score of 75 on a test administered *in English.*)[229]

The only data Eysenck cited of actual relevance to a genetic difference between races came from a study of Australian Aboriginal children. Marion de Lemos had administered a set of Piagetian tests of "conservation," widely accepted by developmental psychologists as marking the beginning of logical thought, to two groups of children—one from Elcho Island, an isolated area that had had very little contact with Europeans, and one from Hermannsburg, an area that had enjoyed much closer contact with Europeans, who had been there for almost a century. (The term *conservation* refers to the realization that an object's weight, volume, or quantity is not affected, that is, is "conserved," by a change in its shape. In a typical test of this sort two identical glasses are filled with the same amount of sugar. The sugar from one of these is then poured successively into a long thin glass, a short wide glass, and four small glasses to see if the child realized that the amount of sugar remained invariant.) In the Hermannsburg group some children were "full-blooded" Aborigines and others, with one European great-grandparent, were seven-eighths Aborigine, though all of them formed a single community and attended the same school; children in the Elcho group were all full Aborigines.[230]

In his description of this study Eysenck referred only to the data from Hermannsburg, reporting that the part-Aboriginal children had performed better on the tests than the full-blooded ones had and concluding that even less than 15 percent white ancestry had produced some substantial differences in intellectual potential. This result was, he wrote, "a prop which environmentalists will find difficult to dislodge," and, indeed, it might have been, had his summary been accurate.[231] When the Elcho "full" children, whom Eysenck had never mentioned, were compared with the Hermannsburg part-Aboriginals, however, the differences almost all disappeared. Shortly after this summary by Eysenck, Jensen gave essentially the same description of the de Lemos study, also omitting any reference to the existence of the Elcho group; in addition, he reproduced a chart from de Lemos, comparing part- and full-Aboriginals, but from the chart's original title the words *Hermannsburg Group* had been carefully excised.[232] The most likely reason for the difference between the two Hermannsburg groups was a different distribution of ages for each group—older children would, of course, be more likely to pass a given test—though de Lemos did not present the data in sufficient detail to investigate this possibility. A replication of this study conducted a short time later, however, ensured that the number of children at each age was the same for part- and full-Aboriginal, and not a single difference was found.[233] Eysenck never mentioned the study again.

The IQ Argument concluded with a lengthy attack on compensatory education as "political playthings," whose abolition would be some kind of favor for black children. Eysenck did acknowledge some moral responsibility to blacks on society's part, but he insisted the real problem, the obstacle to translating these benevolent desires into action, was some small remaining measure of scientific doubt concerning the genetic inferiority of blacks; there was "good (though not conclusive)" evidence on the matter. What was really needed to repay the moral debt to blacks for their centuries of oppression was greater certainty of their genetic disadvantage; only this realization would make effective action possible. Eysenck consequently called upon society to give top priority to expending funds where it would really count—not for compensatory education, which would "only do a disservice to those truly eager to advance the status of the Negro race," but for increased research budgets to clinch the case for their genetic inferiority.[234]

Though Eysenck did not elaborate on exactly *how* convincing proof of their inferiority would help blacks, it was possible to infer the answer from his next book. In *The Inequality of Man* he explained on the very first page that it was written to provide scientific information relevant to "political objectives, such as . . . the creation of communities in which human equality is achieved to a much greater extent than is true of our present societies." Some two hundred and sixty pages later Eysenck concluded that this goal was chimerical because of "man's . . . genetically determined inequality." Biological limits set by nature, he wrote, had produced unavoidable consequences for "our whole thinking about society, about politics and about education," and "attempts to disregard her laws and get our way against her opposition are doomed to failure."[235]

Eysenck's discussion of nature's limits came perilously close to suggesting that political inequality was one of their unavoidable consequences. He strongly recommended an essay written in 1890 by Thomas H. Huxley as "a shrewdly aimed counterblast" to the egalitarians of the time. Huxley's position, which Eysenck quoted with great praise, was that "before drawing [a] sharp line of demarcation between natural and political inequality, might it not be as well to inquire whether they are not intimately connected, in such a manner that the latter is essentially a consequence of the former?"[236] Though Eysenck did not mention it, Huxley's "counterblast" had gone on not only to answer this question in the affirmative but also to proclaim that science supported Aristotle over Rousseau: "Born slave" was closer to biological truth than "born free." Especially incompatible with biological inequality was universal suffrage, which Huxley termed the absurd theory that "while every trade, business or profession requires theoretical training and practical skill, and would go to the dogs if those who carry them on were appointed by the majority of votes of people who know nothing about it and little about them—the management of the affairs of society will be perfectly successful, if only the people who may be trusted to know nothing, will vote into office the people who may be trusted to do nothing."[237] Because Mendelian principles had not yet been discovered, Eysenck remarked that Huxley's arguments were not as strong as they might have been, apparently suggesting that contemporary scientific knowledge should further strengthen the linkage between biological and political inequality.

Despite Huxley's "shrewd aim," Eysenck knew that by the 1970s nature was no longer an acceptable basis for depriving people of political rights, and he found it necessary to redirect the implications of nature's limits. "Status," he explained—social inequality if not political—was now the inevitable consequence of biological inequality: "genetic factors predetermine some people to be capable of being educated to carry out complex and difficult jobs, while they predetermine other people to be incapable of being so educated." One might worry that the latter group would be unsatisfied with their genetically determined lot, frustrated by the unappealing work available to them, and perhaps even jealous of the more enviable occupations of their biological betters. Fortunately, he wrote, genetic determinism encompassed much more than just abilities; it also meant that "different people have different personalities, different temperaments, which suit them to different types of jobs." According to Eysenck, work generally considered hard and dirty, like coal mining or assembly lines, was described in such terms only by writers, whose own personalities would make such jobs unpalatable. Happily, he maintained, the people in the mines and on the assembly lines actually liked their work.[238] Science had finally proven Plato right after all, wrote Eysenck: to achieve true harmony society only had to "scrutinise each child to see what metal had gone to his making, and then allocate or promote him accordingly."[239] Scientific confirmation of their inferiority would apparently assist blacks by ensuring their placement in social and occupational roles appropriate to both their ability and their personality.

"A Living Museum"

The other well-known scientist to rally to Jensen's side on the racial issue was Raymond B. Cattell, a distinguished research psychologist and author of over thirty books and hundreds of articles spanning such diverse fields as personality theory, sociocultural differences, and statistical methodology. Born in England in 1905, he was the only researcher still active in the 1970s who had been prominently involved in eugenics' ancien régime. In the 1930s, with due acknowledgments to the pioneering work of the Nazi ideologue Hans Günther and even Count Joseph Arthur de Gobineau, Cattell offered the standard eugenical characterization of the European races as the key to understanding all history and politics: Nordics were "the most highly evolved in intelligence and stability of temperament," domineering "men of genius" who tended by nature to rule others; Alpines disliked individuality and enterprise and had "no urge to the noble and heroic"; Mediterraneans were vain, gregarious, and unassertive, tending naturally to be conquered or enslaved.[240]

Like his predecessors Francis Galton and Herbert Spencer, Cattell wished to see the evolutionary dynamic become the basis "for a new and nobler structure of scientifically founded religion."[241] Morality would thus become "a branch of natural science," not derived from a speculative rationalism or some mystical inner consciousness but "discovered by an examination of nature"[242] and "calculated according to the facts and principles supplied" by science. Since higher levels of evolution had been scientifically proven to be the goal toward which all living organisms strived, this "true aim of life" would also be the "end and aim of all moral laws" and thus the basis for their derivation. Because evolution was "assured only by our co-operating with Nature in its vigilant and ruthless elimination of the less fit," however, Cattell recognized that the moral laws derived from such a goal "are apparently the exact opposite of those which religion and humanity have bred into our bones." He attained a partial resolution of this apparent paradox by the claim that natural selection acted chiefly on racial groups rather than on individuals, and the racially collective nature of the evolutionary struggle could thus justify "altruistic modes of behavior that are at first sight biologically perverse." That is, qualities like "sympathy, unselfishness, self-sacrifice, and the capacity for enthusiastic co-operation" were morally sound only when employed to help one's own race survive and flourish.[243] Any attempt to extend *intra*-racial kindnesses to people of an "alien" race was "an abominable state of affairs," Cattell warned, which would only destroy the competitive process necessary to determine which races and cultures were biologically superior and fit to survive.[244]

Since race was the basic unit of evolutionary progress, the first law of scientific morality was that there be "no mixture of bloods between racial groups." "In a pure race," Cattell explained "the inheritance of impulses in each individual is bound to be well balanced. The innate forces which are the innate material of character-building must have reached a certain compatibility and potential power of good integration. If two such races inter-breed, the resulting re-shuffling of impulses and psychic forces throws together in each individual a number of items which may or may not be compatible and capable of being organized into a stable unit."[245] In keeping with this scientific gobbledygook, "hybrids," he claimed, were inferior to either parent race, were "frequently positively vicious," were subject to anatomical and glandular disharmonies causing decreased fertility, "exaggerated growth . . . and . . . disproportionately large extremities," and suffered from "seriously defective . . . intellectual and moral development, . . . a fundamental lack of harmony in their character, an abnormal liability to moral conflict and disorder." As an example of such disorders, Cattell cited "the unstable governments" of the Celtic and eastern European peoples, which were a consequence of their mixed, mainly Alpine-Mediterranean blood.[246]

Not only was interbreeding forbidden by evolutionary morality, but races had to be physically separated from each other. In a racially heterogeneous nation, Cattell pointed out, both the fit and the unfit elements were "linked up to sink or swim together," a situation that could result in "parasitism" when a racial group of lesser ability unfairly obtained the advantages produced by a superior group. To remove this obstacle to evolutionary progress, it was necessary to impose racial order; groups had to be "composed entirely of their own types," a goal attained through deliberate racial surgery, ranging from "minor pruning of present national groups" to complete "reconstruction." In the United States, he noted, this meant total segregation for blacks within their own state. The European race, however, had to beware of the Jews, a non-European, introverted race marked by cautiousness, tenacity of purpose, and "a crafty spirit of calculation." Though the Jews were frequently accused of "cowardice, treason and avarice," the more serious problem caused by their presence, according to Cattell, was the "feeling of strangeness" that a European experienced "in regard to these intruders"—an innate sense of racial distance. "Hatred and abhorrence . . . for the Jewish practice of living in other nations instead of forming an independent, self-sustained group of their own" he regarded as the natural response to those who refused "to play the game" correctly. Only "would-be intellectuals," unable to appreciate the biological roots of such sentiments, foolishly branded them "prejudice."[247]

Cattell's greatest ire, however, was reserved for the "race-slumpers," those misguided souls who believed that positions and privileges should be awarded on individual merit regardless of racial background. Such people did not understand, he wrote, that "to treat alien individuals as if they belonged to the same race, simply because their intelligence is on the same high or low level, is a mistake, for constitutional differences of greater importance are being overlooked." These differences in ways of thinking, artistic and cultural ideals, and religious preferences—all rooted in race—were so great, according to Cattell, that an individual had a closer resemblance to every other person "from his own stem" than to any person of another race. Even art Cattell found rooted in the racial temperament, and, concerned that "certain new forms of art" introduced by Jews would not be "intrinsically satisfying" to the English, he warned his compatriots that art from Germany was more racially appropriate, "more in the direct line of our native temperamental strivings." An intelligent Englishman, he concluded, was naturally "more at one" with the less-capable members of his own race than with a Jew who was his intellectual equal; nor "could a less gifted Scot be replaced by an advanced member of the negro race."[248] For Cattell race was always the primary consideration.

The rigid separation of races would make it possible to attain the goal of evolutionary morality: the displacement, even extermination, of backward races by their superiors. There were inevitable instances, Cattell observed, "where it is time to call a halt to a certain line of evolution." In the past, he noted, "surgical operation of lopping off the backward branches of the tree of mankind was done violently and without an anesthetic. The American Indians, the Australian Blacks, the Maoris, the negroes were driven with bloodshed from their lands, as blindly unconscious of the biological rationality of that destiny as were their oppressors." However, he explained, in a more enlightened present the same ends could be achieved by more sensitive, if no less deliberate, means: by birth-control regulation, by sterilization, "and by life in adapted reserves and asylums, must the races which have served their turn be brought to euthanasia."[249] As a result of their "smaller skull capacity, . . . as racially characteristic as the greater projection of . . . [the] heel at the other end of the skeleton," Cattell found blacks to be a naturally inferior group, who, for all their "endearing qualities of humour and religiosity," had "contributed practically nothing to social progress and culture."[250] In such clearly established cases, where there was no hope for improvement, the highest moral considerations dictated that the "more intelligent and alert peoples" should systematically eliminate the "backward" races."[251] While waiting for the inevitable to occur, the advanced countries with their superior races *deserved* to take over the less advanced ones and confiscate their territory. "By evolutionary morals," Cattell observed, shortly after Mussolini invaded North Africa, "the substitution of Italian culture for Abyssinian culture is good."[252] (No doubt, the substitution of Nordic culture would have been better.) In fact, he wrote, national expansion should be "proportional" to national progress, and the most progressive country—the one that was first to adopt eugenic measures officially—had "every prospect of inheriting the earth."[253] The Third Reich would soon act on the same assumption.

Much to Cattell's dismay, however, none of the major ideological influences—journalists, authors, historians, educators, philosophers—was able to understand or appreciate evolutionary morality, and politicians, in particular, he complained, only wished to "debate" instead of "calculate," the skill truly needed by those who would direct society. Only scientists could calculate, and the society therefore had to turn to them for true political wisdom; their introduction to a significant role in the government, Cattell wrote, "is seen to be of the first importance." It was not just any researcher to whom the future could be entrusted, though—it certainly could not be applied scientists, who were busy with the "superficial progress" of "minor improvements" in air travel and electronic communication; only biologists and psychologists were capable of the really important calculations. Organized as a "House of Scientists" in Cattell's plan, they would provide the basic data for the implementation of evolutionary morality: a precise, numerical assessment of each person's worth so an appropriate number of allowable offspring could be assigned; the characteristics on which this worth was based; what privileges or restrictions were appropriate; and methods "to restrict the electorate" to those capable of voting intelligently.[254] Their calculations would thus replace that "moribund morality," which believed in the equal treatment of persons with patently unequal value, with the morality of science. Although the fallacious nature of the former principle was self-evident to Cattell, he offered an obvious example to dispel any belief in its validity: in an unavoidable choice no motorist "would hesitate to run over . . . a feeble minded in preference to a healthy, bright child."[255] The role of science was to instruct society about choices that were not so clear-cut.

Although Cattell was disappointed with the traditional moral sources in his own country, the Third Reich gave him reason to be more hopeful. Germany under Hitler was displaying a sense of social and scientific priorities more in keeping with evolutionary morality. Only in that society—where the Jews, including "Jewish hybrids," were being systematically removed from the professoriat, medical practice, and official positions; where "Jewish" physics and mathematics were distinguished from a more appropriately Aryan approach to science; and where paintings by Jewish artists were displayed as examples of *Entartete Kunst* (degenerate art)—did Cattell find bold action based on biological wisdom. In 1937 he praised the Reich, "where eugenic laws are instantly put into operation," for "being the first to adopt sterilization together with a positive emphasis on racial improvement."[256] Then, a year later, as the newspapers reported the expulsion of Jews from their jobs, the confiscation of their property, and their forced segregation into ghettos and concentration camps, Cattell observed that

the Atlantic democracies are bewildered, envious and hostile at the rise of Germany, Italy and Japan, countries in which individuals have disciplined their indulgences as to a religious purpose . . . in comparison with the vast numbers in our democracies lacking any super-personal aim. Their rise should be welcomed by the religious man as reassuring evidence that in spite of modern wealth and ease, we shall not be allowed to sink into stagnation or adapt foolish social practices in fatal detachment from the stream of evolution.[257]

In a generally uninformed world the Nazis and the fascists provided a beacon of moral light, a model of evolutionary progress to be emulated.

Though Cattell found much to admire in the Third Reich, full-blown evolutionary morality necessitated manipulation of racial groups on a much grander scale, one unimagined even by Spencer or Galton. In the interests of evolutionary progress he proposed that neat experimental designs be imposed on the world. If, for example,

> it is required to discover ... whether the inborn nature of white or yellow peoples is best fitted for progress in the scientific understanding of nature, it would be necessary to divide up world resources between Mongolian and European groups only. We should then start with all other conditions (economic and cultural) approximately equal and observe the course of scientific advance in each group. If now one wished to try out as well a cultural difference, say the social effect of following Christianity on the one hand and Buddhism on the other, it would be necessary to have four groups—a white Buddhist group, a white Christian group, a Mongolian Buddhist group and a Mongolian Christian group.[258]

This was, he emphasized, but a simple illustration; actually, there should be many different racial groups as independent experimental units—four such separate groups in the British Isles alone. In this way a much larger number of variables could be subjected to trial and error and subsequently evaluated, in each case, by scientific comparison: "One group, aiming physically at greater skeletal development, may find itself becoming more susceptible to tuberculosis, or showing a slightly lower average of energy output than another group. Or aiming psychologically at a lesser instinct of self-assertion and greater gregariousness, may find itself producing fewer men of initiative and originality."[259] From the differences that emerged between such groups, scientists would conclude which were superior and which inferior. Since these conclusions would be recognized as fact, ideally the less successful groups would have no reluctance about taking the appropriate eugenic steps; however, in the event of foolish resistance to "controlled evolution," Cattell observed that more forceful means would be in order.

When many social scientists in the postwar period turned from the study of races to the study of racial prejudice, particularly segregation as one of its manifestations, Cattell, now living in the United States, was infuriated. Rather than a reflection of "prejudice," "an attitude which cannot be rationally defended," he maintained that segregation was not only rational but also scientifically imperative. In fact, he wrote—in 1948, when blacks were still systematically excluded from participation in every aspect of U.S. public life—"the very use of the term 'prejudice' as a scientific concept should automatically disqualify the user as a social scientist."[260]

When the controversy over Jensen began, Cattell was naturally outraged by the critics, whom he labeled "ignoracists," persons who refused to recognize that racial differences were genetic in origin. Though he acknowl-

edged that "racists" were "misguided," *ignoracist* was a "more opprobri-
ous term" to Cattell, appropriate for those who had committed an
"error . . . [of] greater immorality."[261] Moreover, the ignoracists confused
research on racial *differences* with conclusions of superiority or inferiority,
something "any thoughtful and biologically educated person" realized
was "meaningless." No mention was made of his own earlier certainty
that blacks were "inferior" and should be systematically eliminated—by
humane measures if possible or force if necessary.

At the same time Cattell was defending Jensen against the scourge of
ignoracism, his own latest work, A *New Morality from Science: Beyondism*,
still insisted that the more "vital" races could not allow the "moribund"
ones to convert the earth into "a living museum"; it was essential that the
"moribund" be "phased out."[262] Though blacks were not mentioned by
name, Cattell now complained about genetic "parasitism," and as an
example he considered a society with two groups: "one type has genes
more favorable to high intelligence and the other resistance to malaria. A
society composed of the first type might succeed as a society by virtue of
its gifts of intelligence (and malaria deaths need not reduce the total
population, granted an appropriate birth rate). On mixing the two, however (in a malarial environment) the differential in immunity endowment
to malaria would result in the intelligent maintainers of the culture being
completely replaced by lower intelligences." Since blacks carry the sickle
cell gene, which also provides malarial immunity, there was little doubt
about the identity of the group with lower intelligence. To ensure that the
relevance of this example to a nonmalarial environment was not missed,
Cattell offered the comparable case of a "welfare society," in which "any
tendency of a group to a birth rate less controlled by social standards—and
this normally happens with the less intelligent and the less temperamentally
foresighted—will result in that genetic sub-group inheriting the society."
Though malaria had not handed society over to blacks, welfare was about
to do so unless there was some "regular cost-accounting" for parasites,
cultural and genetic.[263] Whether their lower intelligence made blacks
"different" or "inferior" would thus seem to be a purely academic distinction to Cattell; in either case they were a parasite on a more "vital" race
and had to be subjected to "genthanasia."

The "*new* morality" of "beyondism" showed no real departure from
Cattell's old ideology, though the racial characterizations were now
expressed with some attempt at subtlety. Instead of the earlier paean to
Nordic dominance, he explained that in the northern European countries
there had been biological selection for "independence of thought and
individualism" and that in those areas long under control of the Roman
Empire there had been selection for "readiness to adapt to orderly
authority," an "authority trusting" genetic mutation. Moreover, the new

work made only one reference to Jews, comparing their "claim to being a Chosen People" with Hitler's assertion of German racial superiority, though there was also an allusion to "mathematical abilities . . . from the Middle East," where Cattell suggested there had been biological selection for "success in accountancy and business."[264]

Once again, the centerpiece of the "new morality from science" was the hubristic claim that all other sources of moral teaching were wrong-headed and that only an appreciation of the evolutionary mechanism could point the way to scientifically derived principles of conduct and define "the finest ways to spend our lives." The intervening thirty-five years had done nothing to improve Cattell's opinion of anyone else. "Few men and fewer women" could appreciate the truth of his message; the mass media could not and consequently had to be "curbed"; literature and art had made no contribution to "moral purpose" and were "irrelevant and malignant" (while dismissing Charles Dickens, George Orwell, and George Bernard Shaw as lacking any moral leadership, Cattell did offer a few examples that lived up to the standards of evolutionary morality: science fiction literature and Star Trek); and economics could be of no value until it was subordinated to the attainment of "ultimate evolutionary goals," producing such policies as steep differentials in earnings, a single flat tax rate for all citizens, and opposition to health insurance. Only the original apostle of Social Darwinism, Herbert Spencer, won Cattell's approval as the one "respectable philosopher who recognized the natural appearance of a 'code of amity' among citizens and a 'code of enmity' among groups." All others only preferred to seduce the public with "such whore phrases as 'social justice and equality,' 'basic freedom' and 'human dignity.' " Faced with such moral incompetence, Cattell saw only one remedy for the society: "to accommodate the will of the majority to an elite of scientific advisors."[265]

One area particularly in need of such scientific supervision was the control of racial intermixture. Though his earlier predictions of wholesale deterioration from interbreeding were now somewhat muted into warnings of "incompatible elements," like those introduced into Anglo-Saxon culture by "the musical beat from the jungle,"[266] Cattell still recommended such rigid genetic separation of races that they "diverge into several distinct non-interbreeding species." If an exception was to be made, however, he emphasized that careful "genetic management . . . in regard to hybridization" was needed. This meant, first, a "shrewd choice" of secondary race to ensure that it had the appropriate properties; then, "an unfettered exercise of the right of self-determination in terms of knowing when firmly to put the lid on and let the melting pot boil . . . to remove the dross"; and, finally, effective eugenic measures "to screen out the many defective combinations," including the "monitoring of gestations" to eliminate not only "physical defect and physiological abnormality but also neurological deviation incompatible with a healthy social life."[267]

For Cattell the purpose of scientific management of different races and cultures was, as always, to test their respective "validities"—to determine which races were to be "hammer" and which "anvil" in the shaping of the future. Once that determination had been made, once it was clear which of two societies was "the more progressive and the more endowed to survive," there was no sense in postponing the inevitable. "In goodness, as in truth," wrote Cattell, "if the right answer is known with greater certainty, there is good reason to apply it with greater rigor. There is no virtue in tolerating known evil." "Failing groups" should either "go to the wall" or be "reconstituted" by outside intervention, while "successful groups" should expand their power, size, and influence.[268] Losing races in the evolutionary competition, Cattell explained, had to give way to their betters, "and genocide, like individual death, is the only way of clearing space."[269]

Because evolutionary progress was best forged in the crucible of racial competition, "external 'charitable' support" rendered to a struggling society by a more successful one and even the successful society's reluctance to expand at the cost of the struggling one were "immoral acts"; to extend the same concern and assistance to other cultures and races that were appropriate for one's own kind "must unquestionably be regarded as a 'heresy.' " (Cattell must have been outraged when concerts that included those "incompatible elements" of black and white musicians raised money to feed starving African children.) Even "culture borrowing," in which an advance developed by one group was shared with another, was to be avoided since it separated the rewards of progress from their genetic origins. In fact, despite his belief in control by a scientific elite, Cattell was concerned that, in their "child-like enthusiasm," many scientists ignored this need for "restriction of discoveries."[270]

Science and political ideology were thus happily united throughout Cattell's career. From the 1930s on he had proclaimed apartheid as a scientifically derived necessity and insisted that scientific conclusions should determine which races were entitled to greater power and territory and which should be "phased out"—indeed, such determinations were the purpose for the study of race. Yet at the same time that he fostered an ideology similar to that which had informed policy in the Reich, Cattell continually maintained that he was an apolitical investigator dedicated only to the pursuit of scientific truths. When other social scientists had complained of his "reactionary" views in 1938, Cattell had responded that that term was political and that he was a scientist with neither knowledge nor interest in such matters.[271] By the 1970s he had converted the very criticisms into a scientific epiphenomenon. It was not just that the critics were mired in politics while he was concerned with more transcendent issues but also that they themselves were victims of evolutionary immaturity. "The brain of man must *itself* evolve," Cattell explained, "before it can understand *why* it should evolve";[272] presumably, his own brain was one of the few to have attained this exalted state.

Cattell's eagerness to offer a scientific foundation for apartheid made him the favorite scientist of the Far Right. Jensen and Eysenck might have provided conclusions about race that others could use to support racist proposals; Cattell was ready to furnish the proposals. Wilmot Robertson, for example, a highly articulate theorist little known outside neo-Nazi circles, has acknowledged his own intellectual debt to Cattell's work. As a member of what he calls "history's greatest gene pool," Robertson has explained that northern Europeans are "best suited to shoulder the main weight of the evolutionary burden"; they have "managed to soar a little higher above the animal kingdom than the other divisions of mankind." Despite this group's genetic superiority, it had been decimated by "two devastating intraracial wars in the first half of the century and the dispossession of the American Majority, the largest reservoir of Northern European genes."[273] Hitler's "failure . . . to establish racial hegemony in Europe . . . was shattering to Northern Europeans both in Europe and America." The last hope for putting "Northern Europeans back on the evolutionary track," according to Robertson, was a "rehabilitated American Majority" bound together by race consciousness, which could be achieved only by liberating them from "the increasing horde of human parasites" in the United States.[274] To deliver "whites of Northern European extraction" from their racial enemies—"an agglomeration of minorities consisting of Jews, dark-skinned Mediterranean whites, Chicanos, Indians, Puerto Ricans and Negroes"—Robertson has proposed a program based directly on Cattell's "beyondism." Each "unassimilable" minority would be forcibly relocated to its own enclave: Asians on the Hawaiian Islands; blacks in sections of the South and in some northern cities; Mexicans in the Southwest; Puerto Ricans in Spanish Harlem and on the island; Jews in sections of New York, Los Angeles, and Miami Beach; and southern Italians and other Mediterranean minorities each in a particular city where they already constitute a sizable segment. "The Utopian States of America," as Robertson termed this system of bantustans, would produce an "ingathering" of northern Europeans, the basis for a biologically correct "world order whose geographical frontiers matched its racial frontiers, once the minority elements were separated out."[275] (The end result of Robertson's plan was illustrated in the December 1984 issue of David Duke's *NAAWP News,* which featured a racially balkanized map of the United States with suggested names for each new territory: for example, "New Africa" in Georgia, Alabama, and Mississippi; "West

Israel" on Long Island and Manhattan; and "Minoria," the rest of the New York metropolitan area for Puerto Ricans, southern Italians, Greeks, and other unassimilable Mediterranean groups.)[276]

Although Cattell's work on "beyondism" received little attention in the scientific community, it was vigorously promoted and distributed by Wilmot Robertson's Howard Allen Press, along with other such "landmark books" as Carleton Putnam's *Race and Reason*.[277] Whether Cattell's claims of political naivete were feigned or sincere, his own pronouncements on race could only further dispel any residual doubts about the true nature of the controversy over Jensenism.

Reinvigoration on the Right

In 1964 a writer in the neo-Nazi periodical *Western Destiny* complained about the lack of discussion in the United States on "how one race rank[s] against another race in ability."[278] At the time the argument for black intellectual inferiority was being articulated primarily by staunch segregationists and was perceived by the public, correctly, as a tactic in the struggle against integration rather than as a bona fide scientific issue. In March 1969 Jensen's *HER* article conferred a new respectability on the racists' favorite topic and catapulted it onto the front page within a matter of days.

Yet the segregationist scientists' sense of vindication was tempered by just the slightest hint of resentment at the attention lavished on Jensen and his supporters for daring to suggest what they had known all along. Amidst their praise for this new hero were occasional reminders that he was a latecomer to the conclusion of black inferiority. In the *Citizen*, the central organ for the southern campaign against integration, Henry Garrett began one column with a Socratic inquiry: "Dr. Garrett, that Dr. Arthur Jensen of the University of California certainly made a splash, didn't he, with his findings? While I am glad to see the publicity given his opinions —that whites are smarter than Negroes—what's so new about that? It seems to me that others, you among them, have been presenting this sort of evidence for a long time?"[279] Elsewhere the *Citizen* characterized Jensen, a nationally recognized scientist, as a "successor" to Frank McGurk, a relatively obscure psychologist and member of the IAAEE Executive Committee active in the scientific campaign against integration.[280]

Jensen provided some balm for these feelings of neglect by regularly acknowledging the segregationists' own contributions to the study of race in the *Mankind Quarterly*—something noted with delight by the original authors—though he gave no indication of the kind of offensive style that characterized the journal devoted to the views of Klansmen and Nazis.

For example, Jensen reported a racial comparison from one *Quarterly* article, omitting the author's observation that Puerto Ricans had performed poorly in part because they were "highly negrified." Nor did he mention that elsewhere in the same issue was a book review extolling the virtues of a well-known Klansman's pamphlet that opposed social and political equality for blacks in America, insisting that the real solution to "the Negro problem in the United States" was to send blacks back to Africa.[281]

Their concern over scientific priority did not prevent Jensen's self-proclaimed predecessors from realizing that his sudden prominence was, most of all, an opportunity. Despite all of the segregationists' own educational efforts, the public's understanding of race was still Ptolemaic; Jensen was their first real hope to make it Copernican. The question was how best to make use of this prestigious new ally.

Despite the segregationists' insistence that Jensen had vindicated their claims, they could not help noticing certain differences between his work and their own, differences that explained why he had "succeeded" where they had failed. Most important, Jensen's research was much more technically sophisticated, especially in its exploitation of behavior-genetic techniques. There were also obvious differences in style. Jensen had no foolish obsession with "amalgamation." He refused to endorse legal segregation. He carefully eschewed the name-calling that was the segregationists' stock-in-trade; he took the positions of his critics seriously and addressed the issues they raised. When it was clear that he had been wrong on a matter of fact, at times he was not reluctant to act in an exemplary fashion. For example, after he made a demonstrably inaccurate statement about Psychologists for Social Action, an organization that had opposed his work, Jensen not only sent them his "humble apology" but also had it printed in the trade paper for the American Psychological Association.[282] The segregationist scientists were like Shaw's Major Saranoff; they *never* apologized.

At first the segregationists attempted to follow in Jensen's technical footsteps, with generally abysmal results. For example, R. Travis Osborne, one of the expert witnesses in the judicial efforts to reverse the *Brown* decision, published a series of studies on the heritabilities of various measures of ability for both blacks and whites. Though he found no differences between the races in these heritabilities, much of the data was just gibberish. Some of the heritability estimates were larger than 1.000, not just slightly greater, which might be attributed to sampling error, but such ridiculous values as 2.840, 3.320, and a staggeringly absurd -11.496. Moreover, all but a handful of the approximately twenty-five heritability values for blacks were not statistically significant; that is, there was no evidence that they were greater than zero.[283] (Though

Osborne presented the appropriate statistics, he provided no indication of their significance, thus omitting the information that would have revealed the study as worthless.) Much to Osborne's ultimate chagrin, the data from his research *were* used in a more methodologically sound investigation. Osborne had been especially interested in a racial blood-group analysis of the test scores, certain that it would "hold surprises" for all those egalitarians with "preconceived ideas of the outcomes."[284] He therefore contributed his own data to be pooled and analyzed with that collected by other researchers (in order to attain an appropriate sample size), and the results were indeed surprising—to Osborne, who found his name, as the third of three authors, on a study concluding that "European genes in Negroes either are not substantially associated with intellectual performance or *actually predict poorer performance*" (emphasis added). The study's introduction noted that "all analyses in the present paper were carried out by the first author," perhaps Osborne's attempt to account for his association with such an unexpected outcome.[285]

Old Money through New Channels

Anxious not to squander the opportunity created by Jensenism but unable to exploit it through their own research, the segregationist academics turned to facilitating the work of the new, more well-known scientific authorities as a more productive tactic. They helped to provide Jensen, Shockley, Eysenck, and Cattell with needed financial support for their research and assistance in disseminating their conclusions beyond the scientific community. In return for this financial and logistic assistance, the segregationists obtained the researchers' prestige for their causes in general and the frequent participation of these prominent scholars in their specific projects. The involvement of mainstream scientists meant that to some extent the racist academics had to moderate their opposition to integration, but this was a small price to pay, especially since the racial battlefield was beginning to shift to such issues as affirmative action, which all of these new authorities did not hesitate to oppose.

The Pioneer Fund, that longtime supporter of efforts to prove the superiority of the original white "stock," provided the resources for these goals in many different ways. It made substantial grants to some scientists; Shockley alone received $179,000 over a period of ten years.[286] It also subsidized a number of nonprofit corporations—all "organized exclusively for educational and scientific purposes" and represented by George Leonard, a lawyer who had told the Supreme Court, on behalf of 375 southern private schools that excluded blacks, that discrimination was "not necessarily a horrible thing"[287]—which seemed to be nothing more than conduits for channeling money to particular researchers. One recipient, for example, the Institute for the Study of Educational Differences, which listed Arthur Jensen as its president, was acknowledged as the source of support for Jensen's later research on race and speed of information processing.[288]

Two other nonprofit corporations supported by the Pioneer Fund, the Foundation for Human Understanding (FHU) and the Testing Research Fund (TRF), acted as publicity agents for works on heredity, intelligence, and race. Directed by Henry E. Garrett, R. Travis Osborne, Frank McGurk, and Ernest van den Haag, all members of the IAAEE and longtime staunch opponents of integration, the FHU and TRF each spent tens of thousands of tax-free dollars to promote books congenial to their viewpoint. They paid for expensive advertisements. For example, when Hans J. Eysenck raved about a new Jensen book containing the *HER* article, the FHU reprinted the review "as a public service" a year later in a full-page ad in the *New York Times Book Review*.[289] They also distributed free copies of books to judiciously chosen target populations. The TRF, for example, bought twenty-eight hundred copies of Jensen's *Straight Talk about Mental Tests* and sent them gratis to college presidents and admissions officers throughout the country.[290] Along with Jensen's usual arguments, these administrators, who determined the future of millions of college applicants each year, could read that the decline in the number of students with high SAT scores was attributable to a declining birthrate among those "ethnic groups" that had contributed most of the top scorers in the past. The FHU also donated copies of Osborne's *Twins: Black and White* (which FHU had published) to university libraries. Dedicated to the memory of Henry Garrett, author of the most repulsive hate pamphlets against school integration, *Twins* was yet another dreary compilation of test scores and heritability estimates (many of these heritability estimates were again not significantly different from zero, a point that Osborne still did not find worth mentioning).[291]

In addition, FHU reprinted, advertised, and distributed such other "classics" as the IAAEE-sponsored *Race and Modern Science* and the English scientist John Baker's *Race*. In language right out of Joseph Arthur de Gobineau's or Madison Grant's work, the slick brochure promoting Baker's book noted that the title provided the "master key" to history and that the book would "not only tell us everything we should know about the major races" but also point out the more "subtle shadings" among whites: "How to tell a Nordic from an Alpine, an Alpine from a Mediterranean, a Jew from a Gentile. How does one race compare with another in intelligence, work concentration, inventiveness, stamina? Which of the various racial traits, both physical and mental, are inherited and which are not? How do the races vary in height, weight, coloration, head shape, even in odor?" "Even antiracists" would benefit from this encyclopedic array of information, the brochure declared, because "it pays to know the arguments of your opponents."[292]

The most ambitious project sponsored by the FHU, however, was the compilation of works resulting in *Human Variation,* a book edited by Osborne, C. E. Noble, and Nathaniel Weyl. Osborne, of course, was a veteran in the anti-integration campaign. Noble, a contributor to the *Citizen* as well as scientific journals, had defended Carleton Putnam and the "expert witnesses" for segregation against criticism from other scientists. A researcher in psychomotor behavior, in 1969 he had claimed that blacks' performance on a test of hand-to-eye coordination was so genetically inferior to the performance of whites that even after fifty practice trials they could not do as well as whites on their first attempt and that blacks' performance with their right hand was always poorer than whites' with their left.[293] (Observation of any National Basketball Association contest will confirm the meaningfulness of these conclusions.)

In the early 1960s Weyl had authored several books on blacks. In a historical review he claimed that every statesman had objected to the presence of blacks on American soil, considering them aliens who could not be assimilated without destroying the cohesion of the Republic. Most of the time, according to Weyl, this conviction had been informed by belief in black inferiority, but even those few who had considered blacks to be mental equals had an aversion to their presence. A consensus had thus existed over the need for wholesale deportation, until forced emigration became impractical after the Civil War. As a substitute, he explained, the nation's leadership turned to segregation to protect the country from the indigestible mass of newly freed blacks, most of them ignorant, intemperate, and vicious. Segregation remained the solution of choice until Franklin Roosevelt, eager to obtain the black vote, began to throw them "sops" and the Supreme Court began to "lean over backward" to render absurd decisions. Despite all the assistance blacks had received since FDR, in Weyl's opinion they had still contributed nothing—a few well-known musicians, though not "in the more demanding" musical areas—and were just not genetically capable of becoming a productive and integral part of American society. Nevertheless, he observed, blacks had made economic progress that bore little relationship to their abilities. "The American Negro," Weyl wrote in 1960, before the passage of most civil rights legislation, "is not underprivileged, but overprivileged."[294]

In another work Weyl traced the reason for blacks' inferiority to their brain, which was not only supposedly smaller but also poorly "integrated" so the frontal lobes, the source of imagination, conceptual thought, and foresight, remained relatively "idle." Lacking these crucial capacities, blacks had naturally "been relegated to an inferior and servile status." To account for their underdeveloped brain, Weyl claimed that a large active brain had been a disadvantage for survival in tropical climates because it placed too much stress on the heart to supply it with oxygen. To this pseudo-Darwinian analysis he appended one other scientific observation in an area that had been overlooked by previous researchers: much of black male anatomy and physiology was more similar to that of European girls than boys, and this physical feminization of black men accounted for their widespread tendency to perform fellatio on each other without guilt or embarrassment.[295]

With such views Weyl soon became a regular contributor to the *Mankind Quarterly* (though the journal did find fault with his observation that a black had a "right to be judged as a human being," terming such an unrealistic proposition an *"ignis fatuus"*).[296] In the *Quarterly* he refined his theory of the relationship between climate and brain size, tracing both to somatotype. The slim "Negroid" body, he noted, was a physiological adaptation to warm climates, producing a greater ratio of skin-surface to body-mass and thus a proportionately larger area for heat loss through sweating. But this slender build, he explained, was also the cause of black intellectual inferiority, because women with a narrower pelvic brim crushed or otherwise traumatized the cranium of large-brained neonates. The process of evolutionary selection had thus produced small-brained blacks as an adaptation to the size of the pelvic brim.[297]

Fresh from this scientific tour de force, Weyl joined with Osborne and Noble to put together *Human Variation*. The collection's introductory essay was contributed by Dwight Ingle, a gracious choice since Ingle had earlier used his editorship of *Perspectives in Biology and Medicine* to publish Weyl's and Noble's diatribes against blacks.[298] Ingle once again emphasized the importance of scientific proof for blacks' genetic inferiority so society would "stop telling Negroids" that their problems were caused by racism. Fifteen years after he had found biology an obstacle to integration, Ingle acknowledged that there had been some individuals who attempted to exploit genetic evidence "to deprive Negroids of equal rights" but maintained that there had been no scientists among them.[299]

Most of the authors in *Human Variation* were members of the *Mankind Quarterly*'s editorial board, though they were now joined by Jensen, who contributed a technical discussion of the effects of nonrandom mating.[300] Perhaps to avoid alienating him from their project, the *Quarterly*'s associates were uncharacteristically restrained. Weyl, for example, chose not to share his momentous discovery of the relationship between intelligence and pelvic brim size. There was, of course, the usual obsession with racial differences. The English psychologist Richard Lynn reported a dizzying list of IQ results from different nationalities—Belgian, French, Scottish, East German, Italian, Spanish, Yugoslavian, Greek, Iranian, and on and on—and concluded that Nordics were intellectually superior to "Caucausoid peoples inhabiting the more southerly latitudes"; with no embarrassment he even cited the World War I army data as corroboration of this result.[301] Another contributor, Robert Lehrke, offered a genetic theory to account for women's diminished representation at the highest levels of accomplishment despite having the same "average" IQ as men. "For the benefit of the ladies," Lehrke acknowledged that the brightest women were on a par with the brightest men; there were just fewer of them.[302] C. D. Darlington concluded the collection with a genetic explanation for the absence of civilization from Africa: the same genes that endowed "Negroids" with immunity to malaria both weakened the reaction to other diseases and produced a belief in witchcraft. Slavery, he noted, had mercifully rescued blacks from the first of these dangers, but the second remained an ongoing obstacle to their development.[303]

Despite the absence of any overtly racist rhetoric in *Human Variation*, there was little doubt about its true purpose. Soon after publication the *Citizen* featured an unsigned discussion praising the book—probably written by one of its three editors, who did not wish to compromise the book's scientific image by appearing in a periodical dedicated to preserving segregation—and provided an address from which it could be obtained. This interest in a work that did not directly label blacks inferior and call for a return to segregation might have been puzzling to the *Citizen*'s less astute readers. To prevent any confusion, the article was accompanied by a gratuitous photograph of William Shockley, who had not been involved in the project but whose scientific opinions on race were well known to the *Citizen*'s audience, in a debate with a black attorney. The picture's caption pointed out the "observable hereditary differences" between the two despite their common academic background and concluded that Shockley's opponents "generally win the debate—for Shockley."[304] Even the scientifically unsophisticated would have no problem decoding the *Citizen*'s interest in this book: *Human Variation* was another biological demonstration of white superiority.

Transition at the Mankind Quarterly

For a long time the segregationist scientists' new, more sophisticated image did not extend to their flagship journal, the *Mankind Quarterly*. Although the addition of Eysenck to its editorial board in 1974 placed a prestigious name on the *Quarterly*'s cover, its rhetoric remained as overtly racist as ever. More than a decade after the civil rights movement, however, blatantly racist appeals were neither effective nor acceptable, especially in a scientific journal, and eventually the *Quarterly* attempted to change its image. In 1978 the anthropologist Robert Gayre of Gayre announced his resignation as editor in chief, informing readers that the journal would be moved to Washington, D.C., where the new editor would be Roger Pearson of the Institute for the Study of Man.[305]

The British-born Pearson, who once reportedly boasted of helping to hide Josef Mengele,[306] had spent the previous twenty years working toward the formation of a Fourth Reich. Only a decade after the war he began publishing the "cultural journal" *Northern World,* in which he complained that nationality had come "to be determined not by descent, not by the common blood ties of a shared biological heritage, but by the accident of geographical location," a situation that had produced "racial chaos." If Nordics were "not to be annihilated as a species," he wrote, they had to "develop a world-wide bond between our own kind" and "begin to think in terms of . . . racial identity." Such a true "Pan-Nordicism" could be achieved "only . . . if we realize the falsity of modern political 'nationality' laws which are playing havoc with our natural loyalties and result too often in mongrelisation at home and fratricidal warfare abroad."[307] In 1958 Pearson established the Northern League in Europe as a rallying ground for former Nazi intellectuals and SS officials, with Hans F. K. Günther as one of its founding members. The Northern League's first conference, held in West Germany, was described by that country's authorities as "national socialism revived."[308]

In the 1960s Pearson immigrated to the United States to join forces with Willis Carto, organizer of the Liberty Lobby. Subsidized by Pioneer grants, their alliance produced a merger of Pearson's *Northern World* with *Right,* edited by Carto under the pseudonym of E. L. Anderson, which became a new publication, *Western Destiny.*[309] To Pearson's call for Nordic purity *Western Destiny* now added Carto's obsession with Jews as "Culture Distorters," "aliens . . . inherently unable to be in tune with our Western Culture and Spirituality."[310] For the Nordic race to survive, wrote Pearson as editor of the new journal, the Culture Distorter, preaching freedom instead of race consciousness, had to be prevented "from capturing the minds, morals and souls of our children."[311] *Western Destiny* regularly blamed the "New York money changers" for causing the "Second Fratricidal War" and the subsequent "Allied War Crimes" against the Reich out of a desire to impose financial slavery on Germany and the world.[312] Pearson also authored tracts on race and eugenics for Carto's Noontide Press. In *Race and Civilization,* for example, he described how the aristocratic Nordic, the "symbol . . . of human dignity," had been forced by "taxes against landholders . . . to intermarry with Jewish and other non-Nordic elements," thus securing the wealth necessary to retain their family estates but sacrificing their "biological heritage" and "thereby renounc[ing] their real claim to nobility."[313]

In the 1970s, however, Pearson began a transition toward greater respectability, eventually becoming a link between neo-Nazi elements and the New Right. After a number of academic appointments he moved to Washington to found the Council on American Affairs and the *Journal of Social and Political Studies* (later expanded to the *Journal of Social, Political and Economic Studies*), which eschewed the old rhetoric of Nordic solidarity in favor of a more mainstream conservative orientation and featured contributions by such public figures as Jack Kemp and Jesse Helms as well as analyses by academics. Pearson soon became a recognized New Right academic himself, serving as an editorial associate for such think tanks as the Heritage Foundation and the American Security Council's Foreign Policy Institute, and his own Council on American Affairs was named the United States Chapter of the World Anti-Communist League (WACL). He used this opportunity to fill the WACL with European Nazis—ex-officials of the Third Reich and Nazi collaborators from other countries during the war as well as new adherents to the cause—in what one journalist called "one of the greatest fascist blocs in postwar Europe."[314]

A respected intellectual in influential circles, who could nevertheless be depended on to keep the neo-Nazi faith, Pearson no doubt seemed the ideal person to take the reins at the *Mankind Quarterly*, which was in the process of a similar transition. At the time of Gayre's departure, such fanatic right-wingers as Robert Kuttner also ended their association with the journal, and a change in its physical composition gave the *Quarterly* a more polished, sophisticated appearance.

Before he could actually take charge of the *Mankind Quarterly*, Pearson's new image began to unravel, however. First, a *New York Times* story on the Pioneer Fund named him as a beneficiary of two grants, noting his earlier incarnation as editor of *Western Destiny* and author of pamphlets on Nordic supremacy.[315] Then, even more damaging, the *Washington Post* published a front-page story on the "Fascist specter" behind the World Anti-Communist League, which was holding its annual conference in Washington at the time, with particular attention to Pearson as the conference chair. The article described the unsavory political nature of some of the participants, such as one official delegation that circulated materials attacking a recent TV show on the Holocaust as "another gigantic campaign of Jewish propaganda to conceal their objectives of world domination." It also detailed Pearson's background, noting that his assistant at the conference, as well as at his own Council on American Affairs, was a former American Nazi party stormtrooper. In addition, when members of the National States Rights party, yet another Nazi-style political group, whose bylaws declared that "Jew-devils have no place in a White Christian nation," showed up at the conference to distribute anti-Jewish tracts, the article reported that Pearson asked them to leave, remarking, "Not that I'm not sympathetic with what you're doing . . . but don't embarrass me and cut my throat." As they departed, he told them to "give my regards" to Edward Fields, their party's national secretary.[316]

Though the exposure of these links left Pearson's throat unscathed, it might have severed his name from the masthead of the *Mankind Quarterly,* whose official editorship he never actually assumed (he was soon dropped from the editorial board of the Heritage Foundation's journal *Policy Review* as well). In the issue after Gayre had named Pearson as his successor, the journal announced that a reorganization was taking place, and when the new editors were named over a year later, Pearson was not among them; an editor on cozy terms with Nazis was hardly in keeping with the *Quarterly*'s renovated image. Though Pearson's name was not displayed on the masthead, he was clearly in charge behind the scenes. The journal was published at the Institute for the Study of Man, where he was both founder and president; subscriptions were ordered there; and manuscripts were submitted there—to the "general editor," a position that was not listed among the *Quarterly*'s official roster of editors, having been replaced by an editorial committee, but was certainly filled by Pearson in practice. In addition to the *Quarterly* itself, Pearson's institute also published articles excerpted from the journal ("Mankind Quarterly Monographs") and books on race, many of them issued under the imprint of "Cliveden Press"—a deft touch by Pearson since those members of the British aristocracy sympathetic to Hitler during the war were known as the "Cliveden Set," named after the location of the Astors' country home, the group's symbolic headquarters.[317] Although more moderate names were now "officially" in charge of the *Mankind Quarterly,* it remained under Pearson's control.

Of course, the new editors were moderate only by the *Quarterly*'s standards. Richard Lynn, for example, had contributed the chapter to *Human Variation* with the latest evidence that Nordics were intellectually superior to southern Europeans. He also had devoted an entire book to a study of national differences in measures of anxiety, closely paralleling Carl C. Brigham's 1923 racial analysis of army test scores. Where Brigham had attributed national differences in intelligence to underlying racial composition, with Nordic countries ranking ahead of Alpine and Mediterranean, Lynn concluded that the order was reversed for anxiety—the calm and well-controlled Nordics ranked lowest, the other races, frantic and hysterical, much higher. Some strained interpretations were necessary to achieve this result. When the Nordic countries turned out to have higher rates of coronary heart disease, this ailment was characterized as an indication of low anxiety. Suicide, a behavior more frequent in the northern European countries, had been explained by the earlier eugenicists as the ultimate exploration of the unknown by adventurous

Nordics, but in Lynn's analysis it was viewed as a consequence of high anxiety. To preserve the appropriate racial ordering in the face of this hostile data, he merely changed the racial composition of the various nationalities: the Irish, for example, who had been labeled predominantly Mediterranean to explain their low IQs were now converted to Nordics to account for their exceptionally low suicide rate. As always, these racial differences had political implications: those in the Nordic countries, Lynn observed, were more fit for constitutional government than were "the abrasive peoples" in the countries of Alpine and Mediterranean extraction.[318] Though untainted by the kind of overt political associations that had marked Pearson, Kuttner, and others, Lynn still had the appropriate obsession with race.

The "new" *Mankind Quarterly* also featured Raymond Cattell as a board member and frequent contributor. The journal thus acquired another prominent scientific name for its masthead, while Cattell obtained an outlet for a stream of works unlikely to be welcome in other scientific publications despite his prestige. One paper, for example, presented his "beyondist" exhortation for humankind to become a number of noninterbreeding species.[319] Another investigated the relationship between personality traits and blood type, the latter variable possibly suggesting a link to race, whose biological—as opposed to social—definition has considered the frequency of various blood groups.[320] Some years earlier a similar study by Cattell published in a medical journal had been subjected to ridicule by other scientists; it was called technically inaccurate, useless, and a waste of journal space. According to one researcher, the "only consolation is that the article is probably harmless, because few readers will take it seriously." At the time Cattell had responded with a plea of nolo contendere: he had not bothered to save the data.[321] When he submitted a new set of data to the same type of analysis, however, he had a friendlier venue for its appearance. The *Mankind Quarterly* would never publish attacks on the chief scientific exponent of evolutionary morality.

In keeping with the *Quarterly*'s improved image, however, its worst rhetorical excesses were now toned down. The threat of "Negrification" or "mongrelization" was replaced by discreet reference to "the presence of black genes amongst segments of the population classified as white," and overt proclamations of Nordic superiority were eliminated, along with the clarion calls for a return to apartheid in the United States.[322] Beneath this Band-Aid of sophistication festered the same racist sore, though. One of the journal's first articles in 1961, "The Evolutionary Basis of Race Consciousness," had explained that interracial hostility was an automatic biological response, whose function was to "prevent interbreeding" and preserve "genetic integrity."[323] A quarter of a century

later an article entitled "The Evolutionary Function of Prejudice" concluded that race prejudice was a deeply rooted biological mechanism
necessary "to preserve the genetic identity of races and sub-species . . . by
inhibiting miscegenation." Indeed, it predicted, the decay of such a
natural barrier would only weaken a society's "survival potential . . . by
promoting anti-evolutionary life-styles together with their concomitant
reproductive abnormalities."[324] In 1986 a scientific journal could still
provide a biological rationale for the activities of a lynch mob.

Though less intemperate in style, the *Mankind Quarterly* also contin-
ued to hammer away at desegregation, publishing a series of articles by
Ralph Scott, a professor of educational psychology at the University of
Northern Iowa; a former vice president of the German-American National
Congress, an organization that extolled the virtues of the Third Reich;[325]
and once a gubernatorial candidate of the American party, another Far
Right group supported by Willis Carto. Scott had also received Pioneer
Fund grants to hold anti-school-integration seminars around the country,
an activity he conducted under a pseudonym.[326] (Amazingly, this record
did not prevent him from being appointed chair of the Iowa Advisory
Commission on Civil Rights by the Reagan administration.) In the *Mankind
Quarterly* Scott scored the "professional bias and ideological imbalance"
of the expert witnesses for the plaintiffs in the *Brown* case, now some
thirty years old, and claimed that desegregation had been harmful to
blacks.[327] If nothing else, the *Quarterly* was certainly perseverative.

The European Right

The attention generated by Jensenism was also a source of encouragement to a rising fascist movement in Europe, where groups were working
to rehabilitate Nordicism as scientific support for neo-Nazi ideologies.
The chief organizer for Britain's National Front, Martin Webster, who had
boasted of creating a "well-oiled Nazi machine," noted that "the most
important factor in the build-up of self-confidence amongst 'racists' . . . was
the publication in 1969 by Professor Jensen in the *Harvard Education
Review.*"[328] The National Front's magazine, *Spearhead,* observed with
satisfaction that Jensen's work had "exploded like a bomb in the ranks of
the environmentalists."[329] When a group of Strasserite Nazis broke from
the National Front's Hitlerite mainstream to form the National party, the
first issue of *Beacon,* the new organization's magazine, featured a personal interview with Eysenck, in which the psychologist noted "a very
close correlation between the different achievements of races and their
present day IQ level."[330]

In particular, Jensen's work was often cited to justify apartheid in
South Africa, which was regarded by racist groups everywhere as the

only remaining nation based on comprehension of "the true nature of Western civilization."[331] Shortly after the *HER* publication A. James Gregor, who had played such an important role in founding the IAAEE and the *Mankind Quarterly*, organized a conference in London with Jensen and Shockley as the featured speakers. In an article on the conference entitled "Moderne Rassentheorie stützt Südafrika" (Modern Racial Theory Supports South Africa) *Nation Europa*, a journal established shortly after World War II by members of the old Nazi elite, reported that Jensen had said blacks and Puerto Ricans were in "last place" in the racial order. Noting that extensive study had not been necessary for South Africa to realize that a "Bantu" could not be "converted" into a European, *Nation Europa* nevertheless found Jensen's work to be a useful scientific confirmation of the necessity of confining blacks to "their own tribal lands."[332]

Although Jensen steered clear of personal involvement with overtly segregationist publications in the United States, he appeared to have few qualms about contributing to fascist journals in other languages. He granted an exclusive interview to *Nation Europa;* the same issue featuring the interview gave high praise to a revisionist work distributed by many neo-Nazi groups claiming that the Holocaust had never occurred but was merely a hoax perpetrated to commit political blackmail and to silence those who would warn Europe about the biological danger of "colored immigration."[333] Though Jensen refused to endorse segregation in the interview, his scientific statements provided ample compensation for this difference over policy. Asked whether different races might not actually be different species, he first acknowledged interfertility as the theoretical criterion for such a decision but then added reservations about its practical validity. Some human races, Jensen declared, differed from one another even more than did some animals of different species. Moreover, he claimed, a measurement of the "genetic distance" between blacks and whites showed a divergence of some forty-six thousand years in their evolutionary history, approximately three times the genetic distance between whites and Orientals.[334] These were observations Jensen had not made elsewhere. He had chosen an interview with fascists to question not only whether blacks were at the same level of evolutionary development as whites but also whether they were even members of the same species.

Nation Europa also sought Jensen's endorsement for the validity of intrawhite racial comparisons, reminding him of Weyl's recent article "The Geography of Stupidity" in the *Mankind Quarterly*, which had examined the army IQ test scores of 1968 draftees and found that the best performance was achieved by inhabitants of states with high concentrations of Nordic elements, especially Scandinavian and German, and low concentrations of Hispanics, Portuguese, and Italians. That is, a publication ideologically committed to Nordic superiority was requesting Jensen's imprimatur for the issue as scientifically respectable. He gave them half a loaf: it was "theoretically" a scientific question but, being of little practical significance in the United States, would not be a sensible use of the country's resources.[335] Neither party in the exchange doubted that an appropriate role of science was to link sociopolitical questions to genetic differences. In the United States this meant studying the "great races" to rationalize blacks' position in the social order; in Europe it might well mean comparing "subgroups" within the white race to support Nordic superiority.

As the European Right reorganized further in the late 1960s and early 1970s, two new academic publications, both clones of the *Mankind Quarterly* appeared, one in Germany and one in France. The three journals seemed like different language franchises for the same ideology. Each carried advertisements for the other two; the same persons regularly served as their board members and appeared as contributors; and sometimes the exact same article would appear in two of these publications simultaneously. In addition, they were all recommended by, and in turn carried advertisements for, such publications as the *Northlander*, the official journal of Pearson's Northern League. *Nouvelle Ecole*, the French journal, included as members of its board Gayre, Pearson, Kuttner, and Garrett. At the World Anti-Communist League meeting chaired by Pearson, a group representing *Nouvelle Ecole* met with William Pierce, a former American Nazi party functionary and author of *The Turner Diaries*, a blueprint for race war used as a model by the neo-Nazi group The Order, which murdered Denver talk-show host Alan Berg in 1984. According to Pierce, now the head of his own neo-Nazi group, the National Alliance, the French publication was "working along lines very close to ours."[336]

Nouvelle Ecole described the Jensen controversy in an article entitled "School Integration and Racial Psychology," a characterization over which he had no control, of course. But a short time later Jensen granted a personal interview to the journal, emphasizing the importance of research on racial difference, though he offered no explicit example of its use.[337] A publication whose readers would also be interested in subscribing to the *Northlander* could certainly trust them to appreciate the practical implications of lower black intelligence.

The German member of the triumvirate was *Neue Anthropologie*, whose first issue in 1973 honored Fritz Lenz, the doyen of *Rassenhygiene*, on his eighty-fifth birthday. Its editor, Jürgen Rieger, had authored the pamphlet *Rasse—ein Problem auch für uns* (Race—a Problem for Us Also), which stressed the importance of preserving Nordic purity. (When

Rieger's book produced a sectarian controversy within the neo-Nazi movement over the proper criteria for defining white subraces, both his critics and defenders agreed, however, that he had relied on the best scientific references on race—IAAEE publications by Kuttner, Garrett, Gregor, and others, which had attained an almost scriptural status among knowledgeable racists; they disagreed over whether his political conclusions were consistent with these established scientific facts.)[338] Several members of the journal's "board of scientific advisers" were also active in the German neo-Nazi party, the NPD (Nationaldemokratische Partei Deutschlands), including one professor whose pamphlet providing a scientific basis for the party's ideology was sent free to new subscribers to *Neue Anthropologie*.[339] Another board member was Donald Swan, also an editor and frequent contributor to the *Mankind Quarterly* as well as a recipient of Pioneer grants. According to the *Nation*, when Swan was arrested for mail fraud in 1966, Nazi "paraphernalia," weapons, and stacks of anti-Semitic, antiblack, and anti-Catholic pamphlets were found in his home.[340] When *Neue Anthropologie*'s publisher sought to establish a "Günther-Circle," the journal knowingly requested readers to help assemble a complete collection of his works by contributing their personal copies of Günther's articles from such prewar journals as *Neues Volk*, an official publication of the Third Reich's Nazi party.[341]

Jensen was extensively involved with *Neue Anthropologie*. Its first issue contained the same interview with him that had earlier appeared in *Nouvelle Ecole*, unsurprising since the editor-interviewer for the latter publication was also a member of the former's "scientific board."[342] Jensen would become a more important resource for *Neue Anthropologie*, however, eventually making regular contributions to the journal, articles that, though largely technical, lent scientific respectability to the surrounding prose—anti-immigrant polemics, favorable reviews of anti-Semitic tracts, tributes to racist scientists from the Nazi era. Then in 1976, in obvious recognition of Jensen's significance to them, *Neue Anthropologie* published a special bibliography of all his works since 1967 (the writing from his earlier "environmentalist" period naturally was of little interest to them).[343] Two issues later Jensen joined the journal's board, his name appearing alongside the neo-Nazis who also graced that body. The association appeared to benefit them more than it harmed him.

According to the sociologist Robert Gordon, who has spoken to Jensen personally about his involvement with *Neue Anthropologie*, Jensen did not have "the foggiest idea who Rieger is, . . . does not read German well, but has never recognized anything in copies of N.A. sent to him to put him on guard . . . [and] has not reviewed any material for the journal or participated in any way other than allowing articles of his published elsewhere to be reprinted in German."[344] Assuming all these claims were true, it only confirmed Jensen's role as an unwitting accomplice to the forces of bigotry; though he had neither duties nor responsibilities as a board member, his name provided a patina of scientific respectability for a journal devoted largely to the restoration of Güntherism. Gordon himself went on to suggest that the journal's characterization as "neo-Nazi" was an exaggeration stemming from Rieger's "disfavor with the small remnants of the Jewish community still residing in Germany," because he had served as defense counsel for a man accused of war crimes. In fact, as an active member of Pearson's Northern League, Rieger told this group dedicated to Nordic solidarity that it was "natural" for "the Teutonic nations . . . of the *same racial extraction* . . . to strive for political union and unity of power" and encouraged its members to "fight for a Teutonic confederation that *must* come." He was also one of the organizers and a featured speaker of a Munich conference entitled "Eternal Penitence for Hitler?"; the other two speakers were both proponents of the theory that the Holocaust was a lie created by Jewish propagandists.[345] In addition Rieger has been the neo-Nazi movement's chief legal counsel, representing, for example, Ernst Zúndel, the author of *The Hitler We Loved*, a book that portrayed Hitler as Germany's salvation and concluded with the declaration "WE LOVE YOU, ADOLF HITLER."[346] Jensen might have been naive, but there was no doubt about the facts.

Of course, the degree of Jensen's complicity, willful or otherwise, in the ideological misuse of his research is in some ways a distraction from the more important point: his considerable efforts to investigate racial differences in intellectual ability produced neither scientific insight nor social benefit. In exchange, as it were, for the political misuse of science, nothing of value was obtained.

Epilogue to Jensenism: New Approaches to Old Obsessions

After the bulk of the controversy over his work had died down, Jensen persevered in his attempts to prove blacks genetically less intelligent than whites. His new research, however, eschewed interest in the heritability of IQ scores in favor of racial differences in the speed of information processing, a measure he considered "related to even more fundamental processes at the interface of brain and behavior, such as errors in the transmission of neural impulses."[347] His first reported study of this type compared the reaction times of blacks and whites to the onset of some sensory stimulus, usually a light. According to Jensen, "simple reaction time"—in which a subject merely has to lift his or her finger off a button the instant a light bulb goes on—was much less g-loaded (i.e., less dependent on general intelligence) than was "choice reaction time"—in which a subject is faced with a number of lights, each with a corresponding button, and must react to the specific one that is turned on; as the number of possible stimuli increases, more information must be processed, and the decision mechanism becomes more complex, elements he claimed were "the essence of *g*." This procedure permitted an exact quantification of stimulus complexity in terms of the number of "bits" of information presented. (A *bit*—short for *binary digit*—is the standard unit of measurement in information theory, defined as the logarithm to the base two of the number of alternatives in a choice situation. A single light thus presents zero bits of information, while two, four, and eight lights involve one, two, and three bits, respectively.) When Jensen compared the performance of blacks and whites on these tests, "the results turn out perfectly in accord with the hypothesis": there was no difference between the two groups in reaction time to a *single* light, but as the number of stimuli grew larger, increasing the number of bits of information and thus the intellectual requirements of the task, "the white-Negro differences in RT [reaction time] increased significantly and linearly with each additional bit."[348]

A somewhat similar result had been obtained more than forty years earlier by two Vanderbilt University professors, Martha Lambeth and Lyle Lanier, but Jensen's outcome was much more impressive for two reasons. First, although the earlier scientists had found greater racial differences in "speed" as the complexity of performance increased, they acknowledged that their judgment of performance was somewhat subjective, especially since some of the tasks involved learned abilities, such as reading. Jensen, in contrast, had a definition of complexity that not only was precise and theoretically based but also allowed tasks that were free of any cultural content. Second, in the earlier study when blacks and whites were matched for IQ score, the differences in speed disappeared. "Indeed," wrote Lambeth and Lanier, "the Negro is usually 'faster' than the white of the same Stanford-Binet score."[349] In Jensen's study the two groups of subjects began "almost perfectly matched in the score distribution on a group verbal test of intelligence," thus "stack[ing] the cards," as he put it, against the hypothesis that the groups would differ in reaction time as the amount of information increased. When such a steadily increasing difference occurred nevertheless, it was all the more astonishing. If blacks performed progressively worse than whites with the same IQ as this culture-free measure of information processing increased, it implied that standardized tests of intelligence *were* biased—in favor of blacks.

By the time Jensen's study on reaction time appeared, Leon Kamin, a professor of psychology at Princeton University, had exposed the fraudulent nature of Sir Cyril Burt's studies on heritability and IQ and was becoming well known for his reanalyses of data collected by other researchers on the same topic. In reanalyzing the data, he often had to request subjects' individual scores from these investigators, who usually responded in the best traditions of science, making their material available to Kamin even though they knew that his analysis might suggest a conclusion opposed to their own. When Kamin read Jensen's work on race and reaction time, he considered the results slightly incredible, implying, as they did, that blacks should be underrepresented in endeavors requiring rapid response to complex visual displays—such as basketball and boxing. He consequently wrote to Jensen, politely requesting to see the data and offering to defray all expenses involved in reproduction.[350] Kamin anticipated no difficulty, especially since Jensen was clearly on record that scientific data should be made public. After his own reanalysis of Burt's data had also judged them useless, Jensen had reflected on the "important lesson" to be derived from this unfortunate episode, offering some recommendations to "aid the advancement of behavioral genetics": data "should be published in full," perhaps as a "general requirement for the publication of studies . . . so that quantitative analytical techniques other than those used by the original authors can be applied to the data by anyone who wishes"; if this was too demanding, at least the data should "be submitted complete in some standard form to the journals publishing the studies . . . , to be permanently preserved in the journals' archives for future workers."[351] Despite this unequivocal statement, Jensen refused Kamin's numerous requests to see the original observations, in effect maintaining that blacks were intellectually inferior to whites on the basis of data that he was unwilling to make available for critics' inspection.

Kamin *was* able to examine more closely some of Jensen's subsequent assertions about race and reaction time. Many of these statements were attributed to other researchers, but when Kamin tracked down the original sources, he often found that they had been seriously distorted. For example, Jensen claimed that "another study . . . of information processing rate . . . has also reported a relatively content-free mental processing task . . . and shows a significant mean black-white difference . . . 75% as large as the black-white difference" on a standard IQ test.[352] However, Kamin found that the cited publication, an obscure technical report from the Naval Postgraduate School, had compared the performance of forty-three whites and twenty-two "nonwhites," but the latter group had actually contained exactly one black subject, along with eleven Hispanics, two Filipinos, four Orientals, one Native American, and three "other."[353]

On another occasion Jensen explained that reaction time was attributable to "brain activity" much more than to sensory-motor functioning: "It is taken for granted . . . that highly skilled athletes should outperform, say university students in all RT tasks. Yet Muhammad Ali, perhaps the greatest boxer of all time, in his prime was found to show a very average RT."[354] That is, a great black athlete was alleged to have a slower reaction time than do most university students because reaction time depends on the brain. Jensen's reference for this assertion was a secondary source.[355] When Kamin found the *original* description of Ali's performance, it stated only that he "was asked to jab at and smash a balsa board 16½ inches away when a light was flashed. Timed with an Omegascope, he did it in 19/100 of a second. His fist actually covered the distance in 4/100 of a second, about the period of an eyeblink."[356] Subtracting the latter time from the former indicated that the actual reaction time to the light was 15/100 of a second, the exact speed that Jensen had termed "the fastest human RT to a single stimulus" in the same paragraph in which he called Ali's reaction time "very average." Though Jensen might have been misled by his secondary source, which implied that the reaction time alone had been 19/100, he should nevertheless have been highly impressed by Ali's performance, having just published a lengthy analysis of the difference between merely lifting a finger from a button at the onset of a light and not only lifting the finger but also moving it to push another button six inches away. Jensen had found that the reaction time—only the time needed to *lift* the finger when the light was presented—was considerably greater in the latter case than in the former, a reflection, he theorized, of "the programming time for the execution of the specific ballistic response required."[357] Indeed, the university students in Jensen's study had needed an average of 30/100 of a second just to lift their finger when they knew an additional six-inch movement would be required. This should have provided an obvious contrast to the 19/100 of a second within which Ali not only lifted his hand but also smashed a target over sixteen inches away.

Eventually, Jensen replicated his study on racial differences in reaction time. This time he did not "stack the cards" against his own hypothesis by matching black and white subjects on IQ score; the blacks had significantly lower scores than the white subjects. From Jensen's point of view, it should now have been easier to replicate the previous result of a steadily increasing difference between the performance of the two groups as the number of bits of information (i.e., the complexity of the choice) increased. He made absolutely no mention of this astonishing conclusion from the earlier study, however. Instead, he noted only that there was no significant difference between the overall reaction times of the two groups (actually, the blacks were a trivial amount *faster* than the whites). Curious about this omission, Kamin requested and this time received—from Philip Vernon, Jensen's coauthor—the original data, which showed that in this case blacks' performance did not decrease relative to whites' as the number of alternatives grew larger; in fact, it became slightly better in comparison. But with no reference to the complete disconfirmation of the earlier "perfect" results, Jensen and Vernon now reported that whites had performed faster than blacks on a number of "measures of speed of information processing" other than reaction time, though only one of these differences was significant. The researchers concluded that the size of the differences "bears some relationship to task complexity," a term for which they now devised an ad hoc definition. That is, the data on simple and choice reaction time, the only measurements based on a precise, theoretical definition of task complexity that could be applied to culturally unbiased stimuli, had provided hostile evidence and were now ignored. As Kamin observed, "Goodbye information theory (indeed, goodbye theory), hello Lambeth and Lanier!"[358]

Jensen's continuing attempt to wrest his conclusion, by hook or crook, even from hostile data raises serious concerns about the investigation of race and intelligence. Self-serving interpretations or the selective use of data may not be entirely unexpected when there is intense disagreement in science. It is more disturbing that a distinguished scientist and member of the National Academy of Sciences does not find the disconfirmation of a previous finding worth mentioning or that he could read a comparison between "whites" and a conglomeration of Hispanics, Filipinos, Orientals, Native Americans, and one black subject, all lumped together as "nonwhites," and then cite it as evidence for the difference between blacks and whites. (Whether such a comparison, if accurately reported, was at all meaningful is another issue.) In addition to what it reveals about the researchers, the obsession over race—an issue having no demonstrable scientific value—also raises larger questions concerning the most effective use of society's scientific resources.

Conclusion:
Science and Safeguards

FOR WELL OVER a hundred years some of the finest scientific researchers with the best academic credentials have investigated racial differences in intelligence, yet this considerable investment of resources has produced precious little of scientific value. There are certainly questions of enormous importance concerning the relationship between intellectual abilities and genetic structure: mapping the human genotype in detail, specifying the neurochemical products involved in central nervous system activity, explaining the functional mechanisms by which they interact with external stimuli. The study of racial differences—even if they *are* genetic—cannot provide any of this information. If indeed it were possible to prove one race more capable than another, it would shed no light on any question of scientific significance.

The question of racial differences in intelligence has now been debated to death; mountains of data have been gathered and processed without altering the arguments on either side one iota. As Philip Vernon, a well-known researcher and Arthur Jensen's coauthor on one of the reaction-time studies, has acknowledged in an unusual display of candor, "The same controversy has been going on for over fifty years, and it is doubtful that any of the protagonists have ever been persuaded to change their views."[1] Quite apart from whether the *answer* would have any scientific value, some scientists have concluded that the *question* is utterly meaningless—that, as one neurobiologist remarked, it makes no more sense than asking "whether the backside of the moon is made of Gorgonzola or of Stilton."[2]

Although the obsession with racial differences has contributed absolutely nothing to our understanding of human intellectual processes, it has performed continuing service as support for political policies—and not benign ones. The imprimatur of science has been offered to justify, first, slavery and, later, segregation, nativism, sociopolitical inequality, class subordination, poverty, and the general futility of social and economic reform. Indeed, during the past century the major ideological foundation for systematic oppression has shifted from religion to science, as the natural order has been invoked to rationalize inequalities previously sanctified by the divine order.

Science and Policy

Though the policies themselves have been tailored to fit the political controversies of their time, the path from scientific investigation to political exploitation has remained essentially the same. The scientists have regularly begun by claiming to be impartial investigators, deriving their authority from putative disinterest as much as from professional expertise. Charles White desired "only . . . to investigate the truth, and to discover what are the established laws of nature"[3] when he concluded blacks were biologically closer to apes than to humans. Karl Pearson had "no axes to grind" when he concluded the Jews were a "parasitic race" that should be excluded from England; his only motivation was "to seek the truth and utter it."[4] Carl C. Brigham presented "not theories or opinions but facts" when he detailed the threat posed by Mediterranean and Alpine immigrants to national progress and welfare.[5] Arthur Jensen's only interest was "to do his research as competently and carefully . . . and to report his methods, results and conclusions as fully and accurately as possible" when he warned that the War on Poverty could lead to the "genetic enslavement" of blacks.[6]

Shielded from any taint of bias by the armor of scientific disinterest, the researchers have proclaimed their work to be of monumental importance. From Henry H. Goddard, who called the World War I army test data "the most important piece of information which mankind has ever acquired about itself," to Raymond Cattell, who insisted that the denial of racial differences has done more harm to human progress than the Nazis did, they have viewed their efforts as a holy cause.[7] Despite this religious fervor, no one has ever suggested how racial comparisons have any scientific value, and the true significance of this research has invariably been the promotion of a "scientific" solution for some social problem, typically in the form of a repressive policy. Yet once offered as the ineluctable consequence of scientific knowledge, the policy—and the scientists whose work is offered to support it—can be dissociated from partisan politics. As Brigham insisted, after finding the latest immigrants genetically inferior to the earlier stock, policy "must of course be dictated by science and not by political expediency."[8] Similarly, Cattell has professed neither knowledge of nor interest in political issues while explaining that apartheid—not in South Africa but in the United States—is a necessary consequence of scientific discoveries.

Some scientists have been reluctant to speculate on the policy implications of their work. On occasion this has been a sham on their part, a ploy to foster the image of disinterest. Louis Agassiz, for example, purportedly began his published treatment of racial differences as a purely scientific question "without reference to politics," leaving it for others to "see what they can do with the results."[9] Yet in his private correspondence he warned against extending equality to blacks. Harry Hamilton Laughlin employed a similar approach, filling the pages of *Eugenical News* with polemics for restrictive immigration while coyly testifying to a congressional committee on immigration that he was there "simply as a scientific investigator to present the facts . . . with the hope that the facts and their analysis might be of use."[10] Arthur Jensen and William Shockley, while denying any political or ideological agenda, have rushed from the laboratory to testify before congressional committees or air their views in the mass media in an obvious attempt to sway public opinion. Even when scientists have been sincerely reticent about interpreting the political significance of their conclusions, others have been only too willing to do it for them—with little objection on the scientists' part. Relentless in his attempts to prove blacks intellectually inferior, Jensen has continually insisted that the advancement of knowledge is his only goal. Yet at the same time he has regularly collaborated with racists and Nazis, remaining mute on their use of his research to further their own goals.

"In Accordance with Modern Knowledge"

There are no tolerable political implications of racial differences in genetic ability if they could be proven to exist. Until the civil rights era of the 1960s there were frequent attempts to discredit the concept of political equality by demonstrating that people were not biologically equal. The alleged contradiction was, of course, illusory. The biological observation is a fact, and a rather trivial one by its very obviousness, though substitution of the word *equal* in place of the more appropriate word *identical* encourages, often intentionally, the perception of human differences as something to be rank ordered on a scale of value instead of being nurtured and appreciated for their diversity. The political assertion is a normative ethical principle about the rights to be enjoyed by all members of a society, an agreement often codified and mandated by a constitution or statutory measure. Biological inequality is empirically demonstrable; political equality is, as Thomas Jefferson observed, a "truth" that is "self-evident." Most of the attempts to link these two domains have, happily, failed. Despite the efforts of the anthropometricians, the eugenicists, and the segregationists, America's democratic political traditions have prevailed, and today universal suffrage, equal rights under law, and the guarantee of other civil liberties to all citizens are no longer up for debate; where demonstrable infringement has occurred, there is generally outrage and fairly prompt redress.

In the modern era the quest to prove blacks genetically less intelligent than whites is still claimed in some quarters to have enormous practical significance. The illustrations of this putative value, however, range from the trivial to the intolerable. Bernard Davis, a professor at Harvard, has, for example, justified such research on the grounds that it has contributed "to public awareness that one cannot determine an individual's capacities by identifying him with an ethnic group,"[11] thus crediting massive research for a "discovery" not only obvious to every sensible layperson but acknowledged by the most rabid racists.

Jensen has remained the causes's most enthusiastic scientific exponent, expressing his "dismay" over the decline in research on the "deficit" in black intelligence,[12] even though he has acknowledged that "an elegant scientific explanation of racial differences in intelligence would not advance science in the least"—the latter observation was actually made by Robert Nichols, a professor of education, in a review of Jensen's work, but in his own reaction to Nichols's essay Jensen stated that "it contains nothing I could disagree with."[13] Yet throughout the twenty years since first raising the issue, he has touted the genetic explanation's practical significance for educational and social problems, though always in vague terms that fail to specify *how* it would be useful. To his credit, Jensen has continually disavowed any treatment of persons in terms of their group identity; however, his regular reminder that even intelligent blacks produce children whose IQ would "regress" toward a black mean some fifteen points lower than that of whites has tended to vitiate his insistence on judgment of individual merit by implying that all blacks are eugenically suspect no matter what their IQ. As Francis Galton observed a century ago, a "gifted" individual might be "an exceptionally good specimen of a poor race, or an average specimen of a high one"; the latter was eugenically preferable because the former's descendants would inevitably "revert towards the typical centre of their own race."[14]

Despite Jensen's lack of specific detail, he seems to believe that the true practical significance of blacks' genetic disadvantage has been, all along, the eugenical implications hinted at in his famous 1969 article. Nineteen years later in a discussion of the pervasive social differences between blacks and whites—in educational achievement, average income, infant deathrate, life expectancy, and involvement in crime—Jensen agreed with Nichols's assessment that "nothing" could be done about these problems and that, consequently, the treatment of each person as an individual was "not really a remedy, but a prescription for ignoring the problem."[15] In Jensen's opinion there was only one effective approach: "the remedy is to control birth rates." Although the exact nature of such a program was to be "decided democratically," he remarked with obvious disappointment that such measures were "almost certainly doomed for the twentieth century, and one can only speculate about conditions in the twenty-first century that may bring about a change in attitudes on this issue."[16] For Jensen, ghettos, with their accompanying social pathology did not result from poverty and racism but from the defective genes of their inhabitants, and, consequently, the true solution was to reduce the black population. Underlying Jensen's egalitarian rhetoric had always lurked this Galtonian perspective, anticipating a time when decisions about who should be precluded from having children could be made "democratically."

A less nuanced view of the contemporary practical implications of racial differences in ability has been offered by Roger Pearson, whose Council for Social and Economic Studies had become, by the 1990s, the origin of a raft of conservative journals and books on race. Though Pearson is no longer overtly associated with neo-Nazi organizations, his latest views on race have continued to reflect his Güntherist roots. In *Race, Intelligence and Bias in Academe,* which featured a lengthy introduction by Hans J. Eysenck, he waxed nostalgic over the days when the European upper classes were still distinctly "Nordic" and scientists understood that the first nation to adopt eugenic measures "would create a true race of supermen." In the United States, too, Pearson saw biological deterioration, as an earlier, eugenically dominated scientific establishment, appropriately concerned with the "threat to white leadership" posed by declining "Nordic fertility," had given way to a "Marxist" science introduced by a clique of Eastern European immigrant radicals—"failed . . . 'intellectuals,'" Pearson called them, who conspired to replace the classic European tradition of rational inquiry with the "Middle Eastern concept of 'the revealed word,'" and whose opposition to eugenic measures was the resistance of "those who have no claim to genetic distinction." Because, according to Pearson, this group of (Jewish) academics together with their political allies in the black community had suppressed the scientific facts about racial differences in order to justify programs designed "to assist those who have been designated 'disadvantaged minorities,'" it was now necessary to revise social legislation "in accordance with modern knowledge concerning human genetics." Specifically, Head Start, all forms of compensatory education, and social welfare programs were a waste of money and should be abandoned. Not only were they doomed to failure by the existence of genetic disparities between the races, but whatever effects they might have would not be "intergenerational." That

is, although the beneficiaries of these programs might enjoy an improvement in their abilities and the conditions of their life, the effect would be
temporary—and consequently meaningless, according to Pearson—since
it could produce no "improvement in the genetic constituency of a
population."[17]

Of course, the claim that various social programs must be eliminated
because of genetic differences does not constitute a deprivation of rights,
at least not in the traditional American view—informed predominantly
by the Enlightenment and the struggle against political tyranny—of
rights as "justiciable" (i.e., as certain freedoms guaranteed to the individual and not subject to violation or contravention by the state). Government does not grant such rights as much as it refrains from interfering
with their exercise.

Recently, however, the rhetoric of rights has been increasingly applied
to such social and economic benefits as housing and medical care,
entitlements that the government really does have to "grant," in other
words, fund. This more expansive—and expensive—notion of rights has
provided very appealing political slogans. In 1991, for instance, Harris
Wofford overcame a forty-point deficit to win a senatorial election against
a better-known opponent by campaigning on the "right" to health care.
The gap between supposed entitlements and actual conditions, however,
makes it evident that these rights are "aspirational" rather than "justiciable."
Naturally, aspirational entitlements do not enjoy the same kind of constitutional protection that justiciable rights do (although education, which is
guaranteed as a right by some state constitutions may be a partial
exception). But whatever degree of legitimacy they may have does not
depend in any way on a scientific demonstration of the genetic merit of
their recipients; nor would proof of genetic shortcoming vitiate the claim
to their benefits. The kind and amount of social support that an affluent
society decides to guarantee to its neediest citizens are an expression of
its humanitarian ideals and its notion of social justice, derived not from
science but from such traditional sources of moral values as religion and
conscience. There are no moral directions in genotypes. To withhold
some program of social assistance—medical, nutritional, educational—from
a group or an individual on the grounds of a suspect genotype would be
properly considered an act of neobarbarism, no more tolerable than the
deprivation of political rights for genetic reasons.

Scientific Rights and Responsibilities

The quest to prove one race genetically less intelligent than others has
been scientifically valueless and socially harmful. Naturally, this harsh

judgment is not applicable to other investigations of genetic differences between races. Unlike the research on intelligence, studies of other traits may focus on genuine "differences," and although there is still the possibility of misuse, there is also the potential for discovering scientific information of great value: the investigation of racial differences and genetic predisposition to sickle cell anemia, malaria, or Tay-Sachs, for example, has greatly increased knowledge about the cause of these diseases.

The research on "innate" intellectual ability and race, however, has been interested not so much in "differences" as in judgments of superiority and inferiority, essentially an application of science to support the (ideological) assumption that some human beings are intrinsically worth more than others. Scientists from the earlier eugenics era felt no need to be subtle about this point. "Science" wrote Karl Pearson, "will not flinch from the conclusion . . . that some . . . races scarce serve in the modern world any other purpose than to provide material for the history of man." William McDougall emphasized that "if Nature has made men of unequal value, the cruelty is hers, not ours, and . . . we do no wrong in ascertaining and recording the facts."[18] Though the language of contemporary scientists has been somewhat less frank, their research has clearly been informed by similar sentiments, continually posing the issue in terms of "genetic equality." Of course, with the exception of monozygotic twins, it is a biological truism that no two individuals are genetically "equal." The alternative to equality in this case, however, has been not "difference" or "diversity" but rather—as in the title of Eysenck's book—the "*in*equality of man," with its implication of a scale of genotypic value that places some groups higher than others. This ongoing obsession with ranking the genetic ability of races has been an enormous waste of scientific time, energy, and resources that could be put to more productive use.

Of course, there is no justification for any attempt to deprive scientists of their rights to expression no matter how objectionable their views might be; true intellectual freedom must allow what the Yale University code calls "the right to think the unthinkable, discuss the unmentionable and challenge the unchallengeable."[19] Moreover, attempts to censor and intimidate are counterproductive; invariably they produce backlash, galvanizing support and sympathy for the victims of suppression and effectively shifting the focus of attention from issues of scientific substance and purpose to the rights to pursue research without harassment. On the frequent occasions that Shockley's public appearances were disrupted by shouting, jeering, or clapping, the draconian nature of his proposals suddenly became less noteworthy to many observers than the deprivation of his right to speak. In response to Jensen's initial allegations of blacks' intellectual inferiority, some opponents of his views foolishly demanded that he be fired from his Berkeley professorship, his classes were disrupted, and he was personally threatened. Just as inexcusable, the editors of *Harvard Educational Review* refused to circulate reprints of his controversial article—not even to Jensen himself—until they could be bound together with the responses of a number of critics.[20] *HER* had apparently decided that the article was too dangerous to be read without comment.

They "Must Mend Their Ways"

Such indefensible tactics soon led to a formal resolution of support for scientists investigating the "role of inheritance in human abilities," signed by fifty well-known researchers. The crafting of this declaration was itself revealing. It was initiated by Jensen and Ellis Page, a professor of educational psychology at the University of Connecticut and an outspoken opponent of affirmative action as "the result of environmentalist assumptions and our failure to examine them critically."[21] In their attempt to enlist the support of scientists whose names would carry weight among intellectuals, they solicited the signature of the noted geneticist Theodosius Dobzhansky. Before he would sign the statement, however, Dobzhansky asked that it include some acknowledgment of the social responsibility of the scientist: "his duty to state publicly that the misuses of his research are just that—misuses. Silence is too easily mistaken for consent. Our position would be much stronger if we make it clear that we deplore the prostitution of our science by racists as a bogus justification of their biases."[22] Dobzhansky's request was ignored, and his signature consequently did not appear on the resolution. (A short time later Dobzhansky published *Genetic Diversity and Human Equality*, in which he repudiated the exploitation of studies on heritability for racist purposes. Jensen's review of the book criticized it for even bringing up the subject of misuse in a scientific book. "Racism," wrote Jensen, "is really a political-ideological matter," and its very mention "mars the otherwise . . . scholarly tone of Dobzhansky's essay."[23] It seemed that Jensen felt not only no responsibility to speak out against the political misuse of science but also irritation that others would not keep silent on the matter.)

The resolution itself contained some instructive ironies. The first sentence of its preface cited the work of Sir Cyril Burt, who had just been named posthumous recipient of psychology's Thorndike Award, drawing "attention again to the great influence played by heredity in important human behaviors." Only months later Burt's work was exposed as fraudulent, and subsequent reprints of the resolution conveniently omitted the first paragraph.[24] The document went on to compare the harassment of the current researchers with the suppression of Galileo, Darwin, Einstein in the Third Reich and Mendelian biologists in Stalinist Russia.

Quite apart from the self-serving nature of this comparison—as if the trivial scientific value of IQ heritabilities, between or within groups, could possibly be compared with the contributions of Galileo, Darwin, and Einstein—no one had actually suppressed the ideas of Jensen, Shockley, and the others. Despite the harassment—in truth, to a considerable degree because of it—their writing appeared everywhere, not just in the scientific journals but in popular magazines, newspapers, and the *Congressional Record.* Also, while this declaration appropriately condemning any scientific suppression was being circulated, some of its signers were attempting to deprive Leon Kamin, the Princeton University professor who had first raised suspicions about Burt's work, of the rightful credit for his discovery because Kamin was an "environmentalist." Kamin had given a number of colloquia throughout the country and an invited address at the Eastern Psychological Association's annual conference, providing a detailed discussion of the evidence for Burt's unreliability. Thousands of copies of the EPA talk were disseminated and the entire professional field was well aware of Kamin's work. After this conference paper had begun to circulate, Jensen rushed an article into print containing a point-by-point consideration of almost every issue Kamin raised. Thereafter, Jensen, Eysenck, Cattell, the Harvard psychologist Richard Herrnstein, who had actually attended one of Kamin's colloquia, and other prominent "hereditarians" who had all previously referred to Burt's work as definitive refused to acknowledge Kamin's precedence, instead citing Jensen as the first to discover Burt's inconsistencies.[25]

Thus, although the resolution seemed merely a reaffirmation of the basic right to freedom of research, in unintentional ways it embodied the lack of concern for social and scientific responsibility that had characterized so much of the research on race and genetics. Naturally, the right to pursue research and to interpret the findings without fear of censure is an important one and should be protected from arbitrary attack. But generations of eugenicists and investigators of race have considered that right an absolute, not to be affected by any questions of morality or possible harm to vulnerable groups and individuals; they have never recognized a situation in which their scientific rights might be qualified by the rights of others. Even when oppressive political forces have proposed policies based on the scientists' claims—often with their endorsement—the researchers have disavowed any responsibility for the results. The German geneticist Fritz Lenz, who had offered a Darwinian explanation for Jews' parasitical nature, dismissed their concerns over his research because "a tranquil and objective discussion of the Jewish problem would best serve the true interests of both sides." Yet after the war he found no reason to regret his earlier pronouncements or to feel any responsibility for the results of the "political biology" that he had urged as the basis for state policy. His work had been completely apolitical;[26] he had been only a scientist, dedicated to the objective investigation of racial differences. Though nothing as horrible as the Nuremberg Laws was promulgated in the United States, it was not for lack of effort on the part of the scientists who campaigned vigorously for legislative recognition of the genetic facts.

The modern eugenicists, on the rare occasion they have acknowledged their predecessors' behavior, have seen only minor scientific errors. Jensen, for example, has dismissed criticisms of the earlier era as merely a few insignificant instances, "handpicked" by "Marxist sociology," in which the "pioneers of psychometrics may have expressed poorly founded and occasionally dogmatic hereditarian opinions concerning intelligence at a time before any adequately developed methodology . . . was available for the genetical analysis of mental test data."[27] He also has tried to sugar-coat earlier excesses, claiming, for example, that in Goddard's famous study of immigrants at Ellis Island, which concluded that huge proportions of Jews, Hungarians, Italians, and Russians were "defective," only those previously "suspected of being 'feebleminded' " were tested. Jensen said the charge that Goddard had intended his percentages to apply to the immigrants from these countries in general was a "shabby slander" created by the opponents of psychological tests. (In fact, in the actual study Goddard had stated that his sample was drawn from "the great mass of 'average immigrants.' ")[28] Though eager to quibble over minutiae, Jensen has been apparently undisturbed that scientists proffered their findings to support the most revolting nativism, the necessity of segregation, and deliberate "genthanasia" for allegedly inferior ethnic groups.

In the face of this dreary history, some of it committed by signers of the resolution, the refusal to include in the statement any word of opprobrium for the misuse of science suggested that the contemporary researchers in the field still wanted their rights only, unburdened by any questions of social responsibility, and still wished to offer their questionable findings as the basis for policy while insisting they were apolitical scientists. When their own words then turned up in the mouths of the Klan and the Nazi party, they still felt no moral imperative to disavow such uses of their work.[29] They were scientists, doing what scientists do: research. What others did with their findings was not their responsibility, not even their business. The resolution's call for unimpeded research was irresistible, but it was only one piece in a larger scientific picture. "Intellectual intolerance is in its way as evil as racial intolerance," noted an editorial on the resolution in the British scientific journal *Nature*, "but some of the signatories must mend their ways."[30]

Suggestions by Scientists

There is thus a dilemma: on the one hand, harassment of scientists and attempts to censor their research are intolerable acts, to be resisted and denounced; on the other, in addition to protecting freedom of inquiry, society has an interest in discouraging the waste of resources on research that is meaningless and divisive and in laying to rest the notion that the innate intellectual inferiority of an ethnic group is a legitimate scientific question. In an intellectually open society such research must be tolerated, but there is a difference between toleration and encouragement.

Some highly respected scientists, no strangers themselves to the ethic and process of scientific investigation, have already expressed misgivings about such research. In her 1973 presidential address to the American Psychological Association, for example, Leona Tyler noted that the issue of racial differences in IQ is both incapable of resolution and subject to misuse in others' hands. In such a case, she suggested, "investigators should give serious thought at the outset to whether the research should be *done.*"[31]

Other scientists have proposed measures that go beyond mere calls to conscience. Seymour Sarason, a professor of psychology at Yale, has recommended an approach modeled after the procedure designed to protect the environment from private enterprise. The traditional attitude toward entrepreneurial freedom has changed dramatically from the time that corporate decisions were relatively unencumbered by social considerations. Today, before acting, a business must submit an environmental impact study, demonstrating that its plans will not adversely affect the lives of others. As Sarason puts it, society says to entrepreneurs, " 'You have an obligation to judge anything you may do by what it does to communities and their citizens. You are not the sole and final arbiter of what can or should be done.' " He suggests that the same principle provide the basis for "examining the tradition of untrammeled scientific inquiry." A prospective line of research would first be judged on the basis of a " 'people's impact report,' . . . if something can be done, it should only be done if the means do not subvert society's view of what is in its best interests." Sarason acknowledges that this approach would be seen "in some quarters . . . as . . . thought control" but notes that legislation for environmental protection elicited a similar reaction when first proposed.[32] There is, however, an important difference between precluding the construction of factories and precluding the conduct of research. Factories may have detrimental physical effects on the surrounding community and have traditionally been subject to regulation by various levels of government; the conduct of research is an act of intellectual inquiry, enjoying the protection of the First Amendment as well as long-cherished tenets of academic freedom.

Possibly more acceptable is the suggestion, made at the height of the Jensen controversy by the research geneticists L. L. Cavalli-Sforza and W. F. Bodmer in *The Genetics of Human Populations*—at the time the most authoritative text in the field—that government funding be withheld from studies of genetic difference in intelligence between races.[33] Denial of financial support *might* be acceptable, depending on how such a decision was reached. The application of political criteria to the judgment of scientific proposals is no more tolerable than the application of Jesse Helms's esthetic sensibilities to the judgment of requests submitted to the National Endowment for the Arts. In both cases the proper mechanism is peer review: other scientists are appropriately charged with the responsibility of evaluating research proposals, just as other artists should evaluate prospective work in their fields of expertise. In exercising this responsibility, however, peer reviewers should bear in mind that much of the research on genetic differences in intelligence between races has been scientifically worthless and socially mischievous. Moreover, they should consider the opportunity cost of resources allocated for such studies: research funds devoted to "proving" blacks less intelligent than whites cannot be used to support some worthier cause. It would thus be perfectly appropriate for such proposals to be rejected, not because the research offends some notion of political correctness but because the peer review process realizes that it is not good science: it does not answer any important scientific question, nor does it have any worthwhile social application.

Naturally, the restriction of public funds would not prevent investigators from turning to other sources, like the Pioneer Fund. Indeed, several recent studies of race and intelligence have relied on such support. Jensen's work on racial differences in reaction time, for example, has been funded by the Institute for the Study of Educational Differences, a nonprofit corporation listing him as president, his wife as vice president, and Ellis Page, co-crafter of the resolution of support for hereditarian research, on its board of directors. The institute, however, appears to be no more than a conduit for channeling money from the Pioneer Fund to Jensen, who received well over $300,000 in research grants by this route during the 1980s.[34]

Science and Subjects

Whatever the source of research funds, a scientist's right to conduct studies on other human beings is not an absolute, completely unaffected by any countervailing interests. Unlike purely theoretical scientists, whose work does not require the participation of human subjects, investigators of racial differences must frequently find individuals willing to be the objects of study; in essence they must "recruit" subjects. In such cases scientists' freedom to pursue research must be constrained to some degree by the rights and interests of their subjects.

In the early days of psychological research the description of recruitment often regarded subjects with unconcealed contempt. In one study of the abilities of a specific college freshman Lewis Terman bluntly explained that the subject had been selected because of his incredible "stupidity."[35] Another psychologist of the time, Albert L. Crane, shared with his colleagues the special problems involved in recruiting blacks for research:

> Only the fellow scientist who has attempted to induce one hundred Southern darkies to offer themselves as subjects in an experiment . . . can have any conception of the difficulties involved in actually getting the subjects into the laboratory. Threats, cajolery, flattery, bribery and every other conceivable ruse within the bounds of reason and the law were resorted to. . . . It was a never-to-be-forgotten experience, the humor and zest whereof, however, more than compensated for the many weary and discouraging hours which it can cost to witness a subject fleeing over the hill in fright or reversing decisions on the foot of the laboratory steps at the last moment.[36]

Aside from these insulting characterizations, which would now be considered an egregious breach of professional ethics, subjects often had further reason to be wary of psychological research. Crane's investigation of race differences in inhibition, for example, supposedly demonstrated that in dangerous situations "the colored man would immediately give vent to his instinctive reactions, whatever they might be, after which (if he escaped without injury) he . . . might pick himself right up and walk off as though nothing had occurred," while the white man, though initially "exercising greater control, . . . would probably be all 'flinchy' for a considerable time to come." This result, obtained "without prejudice," according to Crane, proved that blacks were clearly more fit for perilous work than whites were, though "considerable persuasion might frequently be necessary to induce the colored man to undertake a dangerous pursuit."[37] Even if the stepin-fetchit characterization of his subjects had been omitted, there was still an ethical flaw in Crane's recruitment procedure, one that continues to plague much contemporary research on race: the failure to inform his subjects appropriately before obtaining their consent to participate. Had these black subjects known that the research would provide scientific evidence of their unique fitness for hazardous work, they might have been even less likely to "volunteer."

Informed Consent

The most widely recognized statement of ethical principles in scientific research with human subjects is the Nuremberg Code, issued as a part of the court's judgment in the Nuremberg trial of Nazi doctors who had performed brutal experiments on human beings. The code has served as the prototype for virtually every subsequent major ethical declaration, set of professional standards, and regulatory guidelines on research involving human subjects. The code's first precept states that "the voluntary consent of the human subject is absolutely essential." It goes on to explain that such consent means the subject

> should ... be able to exercise free power of choice, without the intervention of any element of force, fraud, deceit, duress, over-reaching, or other ulterior form of constraint or coercion; and should have sufficient knowledge and comprehension of the elements of the subject matter involved as to enable him to make an understanding and enlightened decision. This latter element requires that before the acceptance of an affirmative decision by the experimental subject there should be made known to him the nature, duration and purpose of the experiment; the method and means by which it is to be conducted; all inconveniences and hazards reasonably to be expected; and the effects upon his health or person which may possibly come from his participation in the experiment.[38]

The code thus went beyond merely proscribing the infliction of injury or harm on subjects in the name of science; it also insisted that subjects be more than mere "guinea pigs" in the investigation, more than passive objects to be "used" like instruments and other experimental equipment. This informed consent, as it is now called, respects the personhood of subjects by treating them as sentient beings concerned with issues beyond simple assurance that their interaction with the researcher will not be hazardous to them.

Subsequent analyses of informed consent by ethicists have all agreed that its underlying principle forbids the use of subjects only as a means to the researcher's end; they must be treated as ends in themselves, autonomous persons with rights to determine what is in their own interest. The means/ends problem is thus resolved by providing subjects with sufficient information to decide that participation meets this self-interest test. As Hans Jonas, a professor of philosophy, explains, the "wrong" of reifying the subject is made into a "right" by

> such authentic identification with the cause that it is the subject's as well as the researcher's cause—whereby his role in its service is not just permitted by him but *willed.* That sovereign will ... to be

valid ... must be autonomous and informed. The latter condition can, outside the research community, only be filled by degrees; but the higher the degree of the understanding regarding the purpose and the technique, the more valid becomes the endorsement of the will. ... Ultimately the appeal for volunteers should seek this free and generous endorsement, the appropriation of the research purpose into the person's own scheme of ends.[39]

Paul Ramsey, a professor of ethics, has similarly suggested that informed consent occurs only when subject and researcher "become joint adventurers in a common cause." He proposes "partnership," with its connotation of a shared goal, as a more appropriate conceptualization of their relationship than "contract," in which one party makes assurances to the other. Alexander Morgan Capron, a legal scholar and the executive director of the President's Commission for the Study of Ethical Problems in Medicine and Biomedical and Behavioral Research, has argued that "the subject who has truly consented has adopted the goals of the research program as his own; as a 'collaborator' with the investigators, the subject is no longer merely a means to someone else's ends but a participant in a process to reach his own ends."[40]

Some of these discussions of informed consent have been primarily concerned with subjects in medical research but not all of them; Capron, for example, was specifically concerned with social science. However, the arguments have even greater force for social research, especially studies on race and intelligence. In the medical case the cause is unarguably beneficial: improving health, curing disease, and saving life. Participation thus appeals to the subject's highest motivations: compassion for the suffering of others; the desire to help the afflicted, to contribute to future generations, even to provide purpose for one's own existence. If subjects must be informed "coadventurers" even in the pursuit of such noble goals, there is all the more reason to insist that their participation be based on an affirmative decision to share the researcher's end when the value of the research is not so universally acknowledged and its purpose is, in fact, repugnant to many persons. As Jonas observes, of all "experimentation with man, medical is surely the most legitimate, psychological the most dubious."[41] Where the case for benefit is weakest, the ethical obligations must be strongest.

Government Regulation

In 1966 the federal government began to take an interest in the formal protection of subjects' rights, enacting the first of what would be a series of measures designed to provide regulatory protection for human subjects of scientific research. The first rules, applicable only to Public Health Service (PHS) grants, mandated the establishment of local committees, eventually known as Institutional Review Boards (IRBs), to monitor the consent process and to ensure, generally, the protection of subjects' rights and welfare. Even these modest requirements produced some protests over government interference with freedom of inquiry, and one outraged researcher actually claimed that the future would "mark 1966 as the year in which all medical progress ceased."[42] Although there was some uncertainty about whether the PHS policy applied to research in the behavioral and social sciences, all confusion on the matter was eliminated in 1971 when the Department of Health, Education, and Welfare (DHEW) issued a more extensive set of guidelines—applicable to all institutions receiving DHEW money for research involving human subjects—on the responsibilities of IRBs, with explicit attention paid to social and behavioral research.[43] In 1974 an even more ambitious set of regulations promulgated by the DHEW listed no exceptions to the requirement of informed consent for all research, prompting numerous complaints from social scientists, especially those engaged in research based on public records or observations of public behavior.[44]

Still unresolved, however, was the ethical basis for these regulations— that is, whether the consent requirement was intended merely to protect subjects from harm or to encode the subject-as-coadventurer spirit of informed consent in the Nuremberg Code and its subsequent interpretations. This distinction was of major significance for social scientists, whose research rarely puts subjects at risk of any physical discomfort, much less damage. If protection from harm was the basis, the great majority of behavioral investigations might well be exempt from the necessity for this kind of regulation. If the Nuremberg concept was to be implemented, however, the regulations should not only protect subjects' welfare but also ensure that they be provided sufficient information about the research to decide whether they wished to "collaborate."

Some social scientists responded to these first regulatory steps with a preemptive strategy, frankly acknowledging the hope that self-monitoring based on the do-no-harm approach would head off government implementation of the more demanding model. Paul Davidson Reynolds, a University of Minnesota sociologist, for example, termed the concept of informed consent "unsatisfactory . . . on a practical level" because he found it "ludicrous" to expect prospective subjects "to make a rational judgment and weigh the risks to himself and the benefits to society of a complex study." Only professionals could judge the value of research, according to Reynolds, and "if social scientists have confidence" that the results "will be useful for mankind, they have no choice but to accept 'discomfort' to the participants as the price for creating scientific knowledge." However, he noted, "if the lay public perceives that social scientists are engaged in thoughtless or damaging research, the reaction, fostered by ignorance and prejudice, will quite likely be a severe restriction or prohibition of any research, *regardless of its potential benefit to society.* This suggests that social scientists have no choice but to prevent such a reaction by developing their own mechanisms of self-control. . . ."[45] To prevent public encroachment onto scientific turf, Reynolds recommended that research be reviewed only by other professionals, who would be "*restricted* to evaluating the potential for 'unnecessary discomfort' of the subjects." This mechanism would produce a list of "approved procedures" that could then be used by any "licensed investigator" regardless of purpose. If a scientist wished to conduct research "which might produce more severe effects on the subjects . . . then he should . . . voluntarily solicit the advice and counsel of a committee of his peers," which would "determine whether the potential benefit of the research was commensurate with the potential risk to the participants" and, if so, "how to select those to be exposed to the risk."[46] In place of an informed consent subjects would thus be protected by their total reduction to objects, means to the researcher's ends, completely deprived of the opportunity for self-determination. Reynolds's proposal made an unintended but rather convincing case for government regulation. Although other social scientists might not have approved of the severely limited autonomy provided for subjects in this scheme, many of them certainly concurred in Reynolds's desire to restrict any regulatory system to the issue of potential harm to subjects.

To resolve the confusion over the ethical basis of federal regulation, in 1974 Congress passed the National Research Act, creating the National Commission for the Protection of Human Subjects of Biomedical and Behavioral Research, a blue-ribbon panel of experts from medicine, law, ethics, and the scientific community. Among other tasks the commission was asked to identify "the basic ethical principles which should underlie the conduct of biomedical and behavioral research involving human subjects," including "the nature and definition of informed consent in various research settings," and to recommend ways to ensure that research was conducted in accordance with these principles.[47] The commission's report—*The Belmont Report*—was unequivocal. It supported a concept of informed consent based on the conviction that subjects "should be treated as autonomous agents . . . capable of deliberation about personal goals and of acting under the direction of such deliberation. . . . To show a lack of respect for an autonomous agent is to repudiate that person's considered judgments, to deny an individual the freedom to act on those considered judgments, or to withhold information necessary to make a considered judgment, when there are no compelling reasons to do so."[48]

The only possible justification for "incomplete disclosure," in the commission's opinion, was the case "where informing subjects of some pertinent aspect of the research is likely to impair the validity," but even here, the report warned, information "should never be withheld for the purpose of eliciting the cooperation of subjects."[49] Clearly, this exemption was not meant to apply to research on racial differences. As one of the resource papers prepared to assist the commission noted, the purpose of providing information was to allow a "prospective subject to decline participation in research the goals of which he does not share . . . for example . . . research that might identify racial or ethnic groups as having certain qualities: e.g., as having lower intelligence than the general population."[50]

In accord with such principles, the commission recommended that with the exception of studies of public records or public behavior informed consent be required in all research involving human subjects: "All information relevant to a decision regarding participation [must] be properly communicated to subjects," including but not limited to "the aims and specific purposes of the research" and "who is funding it." It "frequently . . . can be expected," wrote the commission, "that research will involve an element that is not on the list but about which it can be expected that subjects would want to be informed. Such information should, of course, be communicated to subjects."[51] In addition, the commission recommended that if an institution received any federal funds for research involving human subjects, the ethical regulations should apply not only to that research but also to all other research at that institution involving human subjects. That is, the commission believed, sensibly, that all research sponsored at the same institution by different monies should be subject to uniform ethical standards.

When these recommendations appeared in the *Federal Register* in 1979 as proposed regulations, however, they elicited outrage from some social scientists. The strongest opposition was directed at the extension of regulatory coverage to nonfederally funded research, though there were also complaints about the requirement of informed consent for research involving minimal risks. Two years later the DHEW, now reorganized as the Department of Health and Human Services, acquiesced to the pressure on both counts, issuing final rules that substantially reduced the scope of regulatory coverage by omitting the extension to nonfunded research and by permitting the exemption of broad categories that "present little or no risk of harm to subjects" from any ethical review, including "research involving the use of educational tests (cognitive, diagnostic, aptitude, achievement)."[52] Of course, the permission to exempt did not imply a necessity to do so, and nothing required institutions to confine their interest to ethical responsibilities mandated by government regulation.

Moreover, the rules termed it "of crucial importance" for institutions to employ IRB review of their own volition to all research "regardless of the source of funding," suggesting bluntly that "public funds for research involving human subjects should not be awarded to institutions which are unwilling to demonstrate their dedication to this principle."[53] Nevertheless, in the first year of the new regulations, some 9 percent of institutions with federally funded research still did not routinely mandate IRB review of all studies with human subjects.[54] Of course, depending on where it is conducted, research sponsored by interests like the Pioneer Fund may not be affected by these regulations at all.

Psychologists' Standards

The published professional standards of the American Psychological Association (APA), *Ethical Principles in the Conduct of Research with Human Participants,* also recognize the researcher's responsibility to obtain informed consent from a prospective subject. The principles do acknowledge that an exception might be justified for research in which valid data could not be obtained if the participants had prior knowledge of the hypotheses under investigation—for example, a study of social influence processes could be meaningfully conducted only with subjects who do not anticipate an attempt to influence them. However, even this exception assumes that subjects would decide to cooperate if they *could* be given full information without compromising the validity of the research. According to the principles, the investigator should inform a prospective subject of "all aspects of the research that might reasonably be expected to influence willingness to participate." One cited example is the possibility that the data may reveal something unfavorable about the subject's "valued groups"; another is sponsorship of the research "by an organization with particular goals." The APA's official statement of ethical standards, *The Belmont Report* on the principles underlying government regulatory protection for human subjects, and the ethicists' interpretation of informed consent thus all agree: researchers' rights are in essence derivative from the subjects'; an investigation should not proceed until the subjects make an "understanding and enlightened decision" to offer their cooperation.[55]

Although some social scientists insist that such extensive information should not be mandatory when there is clearly no risk to the subject, even these dissidents typically believe subjects should be apprised of any factors that might reasonably deter their participation. The psychologists Edward Diener and Rick Crandall, for example, have termed the consent requirement "in studies that are entirely harmless . . . probably unrealistic and unnecessary" but at the same time acknowledge that "participants should also be informed of any details that would be likely to influence their willingness to participate. For instance, if the sponsor of the study is an institution the respondent might not approve of (e.g., the Ku Klux Klan) or if the results are to be used to draw conclusions about the respondent's ethnic group, then he should be informed of these details."[56] That is, the reduced standard only applies if, as in the APA's *Principles,* it can reasonably be assumed that a subject would remain a willing collaborator if provided full information. Richard A. Tropp, one of the architects of government policy on the regulation of research involving human subjects and author of one of the papers prepared to assist the National Commission for the Protection of Human Subjects of Biomedical and Behavioral Research, has also argued in favor of "overhaul[ing]" the informed consent model "to make it appropriate to social science" by removing "disabling and unnecessary burdens," such as the requirement to disclose the purpose of the research. Yet he, too, has insisted that subjects "be given all information material . . . to their decision on participation."[57] Albert Reiss, another scientist whose ideas were solicited by the commission, termed the requirement for complete disclosure in behavioral science research "burdensome," but he still emphasized that "subjects should be advised on matters of substance" if the information may prove "objectionable" to some of them.[58] The common thread running through all these views is that even when it may be permissible to abridge the idealized concept of informed consent in the interests of scientific progress, the researcher still has a responsibility to ensure that a subject does not unknowingly participate in a project whose end he or she does not share. A scientist is thus obligated to provide whatever information the *subject* is likely to find relevant, regardless of whether the researcher believes it to be of any significance. Withholding such information deprives subjects of their right to choose participation freely and rationally.

These ethical requirements have obvious implications for research on race. The subjects in such studies are typically of interest not so much for their responses alone but for what those responses suggest to the researcher about the behavior or abilities of their "valued" reference group; in essence the subjects are treated as "representatives" of their race. When, for example, Jensen compares the reaction times of black and white subjects, his purpose is to gather evidence for the hypothesis that there are genetic differences between the races in "fundamental processes at the interface of brain and behavior."[59] Such a study is certainly likely to prove "objectionable" to some subjects. The researcher consequently has an ethical obligation to inform all prospective subjects of the hypothesis and black subjects, in particular, of the possibility that their responses may be used as evidence that their race is less capable than the white race. In addition, if the research has received financial support from the

Pioneer Fund or some similar source, all subjects should be informed of that fact as well as the fund's interests and goals. All this information surely qualifies as "aspects of the research that might reasonably be expected to influence willingness to participate." If provided this information, most blacks probably would not view scientific evidence of their genetic disadvantage as an important contribution to knowledge or social progress, one that would induce them to participate in the research, and many whites also might be disinclined to cooperate with such a purpose. If this essential information is withheld, subjects are prevented from exercising their right to refuse to collaborate in an endeavor that many of them might find meaningless or offensive.

Although threats to freedom of inquiry have quickly elicited ringing affirmations of the rights of scientists, this infringement of subjects' rights has been virtually ignored. Most scientists who conduct research on race and intelligence have demonstrated no interest in subjects' rights and have confined their consideration of ethical issues to scientific platitudes. In an entire paper on the ethics of research on race and intelligence, for example, Linda Gottfredson, a professor of education at the University of Delaware who has argued that socioeconomic inequality between races is the expected outcome of lower black intelligence,[60] did not make a single reference to subjects. Scientists' ethical responsibilities, she explained, were to report their data accurately, avoid ad hominem attacks, zealously protect freedom of inquiry, and above all "speak the truth."[61] A concern for the truth is excellent advice; scientists should begin by telling it to their subjects. Nor did Gottfredson's analysis acknowledge any ethical dilemma regarding the source of support for research, despite the fact that she was the recipient of $174,000 from the Pioneer Fund.[62] In addition to its mandate to inform subjects about the nature of sponsorship if such information might affect willingness to participate, the APA's *Principles* also emphasizes that an "investigator who accepts support from an organization should, therefore, be prepared to associate with its mission."[63]

Only one researcher studying race and intelligence has directly addressed the APA's ethical standards concerning the treatment of subjects. Sandra Scarr has opposed the *Principles'* mandate that subjects be informed of possible outcomes they would find degrading to their "valued groups" on the grounds that subjects deserve protection only as individuals, not against "potential embarrassment" to their ethnic group. According to Scarr, "One cannot be said to be *individually* damaged by research that exposes one's group to criticism or derogation however psychologically painful the implications seem to be."[64] In her view black subjects have no right to be informed of the purpose of research that might make them unwitting accomplices in the devaluation of their race, and, a fortiori, white subjects, whose ethnic group would not experience potential embarrassment, would have no reason to deserve disclosure. In this analysis a scientist's only ethical obligation is to protect subjects from harm; as long as there is no danger to their individual health and safety, the nature of the research is none of their business, even if its purpose violates their deepest values and beliefs. Scarr's position thus runs counter to every ethicist's interpretation of informed consent and is at'diametric odds with the ethical mandate in both the APA's *Principles* and *The Belmont Report* for investigators to provide subjects with all information material to their decision to participate. A consent process that deliberately withholds exactly those details the researcher suspects would deter subjects' participation converts their solicitation into a con game, deceiving subjects into cooperating with an endeavor they would probably regard as repugnant if properly informed. As the ethicist Paul Ramsey has pointed out, a subject can be "wronged" without being "harmed."[65]

Scarr justifies her opposition to the ethical standards of her own professional association by claiming that the APA's principles are not "realistic," especially the advice "to inform one's research participants of the possibly unfavorable outcomes for *all* groups to which they may belong." This quotation, however, is Scarr's—it does not appear in the APA's publication—and it has been crafted to suggest an absurdly unwieldy scenario, in which, again according to Scarr, a researcher would have to inform subjects that the results of a "study may prove embarrassing to them because of their membership in such groups as men, aging adults, Black Americans, New Yorkers, residents in high-rise buildings, gay rights activists, Christian fundamentalists, the Ladies Garment Workers Union, and so forth."[66]

This argument ignores the actual language in the APA's *Principles,* that an investigator should inform subjects "of all aspects of the research that might *reasonably* be expected to influence willingness to participate" (emphasis added). Since the most oppressive and discriminatory policies in U.S. history have traditionally been based on claims of some racial group's innate inferiority, it would be "reasonable" to expect that many subjects' willingness to participate would be influenced by the knowledge that a study intended (yet again) to compare races in ability. When scientific evidence about high-rise residents, fundamentalists, or union members is offered to justify deprivation of their rights or to support policies opposed to their interests, then these subjects, too, could reasonably be expected to refuse participation in research on their groups. As Oliver Wendell Holmes once remarked, "A page of history is worth a volume of logic."[67]

Though Scarr makes no mention of the issue of sponsorship, presumably such information is also not the subjects' due. She does note that researchers are not responsible for the "evil uses" that others make of their results: these "unanticipated (and unanticipatable) consequences of research cannot be held against the investigators."[68] This is extremely naive. When a study is sponsored by the Pioneer Fund, an organization established to prove white superiority, there is nothing "unanticipatable" about how the results will be used. Withholding such information from subjects—especially black subjects—is no different in principle from asking women seeking an abortion to be subjects in a psychological study without mentioning that the research is sponsored by a "pro-life" organization, which will use the results to oppose the right to abortion. A procedure that respects subjects' right to self-determination does not, by omitting crucial information, manipulate them into rendering assistance toward a goal that they perceive as antithetical to their own interests.

Scarr's real concern seems to be not so much that the APA's principles are "unrealistic" but that, if taken seriously, they might be effective, impeding research she considers significant and wishes to encourage. Her criticism appears at the end of an article emphasizing the importance of research on race and gender differences in intellectual functioning, in which she concludes that "misguided protectionism both violates investigators [sic] rights and prevents psychology from developing research information"[69] that could be of great value to minorities. That is, researchers may determine their scientific goals—not to mention their career interests—to be so important that they cannot risk allowing subjects to make an informed decision about participation for fear that an exercise in self-determination might retard scientific progress. This is the ultimate reduction of the subject to an object.

Of course, Scarr may well be right in some cases about the significance of research on race: studies that eschew the obsession with genetic differences in intelligence may eventually prove to have value.[70] Research conducted without proper consideration for the rights of subjects cannot, however, be justified by the importance of the results. As Henry K. Beecher, Dorr Professor of Research at Harvard Medical School, observed in a widely cited article on ethics, "An experiment is ethical or not at its inception; it does not become ethical post hoc."[71] The inability of ends to justify means is a well-known moral postulate; there is no reason that scientific research merits an exemption from it.

"One Fundamental Test"

In the late 1980s J. Philippe Rushton, a professor of psychology at the University of Western Ontario and a recipient of hundreds of thousands of dollars from the Pioneer Fund, offered a "new" theory about race, attributing black intellectual inferiority once again to evolutionary history. Rushton found a combination of reproductive strategy and degree of parental care underlying the phylogenetic scale: at the lower end of the spectrum were species that produce many eggs—perhaps tens of thousands a year—but devote minimal attention to parental care, while at the higher end were species that produce only one infant every few years but invest considerable energy in the offspring's survival. Associated with the latter groups were such traits as greater intelligence, keener competition, greater altruism, and a higher degree of social organization. Applying this same continuum to differences within the human species, Rushton found blacks to rank systematically lower than whites on traits separating humans from other primates—degree of parental care, intelligence, brain size, sexual restraint, and impulse and aggression control, among others. Rushton explained, with no sense of historical irony, that blacks displayed greater similarity to lower species because of their *earlier* evolution; other races, having evolved more recently, were naturally more advanced.[72] Like the paths in an M. C. Escher painting, the data can head off in opposite directions yet invariably lead to the same conclusion.

While a scientist was offering this latest version of the great chain of being, racial conflict, often predicated on the belief that blacks were inferior, remained a pervasive problem, infecting almost every sector of public life in the United States. Some political campaigns attempted to exploit racial fears to attract the "white vote." In 1988 an FBI informant reported that an "unofficial policy" of investigating prominent black officials without probable cause was referred to at the bureau as "Fruemenschen," a German word meaning "primitive men," and was based on "the assumption . . . that black officials are intellectually and socially incapable of governing."[73] On some university campuses racist leaflets have been distributed, decorated with swastikas and bearing such headlines as "Niggers Get Out" or "Get Your Black Asses Back to Africa."[74] Even at Yale Law School, an elite, supposedly enlightened institution, black students received notes from "Yale Students for Racism," describing a crime committed by two black males and concluding, "Now you know why we call you niggers."[75] The National Institute against Prejudice and Violence reported incidents of ethnic violence at 113 colleges in 1990 and estimated that approximately 20 percent of minority students were victimized, a quarter of them enduring more than one instance of harassment.[76]

Worst of all, organized white supremacists were on the rise. The White Aryan Resistance, various Klan sects, the neo-Nazi "skinheads," and a host of other extremist groups were again warning white Americans of the threat posed by biologically less capable races. Twenty-five public access cable channels around the country aired "Race and Reason," a talk show on which host Tom Metzger, a former Grand Dragon in the California Klan and now head of the White Aryan Resistance, interviewed such guests as J. B. Stoner, who was convicted for the 1958 bombing of a black church in Birmingham, Alabama.[77]

For a time David Duke, the Republican Louisiana state legislator who took 55 percent of the white vote in his 1991 campaign for governor despite facing an unprecedented coalition of forces supporting his opponent, became the most visible representative of the new racist movement. In his youth Duke claimed to have espoused a "liberal, humanist viewpoint on race" until a schoolteacher assigned a report on the pros and cons of integration. To gather information, Duke went to the local Citizens' Council library, where he found a "wall of books by scientists, educators, psychologists, doctors, lawyers, anthropologists"—Carleton Putnam's *Race and Reason,* the writings of Henry E. Garrett and Carleton S. Coon, and the work of his "scientific heroes," Arthur Jensen and William Shockley. Now influenced by what he termed "the hard scientific facts about race," Duke joined the Klan, rising to Grand Dragon of the Louisiana chapter and Imperial Wizard of the national organization.[78] He also became a member of the American Nazi party before leaving to form his own organization, the National Association for the Advancement of White People (NAAWP). Eventually Duke chose to abandon white sheets and brown shirts in favor of a more politically respectable wardrobe. After a brief experiment with the Populist party, an electoral coalition of Klansmen, neo-Nazis, and other racists that was supported by Willis Carto's Liberty Lobby, and an even briefer experiment with the Democratic party, he took up political residence on the right wing of the Republican party.

Duke's attempt at mainstream affiliation, however, seemed no more than a tactical maneuver, designed to provide a more respectable front for his continuing racist agenda. Many of his close associates in the Klan left along with him to follow his new political direction, and such recent Klan publications as the *White Patriot,* the "worldwide voice of the Aryan people," have boasted that "David Duke . . . put us into the arena of a national organization."[79] The chairman of his 1988 presidential campaign under the banner of the Populist party was also a former Klan leader and had been the western U.S. commander of the American Nazi party.[80] Until it began to create problems for Duke's new claim to moderation, the *NAAWP News* advertised and distributed a list of "suppressed books," which included such classics of the Nazi movement as *Protocols of the Learned Elders of Zion* and Francis Parker Yockey's *Imperium,* along with the IAAEE's scientific publications and the *Mankind Quarterly.*

Claims of a scientific basis allowed Duke's underlying ideology to merge seamlessly with his new, more moderate image. "High nonwhite birthrates and uncontrolled immigration," which were making the United States "a nation completely controlled and dominated by minorities," supposedly concerned him not for racist but for biological reasons. The average difference of fifteen IQ points between blacks and whites provided scientific proof that "the least capable and least talented people . . . have the highest birthrate," and, he concluded, "that's against evolution."[81] To ensure the nation's biological well-being, Duke maintained, "the best elements in our people . . . the genetic excellence of [the] founding majority" must be promoted and cultivated, and "we must completely alter the welfare system so that it doesn't fuel the exploding non-white birthrate."[82] His specific proposals, as well as much of his current rhetoric, were taken directly from Shockley, who was eulogized in the *NAAWP News* as "one of the great men of our time."[83] In his campaign for the Louisiana legislature Duke declared, in language almost identical with the physicist's, that he was "the only candidate" with "concrete proposals to reduce the illegitimate birthrate and break the cycle of poverty that truly enslaves and harms the black race." Duke, too, would rescue blacks from their own genes by making welfare and other forms of government assistance contingent on sterilization and by offering "cash bonuses" for the procedure.[84]

Only the Roger Pearsons and David Dukes of the world can find practical value in the research on racial differences in intelligence. Such science is the very basis and essence of their ideology, helping to dignify beliefs that would otherwise be held in complete contempt. Every neo-Nazi organization is obsessed with the "scientific evaluation" of races, and their literature regularly refers to the work of such scientists as Jensen, Eysenck, Shockley, Cattell, and now Rushton as the justification for oppressive political positions. At times the scientists have willingly contributed to these publications. Though such an act is, naturally, their right as citizens, no one should be misled into thinking their involvement is anything but political. Even when scientists have maintained a professional distance from the exploitation of their research, their obsession with racial differences has unavoidably lent itself to such use. As the MIT biologist and Nobel Laureate S. E. Luria has observed,

Whenever self-appointed experts state that the problem of impoverishment of IQ is a major problem facing our nation, I see racist eugenics raising once again its ugly head. Behind the urgent scientific necessity to know the truth about those miserable 15 IQ points, on which the whole future of the schools, the nation, and the species is claimed to depend, there is a movement to drop the current efforts toward integrated schools and equalized opportunities for black and white children. If biologists let themselves be enticed into the quicksands of the genetics of IQ, they will end up as the stooges of the forces of racial bigotry.[85]

"In a democracy," wrote the architect Louis Sullivan, "there can be but one fundamental test of citizenship, namely: Are you using such gifts as you possess for or against the people?"[86] If the century and a half of research into racial differences had at least unearthed some shard of scientific fact, political misuse might be the necessary price for scientific progress. Sadly, however, the legitimation of racist ideology has been its major accomplishment. Instead of helping to rationalize attempts to oppress many of their fellow human beings, scientists should be putting their talents to better use.

Notes

Introduction

1. H. E. Garrett, "Negro-White Differences in Mental Ability in the United States," *Scientific Monthly* 65 (1947): 329-33.

2. H. J. Eysenck, *The IQ Argument* (New York: Library Press, 1971), 79.

3. G. W. Albee, "The Politics of Nature and Nurture," *American Journal of Community Psychology* 65 (1982): 5.

4. G. R. Stetson, "Some Memory Tests of Whites and Blacks," *Psychological Review* 4 (1897): 288.

5. C. Burt, "Experimental Tests of General Intelligence," *British Journal of Psychology* 3 (1909): 143-44.

6. A. R. Jensen, "What Is the Question? What Is the Evidence?" in *The Psychologists*, vol. 2, ed. T. S. Krawiec (New York: Oxford University Press, 1974), 222-25.

7. R. M. Bache, "Reaction Time with Reference to Race," *Psychological Review* 2 (1895): 481, 479.

8. A. R. Jensen, "Techniques for Chronometric Study of Mental Abilities," in *Methodological and Statistical Advances in the Study of Individual Differences*, ed. C. R. Reynolds and V. L. Willson (New York: Plenum, 1985), 55.

9. C. B. Davenport and M. Steggerda, *Race Crossing in Jamaica* (Washington, D.C.: Carnegie Institute, 1929), 469.

10. See, for example, R. B. Bean, *The Races of Man* (New York: University Society, 1932), 30-37; and H. F. Osborn, "The Evolution of Human Races," *Natural History* 26 (January-February 1926): 5.

11. C. S. Coon, *The Origin of Races* (New York: Alfred A. Knopf, 1962).

12. H. H. Goddard, "Mental Tests and the Immigrant," *Journal of Delinquency* 2 (1917): 244, 266; the percentages appear in a table on 252.

13. E. M. East, *Heredity and Human Affairs* (New York: Charles Scribner's Sons, 1929), 200, 181, 199.

14. See T. S. Kuhn, *The Structure of Scientific Revolutions* (Chicago: University of Chicago Press, 1962).

15. A. N. de Condorcet, *Sketch for a Historical Picture of the Progress of the Human Mind*, trans. J. Barraclough (London: Weidenfeld and Nicolson, 1955 [1795]), 83.

16. E. Barker, *The Politics of Aristotle* (London: Oxford University Press, 1950), 14.

17. Ibid., 16, 17.

18. T. Hobbes, *Leviathan* (New York: Bobbs-Merrill, 1958 [1651]), 127.

19. K. Pearson and M. Moul, "The Problem of Alien Immigration into Great Britain Illustrated by an Examination of Russian and Polish Jewish Children," *Annals of Eugenics* 1 (1925): 8.

20. Ibid., 124, 125.

21. L. M. Terman, "The Psychological Determinist; or Democracy and the IQ," *Journal of Educational Research* 6 (1922): 62.

22. Unsigned editorial, *American Medicine* (April 1907): 197.

23. P. Popenoe and R. H. Johnson, *Applied Eugenics* (New York: Macmillan, 1933), 302.

24. W. B. Smith, *The Color Line* (New York: Negro Universities Press, 1969 [1905]), 71.

25. A. R. Jensen, "The Price of Inequality," *Oxford Review of Education* 1 (1975): 61.

Chapter 1: "Helping Along the Process"

1. From Carolus Linnaeus's *Systema Naturae*, discussed in P. R. Ehrlich and S. S. Feldman, *The Race Bomb* (New York: Quadrangle, 1977), 16.

2. Quoted in J. S. Haller, Jr., *Outcasts from Evolution* (Urbana: University of Illinois Press, 1971), 5.

3. A good discussion of the great chain can be found in W. D. Jordan, *White over Black* (Chapel Hill: University of North Carolina Press, 1968), 219–38, 482–511.

4. A. Pope, *An Essay on Man*, epistle 4, ver. 49–50, in *The Poems of Alexander Pope*, ed. J. Butt (New Haven, Conn.: Yale University Press, 1977), 537.

5. C. White, *An Account of the Regular Gradation in Man and in Different Animals and Vegetables; and from the Former to the Latter* (London: C. Dilly, 1799), 94–95.

6. Ibid., 82.

7. Ibid., 134–35.

8. Ibid., iii.

9. See, for example, the work of the historian Edward Long, described in Jordan, *White over Black*, 492.

10. Letter from Jefferson to Henri Gregoire, February 25, 1809, in *The Writings of Thomas Jefferson*, vol. 12, ed. A. E. Bergh (Washington, D.C.: Thomas Jefferson Memorial Association, 1907), 254.

11. T. Jefferson, *Notes on the State of Virginia* (New York: Harper and Row, 1964), 133.

12. Quoted in W. S. Jenkins, *Pro-Slavery Thought in the Old South* (Gloucester, Mass.: Peter Smith, 1960), 65.

13. Quoted in ibid., 244.

14. J. H. van Evrie, *Negroes and Negro "Slavery"* (New York: van Evrie, Horton, 1863 [1853]), 89-91.

15. Ibid., 113-14, 122.

16. Ibid., 94-96.

17. S. A. Cartwright, "Report on the Diseases and Physical Peculiarities of the Negro Race," *New Orleans Medical and Surgical Journal* 7 (1851): 692-93.

18. Ibid., 694, 715.

19. Ibid., 707-9.

20. E. Jarvis, "Statistics of Insanity in the United States," *Boston Medical and Surgical Journal* 27 (1842): 119.

21. E. Jarvis, "Statistics of Insanity in the United States," *Boston Medical and Surgical Journal* 27 (1842): 288-82 (different from the article cited in note 20).

22. "Statistics of Population: Table of Lunacy in the United States," *Merchants' Magazine* 8 (1843): 290.

23. "Reflections on the Census of 1840," *Southern Literary Messenger* 9 (1843): 346-47.

24. E. Jarvis, "Insanity among the Coloured Population of the Free States," *American Journal of the Medical Sciences* 7 (1844): 80, 83.

25. Letter from Calhoun to Richard Pakenham, April 18, 1844, in *The Works of John C. Calhoun*, vol. 5, ed. R. K. Cralle (New York: Appleton, 1855), 337.

26. Letter from Agassiz to his mother, quoted in S. J. Gould, "Flaws in a Victorian Veil," *Natural History* 87 (June/July 1978): 24.

27. L. Agassiz, "The Diversity of Origin of the Human Races," *Christian Examiner* 49 (1850): 110, 142.

28. Ibid., 144.

29. S. G. Morton, *Crania Americana* (Philadelphia: J. Dobson, 1839), 253.

30. S. G. Morton, "Observations on the Size of the Brain in Various Races and Families of Men," *Proceedings, Academy of Natural Sciences of Philadelphia* 4 (1849): 221.

31. Morton, *Crania Americana*, 5-7, 54, 65, 93.

32. T. F. Gossett, *Race* (New York: Schocken Books, 1965), 74.

33. A. C. Doyle, "The Adventure of the Blue Carbuncle," in *The Complete Sherlock Holmes* (New York: Literary Guild, 1936), 279.

34. W. Shakespeare, *Troilus and Cressida*, ed. J. J. Campbell (New Haven, Conn.: Yale University Press, 1956), 115-16 (act V, scene 1, line 58). For hat sizes as indications of intelligence, see, for example, J. C. Nott and G. R. Gliddon, *Types of Mankind* (Philadelphia: Lippincott, Grambo, 1854), 452-53. See also Nott's appendix to A. de Gobineau, *The Moral and Intellectual Diversity of Races*, trans. H. Hotz (Philadelphia: J. B. Lippincott, 1856), 469-70.

35. Quoted in W. Stanton, *The Leopard's Spots* (Chicago: University of Chicago Press, 1960), 20.

36. Quoted in S. J. Gould, "Wide Hats and Narrow Minds," *Natural History* 88 (February 1979): 36.

37. S. J. Gould, "Morton's Ranking of Races by Cranial Capacity," *Science* 200 (1978): 503-9.

38. S. J. Gould, *The Mismeasure of Man* (New York: W. W. Norton, 1981), 65, 54.

39. Calhoun is quoted in Stanton, *The Leopard's Spots*, 52. The correspondence between Calhoun and Morton is described by Morton's colleague Josiah C. Nott in Nott and Gliddon, *Types of Mankind*, 51.

40. Quoted in Stanton, *The Leopard's Spots*, 144.

41. J. C. Nott, "Statistics of Southern Slave Populations," *Commercial Review* 4 (1847): 288, 280. See also J. C. Nott, "Physical History of the Jewish Race," *Southern Quarterly Review*, n.s., 5 (1850): 451.

42. Nott and Gliddon, *Types of Mankind*, 457-58.

43. Gould, *The Mismeasure of Man*, 32-33. Gould's discussion of this illustration cites J. C. Nott, *Indigenous Races of the Earth* (Philadelphia: J. B. Lippincott, 1868), as its source; in fact, it appears in *Types of Mankind*, 458.

44. J. C. Nott, "The Negro Race," *Anthropological Review* 4 (1866): 114.

45. Nott and Gliddon, *Types of Mankind*, 79, 404.

46. Nott, "The Negro Race," 106.

47. J. C. Nott, "Natural History of Man in Connection with Negro Slavery," address delivered to the Southern Rights Association of Mobile, reprinted in *De Bow's Review* 10 (1851): 332, 329.

48. Nott and Gliddon, *Types of Mankind*, 373, 398-99.

49. Quoted in Stanton, *The Leopard's Spots*, 153.

50. See, for example, White, *An Account of the Regular Gradation*, 51.

51. Quoted in Gossett, *Race*, 70.

52. T. H. Huxley, "Emancipation—Black and White," in *Lay Sermons, Addresses and Reviews* (New York: Appleton, 1871), 20.

53. Quoted in Gould, *The Mismeasure of Man*, 99.

54. E. Eggleston, *The Ultimate Solution of the American Negro Problem* (Boston: Gorham, 1913), 185.

55. See Gould, *The Mismeasure of Man*, 97-100. A similar distinction was made by Nott to account for the unexpectedly large brains of some Africans and Native Americans: "The negro" and "the semi-civilised and barbarous tribes of Indians" had "capacious" brains, he explained, because among these peoples "the posterior or animal part of the brain greatly preponderates over the anterior or intellectual lobes." Nott, "The Negro Race," 113; see also Nott and Gliddon, *Types of Mankind*, 463-64.

56. The French scientist Paul Broca, quoted in Gould, *The Mismeasure of Man*, 97-98.

57. Haller, *Outcasts from Evolution*, 29.

58. S. J. Gould, "Racism and Recapitulation," *Natural History* 84 (June/July 1975): 21.

59. Cited in Haller, *Outcasts from Evolution*, 54.

60. G. F. Lydston, "Letter to Dr. McGuire: Sexual Crimes among the Southern Negroes Scientifically Considered," *Virginia Medical Monthly* 20 (1893): 118.

61. W. L. Howard, "The Negro as a Distinct Ethnic Factor in Civilization," *Medicine* 9 (1903): 424.

62. *Appendix to the Congressional Globe* (December 18, 1867): 70, 73; the chart appears on 72.

63. Howard, "The Negro as a Distinct Ethnic Factor in Civilization," 423.

64. C. Darwin, *The Origin of Species* (New York: Mentor, 1958), 75.

65. H. Spencer, *The Data of Ethics* (New York: American Publishing, 1879), iii.

66. H. Spencer, *Social Statics* (New York: A. M. Kelley, 1969 [1851]), 322-26.

67. On Spencer's popularity, see Haller, *Outcasts from Evolution,* 128; and Gossett, *Race,* 153.

68. See Holmes's dissenting opinion in *Lochner v. New York* 198 U.S. 75 (1905).

69. Hill, Carnegie, and Rockefeller are quoted in R. Hofstadter, *Social Darwinism in American Thought* (New York: George Braziller, 1959), 45.

70. E. H. Clarke, *Sex in Education* (New York: Arno, 1972 [1873]), 82, 62, 104. It is tempting to explain if not excuse Clarke's assertion as a consequence of the era in which it was made, but almost ninety years of subsequent scientific progress did little to modify the conclusions of Erwin O. Strassman, a medical professor at Baylor University, although they were accompanied by somewhat more sophisticated evidence. "It is my experience," wrote Strassman, "that there is a basic antagonism between the scholastic type of intelligence and the reproductive system in infertile women . . . the bigger the brain, the smaller the breasts, and vice versa, the bigger the breasts, the lower the IQ." E. O. Strassman, "Physique, Temperament and Intelligence in Infertile Women," *International Journal of Fertility* 9 (1963): 311.

71. K. Pearson, *National Life from the Standpoint of Science* (London: Adam and Charles Black, 1905), 21, 46, 64, 26-27.

72. Nott, "The Negro Race," 111.

73. *New York Times,* February 27, 1895, 4.

74. "Philanthropist," "Vital Statistics of Negroes and Mulattoes," *Boston Medical and Surgical Journal* 17 (1842): 168-70.

75. W. B. Smith, *The Color Line* (New York: Negro Universities Press, 1969 [1905]), 192.

76. Eggleston, *The Ultimate Solution of the American Negro Problem,* 185, 89.

77. Smith, *The Color Line,* 187.

78. Lydston, "Letter to Dr. McGuire," 122-23.

79. C. S. Bacon, "The Race Problem," *Medicine* 9 (1903): 338, 342.

80. J. R. Straton, "Will Education Solve the Race Problem?" *North American Review* 170 (1900): 797, 793-94.

81. Smith, *The Color Line,* 110.

82. Eggleston, *The Ultimate Solution of the American Negro Problem,* 249.

83. F. L. Hoffman, *Race Traits and Tendencies of the American Negro* (New York: American Economic Association, 1896), 326, 328.

84. Eggleston, *The Ultimate Solution of the American Negro Problem,* 246.

85. E. W. Gilliam, "The African in the United States," *Popular Science Monthly* 22 (1883): 437, 443-44.

86. Hoffman, *Race Traits and Tendencies of the American Negro*, 2–3, 176.

87. Ibid., 50, 310–11.

88. Smith, *The Color Line*, 175–76, 223.

89. John Sharp Williams, "The Negro and the South," *Metropolitan Magazine* 27 (1907): 146–49.

90. Benjamin R. Tillman, "The Race Question," *Van Norden Magazine* 2 (1907): 19–28.

91. Quoted in Gossett, *Race*, 109–10.

92. J. LeConte, "The Effect of Mixture of Races on Human Progress," *Berkeley Quarterly* 1 (April 1880): 101. Actually, almost the same suggestion had been made some years earlier, in 1864, when an anonymous pamphlet advocated the "melaleuketic" (from the Greek *melas*, black, and *leukos*, white) union of the blacks with the Irish as an "infinite service" to the Irish, who, according to the unnamed author, were "below the level of the most degraded negro" and would be vastly improved by such an "intermingling." The pamphlet turned out to be a hoax, written by two Democratic partisans to embarrass the Republican party; however, its title, *Miscegenation,* became the standard term for a union between members of different races. The 1864 edition of *Miscegenation* was republished in 1970 (Upper Saddles River, N.J.: Literature Press/Gregg Press). On the hoax, see F. G. Wood, *Black Scare* (Berkeley: University of California Press, 1968), 53–80.

93. A. Chase, *The Legacy of Malthus* (New York: Alfred A. Knopf, 1977), 107.

94. E. D. Cope, "Two Perils of the Indo-European," *Open Court* 3 (1890): 2054.

95. E. D. Cope, "What Is Republicanism?" *Open Court* 10 (1896): 4899.

96. E. D. Cope, "The Return of the Negroes to Africa," *Open Court* 3 (1890): 2110.

97. Cope, "What Is Republicanism?" 4897; Cope, "The Return of the Negroes to Africa," 2110.

98. N. S. Shaler, "European Peasants as Immigrants," *Atlantic Monthly* (May 1893): 647, 649.

99. N. S. Shaler, "The Negro Problem," *Atlantic Monthly* (November 1884): 70.

100. Shaler, "European Peasants as Immigrants," 655, 650.

Chapter 2: For a Twentieth the Cost

1. D. W. Forrest, *Francis Galton: The Life and Work of a Victorian Genius* (London: Elek Books, 1974).

2. Quoted in K. Pearson, *The Life, Letters and Labours of Francis Galton*, vol. 1 (Cambridge: Cambridge University Press, 1914–30), 124.

3. Letter from Galton to his sister, April 14, 1840, in ibid., 116.

4. Letter from Galton to his niece, October 28, 1905, in ibid., vol. 3b, 551.

5. F. Galton, "The Measure of Fidget," *Nature* 32 (1885): 174–75.

6. F. Galton, "Number of Strokes of the Brush in a Picture," *Nature* 72 (1905): 198.

7. Pearson, *The Life, Letters and Labours*, vol. 3b, 456–58.

8. F. Galton, "Good and Bad Temper in English Families," *Fortnightly Review* 42 (1887): 21–23.

9. F. Galton, *Natural Inheritance* (London: Macmillan, 1889), 66.

10. F. Galton, "Gregariousness in Cattle and in Men," *Macmillan's Magazine* 23 (1872): 354–55.

11. W. T. Kelvin, "Electrical Units of Measurement," in W. T. Kelvin, *Popular Lectures and Addresses*, vol. 1 (London: Macmillan, 1889), 73.

12. See the series of "Pedigree Plates" on the sleeve of the back cover of Pearson, *The Life, Letters and Labours*, vol. 1.

13. Ibid., 353.

14. Ibid., 355, 357. When Karl Pearson discussed this publication in his hagiographic treatment of Galton's life, Pearson shared his mentor's concern over the "mass of servile intelligences" but also added a note of caution about the other end of the spectrum: as bad as too few self-reliant "fore-oxen" was too many of them. A nation could not be stable if "each ruminant and stolid ox no longer considered the common determination of the herd as binding on his conscience," Pearson explained, and this English scientist, who proudly disclaimed any political bias, cited twentieth-century Ireland as an example of such a problem. Ibid., vol. 2, 75.

15. F. Galton, *Hereditary Genius* (London: Macmillan, 1925 [1892]), 18.

16. Pearson, *The Life, Letters and Labours*, vol. 1, 208.

17. Galton, *Hereditary Genius*, 271.

18. F. Galton, "Statistical Inquiries into the Efficacy of Prayer," *Fortnightly Review* 12 (1872): 130.

19. Galton, *Hereditary Genius*, 249.

20. Ibid., xxvii.

21. Speech at the Royal Society dinner (1886), reprinted in Pearson, *The Life, Letters and Labours*, vol. 2, 201.

22. F. Galton, *English Men of Science* (London: Frank Cass, 1970 [1874]), 12. In *The Tempest* (act IV, scene 1, lines 188–90), Prospero terms Caliban "A devil, a born devil, on whose nature can never stick, on whom my pains / Humanely taken, all, all lost, quite lost."

23. F. Galton, "The Possible Improvement of the Human Breed under the Existing Conditions of Law and Sentiment," *Nature* 64 (1901): 659.

24. Galton, *English Men of Science*, 192, 147–48.

25. Galton, *Hereditary Genius*, x, 22.

26. Ibid., 28.

27. Ibid., 31–32.

28. Letter from Galton to Darwin Galton, February 23, 1851, in Pearson, *The Life, Letters and Labours*, vol. 1, 231–32.

29. Galton, *Hereditary Genius*, 327–28.

30. R. E. Fancher, "Galton in Africa," *American Psychologist* 37 (1982): 713.

31. Galton, *Hereditary Genius*, 35.

32. Ibid., 39.

33. See the biography by R. Grimsley, *Jean d'Alembert* (Oxford: Oxford University Press, 1965).

34. F. Galton, *Inquiries into Human Faculty and Its Development* (New York: AMS Press, 1973 [1907]), 20, 248–54.

35. Letter from Galton to William Bateson, June 12, 1904, in Pearson, *The Life, Letters and Labours*, vol. 3a, 221.

36. F. Galton, "President's Address," *Journal of the Anthropological Institute of Great Britain and Ireland* 18 (1888): 406–7.

37. Galton, *Inquiries into Human Faculty and Its Development*, 17.

38. Galton, *Hereditary Genius*, 1.

39. Socrates, *The Republic of Plato*, trans. A. Bloom (New York: Basic Books, 1968), book 5, 459a-e.

40. L. J. Cappon, ed., *The Adams-Jefferson Letters*, vol. 2 (Chapel Hill: University of North Carolina Press, 1959), 387.

41. F. Galton, "Hereditary Talent and Character," *Macmillan's Magazine* 12 (1865): 165–66.

42. F. Galton, "Hereditary Improvement," *Fraser's Magazine* 7 (1873): 117–18.

43. Ibid., 123, 125, 126.

44. Ibid., 127–28.

45. Ibid., 127, 129.

46. Galton, *Inquiries into Human Faculty and Its Development*, 198.

47. Galton, *Natural Inheritance*, 197–98.

48. Galton, *Inquiry into Human Faculty and Its Development*, 199.

49. Galton, *Hereditary Genius*, xxvi.

50. Letter from Galton to the *Times* (London), June 6, 1873, in Pearson, *The Life, Letters and Labours*, vol. 2, 32–33.

51. Galton, *Inquiries into Human Faculty and Its Development*, 200–201. Commenting on this observation in 1924, Galton's disciple Karl Pearson added that a race had no inherent rights of any kind since its very presence was attained only by displacing an earlier race, and then he suggested the implications of this fact for the negotiations concluded at the end of World War I: "The preliminary discussion of the recent peace terms at Versailles was accompanied by much futile talk about the 'rights' of small nations and of racial units. No small people, because it at present occupies a certain area, can be said to have a 'right' to mineral resources vastly exceeding its own consumption and essential to the needs of a larger adjacent population. Any allotment of lands based solely on 'aboriginal' or even present occupational 'rights' is certain to be called in question by the pressure of race against race. The peace-makers of Versailles lacked the knowledge that springs from a study of evolution." Pearson, *The Life, Letters and Labours*, vol. 2, 264.

52. Galton, "Statistical Inquiries into the Efficacy of Prayer," 135.

53. Galton, "Hereditary Improvement," 119, 120.

54. F. Galton, "The Part of Religion in Human Evolution," *National Review* 23 (1894): 758–61.

55. J. H. Noyes, "Scientific Propagation," in *The Modern Thinker*, vol. 1, ed. D. Goodman (American News, 1870), 118, reprinted in *Eugenics Then and*

Now, ed. C. J. Bajema (Stroudsburg, Penn.: Dowden, Hutchinson and Ross, 1976).

56. Quoted in M. H. Haller, *Eugenics* (New Brunswick, N.J.: Rutgers University Press, 1963), 37.

57. H. H. Noyes and G. W. Noyes, "The Oneida Community Experiment in Stirpiculture," in *Eugenics, Genetics and the Family*, vol. 1, ed. C. Davenport (Baltimore: Williams and Wilkins, 1923), 376, reprinted in *Eugenics Then and Now*, ed. Bajema.

58. H. W. Holland, "Heredity," *Atlantic Monthly* (October 1883): 447, 450, 452.

59. F. Galton, "The Possible Improvement of the Human Breed," 661, 663.

60. F. Galton, "The Possible Improvement of the Human Breed under the Existing Conditions of Law and Sentiment," *Popular Science Monthly* 60 (1902): 218–33.

61. Letter from Galton to Alphonse de Candolle, October 17, 1884, in Pearson, *The Life, Letters and Labours*, vol. 2, 208–9.

62. Letter to Galton from Weismann, February 23, 1889, in ibid., vol. 3a, 340–41.

63. R. S. Cowan, "Nature and Nurture: The Interplay of Biology and Politics in the Work of Francis Galton," *Studies in the History of Biology* 1 (1977): 178.

Chapter 3: Applying Science to Society

1. E. Huntington, *Tomorrow's Children: The Goals of Eugenics* (New York: John Wiley and Sons, 1935), 104–5.

2. See, for example, S. Nearing, *The Super Race* (New York: B. W. Huebsch, 1912). A number of progressive scientists and intellectuals, especially in England, remained supportive of the concept of eugenics but opposed what they saw as its misuse to serve the class and race biases of the capitalist social order. As the *New Statesman and Nation* observed in an editorial on July 25, 1931, "Though exponents and supporters of the eugenist movement . . . have done everything that could well have been done to alienate the sympathy of the working class leaders in this country, the legitimate claims of eugenics are not inherently incompatible with the outlook of the collectivist movement." See also D. Paul, "Eugenics and the Left," *Journal of the History of Ideas* 45 (1984): 567–90; and M. Freeden, "Eugenics and Progressive Thought: A Study in Ideological Affinity," *Historical Journal* 22 (1979): 645–71.

3. A. E. Wiggam, *The New Decalogue of Science* (New York: Blue Ribbon Books, 1923), 110–11.

4. C. B. Davenport, "The Origin and Control of Mental Defectiveness," *Popular Science Monthly* 80 (1912): 90.

5. Wiggam, *The New Decalogue of Science*, 25.

6. S. J. Holmes, "The Decadence of Human Heredity," *Atlantic Monthly* (September 1914): 304.

7. E. M. East, *Heredity and Human Affairs* (New York: Charles Scribner's Sons, 1929), 248.

8. Ibid., 306.

9. H. S. Jennings, "Health Progress and Race Progress," *Journal of Heredity* 18 (1927): 272.

10. W. B. Smith, *The Color Line* (New York: Negro Universities Press, 1969 [1905]), 191.

11. Wiggam, *The New Decalogue of Science*, 67-68.

12. P. Popenoe and R. H. Johnson, *Applied Eugenics* (New York: Macmillan, 1933), 336, 334, 313-14.

13. East, *Heredity and Human Affairs*, 309.

14. Wiggam, *The New Decalogue of Science*, 87.

15. Ibid., 76.

16. East, *Heredity and Human Affairs*, 250.

17. K. Pearson, *The Groundwork of Eugenics* (London: Dulau, 1909), 20-21.

18. C. B. Davenport, "Euthenics and Eugenics," *Popular Science Monthly* 78 (1911): 20.

19. See R. F. Butts and L. A. Cremin, *A History of Education in American Culture* (New York: Henry Holt, 1953), 308.

20. "Race Genetics Problems," *American Breeders Magazine* 2 (1911): 231-32.

21. F. A. Walker, "Restriction of Immigration," *Atlantic Monthly* (June 1896): 823, 828.

22. E. A. Ross, *The Old World in the New* (New York: Century, 1914), 134.

23. W. McDougall, *Is America Safe for Democracy?* (New York: Charles Scribner's Sons, 1921), 150.

24. M. Grant, *The Passing of the Great Race* (New York: Charles Scribner's Sons, 1923), 87.

25. See G. I. Burch and E. Pendell, *Human Breeding and Survival* (New York: Penguin, 1947), 89.

26. H. H. Laughlin, "Full Text for a Model State Law," in *Eugenical Sterilization in the United States* (Chicago: Psychopathic Laboratory of the Municipal Court of Chicago, 1922), 446-47.

27. J. B. S. Haldane, *Heredity and Politics* (New York: W. W. Norton, 1938), 17.

28. W. E. D. Stokes, *The Right to Be Well Born* (New York: C. J. O'Brien, 1917), 48-50, 223-24.

29. "Preachers and Eugenics," *American Breeders' Magazine* 4 (1913): 63. This unsigned editorial was probably written by the geneticist C. B. Davenport, who at the time was secretary of the Committee on Eugenics of the American Breeders' Association, the publisher of the magazine.

30. W. J. Tinkle, "Heredity of Habitual Wandering," *Journal of Heredity* 18 (1927): 548-51.

31. R. N. Salaman, "Heredity and the Jew," *Journal of Genetics* 1 (1911): 279-90.

32. J. G. Wilson, "A Study in Jewish Psychopathology," *Popular Science Monthly* 82 (1913): 264-71.

33. H. E. Jordan, "The Biological Status and Social Worth of the Mulatto," *Popular Science Monthly* 82 (1913): 580.

34. Cited in H. Pilpel, "Family Planning and the Law," *Social Biology*, supplement, 18 (1971): S130.

35. C. B. Davenport, *Heredity in Relation to Eugenics* (New York: Henry Holt, 1913), 6. See also C. B. Davenport, *The Trait Book* (Cold Spring Harbor, N.Y.: Eugenics Record Office, 1912).

36. Davenport, "The Origin and Control of Mental Defectiveness," 88.

37. Davenport, *Heredity in Relation to Eugenics*, 251.

38. C. B. Davenport, "The Effects of Race Intermingling," *Proceedings of the American Philosophical Society* 56 (1917): 366.

39. Quoted in "Amalgamation," *De Bow's Review*, n.s., 4 (1860): 11.

40. L. H. Harris, "A Southern Woman's View," *Independent* (May 18, 1899): 1354.

41. Davenport, "The Effects of Race Intermingling," 367.

42. J. A. Mjöen, "Harmonic and Disharmonic Race Crossings," in *Eugenics in Race and State,* vol. 2 of *Second International Congress of Eugenics (1921), Scientific Papers* (Baltimore: Williams and Wilkins, 1923), 47, 51.

43. C. B. Davenport and M. Steggerda, *Race Crossing in Jamaica* (Washington, D.C.: Carnegie Institute, 1929), 472.

44. W. E. Castle, "Race Mixture and Physical Disharmonies," *Science* 71 (1930): 605.

45. C. B. Davenport, "Heredity, Culpability, Praiseworthiness, Punishment and Reward," *Popular Science Monthly* 83 (1913): 36.

46. Davenport, "Euthenics and Eugenics," 19; C. B. Davenport, "The Racial Element in National Vitality," *Popular Science Monthly* 86 (1915): 332.

47. A. Chase, "False Correlations = Real Deaths: The Great Pellagra Cover-up," in *Genetic Destiny,* ed. E. Tobach and H. M. Proshansky (New York: AMS Press, 1976), 111.

48. East, *Heredity and Human Affairs,* 125, 86.

49. F. A. Woods, "Laws of Diminishing Environmental Influence," *Popular Science Monthly* 76 (1910): 313.

50. F. A. Woods, *The Influence of Monarchs* (New York: Macmillan, 1913), viii, 15.

51. Ibid., 273–75, 303.

52. East, *Heredity and Human Affairs,* 297.

53. E. M. East, "Heredity," in *Biology in Human Affairs,* ed. E. M. East (New York: McGraw-Hill, 1931), 195–96.

54. Ibid., 181.

55. E. M. East, "Population," *Scientific Monthly* 10 (1920): 621.

56. East, *Heredity and Human Affairs,* 260.

57. Davenport, "The Origin and Control of Mental Defectiveness," 87.

58. Davenport, *Heredity in Relation to Eugenics,* 216.

59. F. A. Woods, "The Racial Limitation of Bolshevism," *Journal of Heredity* 10 (1919): 190; F. A. Woods, "War or Peace?" *Forum* 74 (1925): 539.

60. East, "Population," 621.

61. Davenport, *Heredity in Relation to Eugenics,* 263. See also Davenport, "The Origin and Control of Mental Defectiveness," 90.

62. C. B. Davenport, "Report of the Committee on Eugenics," *American Breeders' Magazine* 1 (1910): 27.

63. Jennings, "Health Progress and Race Progress," 274.

64. East, "Heredity," 189. In *Heredity and Human Affairs,* 258, East gives an estimate of twenty-eight million "morons."

65. East, *Heredity and Human Affairs,* 238, 300.

66. East, "Heredity," 189.

67. Ibid., 190.

68. East, *Heredity and Human Affairs,* 300.

69. E. M. East, "Biology and Human Problems," in *Biology in Human Affairs,* ed. East, 10.

70. Quoted in G. E. Allen, "Genetics, Eugenics and Class Struggle," *Genetics,* supplement, 75 (1979): 36-37.

71. See "Statement of Herbert S. Jennings," in *Restriction of Immigration: Hearings before the Committee on Immigration and Naturalization on H.R.5, H.R.101, and H.R.561,* HR 68-1, January 5, 1924, 511-28.

72. E. M. East, *Mankind at the Crossroads* (New York: Charles Scribner's Sons, 1924), vi.

73. R. Pearl, "Breeding Better Men," *World's Work* 15 (1908): 9818-24.

74. R. Pearl, "The Biology of Superiority," *American Mercury* (November 1927): 260.

75. See T. M. Canfield, "The Professionalization of American Psychology," *Journal of the History of the Behavioral Sciences* 9 (1973): 66-75.

76. R. M. Yerkes, "Testing the Human Mind," *Atlantic Monthly* (March 1923): 367, 370.

77. E. L. Thorndike, "Intelligence and Its Uses," *Harper's Magazine* 140 (1920): 235.

78. Wiggam, *The New Decalogue of Science,* 202.

79. H. H. Goddard, *Human Efficiency and Levels of Intelligence* (Princeton, N.J.: Princeton University Press, 1920), vi.

80. C. Spearman, *The Abilities of Man* (New York: Macmillan, 1927), 8.

81. L. M. Terman, "The Mental Test as a Psychological Method," *Psychological Review* 31 (1924): 115-16, 105-6.

82. Ross, *The Old World in the New,* 285-86.

83. McDougall, *Is America Safe for Democracy?* 179-83.

84. See, for example, R. M. Bache, "Reaction Time with Reference to Race," *Psychological Review* 2 (1895): 475-86; and G. R. Stetson, "Some Memory Tests of Whites and Blacks," *Psychological Review* 4 (1897): 285-89.

85. M. J. Mayo, "The Mental Capacity of the American Negro," *Archives of Psychology,* no. 28 (1913): 9.

86. Ibid., 67, 70, 2.

87. J. Morse, "A Comparison of White and Colored Children Measured by the Binet Scale of Intelligence," *Popular Science Monthly* 84 (1914): 79.

88. G. O. Ferguson, "The Psychology of the Negro," *Archives of Psychology,* no. 36 (1916): 84, 125.

89. H. M. Bond, "Some Exceptional Negro Children," *Crisis* 34 (1927): 259; Ferguson, "The Psychology of the Negro," 125-26.

90. C. P. Knight, "The Detection of the Mentally Defective among Immigrants," *Journal of the American Medical Association* 60 (1913): 106–7.

91. H. A. Knox, "The Moron and the Study of Alien Defectives," *Journal of the American Medical Association* 60 (1913): 105–6.

92. Knight, "The Detection of the Mentally Defective among Immigrants," 107. See also the comments by A. W. Stearns and A. J. Nute in a discussion held by the Boston Society of Psychiatry and Neurology, in "Immigration from a Mental Hygienic Standpoint," *Journal of Nervous and Mental Diseases* 52 (1920): 506–7.

93. H. H. Goddard, "The Binet Tests in Relation to Immigration," *Journal of Psycho-Asthenics* 18 (1913/14): 105.

94. Ibid., 106.

95. H. H. Goddard, "The Feeble Minded Immigrant," *Training School Bulletin* 9 (1912): 111.

96. H. H. Goddard, "Feeble-mindedness and Immigration," *Training School Bulletin* 9 (1912): 91.

97. H. H. Goddard, "Mental Tests and the Immigrant," *Journal of Delinquency* 2 (1917): 243–44, 252, 266, 271.

98. R. Pintner, *Intelligence Testing: Methods and Results* (New York: Henry Holt, 1923), 362, 361.

99. Ross, *The Old World in the New,* 98, 101, 117.

100. See, for example, K. Murdoch, "A Study of Race Differences in New York City," *School and Society* 11 (1920): 150; and A. H. Arlitt, "Further Data on the Influence of Race and Social Status on the Intelligence Quotient," *Psychological Bulletin* 18 (1921): 96.

101. F. L. Goodenough, "Racial Differences in the Intelligence of School Children," *Journal of Experimental Psychology* 9 (1926): 393, 391.

102. L. M. Terman, "The Conversation of Talent," *School and Society* 19 (1924): 363.

103. *Psychological Examining in the U.S. Army,* vol. 15 of *Memoirs of the National Academy of Sciences,* ed. R. M. Yerkes (Washington, D.C.: National Academy of Sciences, 1921).

104. S. J. Gould, *The Mismeasure of Man* (New York: W. W. Norton, 1981), 201, 205.

105. F. P. Donnelly, "Have You an American Intelligence?" *America* (July 14, 1923): 295.

106. C. C. Brigham, "Validity of Tests in Examinations of Immigrants," *Industrial Psychology* 1 (1926): 414.

107. Yerkes, "Testing the Human Mind," 364.

108. R. M. Yerkes, in Foreword to C. C. Brigham, *A Study of American Intelligence* (Princeton, N.J.: Princeton University Press, 1923), vii–viii.

109. Brigham, *A Study of American Intelligence,* 111, 96.

110. See W. Z. Ripley, *The Races of Europe* (New York: Appleton, 1899).

111. Brigham, *A Study of American Intelligence,* 159, 190, 197.

112. Ibid., 208, 190.

113. Ibid., 210.

114. R.P. [sic], "Is the Intelligence of the American Nation on the Decline?" *Journal of Educational Psychology* 14 (1923): 184-85.

115. W. C. Bagley, "The Army Tests and the Pro-Nordic Propaganda," *Educational Review* 67 (1924): 185.

116. Ibid., 179, 186-87.

117. K. Young, "Review of *A Study of American Intelligence,*" *Science* 57 (1923): 670.

118. K. Young, *Mental Differences in Certain Immigrant Groups* (Eugene: University of Oregon Press, 1922), 76.

119. K. Young, "Intelligence Tests of Certain Immigrant Groups," *Scientific Monthly* 15 (1922): 429, 420.

120. M. B. Hexter and A. Myerson, "13.77 versus 12.05: A Study in Probable Error," *Mental Hygiene* 8 (1924): 82.

121. Letter from Madison Grant to Maxwell Perkins, March 7 (no year noted but probably written in 1924 from the reference in the letter to Brigham's recently published book), Scribner's Archives, Princeton University Library, Princeton, N.J.

122. McDougall, *Is America Safe for Democracy?* 146, 118-19.

123. W. McDougall, *The Indestructible Union* (Boston: Little, Brown, 1925), 162-64.

124. W. McDougall, *Ethics and Some Modern World Problems* (London: Methuen, 1925), 38.

125. McDougall, *Is America Safe for Democracy?* 78-83, 89, 115, 101.

126. Ibid., 69-70, 105-7.

127. McDougall, *The Indestructible Union,* 135, 151.

128. See A. Chase, *The Legacy of Malthus* (New York: Alfred A. Knopf, 1977), 115.

129. See, for example, R. D. Ward, "Eugenic Immigration," *American Breeders' Magazine* 4 (1913): 96-102. In the same issue, *American Breeders' Magazine* announced its name would change to the *Journal of Heredity,* beginning with the next issue.

130. See M. D. Biddiss, ed., *Gobineau: Selected Political Writings* (New York: Harper and Row, 1970); and J. A. de Gobineau, *The Inequality of Human Races* (New York: Howard Fertig, 1967 [1915]).

131. Grant, *The Passing of the Great Race,* 167, 228.

132. Ibid., 185-87, 29-33, 159-62, 74-75.

133. H. F. Osborn, letter to *New York Times,* April 8, 1924, 18.

134. Grant, *The Passing of the Great Race,* 74, 89, 16, 85.

135. M. Grant, "Closing the Floodgates," in *The Alien in Our Midst,* ed. M. Grant and C. S. Davison (New York: Galton Publishing, 1930), 21. In an ironic turn of events, a generation later a spokesman for the Liberty Lobby, inheritor of the Madison Grant tradition, cited its diverse supporters—with names like Kaczoroski, Nakashima, Pasqualetti, Thibodeau, and Naciopolos—as Americans first, all opposed to liberalizing the immigration laws. See F. Mintz, *The Liberty Lobby and the American Right* (Westport, Conn.: Greenwood, 1985), 91.

136. Grant, *The Passing of the Great Race,* 18, 60.

137. Ibid., 91.

138. Ibid., 79.

139. F. A. Woods, "A Review of Reviews," *Journal of Heredity* 14 (1923): 93.

140. F. Boas, "Inventing a Great Race," *New Republic* 51 (1917): 305.

141. E. Huntington, "Heredity and Human Responsibility," *Yale Review* 6 (1917): 670.

142. T. L. Stoddard, *The Rising Tide of Color against White World-Supremacy* (New York: Charles Scribner's Sons, 1920), 13, 129, 221.

143. T. L. Stoddard, *The Revolt against Civilization* (New York: Charles Scribner's Sons, 1922), 246.

144. Quoted in "Galton Society," *Eugenical News* 10 (1925): 30–31.

145. See M. H. Haller, *Eugenics* (New Brunswick, N.J.: Rutgers University Press, 1963), 156.

146. Brigham, *A Study of American Intelligence*, 184.

147. "The Great American Myth," editorial, *Saturday Evening Post*, May 7, 1921.

148. Quoted in *Eugenical News* 18 (1933): 111.

149. Quoted in *New York Times*, September 15, 1920, 3.

150. Quoted in *New York Times*, October 27, 1921, 11.

151. C. Coolidge, "Whose Country Is This?" *Good Housekeeping* (February 1921): 14.

152. For a detailed discussion of the different approaches to restriction and the joint efforts of scientists and IRL leadership, see F. Samelson, "Putting Psychology on the Map: Ideology and Intelligence Testing," in *Psychology in Social Context*, ed. A. R. Buss (New York: Irvington, 1979), 103–68.

153. A. Johnson, "The Outline of a Policy," *Outlook* 136 (1924): 140.

154. "Statement of Henry H. Laughlin," in *Analysis of America's Modern Melting Pot: Hearings before the Committee on Immigration and Naturalization*, HR 67-3, November 21, 1922, 737, 738. Laughlin's appointment as expert eugenics agent is described on 729; Johnson's comments are on 731.

155. "Statement of Dr. Harry H. Laughlin," in *Europe as an Emigrant-Exporting Continent and the United States as an Immigrant-Receiving Nation: Hearings before the Committee on Immigration and Naturalization*, HR 68-1, March 8, 1924, 1293–97, 1305.

156. Ibid., 1317, 1311.

157. See Grant's letter to Albert Johnson, January 3, 1924, in *Restriction of Immigration: Hearings before the Committee on Immigration and Naturalization on H.R.5, H.R.101, and H.R.561*, HR 68-1, January 5, 1924, 570.

158. C. C. Brigham, "Intelligence Tests of Immigrant Groups," *Psychological Review* 37 (1930): 164.

159. F. L. Babbott, "Presidential Address: Eugenical Research and National Welfare," *Eugenical News* 12 (1927): 94.

160. L. M. Terman, "Feeble-minded Children in the Public Schools of California," *School and Society* 5 (1917): 161, 165.

161. H. H. Goddard, *The Kallikak Family* (New York: Macmillan, 1914), 50, 7.

162. Ibid., 7. The mistaken identification is cited in E. E. Doll, "Deborah Kallikak: 1889-1978, a Memorial," *Mental Retardation* 21 (1983): 30.

163. See J. D. Smith, *Minds Made Feeble* (Rockville Md.: Aspen, 1985), 26.

164. E. Kite, "Mental Defect as Found by the Fieldworker," *Journal of Psycho-Asthenics* 17 (1913): 151-52.

165. Goddard, *The Kallikak Family,* 73, 78, 87, 28.

166. Ibid., 15, 18, 23, 61-62, 30. In 1985 the psychologist J. David Smith tracked down the real name of the Kallikak family and conducted his own investigation of the defective branch. Like any other poor and uneducated family, it had its share of "ne'er-do-wells," according to Smith, but also a number of success stories—teacher, policeman, pilot. The "most recent flowering of the bad seed" was an honor student at a respected midwestern college. Smith, *Minds Made Feeble,* 113.

167. See A. Myerson, *The Inheritance of Mental Disease* (New York: Arno, 1976 [1925]), 77-80.

168. Goddard, *The Kallikak Family,* 77-78; East, *Heredity and Human Affairs,* 105.

169. For definition of the different levels, see H. H. Goddard, "Four Hundred Feeble-minded Children Classified by the Binet Method," *Journal of Psycho-Asthenics* 15 (1910): 26-27.

170. Goddard, *Human Efficiency and Levels of Intelligence,* 34.

171. L. F. Whitney, *The Case for Sterilization* (New York: Frederick A. Stokes, 1934), 145.

172. H. H. Laughlin, *The Legal and Administrative Aspects of Sterilization,* vol. 2 of *Report of the Committee to Study and to Report on the Best Practical Means of Cutting Off the Defective Germ-Plasm in the American Population* (Cold Spring Harbor, N.Y.: Eugenics Record Office, 1914), 133.

173. Whitney, *The Case for Sterilization,* 150.

174. Laughlin, *The Legal and Administrative Aspects of Sterilization,* 144-45. The later elaboration of the model law appears in Laughlin, *Eugenical Sterilization in the United States.*

175. Laughlin, *The Legal and Administrative Aspects of Sterilization,* 25.

176. The testimony is reprinted in H. H. Laughlin, *The Legal Status of Eugenical Sterilization* (Chicago: Municipal Court of Chicago, 1930), 16-17.

177. Whitney, *The Case for Sterilization,* 159.

178. On Carrie Buck's background, see S. J. Gould, "Carrie Buck's Daughter," *Natural History* 93 (July 1984): 17.

179. Laughlin, *The Legal Status of Eugenical Sterilization,* 19.

180. *Buck v. Bell* 274 US 200 (1927). Located in 1980, neither Carrie nor her sister Doris, who had also been sterilized without her knowledge, appeared "mentally deficient." Both women were literate and socially competent, if unsophisticated, citizens. Carrie's daughter, the "third generation of imbeciles," had been an average elementary school student prior to her death at age eight. On Carrie and Doris, see the interview in *Washington Post,* February 23, 1980, 1-2. On Carrie's daughter, see Gould, "Carrie Buck's Daughter," 18.

181. Laughlin, *The Legal Status of Eugenical Sterilization,* 92.

182. See N. Pastore, "The Army Intelligence Tests and Walter Lippmann," *Journal of the History of the Behavioral Sciences* 14 (1978): 317-18.

183. Lippmann's original position appeared in six segments in the *New Republic* 32 (1922): 213-15, 246-48, 275-77, 297-98, 328-30, and 33 (1922):

9-10. Terman's reply appeared in 33 (1922): 116-20, followed by a rejoinder from Lippmann in 33 (1923): 145. A last exchange between them occurred in the letters section, 33 (1923): 201. The entire debate is reprinted in N. J. Block and G. Dworkin, eds., *The IQ Controversy* (New York: Pantheon, 1976), 4-44.

184. P. F. Hall, "Aristocracy and Politics," *Journal of Heredity* 10 (1919): 166-68. See also A. Ireland, "Democracy and the Accepted Facts of Heredity," *Journal of Heredity* 9 (1918): 340-42.

185. E. L. Thorndike, "The Psychology of the Half-educated Man," *Harper's Magazine* 140 (1920): 666, 670.

186. E. L. Thorndike, "Intelligence and Its Uses," *Harper's Magazine* 140 (1920): 235.

187. From the poem "Die das Fleisch wegnehmen vom Tisch," in B. Brecht, *Gedischte*, vol. 4 (Frankfurt: Suhrkamp, 1961), 10; L. M. Terman, "The Psychological Determinist; or Democracy and the IQ," *Journal of Educational Psychology* 6 (1922): 62.

188. Goddard, *The Kallikak Family*, 108.

189. See H. T. Reeves, "The Later Years of a Noted Mental Defective," *Journal of Psycho-Asthenics* 43 (1938): 196-97.

190. H. H. Goddard, *Psychology of the Normal and Subnormal* (New York: Dodd, Mead, 1919), 234; Goddard, *Human Efficiency and Levels of Intelligence*, 99.

191. Goddard, *Psychology of the Normal and Subnormal*, 237-38.

192. Ibid., 243-44; Goddard, *Human Efficiency and Levels of Intelligence*, 99, 126-27.

193. Goddard, *Human Efficiency and Levels of Intelligence*, 100, 32.

194. G. B. Cutten, "The Reconstruction of Democracy," *School and Society* 16 (1922): 478-81.

195. McDougall, *Ethics and Some Modern World Problems*, 156-63.

196. J. M. Cattell, "Science, the Declaration, Democracy," *Scientific Monthly* 24 (1927): 201-2.

197. Letter from Thomas Jefferson to William Charles Jarvis, September 28, 1820, in *The Writings of Thomas Jefferson*, vol. 15, ed. A. E. Bergh (Washington, D.C.: Thomas Jefferson Memorial Association, 1907), 278.

198. Goddard, *The Kallikak Family*, 53.

199. L. M. Terman, V. E. Dickson, A. H. Sutherland, R. H. Franzen, C. R. Tupper, and G. Fernald, *Intelligence Tests and School Reorganization* (Yonkers-on-Hudson, N.Y.: World Book, 1923), 28.

200. L. M. Terman, *The Intelligence of School Children* (Cambridge, Mass.: Riverside, 1919), 269.

201. L. M. Terman, *The Measurement of Intelligence* (Cambridge, Mass.: Riverside, 1916), 24, 17.

202. L. M. Terman, "Adventures in Stupidity: A Partial Analysis of the Intellectual Inferiority of a College Student," *Scientific Monthly* 14 (1922): 24-25.

203. Terman, *The Measurement of Intelligence*, 91-92; Terman, "Adventures in Stupidity," 39-40.

204. Terman, *The Intelligence of School Children*, 268-70, 288.

205. Terman et al., *Intelligence Tests and School Reorganization*, 24.

206. F. N. Freeman, "Sorting the Students," *Educational Review* 68 (1924): 171.

207. Ibid., 170.

208. L. M. Terman, "The Great Conspiracy," *New Republic* 33 (1923): 116.

209. Quoted in N. Pastore, *The Politics of Nature* (New York: Kings Crown, 1949), 94. In his study of the relationship between scientists' opinions on the nature-nurture issue and their political positions, Pastore had categorized Terman as a conservative, and Terman wrote to Pastore contesting the characterization.

210. L. M. Terman, "Were We Born That Way?" *World's Work* 44 (1922): 659, 660; Terman, *The Measurement of Intelligence*, 91-92.

211. Popenoe and Johnson, *Applied Eugenics*, 136.

212. Quoted in D. Gasman, *The Scientific Origins of National Socialism* (London: Macdonald, 1971), 91, 95.

213. See F. Lenz's tribute to Plötz on his seventieth birthday, "Alfred Ploetz zum 70. Geburtstag am 22. August 1930," *Archiv für Rassen- und Gesellschaftsbiologie* 24 (1930): vii-viii.

214. See P. Weindling, "Weimar Eugenics: The Kaiser Wilhelm Institute for Anthropology, Human Heredity and Eugenics in Social Context," *Annals of Science* 42 (1985): 303-18.

215. See the reviews in the *New Statesman and Nation*, October 17, 1931, 482; and in the *Quarterly Review of Biology* 3 (1928): 136. See also reviews in the *Journal of Heredity* 14 (1923): 336; 19 (1928): 122; 22 (1931): 355; and in *Sociology and Social Research* 16 (1932): 281. One of the few critical reviews is by F. H. Hankins, *American Sociological Review* 3 (1938): 147-48, although it was easier to be critical in 1938 than prior to 1933.

216. Quoted in R. J. Lifton, *The Nazi Doctors* (New York: Basic Books, 1986), 46-47. See also F. Wertham, *A Sign for Cain* (New York: Macmillan, 1966), 161.

217. F. Lenz, *Menschliche Auslese und Rassenhygiene (Eugenik)*, vol. 2 of E. Baur, E. Fischer, and F. Lenz, *Menschliche Erblichkeitslehre und Rassenhygiene (Eugenik)*, 4th ed. (Munich: J. F. Lehmanns, 1932), 272-73, 279, 292.

218. Quoted in H. Krausnick, *Anatomy of the SS State*, trans. R. Barry, M. Jackson, and D. Long (New York: Walker, 1965), 16.

219. Lenz, *Menschliche Auslese und Rassenhygiene (Eugenik)*, 503.

220. E. Baur, E. Fischer, and F. Lenz, *Human Heredity*, trans. E. Paul and C. Paul (New York: Macmillan, 1931), 655-56, 666.

221. Ibid., 667-77.

222. Ibid., 693.

223. Ibid., 667-77, 699.

224. H. F. K. Günther, *The Racial Elements of European History* (Port Washington, N.Y.: Kennikat, 1970 [1927]), 51-61, 195.

225. Ibid., 78-79.

226. Ibid., 260, 245, 267.

227. Ploetz quoted in Lenz, "Alfred Ploetz zum 70. Geburtstag," xiii; ibid., vii-viii, xiv. See also Lenz, *Menschliche Auslese und Rassenhygiene (Eugenik)*, 540.

228. Quoted in R. Proctor, *Racial Hygiene* (Cambridge, Mass.: Harvard University Press, 1988), 60.

229. A. Hitler, *Mein Kampf*, trans. Ralph Manheim (Cambridge, Mass.: Riverside, 1971), 402.

230. See Proctor, *Racial Hygiene*, 27, although Proctor gives the date, incorrectly, as 1932.

231. T. Lang, "Der Nationalsozialismus als politischer Ausdruck unserer biologischen Kenntnis," *Nationalsozialistische Monatshefte* 1 (December 1930): 393, 395, 396, 397. The tribute to Ploetz appears in the same issue on 417-18.

232. Reported in *New York Times*, December 8, 1931, 1.

233. Lenz, *Menschliche Auslese und Rassenhygiene (Eugenik)*, 417, 418-19.

234. F. Lenz, "Die Stellung des Nationalsozialismus zur Rassenhygiene," *Archiv für Rassen- und Gesellschaftsbiologie* 25 (1931): 300, 301, 304, 302, 307, 308.

235. "Ansprache des Herrn Reichsministers des Innern Dr. Wilhelm Frick auf der ersten Sitzung des Sachverständigenbeirats für Bevölkerungs-und Rassenpolitik," *Archiv für Rassen- und Gesellschaftsbiologie* 27 (1933): 415, 416.

236. Ibid., 419.

237. Proctor, *Racial Hygiene*, 41.

238. Quoted in B. Müller-Hill, *Murderous Science* (Oxford: Oxford University Press, 1988), 30. Lenz's reservations are also described in the Foreign Letters section of the *Journal of the American Medical Association* 104 (1935): 2110.

239. Quoted in Proctor, *Racial Hygiene*, 105.

240. Quoted in ibid., 45.

241. Quoted in Müller-Hill, *Murderous Science*, 10.

242. E. Rüdin, "Aufgaben und Ziele der Deutschen Gesellschaft für Rassenhygiene," *Archiv für Rassen- und Gesellschaftsbiologie* 28 (1934): 228-29.

243. "Ansprache des Herrn Reichsministers des Innern," 412, 419.

244. See M. Weinrich, *Hitler's Professors* (New York: Yiddish Scientific Institute, 1946), 40-41.

245. See Proctor, *Racial Hygiene*, 197.

246. Foreign Letters section of the *Journal of the American Medical Association* 103 (1934): 501; 106 (1936): 1931-32; 107 (1936): 600-601; 105 (1935): 1998-99. See also Proctor, *Racial Hygiene*, 103, 131-32.

247. K. Holler, "The Nordic Movement in Germany," *Eugenical News* 17 (1932): 119

248. "Eugenical Sterilization in Germany," *Eugenical News* 18 (1933): 89, 90.

249. P. Popenoe, "The German Sterilization Law," *Journal of Heredity* 25 (1934): 257, 259, 260.

250. Whitney, *The Case for Sterilization*, 136-38, 205.

251. Dr. Brauss, Dortmund health officer, quoted in *New York Times*, May 5, 1933, 9.

252. See Proctor, *Racial Hygiene*, 101, 361.

253. W. Frick, "German Population and Race Politics," *Eugenical News* 19 (1934): 33-38.

254. "Eugenics in Germany," *Eugenical News* 19 (1934): 40-43; "Eugenical Propaganda in Germany," 45.

255. "German Eugenics, 1934," *Eugenical News* 19 (1934): 140.

256. Quoted in *New York Times,* August 2, 1933, 6.

257. Grant, *The Passing of the Great Race,* 49.

258. M. Grant, *The Conquest of a Continent* (New York: Charles Scribner's Sons, 1933). On the complimentary copies, see memo from R. V. Coleman to Miss Wyckoff, October 26, 1933, Scribner's Archives, Princeton University Library, Princeton, N.J.; on the claims of Jewish influence, see letters from Scribner's to Grant, April 23, 1934; Grant to Maxwell Perkins, May 14, 1934; and Col. Laurence Timpson to Grant, May 4, 1934, all in the Scribner's Archives. Grant's complaint had some substance; the archives also contain a December 19, 1933, circular from R. E. Gutstadt of the Anti-Defamation League to publishers of Anglo-Jewish periodicals, requesting that they refrain from review or any other comment on the book. On the German version of Grant's book, see Chase, *The Legacy of Malthus,* 343.

259. From Pearl's letter to Lawrence J. Henderson, his friend and colleague at Harvard, quoted in E. Barkan, *The Retreat of Scientific Racism* (Cambridge: Cambridge University Press, 1992), 217.

260. Wilson, "A Study in Jewish Psychopathology," 264–71.

261. Ross, *The Old World in the New,* 145; Brigham, *A Study of American Intelligence,* 208.

262. K. L. Roberts, *Why Europe Leaves Home* (New York: Bobbs-Merrill, 1922); *Boston Sunday Herald,* June 26, 1921, D1.

263. Letter from Galton to the Swiss scientist Alphonse de Candolle, October 17, 1884, in K. Pearson, *The Life, Letters and Labours of Francis Galton,* vol. 2, (Cambridge: Cambridge University Press, 1914–30), 208–9.

264. On Pearson's praise for Hitler, see G. L. Mosse, *Toward the Final Solution* (New York: Howard Fertig, 1978), 76. The characterization of Jews appears in K. Pearson and M. Moul, "The Problem of Alien Immigration into Great Britain Illustrated by an Examination of Russian and Polish Jewish Children," *Annals of Eugenics* 1 (1925): 7, 126.

265. Ross, *The Old World in the New,* 154; C. B. Davenport, "Comparative Social Traits of Various Races," *School and Society* 14 (1921): 348, 345.

266. C. G. Campbell, "The German Racial Policy," *Eugenical News* 21 (1936): 27, 25.

267. The 1938 laws are summarized in Proctor, *Racial Hygiene,* 155.

268. See R. D. Bird and G. Allen, "The Papers of Harry Hamilton Laughlin, Eugenicist," *Journal of the History of Biology* 14 (1982): 352.

269. T. L. Stoddard, *Into the Darkness* (New York: Duell, Sloan, and Pearce, 1940), 285.

270. H. H. Laughlin, *Immigration and Conquest* (New York: Special Committee on Immigration and Naturalization of the Chamber of Commerce of the State of New York, 1939), 20–23, 91–95. On the attempts to waive the regulations, see A. D. Morse, *While 6,000,000 Died* (New York: Random House, 1968).

271. K. Lorenz, "Durch Domestikation verursachte Störungen arteigenen Verhaltens," *Zeitschrift für Angewandte Psychologie und Charakterkunde* 59 (1940): 69, 68.

272. See Wertham, *A Sign for Cain*, 159, 180; and Lifton, *The Nazi Doctors*, 51-66.

273. See Müller-Hill, *Murderous Science*, 23.

274. A. Hitler, *Hitler's Secret Book*, trans. A. Attansio (New York: Grove Press, 1961), 23. See also N. H. Baynes, ed., *The Speeches of Adolph Hitler* (New York: Howard Fertig, 1969), 691-93; and Hitler, *Mein Kampf*, 150, 305-9.

275. On the alternate measures, see Proctor, *Racial Hygiene*, 206.

276. Quoted in Müller-Hill, *Murderous Science*, 39-40.

277. O. F. von Verschuer, "Was kann der Historiker, der Genealoge und der Statistiker zur Erforschung des biologischen Problems der Judenfrage beitragen?" *Forschungen zur Judenfrage* 2 (1937): 218.

278. Quoted in Proctor, *Racial Hygiene*, 211.

279. Quoted in Müller-Hill, *Murderous Science*, 61.

280. Quoted in ibid., 36-37.

281. Quoted in ibid., 80. On the institute and its opening conference, see also Weinrich, *Hitler's Professors*, 98-113.

282. Quoted in Proctor, *Racial Hygiene*, 295.

283. Quoted in Müller-Hill, *Murderous Science*, 61.

284. Quoted in ibid., 79.

285. Wertham, *A Sign for Cain*, 169-74.

286. Quoted in Lifton, *The Nazi Doctors*, 114-17, 31.

287. Ibid., 339-40, 347-48, 357-58, 362; Müller-Hill, *Murderous Science*, 70-73.

288. "Otmar Freiherr von Verschuer 60 Jahre alt," *Homo* 7 (1956): 65-73.

289. Von Verschuer's earlier remarks are quoted in L. C. Dunn, "Cross Currents in the History of Human Genetics," *American Journal of Human Genetics* 14 (1962): 8. Von Verschuer's response appears in a letter to the editor, in ibid., 309-10. Other information on his background is found in P. Weindling, "Race, Blood and Politics," *Times Higher Education Supplement*, July 19, 1985; and in Weindling, "Weimar Eugenics."

290. Quoted in Müller-Hill, *Murderous Science*, 189.

291. Dunn, "Cross Currents in the History of Human Genetics," 8; Lenz, letter to the editor, *Journal of Human Genetics* 14 (1962): 309.

292. In 1943, for example, Fischer coauthored *World Jewry in Antiquity*, which concluded, "Always, at all times, in the first century as in the twentieth, world Jewry is the dream of exclusive world domination on earth and in the hereafter!" Quoted in Weinrich, *Hitler's Professors*, 217.

293. Quoted in *The Race Concept: Results of an Inquiry* (Paris: UNESCO, 1952), 30-31, 46, 50.

294. Quoted in ibid., 32.

295. Quoted in ibid., 35.

296. See, for example, H. Morgenthau, *Ambassador Morgenthau's Story* (New York: Doubleday, 1918); D. Corn, "Report from the Inferno," *Nation* (May 28, 1990): 748-49; and Wertham, *A Sign for Cain*, 140

297. J. von Lang, ed., *Eichmann Interrogated: Transcipts from the Archives*

of the Israeli Police, trans. R. Manheim (New York: Farrar, Straus, and Giroux, 1983), 149, 91.

298. At about the same time, a procedure for legally killing "feebleminded" in the United States was recommended by Dr. Foster Kennedy. Only "those hopeless ones who should never have been born—Nature's mistakes"—were to "be relieved of the burden of living" in Kennedy's plan. F. Kennedy, "The Problem of Social Control of the Congenital Defective," *American Journal of Psychiatry* 99 (1942): 14, 15.

299. Wertham, *A Sign for Cain,* 157, 160.

300. Popenoe and Johnson, *Applied Eugenics,* 302-3.

301. See Chase, *The Legacy of Malthus,* 299-300.

302. "White America," *Eugenical News* 9 (1924): 3; E. S. Cox, "Repatriation of the American Negro," *Eugenical News* 21 (1936): 133-38.

303. E. A. Hooten, *Apes, Men and Morons* (New York: G. P. Putnam's Sons, 1937), 229-31.

304. E. L. Thorndike, *Human Nature and the Social Order* (New York: Macmillan, 1940), 582, 596-97, 352.

305. Ibid., 371-73, 370.

306. Ibid., 959, 488, 492, 670, 953.

307. Ibid., 690, 691

Chapter 4: Science Giveth and It Taketh Away

1. From the UNESCO Statement on Race, issued in Paris, July 18, 1950, reprinted in UNESCO's *The Race Question in Modern Science* (New York: Columbia University Press, 1961), 498.

2. From the UNESCO Statement on Race, issued in Paris, June 8, 1951, reprinted in ibid., 504.

3. T. Hobbes, *Leviathan* (New York: Bobbs-Merrill, 1958 [1651]), 127.

4. O. Klineberg, "Race and Psychology," in UNESCO, *The Race Question in Modern Science,* 423. See also O. Klineberg, "Race and I.Q." *UNESCO Courier* (November 1971): 6.

5. For a detailed account of the black experience under segregation, see N. R. McMillen, *Dark Journey: Black Mississippians in the Age of Jim Crow* (Urbana: University of Illinois Press, 1989).

6. J. Bardin, "The Psychological Factor in Southern Race Problems," *Popular Science Monthly* 83 (1913): 373.

7. Quoted in *New York Times,* October 27, 1921, 11.

8. The supposedly degenerative consequences of interracial liaisons has been a source of alarm to some whites at least as far back as the Elizabethan era. Iago taunted Brabantio (*Othello,* I, i, lines 87-92, 110-13) with the thought that "Even now, now, very now, an old black ram / Is tupping your white ewe. Arise, Arise! / . . . the devil will make a grandsire of you. / . . . you'll / have your daughter covered with a Barbary horse; / you'll have your nephews neigh to you; you'll have / coursers for cousins and gennets for germans." (Coursers and *gennets* were types of horses; *germans* was a term for near relatives.)

9. W. J. Cash, *The Mind of the South* (New York: Alfred A. Knopf, 1941), 116.

10. "Amalgamation," *De Bow's Review,* n.s., 4 (July 1860): 14; W. B. Smith, *The Color Line* (New York: Negro Universities Press, 1969 [1905]), 24.

11. See W. D. Zabel, "Interracial Marriage and the Law," *Atlantic Monthly* (October 1965): 79.

12. Cash, *The Mind of the South,* 116.

13. From South Carolina, *Briggs v. Elliott* 98 F. Supp 529 (1951) and 103 F. Supp 920 (1952); from Virginia, *Davis v. School Board of Prince Edward County* 103 F. Supp 337 (1952); from Delaware, *Gebhart v. Belton* 91 A.2d 137, 152 (1952); from Kansas, *Brown v. Board of Education of Topeka* 98 F. Supp 797 (1951).

14. See R. Kluger, *Simple Justice* (New York: Alfred A. Knopf, 1976), 540.

15. M. Deutscher and I. Chein, "The Psychological Effects of Enforced Segregation: A Survey of Social Science Opinion," *Journal of Psychology* 26 (1948): 259, 260.

16. See "Stress Claims Are Making Business Jumpy," *Business Week* (October 14, 1985): 44.

17. Deutscher and Chein, "The Psychological Effects of Enforced Segregation," 279, 285.

18. I. Chein, "What Are the Psychological Effects of Segregation under Conditions of Equal Facilities?" *International Journal of Opinion and Attitude Research* 3 (1949): 230.

19. See Kluger, *Simple Justice,* a thorough and fascinating account of the legal campaign to overturn segregated schools, which includes a detailed discussion of the roles played by each of the scientists.

20. K. B. Clark and M. P. Clark, "Racial Identification and Preference in Negro Children," in *Readings in Social Psychology,* ed. E. E. Maccoby, T. M. Newcomb, and E. L. Hartley (New York: Holt, Rinehart and Winston, 1958), 602; Clark's testimony quoted in Kluger, *Simple Justice,* 354.

21. "The Effects of Segregation and the Consequences of Desegregation: A Social Science Statement," appendix to appellants' briefs in *Brown v. Board of Education,* reprinted in *Minnesota Law Review* 37 (1953): 435.

22. Clark and Clark, "Racial Identification and Preference in Negro Children," 602–11.

23. Quoted in L. Friedman, *Argument: The Oral Argument before the Supreme Court in Brown v. Board of Education* (New York: Chelsea House, 1969), 58–59.

24. Even in cases where specific harmful effects could be documented, judges have relied on their knowledge as human beings rather than on scientific evidence to make constitutional judgments. The Eighth Circuit Court of Appeals, for example, needed no testimony from a gastroenterologist to determine that subjecting inmates to enforced medication with a drug that induced vomiting for an extended period of time violated the Eighth Amendment prohibition against cruel and unusual punishment. See *Knecht v. Gillman* 488 F.2d 1136 (1973).

25. Quoted in Friedman, *Argument,* 65.

26. *Brown v. Board of Education* 347 U.S. 493–94 (1954).

27. *Plessy v. Ferguson* 163 U.S. 551 (1896).

28. E. Cahn, "Jurisprudence," *New York University Law Quarterly* 30 (1955): 160.

29. The quotation is from *Plessy v. Ferguson*. In the interview described in Kluger, *Simple Justice*, 706, Warren paraphrased it as, "If there was any harm intended, it was solely in the mind of the Negro."

30. *New York Times*, May 18, 1954, 1.

31. Quoted in Cahn, "Jurisprudence," 157.

32. K. B. Clark, "Desegregation: An Appraisal of the Evidence," *Journal of Social Issues* 9 (1953): 3, 8.

33. K. B. Clark, "The Desegregation Cases: Criticisms of the Social Scientist's Role," *Villanova Law Review* 5 (1959): 234.

34. K. B. Clark, "The Social Scientist as an Expert Witness in Civil Rights Litigation," *Social Problems* 1 (1953): 10.

35. Quoted in *New York Times*, June 11, 1972, 37.

36. P. Kurland, "The Legal Background of the School Segregation Cases," in K. B. Clark, *Prejudice and Your Child* (Boston: Beacon, 1963), 154, 143.

37. P. L. Rosen, *The Supreme Court and Social Science* (Urbana: University of Illinois Press, 1972), 187, 153.

38. Cahn, "Jurisprudence," 167.

39. Clark, "Desegregation: An Appraisal of the Evidence," 9-76. See also K. B. Clark, "The Social Scientists, the Brown Decision, and Contemporary Confusion," Preface to Friedman, *Argument*, xxxvii; and K. B. Clark, "The Role of the Social Sciences in Desegregation," Appendix 5 in Clark, *Prejudice and Your Child*, 214-19.

40. *Brown v. Board of Education* 349 U.S. 301 (1954).

41. See *Congressional Record* (May 27, 1954): 7251-57; (July 23, 1954): 11522-27; (May 25, 1955): 6963-64; (May 26, 1955): 7120-24.

42. E. Cook and W. I. Potter, "The School Segregation Cases: Opposing the Opinion of the Supreme Court," *American Bar Association Journal* 42 (1956): 316.

43. C. Putnam, *Race and Reason* (Washington, D.C.: Public Affairs Press, 1961), 97-98, 35.

44. The Twain quote is from *Pudd'nhead Wilson* (New York: Harper and Brothers, 1922), 12. On interracial laws, see Zabel, "Interracial Marriage and the Law"; and *U.S. News and World Report* (October 26, 1964): 10.

45. *Loving v. Virginia* 388 U.S. 1 (1966).

46. H. R. Sass, "Mixed Schools and Mixed Blood," *Atlantic Monthly* (November 1956): 49.

47. *New York Times*, September 3, 1963, 27; *New York Times*, September 4, 1963, 27. The woman, Charlayne Hunter, later became the well-known journalist Charlayne Hunter-Gault.

48. W. C. George, *The Biology of the Race Problem* (Report prepared by Commission of the Governor of Alabama, distributed by the National Putnam Letters Committee, New York, 1962), 64.

49. E. van den Haag, "Social Science Testing in the Desegregation Cases—A Reply to Professor Kenneth Clark," *Villanova Law Review* 6 (1960): 71.

50. "Testimony on South West Africa," *Pleadings, International Court of Justice* 10 (1966): 130-82, 425-79.

51. A. J. Gregor, "On the Nature of Prejudice," *Eugenics Review* 52 (1961): 219, 222.

52. A. J. Gregor, "The Law, Social Science, and School Segregation: An Assessment," *Case-Western Reserve Law Review* 14 (1963): 629, 635.

53. C. P. Armstrong and A. J. Gregor, "Integrated Schools and Negro Character Development," *Psychiatry* 27 (1964): 70.

54. F. C. J. McGurk, "A Scientist's Report on Race Differences," *U.S. News and World Report* (September 21, 1956): 96, 92.

55. "Statement by 18 Social Scientists," *U.S. News and World Report* (October 26, 1956): 74-75.

56. For Garrett's opinion of Clark, see Kluger, *Simple Justice,* 502. Clark's contributions are summarized in *American Psychologist* 43 (1988): 263-64.

57. H. E. Garrett, letter to the editor, *Science* 101 (1945): 16-17, 404-6; H. E. Garrett, "Negro-White Differences in Mental Ability in the United States," *Scientific Monthly* 65 (1947): 333.

58. H. E. Garrett, letter to the editor, *Science* 135 (1962): 984.

59. H. E. Garrett, "The Scientific Racism of Juan Comas," *Mankind Quarterly* 2 (1961): 106.

60. H. E. Garrett, "Klineberg's 'Negro-White Differences in Intelligence Test Performance,' " *Mankind Quarterly* 4 (1964): 222.

61. H. E. Garrett, "Review of *Heredity and the Nature of Man* (by T. Dobzhansky)," *Mankind Quarterly* 6 (1966): 241.

62. H. E. Garrett, letter to the editor, *Current Anthropology* 2 (1961): 320.

63. Interview with Garrett, *U.S. News and World Report* (November 18, 1963): 93.

64. H. E. Garrett, "The Equalitarian Dogma," *Mankind Quarterly* 1 (1961): 253, 254, 255.

65. See Grant's letter to Maxwell Perkins, March 7 (no year given but probably 1924), complaining about Boas, in Scribner's Archives, Princeton University Library, Princeton, N.J.

66. Garrett, "The Equalitarian Dogma," 256, 257.

67. D. J. Ingle, letter to the editor, *Science* 133 (1961): 960; D. J. Ingle, *I Want to See the Elephant* (New York: Vantage, 1963), 205-28 (quote on 205).

68. *U.S. News and World Report* (September 16, 1963): 96-97.

69. D. J. Ingle, letter to the editor, *Science* 146 (1964): 1530. See also D. J. Ingle, "Racial Differences and the Future," *Science* 146 (1964): 376-78.

70. Ingle, *I Want to See the Elephant,* 79.

71. Noted in R. J. Sickels, *Race, Marriage and the Law* (Albequerque: University of New Mexico Press, 1972), 105.

72. H. E. Garrett, "One Psychologist's View of 'Equality of the Races,' " *U.S. News and World Report* (August 14, 1961): 72-74. Though retitled in the magazine, this was the same article that appeared in *Perspectives in Biology and Medicine* as "The Equalitarian Dogma."

73. Ingle, *I Want to See the Elephant,* 299-300.

74. H. E. Garrett, "The Equalitarian Dogma," *Perspectives in Biology and Medicine* 4 (1961): 480.

75. D. J. Ingle, "Editorial: Science versus Value Commitments," *Perspectives in Biology and Medicine* 4 (1961): 392.

76. H. E. Garrett, letter to the editor, *Perspectives in Biology and Medicine* 5 (1961): 264.

77. See Ingle's letters to the readers, *Perspectives in Biology and Medicine* 5 (1962): 130–31, 382–84.

78. Ingle, "Racial Differences and the Future," 378.

79. Putnam, *Race and Reason*, 21, 8, 9.

80. Ibid., 16.

81. Ibid., 23.

82. Garrett, "The Scientific Racism of Juan Comas," 106.

83. C. Putnam, *Race and Reality* (Washington, D.C.: Public Affairs Press, 1967), 21, 24. Announcing the "real names" of Jews was a common tactic to imply an un-American background, especially during the McCarthy era. When, for example, a petition on behalf of the Hollywood Ten was forwarded to Congress, Representative John Rankin from Mississippi reported the true identities of some of the famous signers: June Havoc was really June Hovick; Danny Kaye's real name was David Daniel Kaminsky; Eddie Cantor was born Edward Isskowitz; and Edward G. Robinson was, in fact, Emanuel Goldenberg. "There are others too numerous to mention," the Congressman declared; "they are attacking the [House Un-American Affairs] Committee for doing its duty in trying to protect this country and save the American people from the horrible fate the Communists have meted out to the unfortunate Christian people of Europe." Quoted in V. S. Navasky, *Naming Names* (New York: Penguin, 1981), 369.

84. Putnam, *Race and Reason*, 47–48, 86.

85. Ibid., 117, 28.

86. Ibid., 7, 19, 20.

87. Quoted in *New York Times*, December 2, 1961, 47.

88. Putnam, *Race and Reason*, 94, 92, 68; Putnam, *Race and Reality*, 172.

89. See N. R. McMillen, *The Citizens' Council* (Urbana: University of Illinois Press, 1971), 166.

90. On the Virginia resolution, see *New York Times*, February 18, 1962, 62. The resolutions in Louisiana and Mississippi were reported in *Science* 134 (1961): 1868. For Byrd's note, see the addendum to T. Dobzhansky, "A Bogus 'Science' of Race Prejudice," *Journal of Heredity* 52 (1961): 190.

91. Dobzhansky, "A Bogus 'Science' of Race Prejudice," 189–90.

92. Quoted in M. H. Fried, letter to the editor, *New York Times*, October 10, 1962, 46.

93. Reprinted in *Current Anthropology* 4 (1962): 445.

94. Described in Putnam, *Race and Reality*, 32.

95. Patterson's telegram was quoted in *New York Times*, September 28, 1960, 1. On the grant, see *New York Times*, November 3, 1961, 45; and *Science* 134 (1961): 1868.

96. George, *The Biology of the Race Problem*, 1, 13.

97. R. B. Bean, "Some Racial Peculiarities of the Negro Brain," *American Journal of Anatomy* 5 (1906): 380.

98. Ibid., 409.

99. Unsigned editorial, *American Medicine* (April 1907): 197-98.

100. R. B. Bean, "The Negro Brain," *Century* 50 (1906): 784, 779-80.

101. F. P. Mall, "On Several Anatomical Characters of the Human Brain," *American Journal of Anatomy* 9 (1909): 1-32.

102. George, *The Biology of the Race Problem*, 30-32.

103. C. S. Coon, *The Origin of Races* (New York: Alfred A. Knopf, 1962).

104. Putnam, *Race and Reality*, 75.

105. George, *The Biology of the Race Problem*, 60-63.

106. On the fossil evidence, see S. J. Gould, *The Flamingo's Smile* (New York: W. W. Norton, 1985), 192. On the analysis of mitochondrial DNA, see R. L. Cann, M. Stoneking, and A. C. Wilson, "Mitochondrial DNA and Human Evolution," *Nature* 325 (1987): 31-36.

107. R. B. Bean, *The Races of Man* (New York: University Society, 1932), 37, 30-35.

108. See, for example, H. F. Osborn, "The Evolution of Human Races," *Natural History* 26 (January-February 1926): 5.

109. George, *The Biology of the Race Problem*, 1, 78-79.

110. Ibid., 85, 86.

111. "Science and the Race Problem," Report of the AAAS Committee on Science in the Promotion of Human Welfare, *Science* 142 (1963): 560, 559.

112. Putnam, *Race and Reality*, 66.

113. *New York Times*, October 3, 1962, 33.

114. Quoted in I. A. Newby, *Challenge to the Court* (Baton Rouge: Louisiana State University Press, 1969), 196-97.

115. *Stell v. Savannah-Chatham Board of Education* 220 F. Supp 676 (1963).

116. Ibid., 668-75.

117. Putnam, *Race and Reality*, 75; "Mixing Schools: Why One Federal Court Refused," *U.S. News and World Report* (May 27, 1963): 88-90; Putnam, *Race and Rality*, 82, 83.

118. *Stell v. Savannah-Chatham County Board of Education* 333 F. 2d 61 (1964).

119. *Evers v. Jackson School District* 232 F. Supp 241 (1964).

120. H. E. Garrett, *Race: A Reply to Race and Intelligence: A Scientific Evaluation by the Anti-Defamation League of B'Nai Brith* (Washington, D.C.: National Putnam Letters Committee, 1964), 8.

121. H. E. Garrett, *How Classroom Desegregation Will Work*, reprinted in *Citizen* (October 1965): 13-14.

122. Quoted in *Newsweek* (May 30, 1966): 63.

123. H. E. Garrett, *Breeding Down* (Richmond, Va.: Patrick Henry Press, n.d.), 4.

124. Noted in S. L. Chorover, *From Genesis to Genocide* (Cambridge, Mass.: MIT Press, 1979), 48.

125. H. E. Garrett, *IQ and Racial Differences* (Cape Canaveral, Fla.: Howard Allen, 1973), 6; H. H. Goddard, *Human Efficiency and Levels of Intelligence* (Princeton, N.J.: Princeton University Press, 1920), 99.

126. E. Baur, E. Fischer, and F. Lenz, *Human Heredity,* trans. E. Paul and C. Paul (New York: Macmillan, 1931), 675.

127. A. Hitler, *Mein Kampf,* trans. Ralph Manheim (Cambridge, Mass.: Riverside, 1943), 316, 325.

128. For example, the *New Order*—the newsletter of an American group that calls itself the "NSDAP/Auslandsorganisation" (foreign organization of the Third Reich's Nazi party) "acknowledge[s] Adolf Hitler as our Führer and strive[s] to continue his work" (no. 96 [January/February 1992]: 3)—recommends *Race and Reason* to its readers, along with *The Hitler We Loved and Why, Hitler at My Side,* and Henry E. Garrett's *I.Q. and Racial Differences* (no. 94 [September/October 1991]: 2).

129. F. P. Yockey, *Imperium* (New York: Truth Seeker, 1962). The characterization of *Imperium* is from J. George and L. Wilcox, *Nazis, Communists, Klansmen, and Others on the Fringe* (Buffalo, N.Y.: Prometheus Books, 1992), 252. The quote from Carto appears in C. H. Simonds, "The Strange Story of Willis Carto," *National Review* (September 10, 1971): 979.

130. "Statement of Dr. Robert Kuttner," in *Hearings before Subcommittee No. 5 of the Committee on the Judiciary on Miscellaneous Proposals regarding the Civil Rights of Persons within the Jurisdiction of the United States,* HR 88-1, July 19, 1963, 1954-65, 1971.

131. R. E. Kuttner, "Northern Light on Southern Scene," Address to the New Orleans Leadership Conference, reprinted in *Citizen* (December 1972): 24.

132. See the welcome to "the new *Mercury,*" telling the readership from these other publications that "they will see many of their friends on our new Board of Contributing Editors, so they should feel at home," in *American Mercury* (June 1966): 8.

133. F. P. Mintz, *The Liberty Lobby and the American Right* (Westport, Conn.: Greenwood, 1985), 105; R. E. Kuttner, "What Do We Owe the Negroes?" *American Mercury* (March 1967): 8-9.

134. A. J. Gregor, "Nationalism Socialism and Race," *European* 11 (1958): 284-86.

135. The certificate of incorporation (February 21, 1959), Judge Shapiro's memorandum on application (May 13, 1959), Avins's memorandum of law in support of application (June 3, 1959), and Judge Shapiro's responding memorandum in matter of application (July 9, 1959) are all on file in Supreme Court of the Borough of Queens, Queens, N.Y.

136. Articles of incorporation of the IAAEE (April 23, 1959) are on file with the State Tax Commission of Maryland.

137. *Time* (June 16, 1947): 29.

138. See D. Perkins's review of Tansill's *Back Door to War,* "FDR Gets the Blame," *New York Times,* May 11, 1952, VII, 3.

139. The Executive Committee and, eventually, the "founders" are listed at the beginning or end of each IAAEE "Reprint."

140. Certificate of incorporation of the Pioneer Fund (February 27, 1937) is on file with the Department of State, State of New York.

141. Reported in R. W. May, "Genetics and Subversion," *Nation* 190 (May 14, 1960): 420-21.

142. The IAAEE's "Statement of Aims and Objectives" is also found on the inside cover of its "Reprints."

143. J. Scudder, S. B. Bhonslay, A. Himmelstein, and J. G. Gorman, "Sensitising Antigens as Factors in Blood Transfusions," *Mankind Quarterly* 1 (1960): 99–100.

144. R. Gayre, *Teuton and Slav on the Polish Frontier* (London: Eyre and Spottiswoode, 1944), 30, 11–12.

145. See M. Billig, *Psychology, Racism and Fascism*, Searchlight Booklet (Birmingham, England: A.F.&R. Publications, 1979), 7, 13.

146. R. Gayre of Gayre, "Review of Gunther's *The Religious Attitudes of the Indo-Europeans,*" *Mankind Quarterly* 9 (1969): 143–44.

147. See B. Skerlj's letter to the editor, quoting Gayre's reaction to any suggestion of association with the term *Nazi*, in *Man* 60 (1960): 172.

148. R. Gayre, "A Reply to *Challenge to the Court,*" in Newby, *Challenge to the Court*, 319.

149. R. R. Gates, *Heredity in Man* (London: Constable, 1929), 329.

150. N. A. Thompson, letter to the editor, *Eugenics Review* 27 (1936): 351.

151. R. R. Gates, letter to the editor, *Nature* 170 (1952): 896.

152. D. Purves, "The Evolutionary Basis of Race Consciousness," *Mankind Quarterly* 1 (1960): 53–54.

153. E. R. Hall, "Zoological Subspecies of Man," *Mankind Quarterly* 1 (1960): 115–19.

154. Skerlj's resignation and Gates's response are both described in the Skerlj's letter to the editor, *Man* 60 (1960): 172.

155. E. Nevin, "The Black Brainwash in America," *Mankind Quarterly* 7 (1967): 233, 234.

156. W. A. Massey, "The New Fanatics," *Mankind Quarterly* 3 (1962): 79–81.

157. E. E. Hoyt, "The Family of Mankind—Some New Light?" *Mankind Quarterly* 2 (1961): 14.

158. W. Arnold, "The Evolution of Man in Relation to That of the Earth," *Mankind Quarterly* 10 (1969): 90, 94, 96.

159. R. Ford, "Review of E. S. Cox's *White America,*" *Mankind Quarterly* 7 (1966): 118–19. The review also praised *White America*'s "tersely presented style with clear cut austerity of phrasing." Ironically, Madison Grant had attempted to convince Scribner's to publish the book in 1924, only to be told by the publisher that the work was "highly regarded" for its "serious tone" but that Cox just "does not know . . . how to write." Grant acknowledged that "I am afraid what you say about Mr. Cox's book is only too true." Quotes from correspondence between Madison Grant and Maxwell Perkins, November 7, 13, and 14, 1924, in Scribner's Archives, Princeton University Library, Princeton, N.J.

160. H. B. Isherwood, "Review of E. Young's *Two World's—Not One: Race and Civilization,*" *Mankind Quarterly* 11 (1970): 61.

161. Young's book and the South African Broadcasting Company are both quoted in C. C. Aronsfeld, "The Theory of Prejudice," *Patterns of Prejudice* 5 (1971): 26.

162. R. Gayre of Gayre, "Review of R. P. Oliver's *Christianity and the Survival of the West,*" *Mankind Quarterly* 15 (1975): 227.

163. *Eugenics Review* 52 (1960): 136.

164. R. E. Kuttner, ed., *Race and Modern Science* (New York: Social Science Press, 1967), dedication page, xv.

165. L. C. Dunn, "Review of *Race and Modern Science,*" *Eugenics Quarterly* 15 (1968): 298.

166. C. Gini, "Race and Sociology," in *Race and Modern Science,* ed. Kuttner, 264, 270-71; A. J. Gregor, "Evolutionary Theory, Race and Society," in ibid., 279, 287; L. Gedda, "A Study of Racial and Subracial Crossing," in ibid., 123.

167. The literature list is available from Noontide Press, Los Angeles, Calif.

168. On the *The Protocols of the Learned Elders of Zion,* see N. Cohn, *Warrant for Genocide* (London: Eyre and Spottiswoode, 1967); and C. Sykes, "The Protocols of the Elders of Zion," *History Today* 17 (1967): 81-88.

169. See, for example, H. Kiesel, "Race, the 'Nation of Europe' and Ideology: A Critique," *Mankind Quarterly* 12 (1971): 114.

170. W. Robertson, *Ventiliations* (Cape Canaveral, Fla.: Howard Allen, 1974), 73.

Chapter 5: "Unaided by Eugenic Foresight"

1. R. E. Kuttner, letter to the editor, *Perspectives in Biology and Medicine* 11 (1968): 707.

2. W. B. Smith, *The Color Line* (New York: Negro Universities Press, 1969 [1905]), 237, 246.

3. P. Popenoe, "The Lockstep in the Schools," *Journal of Heredity* 18 (1927): 63.

4. A. E. Wiggam, *The New Decalogue of Science* (New York: Blue Ribbon Books, 1923), 76.

5. L. Hogben, *Nature and Nurture* (New York: W. W. Norton, 1939), 33.

6. D. J. Ingle, "Racial Differences and the Future," *Science* 146 (1964): 378.

7. D. J. Ingle, *I Want to See the Elephant* (New York: Vantage, 1963), 213.

8. D. J. Ingle, *Who Should Have Children?* (New York: Bobbs-Merrill, 1973), 115, 102. Though Ingle's suggestion might have seemed farfetched at the time, in December 1990 the Food and Drug Administration approved Norplant, a set of matchstick-size capsules that after being implanted just beneath the skin of a woman's upper arm would slowly release a long-term contraceptive into the bloodstream. The approval was immediately followed by a discussion of "incentives" that might be offered to welfare mothers to use the new technique. See *Time* (December 24, 1990): 66; and the editorial in *Philadelphia Inquirer,* December 12, 1990.

9. See [D. Dickson,] "Case for the Plaintiff," *New Scientist* (February 22, 1973): 434.

10. Shockley's address is reprinted in *Genetics and the Future of Man,* ed. J. D. Roslansky (New York: Appleton-Century-Crofts, 1965), 67.

11. Ibid., 70, 71, 91, 95, 68, 90.

12. Ibid., 98, 100, 101.

13. Interview with Shockley, *U.S. News and World Report* (November 22, 1965): 68–71.

14. W. F. Bodmer, A. T. Ganeson, L. A. Herzenberg, J. Lederberg, E. C. Leventhal, E. M. Shooter, and S. Varon (faculty of the Department of Genetics, Stanford University), letter to the editor, *Stanford M.D.* (October 1966), reprinted in *Congressional Record* (December 20, 1969): 40527.

15. In W. Shockley (and four others), letter to members of the National Academy of Sciences, April 23, 1969, reprinted in O. Gillie, *Who Do You Think You Are?* (New York: Dutton, 1976), 105.

16. W. F. Bodmer at al., letter to the editor, 40927; W. B. Shockley, letter to the editor, *Stanford M.D.* (October 1966), reprinted in *Congressional Record* (December 20, 1969): 40527.

17. W. Shockley, "Possible Transfer of Metallurgical and Astronomical Approaches to Problem of Environment versus Heredity," *Science* 154 (1966): 428.

18. W. Shockley, "A 'Try Simplest Cases' Approach to the Heredity-Poverty-Crime Problem," *Proceedings, National Academy of Sciences* 57 (1967): 1767–68.

19. W. Shockley, "Dysgenics, Geneticity, Raceology: A Challenge to the Intellectual Responsibility of Educators," *Phi Delta Kappan* 53, special supplement (January 1972): 305.

20. Shockley, "A 'Try Simplest Cases' Approach," 1769–71.

21. W. Shockley, letter to the editor, *Scientific American* 224 (January 1971): 6. See also W. Shockley, "Negro IQ Deficit: Failure of a 'Malicious Coincidence' Model Warrants New Research Proposals," *Review of Educational Research* 41 (1971): 245.

22. Shockley, "A 'Try Simplest Cases' Approach," 1770. In an interview with *Playboy* (August 1980): 96, 102, Shockley would substitute "unwarranted" and "unfair" for "unreasonable," but he intended the same interpretation.

23. "A Statement by the Council of the Academy," *Proceedings, National Academy of Sciences* 59 (1968): 653–54.

24. P. Handler, letter to Congressman John R. Rarick, May 15, 1972, reprinted in *Congressional Record* (September 7, 1972): 29785.

25. W. Shockley, "Human Quality Problems and Research Taboos," in *New Concepts and Directions in Education*, ed. J. A. Pintus (Greenwich, Conn.: Educational Records Bureau, 1968), 87–88. A dozen years later the Aztec Indian anecdote was retold verbatim in Shockley's interview with *Playboy* (August 1980): 81.

26. [D. P. Moynihan,] *The Negro Family* (Washington, D.C.: Office of Policy, Planning and Research, U.S. Department of Labor, March 1965), 35; R. deNeufville and C. Conner, "How Good Are Our Schools?" *American Education* 2 (October 1966): 6. Shockley's claim about the scientific basis of the antipoverty programs appeared in "Human Quality Problems and Research Taboos," 86. D. J. Ingle made essentially the same point in his letter to readers, *Perspectives in Biology and Medicine* 10 (1967): 682.

27. Shockley, "Human Quality Problems and Research Taboos," 84–85, 90, 94.

28. M. Scriven, "The Values of the Academy," *Review of Educational Research* 40 (1971): 546; Shockley, "Negro IQ Deficit," 243.

29. W. Shockley, "'Cooperative Correlation' Hypothesis for Racial Differences in Earning Power," *Proceedings, National Academy of Sciences* 66 (1970): 245. Actually Shockley's interpretation misses an important element of correlational analysis. A low correlation between IQ and other desirable traits would indicate that the low values of each variable as well as the high ones are not systematically associated. A smaller correlation for blacks would therefore also suggest that an IQ decrement does not "pull down" with it other personality traits valuable for earning power. According to Shockley's own analysis, without prejudice low IQ blacks should earn more than low IQ whites.

30. Shockley, "Human Quality Problems and Research Taboos," 86.

31. R. E. Kuttner and A. B. Lorincz, "Utilization of Accentuated Environmental Inequalities in Research on Racial Difference," *Science* 160 (1968): 439.

32. Reported by B. Wallace, "Genetics and the Great IQ Controversy," *American Biology Teacher* 37 (January 1975): 12.

33. W. Shockley, letter to Forum members (Forum for Contemporary History, publisher of *Journal of the Forum for Contemporary History*, later to become *Skeptic*), April 23, 1973, disseminated by Foundation for Research and Education on Eugenics and Dysgenics, Stanford, Calif.

34. W. Robertson, *The Dispossessed Majority* (Cape Canaveral, Fla.: Howard Allen, 1972). Kuttner's review appeared in *Mankind Quarterly* 14 (1973): 118-19.

35. W. Shockley, "Crime and Dysgenics," *Skeptic* (November-December 1974): 51.

36. See, for example, J. J. Synon, "Dr. Shockley's Honesty Shocks Establishment," *Citizen* (January 1967): 6-7; and J. J. Synon, "Are Scientists Afraid to Face All the Facts?" *Citizen* (July-August 1968): 10.

37. Quoted in C. Rogers, "The Moral Postulates of a Racist," *Christian Century* 91 (April 10, 1974): 388.

38. Interview with *Playboy* (August 1980): 94.

39. Quoted by L. F. Aarons in *Washington Post*, March 12, 1972, A11.

40. An excellent discussion of "operating" by scientists in general and Shockley in particular appears in A. Goodell, *The Visible Scientists* (Ann Arbor, Mich.: University Microfilm, 1975), especially 316.

41. Rogers, "The Moral Postulates of a Racist," 387.

42. See the introduction to the *Playboy* interview (August 1980): 70.

43. Quoted in R. Fleming, "The Nobel Sperm Bank: Cure for a Vanishing Race," *Encore* 9 (May 1980): 32; see also Shockley's comments in the *Playboy* interview (August 1980): 81.

44. Shockley, "Dysgenics, Geneticity, Raceology," 305-6.

45. After frequently suggesting the similarity between his opponents and Nazis, Shockley became enraged when a reporter compared one of his eugenical proposals with policy under the Third Reich and brought a 2.5 million dollar libel suit. After an eight-day trial featuring considerable technical testimony, the jury rendered the Solomon-like verdict that Shockley had indeed been libeled and awarded him appropriate compensation for the damage to his reputation: one

dollar. See *Time* (September 24, 1984): 62; and *New York Times*, September 6, 1984, A16.

46. Shockley, "Dysgenics, Geneticity, Raceology," 307.

47. *Playboy* interview (August 1980): 82, 100.

48. W. Shockley, letter to the editor, *Presbyterian Life* 25 (February 1, 1972): 38.

49. Shockley, "Dysgenics, Geneticity, Raceology," 306.

50. W. Shockley, "The Moral Obligation to Diagnose the American Negro Tragedy of Statistical IQ Deficit" (Paper presented at New York University, April 7, 1974), 5. Actually, Shockley first mentioned the bounty hunter concept in an interview with the *National Enquirer*, but when the phrase did not appear in the published story, he presented it in a press release. See Goodell, *The Visible Scientists*, 339-40.

51. W. Shockley, "Society Has a Moral Obligation to Diagnose Tragic Racial IQ Deficits" (Paper presented at Case-Western Reserve, September 15, 1974), 5.

52. W. Shockley, letter to the editor, *Palo Alto Times*, December 28, 1967, reprinted in Gillie, *Who Do You Think You Are?* 195.

53. Quoted in letter from IRS to FREED, April 19, 1973, disseminated by the Foundation for Research and Education on Eugenics and Dysgenics, Stanford, Calif.

54. W. Shockley, "Inquiry to Potential FREED Supporters," November 30, 1974, disseminated by the Foundation for Research and Education on Eugenics and Dysgenics, Stanford, Calif.

55. "Fund Backs Controversial Study of 'Race Betterment,'" *New York Times*, December 11, 1977, 76.

56. [Dickson,] "Case for the Plaintiff," 436.

57. V. Royster, editorial, *Wall Street Journal*, May 22, 1968, 18.

58. Quoted in M. Rogers, "Brave New William Shockley," *Esquire* (January 1973): 152.

59. *New York Times*, March 4, 1980, A14. On the sperm bank, see A. Walmsley, "The Genius Babies," *MacLean's* (September 2, 1985): 6; and *New York Times*, March 1, 1980, 6.

60. J. Hirsch, "Behavior-genetic Analysis and the Study of Man," in *Science and the Concept of Race*, ed. M. Mead, T. Dobzhansky, E. Tobach, and R. E. Light (New York: Columbia University Press, 1968), 37.

61. The phone call is reported in J. Hirsch, "To 'Unfrock the Charlatans,'" *Sage Race Relations Abstracts* 6 (1981): 6-7.

62. A. R. Jensen, "The Culturally Disadvantaged: Psychological and Educational Aspects," *Educational Research* 10 (1967): 10.

63. A. R. Jensen, "Comment," *American Psychologist* 29 (1974): 467.

64. A. R. Jensen, "What Is the Question? What Is the Evidence?" in *The Psychologists*, vol. 6, ed. T. S. Krawiec (New York: Oxford University Press, 1974), 209-10.

65. C. L. Burt, "The Inheritance of Mental Ability," *American Psychologist* 13 (1958): 1-15.

66. Jensen, "What Is the Question? What Is the Evidence?" 233-34.

67. See, for example, C. Burt, "The Genetic Determination of Differences in

Intelligence: A Study of Monozygotic Twins Reared Apart and Together," *British Journal of Psychology* 57 (1966): 137–53; and C. Burt, "Intelligence and Social Mobility," *British Journal of Statistical Psychology* 14 (1961): 3–24. On the fraud, see L. Hearnshaw, *Cyril Burt, Psychologist* (Ithaca, N.Y.: Cornell University Press, 1979).

68. Jensen, "What Is the Question? What Is the Evidence?" 234.

69. Jensen, "The Culturally Disadvantaged," 5–6.

70. A. R. Jensen, "Social Class, Race and Genetics: Implications for Education," *American Educational Research Journal* 5 (1968): 23.

71. Ibid., 30.

72. A. R. Jensen, "The Culturally Disadvantaged and the Heredity-Environment Uncertainty," in *Disadvantaged Child*, vol. 2, ed. J. Hellmuth (New York: Brunner-Mazel, 1968), 54.

73. A. R. Jensen, "How Much Can We Boost IQ and Scholastic Achievement?" *Harvard Educational Review* 39 (1969): 111; see also Jensen, "Social Class, Race and Genetics," 34–36.

74. Jensen, "The Culturally Disadvantaged," 5.

75. Jensen, "Social Class, Race and Genetics," 5.

76. Ibid., 38.

77. The entire outline is published in A. R. Jensen, *Genetics and Education* (New York: Harper and Row, 1972), 11.

78. Jensen, "How Much Can We Boost IQ and Scholastic Achievement?" 2, 3.

79. See U.S. Commission on Civil Rights, *Racial Isolation in the Public Schools* (Washington, D.C.: U.S. Government Printing Office, 1967), 120–40.

80. See, for example, the reports on Title I in *Inequality in Education* (Harvard Center for Law and Education): M. G. Yudof, "The New Deluder Act: A Title I Primer," no. 2 (December 5, 1969): 1–2, 5–8; and J. T. Murphy, "Title I: Bureaucratic Politics and Poverty Politics," no. 6 (November 13, 1970): 12–15.

81. Jensen, "The Culturally Disadvantaged," 19.

82. Head Start's chaotic beginning is described in J. B. Richmond, "For the Child of Poverty," *American Child* 48 (1966): 5–10.

83. Jensen, "How Much Can We Boost IQ and Scholastic Achievement?" 105. On the long-term effects of Head Start, see, for example, J. R. Berrveta-Clement, L. J. Schweinhart, W. S. Barnett, A. S. Epstein, and D. P. Weikart, *Changed Lives: The Effects of the Perry Pre-School Program on Youths through Age Nineteen*, Monograph No. 8 (Ypsilanti, Mich.: High/Scope, 1984). Longitudinal evaluations of Head Start produced a dramatic reversal in attitudes toward preschool assistance. The *Wall Street Journal*, November 29, 1984, 34, which had been no friend to the program at its inception, announced that preschool education was an "investment, . . . producing more productive citizens and preventing major public-welfare expenditures in later years."

84. Jensen, "How Much Can We Boost IQ and Scholastic Achievement?" 78.

85. Ibid.

86. Ibid., 82.

87. R. C. Lewontin, "Race and Intelligence," *Bulletin of the Atomic Scientists* 26 (March 1970): 7.

88. A. R. Jensen, *Educability and Group Differences* (New York: Harper and Row, 1973), 363.

89. Quoted in S. P. R. Rose, "Scientific Racism and Ideology," in *Racial Variation in Man*, ed. F. J. Ebling (New York: John Wiley, 1975), 202.

90. L. F. Whitney, *The Case for Sterilization* (New York: Frederick A. Stokes, 1934), 153.

91. Jensen, "How Much Can We Boost IQ and Scholastic Achievement?" 93.

92. Ibid., 95.

93. J. Fincher, "Arthur Jensen: In the Eye of the Storm," *Human Behavior* (March/April 1972): 22.

94. Jensen, "How Much Can We Boost IQ and Scholastic Achievement?" 116-17.

95. Jensen, *Genetics and Education*, 13.

96. A. R. Jensen, "Rejoinder: The Promotion of Dogmatism," *Journal of Social Issues* 25 (1969): 212.

97. "Can Negroes Learn the Way Whites Do?" *U.S. News and World Report* (March 10, 1969): 48-51.

98. "Born Dumb?" *Newsweek* (March 31, 1969): 84; "Intelligence: Is There a Racial Difference?" *Time* (April 11, 1969): 54.

99. L. Edson, "Jensenism, n. The Theory That IQ Is Largely Determined by the Genes," *New York Times Magazine* (August 31, 1969): 10-11, 40-47.

100. Jensen, *Genetics and Education*, 13-14.

101. Edson, "Jensenism," 43.

102. Jensen, *Genetics and Education*, 356-64.

103. See the series on Jensen's impact by E. Garfield in *Current Contents:* "The 100 Articles Most Cited by Social Scientists, 1969-1977," no. 32 (August 7, 1978); "High Impact Science and the Case of Arthur Jensen," no. 41 (October 9, 1978); "The 100 Most Cited SSCI Authors," no. 45 (November 6, 1978).

104. G. Piel, ". . . Ye May Be Mistaken," in *Genetic Destiny*, ed. E. Tobach and H. M. Proshansky (New York: AMS Press, 1976), 132; see also the quotes in B. Rice, "The High Cost of Thinking the Unthinkable," *Psychology Today* (December 1973): 91.

105. J. Hirsch, "Jensenism: The Bankruptcy of 'Science' without Scholarship," *Educational Theory* 25 (1969): 220.

106. At its 1971 convention the American Anthropological Association formally resolved "to condemn as dangerous and unscientific the racist . . . theories of genetic inferiority propagated by . . . Arthur Jensen" (quoted in Rice, "The High Cost of Thinking the Unthinkable," 93). A petition opposing racism, circulated by Psychologists for Social Action, was reprinted in their *Newsletter* (December 1973): 12. The claim by Jensen (*Genetics and Education*, 39) that the petition called for his censure or expulsion from the American Psychological Association was false, and he later apologized for the accusation.

107. See E. Alfert, "Comment on: The Promotion of Prejudice," *Journal of Social Issues* 25 (1969): 208.

108. J. Ehrlichman, *Witness to Power* (New York: Simon and Schuster, 1982), 222.

109. *New York Times*, August 31, 1969, IV, 1.

110. Ehrlichman, *Witness to Power,* 133.

111. Quotes from J. Neary, "A Scientist's Variation on a Disturbing Racial Theme," *Life* (June 12, 1970): 58d.

112. E. Zigler, "Has It Really Been Demonstrated That Compensatory Education Is without Value?" *American Psychologist* 30 (1975): 936.

113. See the transcript of Nixon's veto statement in *New York Times,* January 27, 1970, 24; and his message to Congress on educational reform in *New York Times,* March 4, 1970, 28.

114. Ehrlichman, *Witness to Power,* 223, 233.

115. Quoted in *Boston Globe,* January 4, 1992, 1, 8.

116. Quoted in Neary, "A Scientist's Variation on a Disturbing Racial Theme," 61.

117. *Newsweek* (June 2, 1969): 69. Jensen's first-person account of his harassment is detailed in *Genetics and Education,* 44-46.

118. A. Edel, "The Scientist and His Findings: Some Problems in Social Responsibility," in *Genetic Destiny,* ed. Tobach and Proshansky, 42-43.

119. Letter from Tobach to Jerry Hirsch, quoted in Hirsch, "Jensenism," 6.

120. Lewontin, "Race and Intelligence," 2.

121. Editorial in *Jackson [Mississippi] Daily News,* February 17, 1967, reprinted as "Dixie Crossroads Editor Sees Putnam Vindicated," *Citizen* (April 1967): 71.

122. See W. F. Brazziel, "A Letter from the South," *Harvard Educational Review* 39 (1969): 348.

123. *Congressional Record* (May 28, 1969): 14189-217. For Rarick's background, see M. Barone, G. Ujifusa, and D. Matthews, *The Almanac of American Politics* (Boston: Gambit, 1974), 398; and B. R. Epstein and A. Forster, *The Radical Right* (New York: Vintage, 1967), 69-70.

124. *Race and Integration: Scientists Speak Out* (Denham Springs, La.: Invisible Empire Knights of the Ku Klux Klan, n.d.).

125. See S. Rose, J. Hambley, and J. Haywood, "Science, Racism and Ideology," *Socialist Register, 1973* (1973): 236, 257 (note 5).

126. Quoted in *Science News* 95 (April 5, 1969): 326.

127. The response to Garrett, "Statement on Race and Intelligence from the Society for the Psychological Study of Social Issues," appears in *Perspectives in Biology and Medicine* 5 (1961): 129-30. The response to Jensen was made in a press release on May 27, 1969, and published as "SPSSI Council Statement on Race and Intelligence," *Journal of Social Issues* 25 (1969): 1-3, and as "Statement by SPSSI on Current IQ Controversy," *American Psychologist* 24 (1969): 1039-40.

128. Quoted in "An Interview with Arthur R. Jensen," *Center Magazine* 2 (1969): 77.

129. Ibid., 79.

130. W. A. Massey, "The New Fanatics," *Mankind Quarterly* 3 (1962): 81, 79.

131. Smith, *The Color Line,* 15.

132. J.C.N., letter to the *Southern Quarterly Review,* n.s., 5 (1850): 450-51.

133. "Statement of R. T. Osborne," in *Emergency School Aid Act of 1970: Hearings before the General Subcommittee on Education and Labor on H.R. 17846 and Related Bills,* HR 91-2, June 29, 1970, 461.

134. "Statement of W. B. Shockley," in ibid., 439, 436.

135. "Statement of A. R. Jensen," in ibid., 335, 340, 338.

136. Ibid., 339, 361.

137. Ibid., 369-70. The statements by Jensen and van den Haag reprinted by Rarick appear in *Congressional Record* (July 1, 1970): 22519-26.

138. Quoted in *Times* (London), September 19, 1974, 18.

139. A. R. Jensen, "Reducing the Heredity-Environment Uncertainty: A Reply," *Harvard Educational Review* 39 (1969): 461.

140. Cited in M. Levitas, *America in Crisis* (New York: Holt, Rinehart and Winston, 1969), 66.

141. Jensen, *Educability and Group Differences,* 364, 21.

142. A. R. Jensen, "The Price of Inequality," *Oxford Review of Education* 1 (1975): 61.

143. Ibid., 60. The basis for this claim on Jensen's part was the Coleman Report (*Equality of Educational Opportunity* [Washington, D.C.: Office of Education, 1966]), which a decade earlier had found fairly small differences in laboratory facilities, textbooks, accreditation, and other areas between mostly white and mostly black schools. Coleman, however, specifically did not compare per pupil expenditures, the summary measure of resource allocation, which indicated shameful disparities in funding. Within the three years prior to Jensen's *HER* article, there had been a number of judicial challenges to funding inequities throughout the country, each noting that poorer school districts with large minority populations typically expended much less money per student than more affluent districts did. In New Jersey, for example, even after federal and state assistance, Englewood Cliffs, a school system with less than 2 percent minorities, was spending more than double the amount of money per student than Camden, which had 73 percent minorities and a much higher property-tax rate. The prevalence of such data had led judges in New Jersey (*Robinson v. Cahill* 118 N.J. Super 223 [1972]), California (*Serrano v. Priest,* 487 P.2d 1241 [1971]), and Texas to rule the systems for funding public education in those states to be discriminatory and violative of the state's constitution. The Texas case was appealed to the Supreme Court, which barely ruled (five to four) that inequitable funding of local school systems was not in violation of the U.S. Constitution. The majority opinion, referring sympathetically to "weary taxpayers already resisting tax increases," seemed as concerned with practical considerations as it was with constitutional issues (*San Antonio v. Rodriguez,* 411 U.S. 57 [1972]).

144. A. R. Jensen, "The Nature of Intelligence and Its Relation to Learning," *Melbourne Studies in Education, 1978* (1978): 130-31.

145. A. R. Jensen, "Equality and Diversity in Education," in *Education, Inequality and National Policy,* ed. N. F. Ashline, T. R. Pezzullo, and C. I. Norris (Lexington, Mass.: D. C. Heath, 1976), 131.

146. Quoted in *Intellect* 104 (April 1976): 486.

147. Jensen, "The Price of Inequality," 63, 68-69. Ironically, however, Jensen once described the model admissions process at "selective colleges" as "initial screening . . . to obtain a pool of applicants with promising academic qualifications, who can then be screened further, giving consideration to nonacademic criteria," among which he listed "a wide diversity of backgrounds—ethnic, cultural, social

class and geographic." This procedure is the embodiment of the affirmative action concept. See A. R. Jensen, *Straight Talk about Mental Tests* (New York: Free Press, 1981), 44.

148. See, for example, N. Glazer, *Affirmative Discrimination: Ethics, Inequality and Public Policy* (New York: Basic Books, 1975); and B. Gross, *Discrimination in Reverse* (New York: New York University Press, 1978).

149. Quoted in Jensen, *Genetics and Education*, 43. Though Jensen does not provide the source of the quote, his description in ibid., 28-29, makes clear that it is Deutsch.

150. M. Deutsch, "Happenings on the Way Back to the Forum: Social Science, IQ and Race Differences Revisited," *Harvard Educational Review* 39 (1969): 524.

151. A. R. Jensen, "The IQ Controversy: A Reply to Layzer," *Cognition* 1 (1972): 449-50.

152. C. Spearman, "'General Intelligence,' Objectively Determined and Measured," *American Journal of Psychology* 15 (1904): 201-93; see also C. Spearman, "The Theory of Two Factors," *Psychological Review* 21 (1914): 101-15.

153. On the extension of *g*, see Jensen, "The Nature of Intelligence and Its Relation to Learning," 118; and A. R. Jensen, "*g:* Outmoded Theory or Unconquered Frontier," *Creative Science and Technology* 2 (1979): 18. For Gould's characterization, see S. J. Gould, "Jensen's Last Stand," *New York Review of Books* (May 1, 1980): 41; and S. J. Gould, *The Mismeasure of Man* (New York: W. W. Norton, 1981), 317-19.

154. E. G. Boring, "Intelligence as the Tests Test It," *New Republic* 35 (1923): 35.

155. Jensen, "How Much Can We Boost IQ and Scholastic Achievement?" 5, 19.

156. A. R. Jensen, "Raising the IQ: The Ramey and Haskins Study," *Intelligence* 5 (1981): 39.

157. According to R. J. Sternberg, *The Triarchic Mind* (New York: Viking, 1988), 211, this result is "reported by several researchers." See Sternberg's citations.

158. S. B. Sarason, *Psychology Misdirected* (New York: Free Press, 1981), 183.

159. Jensen, "The Nature of Intelligence and Its Relation to Learning," 116; Jensen, "*g:* Outmoded Theory or Unconquered Frontier," 18.

160. Cited by B. S. Bloom, "Testing Cognitive Ability and Achievement," in *Handbook of Research on Testing*, ed. N. C. Gage (Chicago: Rand-McNally, 1963), 384.

161. D. Feldman, *Nature's Gambit: Child Prodigies and the Development of Human Potential* (New York: Basic Books, 1986).

162. The comment on the death of intelligence research was made by Lee Cronbach, a Stanford professor, to Robert J. Sternberg, his graduate student at the time. Sternberg, *The Triarchic Mind*, 4.

163. H. Gardner, *Frames of Mind* (New York: Basic Books, 1983).

164. K. Pearson, *The Groundwork of Eugenics* (London: Dulau, 1909), 19.

165. F. A. Woods, "Mental and Moral Heredity in Royalty," *Popular Science Monthly* 62 (1909): 503.

166. M. R. Berube, "Jensen's Complaint," *Commonweal* (October 10, 1969): 42.

167. J. A. Ward and H. R. Hetzel, *Biology Today and Tomorrow* (St. Paul, Minn.: West Publishing, 1980), 302; J. B. Jenkins, *Genetics* (Boston: Houghton Mifflin, 1979), 126.

168. H. J. Eysenck, *The IQ Argument* (New York: Library Press, 1971), 67.

169. A. M. Colman, "Scientific Racism and the Evidence on Race and Intelligence," *Race* 14 (1972): 45.

170. J. H. Edwards, "Review of *Developmental Human Behavior Genetics,*" *Annals of Human Genetics* 40 (1976): 142. Heat is conceptualized by modern physics as the energy resulting from the random collision of molecules against each other.

171. H. J. Eysenck, *Know Your Own IQ* (Baltimore: Penguin, 1962), 37.

172. H. J. Eysenck vs. L. Kamin, *The Intelligence Controversy* (New York: John Wiley, 1981), 59.

173. Jenkins, *Genetics,* 166.

174. Jensen, "How Much Can We Boost IQ and Scholastic Achievement?" 45.

175. For example, A. E. Wiggins, *The New Decalogue of Science* (New York: Blue Ribbon Books, 1923), 655-66.

176. A. R. Jensen, "The Meaning of Heritability in the Behavioral Sciences," *Educational Psychologist* 11 (1975): 173.

177. Jensen, "How Much Can We Boost IQ and Scholastic Achievement?" 59.

178. A. R. Jensen, "Race and the Genetics of Intelligence: A Reply to Lewontin," *Bulletin of the Atomic Scientists* 26 (May 1970): 24.

179. R. C. Lewontin, "Further Remarks on Race and the Genetics of Intelligence," *Bulletin of the Atomic Scientists* 26 (May 1970): 24.

180. O. Kempthorne, "Logical, Epistemological and Statistical Aspects of the Nature-Nurture Data Interpretation," *Biometrics* 34 (1978): 19.

181. P. B. Medawar, "Unnatural Science," *New York Review of Books* (February 3, 1977): 14.

182. J. M. Horn, J. C. Loehlin, and L. Willerman, "Intellectual Resemblance among Adoptive and Biological Relatives: The Texas Adoption Project," *Behavior Genetics* 9 (1979): 196.

183. L. G. Humphrey, "The Construct of General Intelligence," *Intelligence* 3 (1979): 115.

184. C. Jencks, M. Smith, H. Alland, M. J. Bane, D. Cohen, H. Gintis, B. Heyns, and S. Michelson, *Inequality* (New York: Basic Books, 1972), 315; S. Scarr and R. A. Weinberg, "Intellectual Similarities within Families of Both Adopted and Biological Children," *Intelligence* 1 (1977): 185. For the reanalyses, see H. F. Taylor, *The IQ Game* (New Brunswick, N.J.: Rutgers University Press, 1980), 41-60.

185. Jencks et al., *Inequality,* 76. Eight years later Jencks's opinion had not changed; see C. Jencks, "Heredity, Environment and Public Policy Reconsidered," *American Sociological Review* 45 (1980): 723.

186. L. Eaves, "Review of *Genetics and Education,*" *Heredity* 30 (1973): 251-52.

187. Jensen, "The IQ Controversy," 433.

188. Ibid., 434.

189. Jensen, "The Meaning of Heritability in the Behavioral Sciences," 175.

190. See, for example, S. Scarr, "From Evolution to Larry P, or What Shall We Do about IQ Tests," *Intelligence* 2 (1978): 336; and S. Scarr-Salapatek, "Race, Social Class, and IQ," *Science* 174 (1971): 1294.

191. Lewontin, "Race and Intelligence," 7–8, contains a particularly good illustration of this point.

192. Jensen, *Educability and Group Differences*, 144.

193. Ibid., 136.

194. A. R. Jensen, "A Reply to Gage," *Phi Delta Kappan* 53 (1972): 421.

195. Eaves, "Review of *Genetics and Education*," 251–52.

196. Jensen, *Genetics and Education*, 162.

197. J. C. DeFries, "Quantitative Aspects of Genetics and Environment in the Determination of Behavior," in *Genetics, Environment and Behavior*, ed. L. Ehrman, G. S. Omenn, and E. Caspari (New York: Academic Press, 1972), 11.

198. A. R. Jensen, "Comment," and J. C. DeFries, "Reply to Professor to Jensen," both in ibid., 23–24.

199. A. R. Jensen, "The Current Status of the IQ Controversy," *Australian Psychologist* 13 (1978): 19.

200. Jensen, *Straight Talk about Mental Tests*, xi–xii.

201. Jensen's *Educability and Group Differences* is devoted almost entirely to this purpose.

202. Jensen, "The Current Status of the IQ Controversy," which was a reprint of his lecture delivered at Australian universities.

203. P. Mackenzie, "Explaining Race Differences in IQ," *American Psychologist* 39 (1984): 1223; see also Mackenzie's letter to the editor, *Behavior Genetics* 10 (1980): 225–33.

204. L. L. Cavalli-Sforza and W. F. Bodmer, *The Genetics of Human Populations* (San Francisco: W. H. Freeman, 1971), 800.

205. A. R. Jensen, "Let's Understand Skodak and Skeels, Finally," *Educational Psychologist* 10 (1973): 34.

206. S. Scarr and R. A. Weinberg, "IQ Test Performance of Black Children Adopted by White Families," *American Psychologist* 31 (1976): 736.

207. These studies are summarized in J. C. Loehlin, G. Lindzey, and J. N. Spuhler, *Race Differences in Intelligence* (San Francisco: W. H. Freeman, 1975), 120–32.

208. S. Scarr, A. J. Pakstis, S. H. Katz, and W. B. Barker, "Absence of a Relationship between Degree of White Ancestry and Intellectual Skills within a Black Population," *Human Genetics* 39 (1977): 82.

209. Quoted in *San Francisco Examiner*, January 24, 1973, 54.

210. Jensen, "The Current Status of the IQ Controversy," 22.

211. S. Scarr, *Race, Social Class and Individual Differences in IQ* (Hillsdale, N.J.: Lawrence Erlbaum, 1981), 525.

212. A. R. Jensen, "Obstacles, Problems and Pitfalls in Differential Psychology," in Scarr, *Race, Social Class and Individual Differences in IQ*, 507–11.

213. Ibid., 500, 499. Scarr's statement is in the same work, 435.

214. R. A. McConnell, "The Future Revisited," *Bioscience* 20 (1970): 903, 904.

215. Eysenck, *The IQ Argument,* 76.

216. H. J. Eysenck, "Personality, Cancer and Cardiovascular Disease: A Causal Analysis," *Personality and Individual Differences* 6 (1985): 535-56; H. J. Eysenck, *The Causes and Effects of Smoking* (Beverly Hills, Calif.: Sage, 1980); H. J. Eysenck, *Smoking, Personality, and Stress: Psychosocial Factors in the Prevention of Cancer and Coronary Heart Disease* (New York: Springer-Verlag, 1991). Reviewers of *Smoking, Personality, and Stress* concluded that "Eysenck's real goal is not to evaluate the role of smoking in disease. Rather he seems more interested in justifying and defending tobacco use. It is hard to discern a theoretical or scholarly intent here." T. B. Baker and M. C. Fiore, "Elvis Is Alive, the Mafia Killed JFK, and Smoking Is Good for You," *Contemporary Psychology* 37 (1992): 1016.

217. H. J. Eysenck, "Some Recent Studies of Intelligence," *Eugenics Review* 40 (1948): 21.

218. H. J. Eysenck, letter to editor, *New Statesman* (April 27, 1973): 616.

219. Eysenck vs. Kamin, *The Intelligence Controversy,* 88-89.

220. H. J. Eysenck, *The Inequality of Man* (London: Temple Smith, 1973), 111.

221. H. J. Eysenck, "The Dangers of the New Zealots," *Encounter* 39 (1972): 81, 83.

222. See for example, Eysenck, *The IQ Argument,* 3.

223. H. J. Eysenck, "When Is Discrimination?" in *Black Paper,* ed. C. B. Cox and R. Boyson (London: Broadwick, 1977), 97.

224. See the ad for the book in *New York Times,* October 6, 1971, 41.

225. Eysenck, *The IQ Argument,* 1.

226. Ibid., 3-4, 113.

227. Ibid., 12. Eysenck began one chapter with an amusing comparison of "Jensenism" with "Jansenism," a doctrine proposed by Cornelius Jansen, bishop of Ypres, and condemned as heresy by Pope Innocent X in 1653. Both the wit and erudition were in marked contrast with Eysenck's usual dry prose style, and no wonder—the paragraph had been lifted from an article by the Harvard geneticist Richard Lewontin. There was an interesting Freudian postscript to this plagiarism, however. Later in the same chapter Eysenck presented a five-page quotation from a publication by Jensen, written in response to the Lewontin article. A paragraph in the middle of this excerpt had begun, "I agree with Lewontin that these assumptions," but in Eysenck's reprinting the first five words were deleted without ellipsis, so the paragraph now began with "These assumptions," thus ensuring that his own readers would remain unaware of Lewontin. In one of the few specific references provided in the text of the book, Eysenck gave the March 1970 issue of the *Bulletin of the Atomic Scientists* as the source of this quote from Jensen, but the citation was incorrect; the Jensen article had not appeared until May. The March issue did, however, contain the Lewontin article.

228. Ibid., 42-43, 123.

229. See B. McGonigle and S. McPhilemy, "Genesis of an Irish Myth," *Times Higher Education Supplement* (September 13, 1974).

230. M. M. DeLemos, "The Development of Conservation in Aboriginal Children," *International Journal of Psychology* 4 (1969): 255–69.

231. Eysenck, *The IQ Argument,* 95–97.

232. Jensen, *Educability and Group Differences,* 316.

233. P. R. Dasen, "The Development of Conservation in Aboriginal Children: A Replication Study," *International Journal of Psychology* 7 (1972): 75–85.

234. Eysenck, *The IQ Argument,* 129.

235. Eysenck, *The Inequality of Man,* 11, 270.

236. Ibid., 17, 19.

237. T. H. Huxley, "On the Natural Inequality of Man," *Nineteenth Century* (January 1890): 9–12.

238. Eysenck, *The Inequality of Man,* 223, 266–67.

239. H. J. Eysenck, Introduction to F. Galton, *Hereditary Genius* (London: Julian Freedman, 1978 [1869]), i.

240. R. B. Cattell, *Psychology and Social Progress* (London: C. W. Daniel, 1933), 40–45, 59, 87.

241. R. B. Cattell, *Psychology and the Religious Quest* (London: Thomas Nelson, 1938), 61.

242. Cattell, *Psychology and Social Progress,* 175.

243. Cattell, *Psychology and the Religious Quest,* 87–89, 91.

244. Cattell, *Psychology and Social Progress,* 69.

245. Ibid., 155, 63.

246. Ibid., 62, 63.

247. Ibid., 75, 81, 76, 47–48, 70.

248. Ibid., 66.

249. Ibid., 360; Cattell, *Psychology and the Religious Quest,* 145.

250. Cattell, *Psychology and the Religious Quest,* 94; R. B. Cattell, *The Fight for Our National Intelligence* (London: P. S. King, 1937), 56.

251. Cattrell, *Psychology and Social Progress,* 360.

252. Cattell, *The Fight for Our National Intelligence,* 68.

253. Cattell, *Psychology and Social Progress,* 410.

254. Ibid., 248–93, 317–41.

255. Cattell, *The Fight for Our National Intelligence,* 67–68.

256. Ibid., 88–89, 141.

257. Cattell, *Psychology and the Religious Quest,* 149.

258. Cattell, *Psychology and Social Progress,* 364.

259. Ibid., 359.

260. R. B. Cattell, "Ethics and the Social Sciences," *American Psychologist* 3 (1948): 195.

261. R. B. Cattell, "The Structure of Intelligence in Relation to the Nature-Nurture Controversy," in *Intelligence,* ed. R. Cancro (New York: Grune and Stratton, 1971), 5

262. R. B. Cattell, *A New Morality from Science: Beyondism* (New York: Pergamon, 1972), 220–21.

263. Ibid., 153, 154.

264. Ibid., 168, 262, 143.

265. Ibid., 38, xii, 426, 429, 451–52, 362–63, 175, 411, 340.

266. In a gratifying coincidence, on the day I read *Beyondism* Paul Simon's magnificent *Graceland* won the Grammy for best record album of the year; many of its songs featured the combined efforts of Simon and such African performers as Joseph Shabalala and Ladysmith Black Mambazo. Fortunately for most of us, musicians do not yet appreciate evolutionary morality.

267. Ibid., 211, 298, 146, 172, 161.

268. Ibid., 421, 95.

269. R. B. Cattell, "Ethics and the Social Sciences: The Beyondist Solution," *Mankind Quarterly* 19 (1978): 308, 305.

270. Cattell, *A New Morality from Science,* 178, 102, 234.

271. R. B. Cattell, "Response to Dr. Neff," *Psychologists' League Journal* 11 (1938), reprinted in *Social Action* (Newsletter of Psychologists for Social Action) 7 (July 1974): 2.

272. Cattell, *A New Morality from Science,* 431-32.

273. W. Robertson, *Ventilations* (Cape Canaveral, Fla.: Howard Allen, 1974), 110; Robertson, *The Dispossessed Majority,* 555.

274. Robertson, *Ventilations,* 76, 108; Robertson, *The Dispossessed Majority,* 555.

275. Robertson, *Ventilations,* 55, 96-109 (description of the relocation plan); Robertson, *The Dispossessed Majority,* 556.

276. The map is reprinted in J. Ridgeway, *Blood in the Face* (New York: Thunder's Mouth, 1990), 150-51.

277. Entitled "Books That Speak for the Majority," the literature list from Robertson's Howard Allen publishers (Cape Canaveral, Fla., n.d.) included Cattell's *A New Morality from Science,* Robertson's own books, and reprints of books by Madison Grant and T. Lothrop Stoddard and of Carleton Putnam's "two lasting contributions to social science . . . Modern Classics on the Negro Problem."

278. W. Massey, "Are All Races Equal?" *Western Destiny* 9 (July 1964): 10.

279. H. E. Garrett, "What Is the Answer?" *Citizen* (January 1970): 21.

280. In the caption under Jensen's picture, *Citizen* (January 1978): 14.

281. N. Weyl, "Some Comparative Performance Indexes of American Ethnic Minorities," *Mankind Quarterly* 9 (1969): 109; the book review of E. S. Cox's *Lincoln's Negro Policy* appears on 140. Jensen cites the article and reproduces some of its data in *Educability and Group Differences,* 252, 287. Weyl's review of Jensen's book in *Mankind Quarterly* 15 (1975): 228, took obvious pains to note that Jensen cited his article.

282. In *Genetics and Education,* 39, Jensen had erroneously claimed that Psychologists for Social Action had circulated a petition calling for his censure or expulsion from APA. His apology appeared in the *APA Monitor* (April 1974): 2.

283. R. T. Osborne and A. J. Gregor, "Racial Differences in Heritability Estimates for Tests of Spatial Ability," *Perceptual and Motor Skills* 27 (1968): 738. See also R. T. Osborne and F. Miele, "Racial Differences in Environmental Influences on Numerical Ability as Determined by Heritability Estimates," *Perceptual and Motor Skills* 28 (1969): 537. The absurd negative value occurred because the correlation between nonidentical twins was much larger than the correlation between identical twins, suggesting that greater genotypic similarity was producing *less* phenotypic similarity.

284. R. T. Osborne and D. E. Suddick, "Blood Type Gene Frequency and Mental Ability," *Psychological Reports* 29 (1971): 1248.

285. J. C. Loehlin, S. G. Vanderberg, and R. T. Osborne, "Blood Group Genes and Negro-White Ability Differences," *Behavior Genetics* 3 (1973): 265, 264.

286. "Fund Backs Controversial Study of 'Race Betterment,'" 76.

287. Quoted in *New York Times,* April 27, 1976, 14.

288. P. A. Vernon and A. R. Jensen, "Individual and Group Differences in Intelligence and Speed of Information Processing," *Personality and Individual Differences* 5 (1984): 423; the institute's support is noted in the Acknowledgment.

289. The directors of the organizations are listed in their incorporation papers filed with the Washington, D.C., Recorder of Deeds. The ad appeared in *New York Times Book Review,* September 1, 1974, 15.

290. On the free distribution of *Straight Talk* and other activities of the nonprofit corporations funded by the Pioneer Fund, see B. Mehler, "The New Eugenics," in *Biology as Destiny* (Cambridge, Mass.: Science for the People, 1984), 26–27.

291. R. T. Osborne, *Twins: Black and White* (Athens, Ga.: Foundation for Human Understanding, 1980).

292. Brochure advertising *Race* (Foundation for Human Understanding, PO Box 5712, Athens, Ga., n.d.).

293. C. E. Noble, "Race, Reality and Experimental Psychology," *Perspectives in Biology and Medicine* 13 (1969): 10–30.

294. N. Weyl and W. Marina, *American Statesmen on Slavery and the Negro* (New Rochelle, N.Y.: Arlington, 1971); N. Weyl, *The Negro in American Civilization* (Washington, D.C.: Public Affairs Press, 1960), 136, 137.

295. Ibid., 148–67, 233–34.

296. See J. B. Fox, "Review of N. Weyl's *The Negro in American Civilization,*" *Mankind Quarterly* 1 (1961): 225.

297. N. Weyl, "Pelvic Brim and Brain Size," *Mankind Quarterly* 18 (1977): 119–24; see also N. Weyl, "Racial Differences in the Range of Brain Capacity," *Mankind Quarterly* 11 (1970): 215–19.

298. N. Weyl, "Some Genetic Aspects of Plantation Slavery," *Perspectives in Biology and Medicine* 13 (1970): 618–25; Noble, "Race, Reality and Experimental Psychology."

299. D. J. Ingle, "Fallacies in Arguments on Human Differences," in *Human Variation: The Biopsychology of Age, Race and Sex,* ed. R. T. Osborne, C. E. Noble, and N. Weyl (New York: Academic Press, 1978), 25.

300. A. R. Jensen, "Genetic and Behavioral Effects of Nonrandom Mating," in ibid., 51–106.

301. R. Lynn, "Ethnic and Racial Differences in Intelligence: International Comparisons," in ibid., 261–86.

302. R. G. Lehrke, "Sex Linkage: A Biological Basis for Greater Male Variability in Intelligence," in ibid., 193.

303. C. D. Darlington, "Epilogue: The Evolution and Variation of Human Intelligence," in ibid., 379–84.

304. *Citizen* (November 1978): 18–19.

305. R. Gayre of Gayre, Foreword, *Mankind Quarterly* 19 (1978): 3.

306. S. Anderson and J. L. Anderson, *Inside the League* (New York: Dodd, Mead, 1986), 93.

307. R. Pearson, "Pan-Nordicism as a Modern Policy," *Northern World* 3 (March–April, 1959): 4, 5, 6.

308. Quoted in Anderson and Anderson, *Inside the League*, 94.

309. On Carto's use of the name "E. L. Anderson," see C. H. Simonds, "The Strange Story of Willis Carto," *National Review* (September 10, 1971): 982.

310. E. L. Anderson [W. Carto], "A Word from the Publisher," *Western Destiny* 9 (June 1964): 3. (This was the first issue of the journal under this name.)

311. R. Pearson, editorial, *Western Destiny* 10 (November 1965): 3.

312. M. F. Connors, "Allied War Crimes," *Western Destiny* 9 (July 1964): 12–13; A. Paul, "Hitler's Economic Policies," *Western Destiny* 11 (April 1966): 7–8.

313. R. Pearson, *Race and Civilization* (Jackson, Miss.: New Patriot, 1966), 122.

314. Anderson and Anderson, *Inside the League*, 100.

315. "Fund Backs Controversial Study of 'Race Betterment,'" 76.

316. P. Valentine, "The Fascist Specter behind the World Anti-Red League," *Washington Post*, May 28, 1978, C1–2; the bylaws of the National States Rights party are quoted in J. George and L. Wilcox, *Nazis, Communists, Klansmen, and Others on the Fringe* (Buffalo, N.Y.: Prometheus Books, 1992), 353. George and Wilcox's work quotes an article by Fields which maintains that "every Jew who holds a position of power or authority must be removed from that position. If this does not work, then we must establish (the) Final Solution" (383).

317. On the Cliveden Set's sympathies for Hitler, see *New York Times*, April 17, 1938, E4.

318. R. Lynn, *Personality and National Character* (New York: Pergamon, 1971). See also R. Lynn, "National and Racial Differences in Anxiety," *Mankind Quarterly* 11 (1971): 205–14.

319. Cattell, "Ethics and the Social Sciences: The Beyondist Solution."

320. R. B. Cattell, C. J. Brackenbridge, J. Case, D. N. Propert, and A. J. Sheehy, "The Relation of Blood Types to Primary and Secondary Personality Traits," *Mankind Quarterly* 21 (1980): 35–51.

321. R. B. Cattell, H. B. Young, and J. D. Hundleby, "Blood Groups and Personality Traits," *American Journal of Human Genetics* 16 (1964): 397–401; the critical comments appear in the same journal in letters to the editor from A. S. Weiner, 17 (1965): 369–70; and H. W. Norton, 23 (1971): 225 (the quoted criticism comes from Weiner, 370); Cattell's reply also appears in a letter to the editor, 24 (1972): 485.

322. See "Review of A. R. Jensen's *Straight Talk about Mental Tests*," *Mankind Quarterly* 22 (1982): 262.

323. D. Purves, "The Evolutionary Basis of Race Consciousness," *Mankind Quarterly* 1 (1960): 53–54.

324. A. McGregor, "The Evolutionary Function of Prejudice," *Mankind Quarterly* 26 (1986): 283, 281.

325. See R. Bellant, *Old Nazis, the New Right and the Reagan Administration* (Cambridge, Mass.: Political Research Associates, 1986), 46.

326. B. Mehler, "Rightists on the Rights Panel," *Nation* (May 7, 1988): 640-41; "Fund Backs Controversial Study of 'Racial Betterment,'" 76.

327. R. Scott, "Law and the Social Sciences: The U.S. Experiment in Enforced School Integration," *Mankind Quarterly* 22 (1982): 275. Scott published four subsequent articles in the same journal opposing integrated schools: "School Achievement and Desegregation: Is There a Linkage?" 24 (1983): 61-81; "Productive Factors for Increased Levels of Learning," 24 (1984): 257-91; "Desegregatory Effects in Charlotte-Mecklenburg County Schools Longitudinal Demographics on Black Achievement and Middle Class Flight," 25 (1984): 47-69; and "Sex and Race Achievement Profiles in a Desegregated High School in the Deep South," 25 (1985): 291-302. All of Scott's articles were later published by Pearson's Council for Social and Economic Studies as *Education and Ethnicity: The U.S. Experiment in School Integration* (McLean, Va.: CSES, 1987).

328. Quoted by S. Rose, letter to the editor, *Nature* 274 (1978): 738.

329. Quoted in C. C. Aronsfeld, "The Theory of Prejudice," *Patterns of Prejudice* 5 (1971): 27.

330. "Interview with Prof. Hans Eysenck," *Beacon* (February 1977): 8. When the biologist Steven Rose pointed out that Eysenck had had a personal interview with *Beacon,* Eysenck said it was "untrue, although I am sure he made the allegation in good faith" (letter to the editor, *Nature* 274 [1978]: 738). The probable explanation for this cryptic and highly atypical response—Eysenck rarely acknowledged good faith on his opponent's part—was hinted at in *Beacon*'s introduction, which stated that *"some time ago* we interviewed Prof. Eysenck" (emphasis added). Since this was the publication's first issue, the interview must have originally taken place for a different purpose and then wound up in *Beacon.* Most likely, the interview was done by someone associated with the *Mankind Quarterly* who later became involved with the National party.

331. Editorial, *Western Destiny* 10 (November 1965): 3.

332. "Moderne Rassentheorie stützt Südafrika," *Nation Europa* (October 1971): 43, 46.

333. H. Stein's review of *Did Six Million Really Die?* in *Nation Europa* (September 1975): 62.

334. "Exklusivinterview mit Prof. A. Jensen: Rasse und Begabung," in ibid., 25.

335. Ibid., 26-27.

336. On William Pierce, *The Turner Diaries,* and The Order, see J. Coates, *Armed and Dangerous* (New York: Hill and Wang, 1987), especially 48-51, 214-15; and D. Vaughn, "Terror on the Right," *In These Times,* March 13-19, 1985, 12-13. Pierce was quoted in Valentine, "The Fascist Specter behind the World Anti-Red League," C-1.

337. A. de Benoist, "Integration Scolaire et Psychologie Raciale," *Nouvelle Ecole,* no. 10 (1969): 75-81; the interview appeared in *Nouvelle Ecole,* no. 18 (1972).

338. J. Rieger, *Rasse-ein Problem auch für uns* (Hamburg: published by the

author, 1969). For the criticism, see H. Singer, "National Ideology or Science?" *Mankind Quarterly* 11 (1970): 61-63; the response appears in H. Kiesel, "Race, the 'Nation of Europe' and Ideology," *Mankind Quarterly* 12 (1971): 111-15.

339. The pamphlet was R. Kosiek, *Das Volk in seiner Wirklichkeit*; see "Werbegeschenk," *Neue Anthropologie* 5 (1977): 96.

340. Mehler, "Rightists on the Rights Panel," 641.

341. "Hans F. K. Günther Archiv," *Neue Anthropologie* 5 (1977): 96.

342. "Ist die Wahrheit verwerflich? Ein Gespräch von Alain de Benoist mit Arthur R. Jensen," *Neue Anthropologie* 1 (1973): 24-25.

343. "Jensen-Bibliographie," *Neue Anthropologie* 4 (1976): 44-46.

344. R. A. Gordon, letter to the author, January 1, 1988.

345. Quoted in M. Billig, *Psychology, Racism and Fascism*, Searchlight Booklet (Birmingham, England: A.F.&R. Publications, 1979), 20.

346. Quoted in D. Lipstadt, *Denying the Holocaust* (New York: Free Press, 1993), 157-58. On Rieger's representation, see also Zündel's letter in *Liberty Bell* (September 1991): 31-32.

347. Vernon and Jensen, "Individual and Group Differences in Intelligence and Speed of Information Processing," 412.

348. A. R. Jensen, "Race and Mental Ability," in *Racial Variation in Man*, ed. Ebling, 103.

349. M. Lambeth and L. H. Lanier, "Race Differences in Speed of Reaction," *Pedagogical Seminary and Journal of Genetic Psychology* 42 (1933): 289.

350. Personal interview with Leon Kamin, August 1979.

351. A. R. Jensen, "Kinship Correlations Reported by Cyril Burt," *Behavior Genetics* 4 (1974): 26-27.

352. Vernon and Jensen, "Individual and Group Differences in Intelligence and Speed of Information Processing," 419.

353. L. Kamin and S. Grant-Henry, "Reaction Time, Race and Racism," *Intelligence* 11 (1987): 304.

354. A. R. Jensen, "Techniques for Chronometric Study of Mental Abilities," in *Methodological and Statistical Advances in the Study of Individual Differences*, ed. C. R. Reynolds and V. L. Willson (New York: Plenum, 1985), 55.

355. S. W. Keele, *Attention and Human Performance* (Pacific Palisades, Calif.: Goodyear Publishing, 1973), 76.

356. Quoted in Kamin and Grant-Henry, "Reaction Time, Race and Racism," 301.

357. A. R. Jensen, "Reaction Time and Psychometric *g*," in *A Model for Intelligence*, ed. H. J. Eysenck (Berlin: Springer-Verlag, 1982), 102.

358. Vernon and Jensen, "Individual and Group Differences in Intelligence and Speed of Information Processing," 418; Kamin and Grant-Henry, "Reaction Time, Race and Racism," 303.

Conclusion

1. P. E. Vernon, *Intelligence: Heredity and Environment* (San Francisco: W. H. Freeman, 1979), vii.

2. S. Rose, "The Limits to Science," *Science for the People* (November-December 1984): 26.

3. C. White, *An Account of the Regular Gradation in Man and in Different Animals and Vegetables; and from the Former to the Latter* (London: C. Dilly, 1799), 1.

4. K. Pearson and M. Moul, "The Problem of Alien Immigration into Great Britain Illustrated by an Examination of Russian and Polish Jewish Children," *Annals of Eugenics* 1 (1925): 8, 125; K. Pearson and E. M. Elderton, Foreword, *Annals of Eugenics* 1 (1925): 2.

5. R. M. Yerkes, Foreword to C. C. Brigham, *A Study of American Intelligence* (Princeton, N.J.: Princeton University Press, 1923), vii.

6. A. R. Jensen, *Educability and Group Differences* (New York: Harper and Row, 1973), 39.

7. Quoted in J. D. Smith, *Minds Made Feeble: The Myth and Legacy of the Kallikaks* (Rockville, Md.: Aspen Systems, 1985), 132; R. B. Cattrell, "The Structure of Intelligence in Relation to the Nature-Nurture Controversy," in *Intelligence*, ed. R. Cancro (New York: Grune and Stratton, 1971), 5.

8. Brigham, *A Study of American Intelligence*, 210.

9. L. Agassiz, "The Diversity of Origin of the Human Races," *Christian Examiner* 49 (1850): 110, 111.

10. "Statement of H. H. Laughlin," in *Europe as an Emigrant-Exporting Continent and the United States as an Immigrant-Receiving Nation: Hearings before the Committee on Immigration and Naturalization*, HR 68-1, March 8, 1924, 1318.

11. B. D. Davis, "The Moralistic Fallacy," *Nature* 272 (1978): 390.

12. A. R. Jensen, "Differential Psychology: Towards Consensus," in *Arthur Jensen: Consensus and Controversy*, ed. S. Mogdil and C. Mogdil (New York: Falmer, 1987), 375.

13. Nichols's comment appears in R. Nicols, "Racial Differences in Intelligence," in *Arthur Jensen: Consensus and Controversy*, ed. Mogdil and Mogdil, 217. Jensen's response is in Jensen, "Differential Psychology: Towards Consensus," 377.

14. F. Galton, *Inquiries into Human Faculty and Its Development* (New York: AMS Press, 1973 [1907]), 198.

15. Again, the statement was actually made by Nichols, "Racial Differences in Intelligence," 215; and again, Jensen, in his response, "Differential Psychology: Towards Consensus," 377, noted his thorough agreement.

16. Jensen, "Differential Psychology: Towards Consensus," 378.

17. R. Pearson, *Race, Intelligence and Bias in Academe* (Washington, D.C.: Scott-Townsend, 1991), 76, 60, 63, 101-10, 128-29, 98, 10-11, 298.

18. Pearson and Elderton, Foreword, 3; W. McDougall, *Is America Safe for Democracy?* (New York: Charles Scribner's Sons, 1921), 23.

19. Quoted in C. V. Woodward, "Freedom and the Universities," *New York Review of Books* (July 18, 1991): 32.

20. A. R. Jensen, *Genetics and Education* (New York: Harper and Row, 1973), 25-27.

21. See "Discussion," in *Racial Variation in Man*, ed. F. J. Ebling (New York:

John Wiley, 1975), 129.

22. Quoted in J. Hirsch, "To 'Unfrock the Charlatans,' " *Sage Race Relations Abstracts* 6 (1981): 20.

23. A. R. Jensen, "Review of T. Dobzhansky's *Genetic Diversity and Human Equality,* " *Perspectives in Biology and Medicine* 17 (1974): 433.

24. E. B. Page, "Behavior and Heredity," *American Psychologist* 27 (1972): 660; see, for example, H. J. Eysenck, "The Dangers of the New Zealots," *Encounter* 39 (1972): 88-89.

25. L. J. Kamin, "Heredity, Intelligence, Politics and Psychology" (Address to the Annual Meeting of the Eastern Psychological Association, April 1973); portions of the address were reprinted in *The IQ Controversy,* ed. N. J. Block and G. Dworkin (New York: Pantheon, 1976), 242-64, 374-82. Jensen's preemptive strike was "Kinship Correlations Reported by Cyril Burt," *Behavior Genetics* 4 (1974): 1-28. The initial draft of Jensen's article was received by *Behavior Genetics* on April 26, and the final version was accepted for publication on May 22, allowing a total of 26 days for submission to reviewers, receipt of their recommendations, forwarding of the comments to Jensen, and his revision and return of the manuscript. As the behavior geneticist Jerry Hirsch has pointed out in "To 'Unfrock the Charlatans,' " 27, articles from the three previous volumes undergoing the same process required an average of 119 days, with a minimum of 38 and a maximum of 233. On refusing to give Kamin credit, see, for example, R. J. Herrnstein, "IQ Testing and the Media," *Atlantic Monthly* (August 1982): 70; H. J. Eysenck, *The Structure and Measurement of Intelligence* (Berlin: Springer-Verlag, 1979), 229; H. J. Eysenck, letter to the editor, *American Psychologist* 32 (1977): 674-75; H. J. Eysenck, letter to the editor, *Bulletin of the British Psychological Society* 30 (1977): 22; and R. B. Cattell, "Review of *Cyril Burt, Psychologist* (by L. Hearnshaw)," *Behavior Genetics* 10 (1980): 318.

26. E. Baur, E. Fischer, and F. Lenz, *Human Heredity,* trans. E. Paul and C. Paul (New York: Macmillan, 1931), 674; F. Lenz, letter to the editor, *American Journal of Human Genetics* 14 (1962): 309.

27. A. R. Jensen, "The Debunking of Scientific Fossils and Straw Persons," *Contemporary Education Review* 1 (1982): 129.

28. Jensen, "Differential Psychology: Towards Consensus," 372; H. H. Goddard, "Mental Tests and the Immigrants," *Journal of Delinquency* 2 (1917): 244.

29. In an interesting consistency the resolution itself was eventually misused, again with no sign of concern from its supporters. It had stated a belief in the strength of hereditary influences and had encouraged research on the topic but had said nothing about group differences in intelligence or any other trait. Nevertheless, Richard Lynn, who replaced R. Gayre of Gayre as editor of the *Mankind Quarterly,* referred to the statement, in a book containing a chapter written by Jensen, as a "counter-resolution" to claims that there were no racial differences in "innate mental characteristics." If Jensen noticed this inaccurate description of his resolution, he made no attempt to correct it. See R. Lynn, "Ethnic and Racial Differences in Intelligence: International Comparisons," in *Human Variation: The Biopsychology of Age, Race and Sex,* ed. R. T. Osborne, C. E. Noble, and N. Weyl (New York: Academic Press, 1978), 262.

30. Editorial, *Nature* 239 (1972): 2.

31. L. Tyler, "Design for a Hopeful Psychology," *American Psychologist* 28 (1973): 1026.

32. S. B. Sarason, "If It Can Be Studied or Developed, Should It Be?" *American Psychologist* 39 (1984): 481.

33. L. L. Cavalli-Sforza and W. F. Bodmer, *The Genetics of Human Populations* (San Francisco: W. H. Freeman, 1971), 801-2.

34. According to Pioneer's IRS returns, the Institute for the Study of Educational Differences was awarded $310,500 in the years 1984-86.

35. L. M. Terman, "Adventures in Stupidity: A Partial Analysis of the Intellectual Inferiority of a College Student," *Scientific Monthly* 14 (1922): 24.

36. A. L. Crane, "Race Differences in Inhibition," *Archives of Psychology,* no. 63 (1923): v-vi.

37. Ibid., 84.

38. *United States v. Karl Brandt,* judgment reprinted in J. Katz, *Experimentation with Human Beings* (New York: Russell Sage, 1972), 305.

39. H. Jonas, "Philosophical Reflections on Experimenting with Human Subjects," in *Experimentation with Human Subjects,* ed. P. A. Freund (New York: George Braziller, 1970), 19.

40. P. Ramsey, *The Patient as Person* (New Haven, Conn.: Yale University Press, 1970), 6; A. M. Capron, "Is Consent Always Necessary in Social Science Research?" in *Ethical Issues in Social Science Research,* ed. T. L. Beauchamp, R. R. Faden, R. J. Wallace, and L. Walters (Baltimore: Johns Hopkins University Press, 1982), 220.

41. Jonas, "Philosophical Reflections on Experimenting with Human Subjects," 1.

42. P. J. Burnham, letter to the editor, *Science* 152 (1966): 448.

43. See Department of Health, Education, and Welfare, *The Institutional Guide to DHEW Policy on Protection of Human Subjects* (Washington, D.C.: Department of Health, Education, and Welfare, 1971).

44. See "Protection of Human Subjects," *CFR,* Title 45, Part 46, May 30, 1974, 18914-20.

45. P. D. Reynolds, "On the Protection of Human Subjects and Social Science," *International Journal of Social Science* 24 (1972): 706, 694.

46. Ibid., 709, 715.

47. See National Research Service Award Act of 1974, Public Law 93-348, July 12, 1974, 349.

48. National Commission for the Protection of Human Subjects of Biomedical and Behavioral Research, *The Belmont Report: Ethical Principles and Guidelines for the Protection of Human Subjects in Research,* DHEW Publication No. (OS) 78-0012 (Washington, D.C.: Department of Health, Education, and Welfare, [1978]), 4-5.

49. Ibid., 12.

50. R. J. Levine, "The Nature and Definition of Informed Consent in Various Research Settings," in *Appendix to the Belmont Report: Ethical Principles and Guidelines for the Protection of Human Subjects in Research,* vol. 1, DHEW

Publication No. (OS) 78-0013 (Washington, D.C.: Department of Health, Education, and Welfare, [1978]), 10.

51. National Commission for the Protection of Human Subjects of Biomedical and Behavioral Research, *Report and Recommendations: Institutional Review Boards,* DHEW Publication No. (OS) 78-0008 (Washington, D.C.: Department of Health, Education, and Welfare, [1978]), 20-21, 25-26.

52. "Protection of Human Subjects," *CFR,* Title 45, Part 46, October l, 1987, ed., 133.

53. "Final Regulations Amending Basic HHS Policy for the Protection of Human Research Subjects," *Federal Register* 46 (January 26, 1981): 8369.

54. See S. J. Ceci, D. Peters, and J. Plotkin, "Human Subjects Review, Personal Values and the Regulation of Social Science Research," *American Psychologist* 40 (1985): 995.

55. American Psychological Association, *Ethical Principles in the Conduct of Research with Human Participants* (Washington, D.C.: American Psychological Association, 1982), 5-6, 74.

56. E. Diener and R. Crandall, *Ethics in Social and Behavioral Research* (Chicago: University of Chicago Press, 1978), 42-43.

57. R. A. Tropp, "A Regulatory Perspective on Social Science Research," in *Ethical Issues in Social Science Research,* ed. Beauchamp et al., 410. Many of the participants in the Brookings conference on social experimentation have offered the same argument; see A. M. Rivlin and P. M. Timpane, eds., *Ethical and Legal Issues of Social Experimentation* (Washington, D.C.: Brookings Institution, 1975).

58. A. Reiss, "Selected Issues in Informed Consent and Confidentiality with Special Reference to Behavioral/Social Science Research/Inquiry," in *Appendix to The Belmont Report: Ethical Principles and Guidelines for the Protection of Human Subjects of Research,* vol. 2, DHEW Publication No. (OS) 78-0014 (Washington, D.C.: Department of Health, Education, and Welfare, [1978]), 39-40.

59. P. A. Vernon and A. R. Jensen, "Individual and Group Differences in Intelligence and Speed of Information Processing," *Personality and Individual Differences* 5 (1984): 412.

60. L. S. Gottfredson, "Societal Consequences of the *g* Factor in Employment," *Journal of Vocational Behavior* 29 (1986): 398-406.

61. L. S. Gottfredson, "Breaching Taboos: A Personal Perspective" (Paper presented at the Annual Meeting of the American Psychological Association, New York, N.Y., August 31, 1987).

62. See "Group's Grants Assailed at U of Del," *Philadelphia Inquirer,* December 21, 1989, 1b. According to *Time* (April 1, 1991): 67, Gottfredson was later prohibited by the University of Delaware from accepting any further money from the Pioneer Fund because the foundation's activities were "incompatible with the university's mission"; however, *Time* erroneously reported that she was engaged in educational research unrelated to possible hereditary differences in intelligence between races.

63. American Psychological Association, *Ethical Principles in the Conduct of Research with Human Participants,* 23.

64. S. Scarr, "Race and Gender as Psychological Variables," *American Psychologist* 43 (1988): 58.

65. Ramsey, *The Patient as Person,* 37.

66. Scarr, "Race and Gender as Psychological Variables," 59.

67. *New York Trust Company v. Eisner,* 256 U.S. 349 (1921).

68. Scarr, "Race and Gender as Psychological Variables," 58.

69. Ibid., 59.

70. The record, however, is not encouraging. One survey of all psychological research in a six-month period on the problems of blacks found that 82 percent of these studies suggested an interpretation "in terms of personal shortcomings." Some of the conclusions, admittedly "extreme examples," were truly bizarre. For example, according to the survey, one researcher "evaluated inner-city black youths' sense of rhythm, tonal memory, and other musical talents, finding them 'markedly deficient' by test standards." Another study on "white reformatory girls' preference for Negro men" concluded that the attraction resulted from the formers' feelings of worthlessness and social rejection. See N. Caplan and S. D. Nelson, "On Being Useful: The Nature and Consequences of Psychological Research on Social Problems," *American Psychologist* 28 (1973): 205.

71. H. K. Beecher, "Ethics and Clinical Research," *New England Journal of Medicine* 274 (1966): 1360.

72. J. P. Rushton, "Race Differences in Behavior: A Review and Evolutionary Analysis," *Personality and Individual Differences* 9 (1988): 1009-24; J. P. Rushton, "Do r-K Strategies Underlie Human Race Differences?" *Canadian Psychology* 32 (1991): 29-42.

73. D. Gilliam, "The FBI and Black Leaders," *Washington Post,* January 18, 1988, 10.

74. *Time* (April 6, 1987): 57.

75. Quoted in S. L. Carter, *Reflections of an Affirmative Action Baby* (New York: Basic Books, 1991), 172.

76. H. J. Ehrlich, *Campus Ethnoviolence and the Policy Options,* Institute Report No. 4 (Baltimore, Md.: National Institute against Prejudice and Violence, 1990).

77. In the interview Stoner waved a medical text and called it "a medically proven fact" that whites contacted AIDS by having sex with a "Negroid." R. D. Purvis, *Bigotry and Cable TV* (Baltimore: National Institute against Prejudice and Violence, 1988), 18-19.

78. See M. Zatarain, *David Duke* (Gretna, La.: Pelican, 1990), 76-82; the description of his early visit to the Citizens' Council comes from Hodding Carter's interview with Duke in a PBS documentary on "Frontline."

79. *White Patriot,* no. 86 (n.d.): 10.

80. J. Ridgeway, *Blood in the Face* (New York: Thunder's Mouth, 1990), 153.

81. Quoted in ibid., 156.

82. D. Duke, "The New White Minority," *NAAWP News,* no. 37 (n.d.): 1-2; fundraising letter for NAAWP signed by Duke (no date).

83. *NAAWP News,* no. 57 (n.d.): 7.

84. Quoted by Z. Nauth in *In These Times,* February 15-21, 1989, 6. See

also Duke's statements in an interview by *Hustler* reprinted in *NAAWP News,* no. 37 (n.d.): 5, and in his undated fundraising letters for NAAWP.

85. S. E. Luria, "What Can Biologists Solve?" *New York Review of Books* 21 (February 7, 1974): 27.

86. Quoted in the preface to F. O. Matthiesson, *American Renaissance* (London: Oxford University Press, 1941), xv-xvi.

Index

FHU. *See* Foundation for Human Understanding
Fields, Edward, 258
Fifteenth Amendment (U.S. Constitution), 34
"Final Solution," 31, 127-28, 131. *See also* extermination; Holocaust
Fischer, Eugen, 112, 116, 118, 120-23, 125, 128-29, 131, 178
Folk, 171
foreigners. *See* immigrants; *names of specific national or ethnic groups*
Foreign Policy Institute (American Security Council), 257
Foundation for Human Understanding (FHU), 252-53
Foundation for Research and Education on Eugenics and Dysgenics (FREED), 193-94
Fourteenth Amendment (U.S. Constitution), 34, 145, 147, 148, 168
France, 132. *See also* French people
franchise. *See* voting rights
Frankfurter, Felix, 145
Frankfurt University, 130
Frankish dynasties, 89
free blacks, 14-16
FREED. *See* Foundation for Research and Education on Eugenics and Dysgenics
Freeden, M., 305n.2
Freeman, Edward A., 34
Freeman, Frank N., 108-9
free speech. *See* censorship
Freigabe der Vernichtung lebensunwerten Leben, Die (Binding and Hoche), 112
French people, 21, 87
Frenkel-Brunswik, Else, 143
Freud, Sigmund, 233
Frick, Wilhelm, 119, 121, 124
frontal lobes. *See* brains
"Frontline" (TV program), 348n.78

Galileo, 89, 188, 191, 192, 276-77
Galton, Francis (Sir), 86; influence of, 51-53; on Jews, 125; social agenda of, 45-49, 59, 183, 239, 243, 272-73; statistical interests of, 5, 6, 37-38, 67
Galton Society, 71, 88, 92, 134
Ganeson, A. T., 327n.14
Gardner, Howard, 220
Garfield, E., 331n.103
Garibaldi, Giuseppi, 89

Garrett, Henry E., 158; credentials of, 1, 153; denunciations of, 211; as IAAEE member, 173-74, 252; and *Mankind Quarterly*, 175; and *Nouvelle Ecole*, 262; as racist leader, 172, 209, 249; and segregation, 153-57, 160, 161, 167, 170, 182; works by, 1, 2, 169, 206, 263, 293
Gates, R. Ruggles, 175, 176, 178
Gayre of Gayre, Robert, 174-75, 177, 255-58, 262
Gebhart v. Belton, 319n.13
genetic defects: chemical therapy for, 57, 71, 184; eugenicists' analysis of, 63-64, 67-70, 99, 119-20, 122-23; immigration opponents' concerns about, 95; Shockley on, 184. *See also* epileptics; feebleminded people; *names of specific genetic defects and diseases*
genetic determinism, 66-67, 234-38. *See also* "genetic enslavement"
genetic differences. *See* racial differences research
Genetic Diversity and Human Equality (Dohzhansky), 276
"genetic enslavement" (of blacks), 187, 192, 197, 204, 270. *See also* genetic determinism
Genetic Health Court (Germany), 120
geneticists, 129-30, 138, 185, 186, 187. *See also* genetics
genetics, 62, 67, 71; in Germany, 112-13, 118-19. *See also* biology; heredity
Genetics (Jenkins), 223
Genetics of Human Populations, The (Cavalli-Sforza and Bodmer), 230, 280
geniuses, 219-20
"genthanasia." *See* extermination
"Geography of Stupidity, The" (Weyl), 261-62
George, J., 341n.316
George, Wesley Critz, 162-68
German-American National Congress, 260
German Anthropological Association, 130-31
German people. *See* Teutonic types
German Society for Anthropology, 130-31
Germany, 68, 89, 111, 113, 117, 174; eugenics movement in, 52, 111-33; reunification of, 176-77. *See also* National Socialism; racial purity; Teutonic types
germ plasm (continuity of), 52, 62
Gessellschaft für Rassenhygiene, 111

WILLIAM H. TUCKER is a graduate of Bates College in Lewiston, Maine, and received his M.A. and Ph.D. in psychology from Princeton University. He is currently an associate professor of psychology at Rutgers University in Camden, New Jersey, where he received the Rutgers College Public Service Award for his work in the Camden community.